THE PHILOSOPHY OF GRAMMAR

By Otto Jespersen

ESSENTIALS OF ENGLISH GRAMMAR

LANGUAGE

HOW TO TEACH A FOREIGN LANGUAGE

A MODERN ENGLISH GRAMMAR
Seven Volumes

NOVIAL LEXIKE

MANKIND, NATION AND INDIVIDUAL

THE PHILOSOPHY
OF GRAMMAR

BY
OTTO JESPERSEN

LONDON
GEORGE ALLEN & UNWIN LTD

FIRST PUBLISHED IN 1924
REPRINTED 1925, 1929, 1935, 1948, 1951, 1955, 1958 AND 1963

PRINTED IN GREAT BRITAIN BY
UNWIN BROTHERS LIMITED, WOKING AND LONDON

*To my old friend
and everwilling helper*

G. C. MOORE SMITH

PREFACE

Il faut beaucoup de philosophie pour savoir observer une fois ce qu'on voit tous les jours.—ROUSSEAU.

THIS book has taken long in making, and like other pet children, it has borne many names. When I gave the first crude sketch of it as a series of lectures at Columbia University in 1909–10, I called it an Introduction to English Grammar; in the preface of the second volume of my *Modern English Grammar* (1914) I was rash enough to refer to " a forthcoming book on *The Basis of Grammar* "; in *Language* (1922) I spoke of it again as " a future work, to be called, probably, *The Logic of Grammar*," and now at last I venture to present it under the perhaps too ambitious title of " The Philosophy of Grammar." It is an attempt at a connected presentation of my views of the general principles of grammar, views at which I have arrived after long years in which I have studied various languages and have been preparing an extensive work on English Grammar, of which I have so far been able to bring out only two volumes.

I am firmly convinced that many of the shortcomings of current grammatical theory are due to the fact that grammar has been chiefly studied in connexion with ancient languages known only through the medium of writing, and that a correct apprehension of the essential nature of language can only be obtained when the study is based in the first place on direct observation of living speech and only secondarily on written and printed documents. In more than one sense a modern grammarian should be *novarum rerum studiosus*.

Though my concern has been primarily with linguistic study, I have ventured here and there to encroach on the territory of logic, and hope that some parts of my work may contain things of interest to logicians; for instance, the definition of proper names (Ch. IV), the discussion of the relation between substantive and adjective (Chs. V and VII), the definition of ' abstracts ' as nexus-words (Ch. X), the relation of subject and predicate (Ch. XI), and the tripartitions in the chapter on Negation (Ch. XXIV).

7

I have had many difficulties to contend with in writing this book; one of these is the proper arrangement of my chapters, inasmuch as the subjects they deal with interlock and overlap in the most bewildering way. My endeavour has been to avoid as far as possible references to *subsequent* sections, but it is to be feared that the order in which different topics are presented may here and there appear rather arbitrary. I must also ask the reader's indulgence for my inconsistency in sometimes indicating and sometimes not indicating the exact place where I have found a passage which I quote as an example of some grammatical phenomenon. This has not been found as necessary here as in my *Grammar*, where it is my principle to give exact references to all passages quoted; but many of the phenomena mentioned in this volume are such that examples may be easily found in almost any book written in the language concerned.

OTTO JESPERSEN.

UNIVERSITY OF COPENHAGEN,
    January 1924

Since this book was first published (in 1924) I have carried out and further developed some of the ideas it contains in volumes 3 and 4 of my *Modern English Grammar* and in *Essentials of English Grammar* to which the reader may therefore be referred.

O. J.

LUNDEHAVE,
    HELSINGOR (ELSINORE).
November 1934

CONTENTS

ABBREVIATIONS OF BOOK TITLES, ETC.

Asboth Gramm = O. Asboth, *Kurze russische Grammatik*, Leipzig 1904.

Bally LV = Ch. Bally, *Le Langage et la Vie*, Genève 1913.

St = *Traité de Stylistique Française*, Heidelberg 1909.

Bloomfield SL = L. Bloomfield, *An Introduction to the Study of Language*, New York 1914.

Boyer et Speranski M = P. Boyer et N. Speranski, *Manuel pour l'Étude de la Langue Russe*, Paris 1905.

Bradley ME = H. Bradley, *The Making of English*, London 1904.

Bréal M = M. Bréal, *Mélanges de Mythologie et de Linguistique*, Paris 1882.

S = *Essai de Sémantique*, Paris 1897.

Brugmann Es = K. Brugmann, *Ursprung des Scheinsubjekts 'es,'* Leipzig 1914.

KG = *Kurze Vergleichende Grammatik*, Strassburg 1904.

VG = *Grundriss der Vergleichenden Grammatik*, 2te Ausg., Strassburg 1897 ff.

Versch = *Verschiedenheiten der Satzgestaltung*, Leipzig 1918.

Brunot PL = F. Brunot, *La Pensée et la Langue*, Paris 1922.

ChE = O. Jespersen, *Chapters on English*, London 1918.

Curme GG = G. O. Curme, *A Grammar of the German Language*, 2nd ed., New York 1922.

Dan. = Danish.

Delbrück GNS = B. Delbrück, *Grundlagen der Neuhochdeutschen Satzlehre*, Berlin 1920.

Synt. = *Vergleichende Syntax der Indogermanischen Sprachen*, Strassburg 1893.

Deutschbein SNS = M. Deutschbein, *System der Neuenglischen Syntax*, Cöthen 1917.

Diez GRS = F. Diez, *Grammatik der Romanischen Sprachen*, 4te Aufl., Bonn 1876.

E. = English.

Eliot FG = C. N. E. Eliot, *A Finnish Grammar*, Oxford 1890.

ESt = *Englische Studien*.

Falk & Torp DNS = Hjalmar Falk og Alf Torp, *Dansk-norskens syntax*, Kristiania 1900.

Fr. = French.

G. = German.

Gabelentz Spr = G. v. d. Gabelentz, *Die Sprachwissenschaft*, Leipzig 1891.

Ginneken LP = J. v. Ginneken, *Principes de Linguistique Psychologique*, Amsterdam, Paris 1907.

11

Gr. = Greek.

GS = O. Jespersen, *Growth and Structure of the English Language*, 4th ed., Leipzig and Oxford 1923.

Hanssen Sp. Gr. = F. Hanssen, *Spanische Grammatik*, Halle 1910.

IF = *Indogermanische Forschungen.*

It. = Italian.

Keynes FL = J. N. Keynes, *Studies and Exercises in Formal Logic*, 4th ed., London 1906.

KZ = Kuhn's *Zeitschrift für Vergleichende Sprachforschung.*

Lang. (Language) = O. Jespersen, *Language, its Nature, Development and Origin*, London 1922.

Lat. = Latin.

LPh = O. Jespersen, *Lehrbuch der Phonetik*, 3te Aufl., Leipzig 1920.

Madvig Kl = J. N. Madvig, *Kleine Philologische Schriften*, Leipzig 1875.

MEG = O. Jespersen, *Modern English Grammar*, Heidelberg 1909, 1914.

Meillet Gr = A. Meillet, *Aperçu d'une Histoire de la Langue Grecque*, Paris 1913.

LI = *Introduction à l'étude des Langues Indo-Européennes*, 2e éd., Paris 1908.

LH = *Linguistique Historique et Linguistique Générale*, Paris 1921.

Meyer-Lübke Einführ. = W. Meyer-Lübke, *Einführung in das Studium der Romanischen Sprachwissenschaft*, 2te Aufl., Heidelberg 1909.

Mikkelsen DO = Kr. Mikkelsen, *Dansk Ordföjningslære*, København 1911.

Misteli = F. Misteli, *Characteristik der hauptsächl. Typen des Sprachbaus*, Berlin 1892.

MSL = *Mémoires de la Société de Linguistique.*

Fr. Müller Gr. = Friedrich Müller, *Grundriss der Sprachwissenschaft*, Wien 1876.

NED = *A New English Dictionary*, by Murray, etc., Oxford 1884 ff.

Negation = O. Jespersen, *Negation in English and Other Languages*, København 1917 (Videnskabernes selskab, Høst).

Noreen VS = A. Noreen, *Vårt Språk*, Lund 1903 ff.

Nygaard NS = M. Nygaard, *Norrøn Syntax*, Kristiania 1906.

Nyrop Gr. = Kr. Nyrop, *Grammaire Historique de la Langue Française*, Copenhague 1914 ff.

OE = Old English.

OFr. = Old French.

OHG = Old High German.

ON = Old Norse.

Onions AS = C. T. Onions, *An Advanced English Syntax*, London 1904.

Paul Gr = H. Paul, *Deutsche Grammatik*, Halle 1916 ff.

P = *Prinzipien der Sprachgeschichte*, 7te Aufl., Halle 1909.

PBB = (Paul und Braune), *Beiträge zur Geschichte der deutschen Sprache.*

Pedersen GKS = H. Pedersen, *Vergl. Grammatik der keltischen Sprachen*, Göttingen 1909.

RG = *Russisk Grammatik*, København 1916.

PhG = O. Jespersen, *Phonetische Grundfragen*, Leipzig 1904.

Poutsma Gr = H. Poutsma, *A Grammar of Late Modern English*, Groningen 1904 ff.

Schleicher NV = A. Schleicher, *Nomen und Verbum*, Leipzig 1865.

Schuchardt Br = *Hugo Schuchardt-Brevier*, v. L. Spitzer, Halle 1922.

Sh. = Shakespeare.

Sheffield GTh = A. D. Sheffield, *Grammar and Thinking*, New York 1912.

Simonyi US = S. Simonyi, *Die Ungarische Sprache*, Strassburg 1907.

Sonnenschein = E. A. Sonnenschein, *A New English Grammar*, Oxford 1921 f.

Sp. = Spanish.

Spr. L. = O. Jespersen, *Sprogets Logik*, København 1913.

Steinthal Charakteristik = H. Steinthal, *Charakteristik der hauptsächl. Typen des Sprachbaues*, Berlin 1860.

Stout AP =G. F. Stout, *Analytic Psychology*, London 1902.

Streitberg GE = W. Streitberg, *Gotisches Elementarbuch*, 5te Aufl., Heidelberg 1920.

Sweet CP = H. Sweet, *Collected Papers*, Oxford 1913.

NEG = *A New English Grammar*, Oxford 1892, 1898.

Tegnér G = E. Tegnér, *Om Genus i Svenskan*, Stockholm 1892.

TG = *The Terminology of Grammar*, by the Joint Committee (1911), 7th impr. 1922.

Tobler VG = A. Tobler, *Vermischte Beiträge zur Französischen Grammatik*, 3te Aufl., Leipzig 1921.

US = United States.

Vendryes L = J. Vendryes, *Le Langage*, Paris 1921.

Vg. = Vulgar.

Vondrák SG = W. Vondrák, *Vergleichende Slavische Grammatik*, Göttingen 1906.

Wackernagel VS = J. Wackernagel, *Vorlesungen über Syntax*, Basel 1920.

Wegener U = Ph. Wegener, *Untersuchungen über die Grundfragen des Sprachlebens*, Halle 1885.

Western R = A. Western, *Norsk Riksmåls-grammatikk*, Kristiania 1921.

Wilmanns DG = W. Wilmanns, *Deutsche Grammatik*, Strassburg 1897 ff.

Wundt S = W. Wundt, *Die Sprache*, Leipzig 1900.

PHONETIC SYMBOLS

ǀ stands before the stressed syllable.
· indicates length of the preceding sound.

[aˑ] as in *alms*.
[ai] as in *ice*.
[au] as in *house*.
[æ] as in *hat*.
[ei] as in *hate*.
[ɛ] as in *care*; Fr. *tel*.
[ə] indistinct vowels.
[i] as in *fill*; Fr. *qui*.
[iˑ] as in *feel*; Fr. *fille*.
[o] as in Fr. *seau*.
[ou] as in *so*.
[ɔ] open *o*-sounds.
[u] as in *full*; Fr. *fou*.
[uˑ] as in *fool*; Fr. *épouse*.

[y] as in Fr. *vu*.
[ʌ] as in *cut*.
[ø] as in Fr. *feu*.
[œ] as in Fr. *sœur*.
[~] French nasalization.
[c] as in G. *ich*.
[x] as in G., Sc. *loch*.
[ð] as in *this*.
[j] as in *you*.
[þ] as in *thick*.
[ʃ] as in *she*.
[ʒ] as in *measure*.
['] in Russian palatalization, in Danish glottal stop.

THE PHILOSOPHY OF GRAMMAR

CHAPTER I

LIVING GRAMMAR

Speaker and Hearer. Formulas and Free Expressions. Grammatical Types.
Building up of Sentences.

Speaker and Hearer.

THE essence of language is human activity—activity on the part of
one individual to make himself understood by another, and activity
on the part of that other to understand what was in the mind of
the first. These two individuals, the producer and the recipient
of language, or as we may more conveniently call them, the speaker
and the hearer, and their relations to one another, should never
be lost sight of if we want to understand the nature of language
and of that part of language which is dealt with in grammar. But in
former times this was often overlooked, and words and forms were
often treated as if they were things or natural objects with an
existence of their own—a conception which may have been to a great
extent fostered through a too exclusive preoccupation with written
or printed words, but which is fundamentally false, as will easily
be seen with a little reflexion.

If the two individuals, the producer and the recipient of language,
are here spoken of as the speaker and the hearer respectively,
this is in consideration of the fact that the spoken and heard word
is the primary form for language, and of far greater importance
than the secondary form used in writing (printing) and reading.
This is evidently true for the countless ages in which mankind had
not yet invented the art of writing or made only a sparing use of
it ; but even in our modern newspaper-ridden communities, the
vast majority of us speak infinitely more than we write. At any
rate we shall never be able to understand what language is and
how it develops if we do not continually take into consideration
first and foremost the activity of speaking and hearing, and if we
forget for a moment that writing is only a substitute for speaking.

A written word is mummified until someone imparts life to it by transposing it mentally into the corresponding spoken word.

The grammarian must be ever on his guard to avoid the pitfalls into which the ordinary spelling is apt to lead him. Let me give a few very elementary instances. The ending for the plural of substantives and for the third person singular of the present tense of verbs is in writing the same -s in such words as *ends, locks, rises,* but in reality we have three different endings, as seen when we transcribe them phonetically [endz, lɔks, raiziz]. Similarly the written ending -*ed* covers three different spoken endings in *sailed, locked, ended,* phonetically [seild, lɔkt, endid]. In the written language it looks as if the preterits *paid* and *said* were formed in the same way, but differently from *stayed,* but in reality *paid* and *stayed* are formed regularly [peid, steid], whereas *said* is irregular as having its vowel shortened [sed]. Where the written language recognizes only one word *there,* the spoken language distinguishes two both as to sound and signification (and grammatical import), as seen in the sentence "There [ðə] were many people there ['ðɛ·ə]." Quantity, stress, and intonation, which are very inadequately, if at all, indicated in the usual spelling, play important parts in the grammar of the spoken language, and thus we are in many ways reminded of the important truth that grammar should deal in the first instance with sounds and only secondarily with letters.

Formulas and Free Expressions.

If after these preliminary remarks we turn our attention to the psychological side of linguistic activity, it will be well at once to mention the important distinction between formulas or formular units and free expressions. Some things in language—in any language—are of the formula character ; that is to say, no one can change anything in them. A phrase like "How do you do ? " is entirely different from such a phrase as "I gave the boy a lump of sugar." In the former everything is fixed : you cannot even change the stress, saying "How *do* you do ? " or make a pause between the words, and it is not usual nowadays as in former times to say "How does your father do ? " or "How did you do ? " Even though it may still be possible, after saying "How do you do ? " in the usual way to some of the people present, to alter the stress and say "And how do *you* do, little Mary ? " the phrase is for all practical purposes one unchanged and unchangeable formula. It is the same with "Good morning ! ", "Thank you," "Beg your pardon," and other similar expressions. One may indeed analyze such a formula and show that it consists of several words, but it is felt and handled as a unit, which may often mean something quite different from the meaning of the component words taken separately; "beg your pardon," for instance, often means "please repeat what you said, I did not catch it exactly"; "how do you do?" is no longer a question requiring an answer, etc.

It is easy to see that "I gave the boy a lump of sugar" is of a totally different order. Here it is possible to stress any of the essential words and to make a pause, for instance, after "boy," or to substitute "he" or "she" for "I," "lent" for "gave," "Tom" for "the boy," etc. One may insert "never" and make other alterations. While in handling formulas memory, or the repetition of what one has once learned, is everything, free expressions involve another kind of mental activity; they have to be created in each case anew by the speaker, who inserts the words that fit the particular situation. The sentence he thus creates may, or may not, be different in some one or more respects from anything he has ever heard or uttered before; that is of no importance for our inquiry. What is essential is that in pronouncing it he conforms to a certain pattern. No matter what words he inserts, he builds up the sentence in the same way, and even without any special grammatical training we feel that the two sentences

> John gave Mary the apple,
> My uncle lent the joiner five shillings,

are analogous, that is, they are made after the same pattern. In both we have the same type. The words that make up the sentences are variable, but the type is fixed.

Now, how do such types come into existence in the mind of a speaker? An infant is not taught the grammatical rule that the subject is to be placed first, or that the indirect object regularly precedes the direct object; and yet, without any grammatical instruction, from innumerable sentences heard and understood he will abstract some notion of their structure which is definite enough to guide him in framing sentences of his own, though it is difficult or impossible to state what that notion is except by means of technical terms like subject, verb, etc. And when the child is heard to use a sentence correctly constructed according to some definite type, neither he nor his hearers are able to tell whether it is something new he has created himself or simply a sentence which he has heard before in exactly the same shape. The only thing that matters is that he is understood, and this he will be if his sentence s in accordance with the speech habits of the community in which he happens to be living. Had he been a French child, he would have heard an infinite number of sentences like

> Pierre donne une pomme à Jean,
> Louise a donné sa poupée à sa sœur, etc.,

and he would thus have been prepared to say, when occasion arose, something like

Il va donner un sou à ce pauvre enfant.

And had he been a German boy, he would have constructed the corresponding sentences according to another type still, with *dem* and *der* instead of the French *à*, etc. (Cf. *Language*, Ch. VII.)

If, then, free expressions are defined as expressions created on the spur of the moment after a certain type which has come into existence in the speaker's subconsciousness as a result of his having heard many sentences possessing some trait or traits in common, it follows that the distinction between them and formulas cannot always be discovered except through a fairly close analysis; to the hearer the two stand at first on the same footing, and accordingly formulas can and do play a great part in the formation of types in the minds of speakers, the more so as many of them are of very frequent occurrence. Let us take a few more examples.

" Long live the King ! " Is this a formula or a free expression ? It is impossible to frame an indefinite number of other sentences on the same pattern. Combinations such as " Late die the King ! " or " Soon come the train ! " are not used nowadays to express a wish. On the other hand, we may say " Long live the Queen " or " the President " or " Mr. Johnson." In other words, the type, in which an adverb is placed first, then a subjunctive, and lastly a subject, the whole being the expression of a wish, has totally gone out of the language as a living force. But those phrases which can still be used are a survival of that type, and the sentence " Long live the King " must therefore be analyzed as consisting of a formula " Long live," which is living though the type is dead, + a subject which is variable. We accordingly have a sentence type whose use is much more restricted in our own days than it was in older English.

In a paper on ethics by J. Royce I find the principle laid down " Loyal is that loyally does." This is at once felt as unnatural, as the author has taken as a pattern the proverb " Handsome is that handsome does " without any regard to the fact that whatever it was at the time when the sentence was first framed, it is now to all intents and purposes nothing but a formula, as shown by the use of *that* without any antecedent and by the word-order.

The distinction between formulas and free expressions pervades all parts of grammar. Take morphology or accidence : here we have the same distinction with regard to flexional forms. The plural *eyen* was going out of use in the sixteenth century ; now the form is dead, but once not only that word, but the type according

to which it was formed, were living elements of the English language.
The only surviving instance of a plural formed through the addition
of -*en* to the singular is *oxen*, which is living as a formula, though its
type is extinct.   Meanwhile, *shoen, fone, eyen, kine* have been supplanted by *shoes, foes, eyes, cows* ; that is, the plural of these words
has been reshaped in accordance with the living type found in
kings, lines, stones, etc.   This type is now so universal that all new
words have to conform to it : *bicycles, photos, kodaks, aeroplanes,
hooligans, ions, stunts*, etc.   When *eyes* was first uttered instead of
eyen, it was an analogical formation on the type of the numerous
words which already had -*s* in the plural.   But now when a child
says *eyes* for the first time, it is impossible to decide whether he is
reproducing a plural form already heard, or whether he has learned
only the singular *eye* and then has himself added -*s* (phonetically
[z]) in accordance with the type he has deduced from numerous
similar words.   The result in either case would be the same.   If it
were not the fact that the result of the individual's free combination
of existing elements is in the vast majority of instances identical
with the traditional form, the life of any language would be ham-
pered ; a language would be a difficult thing to handle if its speakers
had the burden imposed on them of remembering every little item
separately.

It will be seen that in morphology what was above called a
" type " is the same thing as the principle of what are generally
called regular formations, while irregular forms are " formulas."

In the theory of word-formation it is customary to distinguish
between productive and unproductive suffixes.   An example of a
productive suffix is -*ness*, because it is possible to form new words
like *weariness, closeness, perverseness*, etc.   On the contrary -*lock*
in *wedlock* is unproductive, and so is -*th* in *width, breadth, health*, for
Ruskin's attempt to construct a word *illth* on the analogy of *wealth*
has met with no success, and no other word with this ending seems
to have come into existence for several hundred years.   This is a
further application of what we said above : the type adjective
+ -*ness* is still living, while *wedlock* and the words mentioned in -*th*
are now formulas of a type now extinct.   But when the word *width*
originated, the type was alive.   At that far-off time it was possible
to add the ending, which was then something like -*iþu*, to any
adjective.   In course of time, however, the ending dwindled down
to the simple sound þ(*th*), while the vowel of the first syllable was
modified, with the consequence that the suffix ceased to be productive, because it was impossible for an ordinary man, who was not
trained in historical grammar, to see that the pairs *long : length,
broad : breadth, wide : width, deep : depth, whole : health, dear : dearth*,
represented one and the same type of formation.   These words

were, accordingly, handed down traditionally from generation to
generation as units, that is, formulas, and when the want was felt
for a new 'abstract noun' (I use here provisionally the ordinary
term for such words), it was no longer the ending -*th* that was
resorted to, but -*ness*, because that offered no difficulty, the adjective
entering unchanged into the combination.

With regard to compounds, similar considerations hold good.
Take three old compounds of *hūs* 'house,' *hūsbōnde, hūsþing,
hūswīf*. These were formed according to the usual type found in
innumerable old compounds ; the first framers of them conformed
to the usual rules, and thus they were at first free expressions.
But they were handed down as whole, indivisible words from
generation to generation, and accordingly underwent the usual
sound changes ; the long vowel *ū* was shortened, [s] became voiced
[z] before voiced sounds, [þ] became [t] after [s], [w] and [f] disappeared, and the vowels of the latter element were obscured, the
result being our present forms *husband, husting(s), hussy*, phonetically
[hʌzbənd, hʌstiŋz, hʌzi]. The tie, which at first was strong between
these words and *hūs*, was gradually loosened, the more so because
the long *u* had here become a diphthong, *house*. And if there was
a divergence in form, there was as great a divergence in meaning,
the result being that no one except the student of etymology would
ever dream of connecting *husband, hustings*, or *hussy* with *house*.
From the standpoint of the living speech of our own days the three
words are not compound words ; they have, in the terminology here
employed, become formulas and are on a par with other disyllabic
words of obscure or forgotten origin, such as *sopha* or *cousin*.

With regard to *huswif* there are, however, different degrees
of isolation from *house* and *wife*. *Hussy* [hʌzi] in the sense
'bad woman' has lost all connexion with both ; but for the
obsolete sense 'needle-case' old dictionaries record various forms
showing conflicting tendencies : *huswife* [hʌzwaif], *hussif* [hʌzif],
hussive ; and then we have, in the sense of 'manager of a house,'
housewife, in which the form of both components is intact, but this
appears to be a comparatively recent re-formation, not recognized,
for instance, by Elphinston in 1765. Thus the tendency to make
the old compound into a formula was counteracted more or less
by the actual speech-instinct, which in some applications treated
it as a free expression : in other words, people would go on combining the two elements without regard to the existence of the
formular compounds, which had become more or less petrified in
sound and in meaning. This phenomenon is far from rare :
grindstone as a formula had become [grinstən] with the usual
shortening of the vowel in both elements, but the result of a free
combination has prevailed in the current pronunciation [graind-

stoun] ; in *waistcoat* the new [weistkout] is beginning to be used instead of the formular [weskət] ; *fearful* is given as sounding ' ferful ' by eighteenth-century orthoepists, but is now always [fiəf(u)l]. For other examples see MEG I, 4. 34 ff.

Something similar is seen in words that are not compounds. In Middle English we find short vowels in many comparatives : *deppre, grettre* as against *deep, great (greet).* Some of these comparatives became formulas and were handed down as such to new generations, the only surviving instances being *latter* and *utter,* which have preserved the short vowels because they were isolated from the positives *late* and *out* and acquired a somewhat modified meaning. But other comparatives were re-formed as free combinations, thus *deeper, greater,* and in the same way we have now *later* and *outer,* which are more intimately connected with *late* and *out* than *latter* and *utter* are.

Stress presents analogous phenomena. Children, of course, learn the accentuation as well as the sounds of each word : the whole of the pronunciation of a word is in so far a formular unit. But in some words there may be a conflict between two modes of accentuation, because words may in some instances be formed as free expressions by the speaker at the moment he wants them. Adjectives in *-able, -ible* as a rule have the stress on the fourth syllable from the ending in consequence of the rhythmic principle that the vowel which is separated by one (weak) syllable from the original stress is now stressed, thus 'despicable[1] (originally as in French |despi'cable), 'comparable, 'lamentable, 'preferable, etc. In some of these the rhythmic principle places the stress on the same syllable as in the corresponding verb : con|siderable, 'violable. But in others this is not so, and a free formation, in which the speaker was thinking of the verb and then would add *-able,* would lead to a different accentuation : the adjective corresponding to ac|cept was 'acceptable in Shakespeare and some other poets, and this formula still survives in the reading of the Prayer Book, but otherwise it now is reshaped as ac|ceptable ; *refutable* was ['refjutəbl], but now it is more usual to say [ri'fju·təbl] ; 'respectable has given way to re|spectable ; Shakespeare's and Spencer's |detestable has been supplanted by de|testable, which is Milton's form ; in *admirable* the new [əd'mairəbl] has been less successful in supplanting ['ædmirəbl], but in a great many adjectives analogy, i.e. free formation, has prevailed entirely : a'greeable, de'plorable, re'markable, irre'sistible. In words with other endings we have the same conflict : |confessor and con|fessor, ca|pitalist and 'capitalist, de|monstra-

---

[1] Full stress is here indicated by a short vertical stroke above, and half-stress by a short vertical stroke below—these marks placed *before* the beginning of the stressed syllable in accordance with the practice now followed by most phoneticians.

tive and ˈ*demonstrative*, etc., sometimes with changes of meaning, the free formation following not only the accent, but also the signification of the word from which it is derived, while the formula has been more or less isolated. (Examples see MEG Ch. V.) The British *advertisement* [ədˈvə·tizmənt] shows the traditional formula, the American pronunciation [ˌædvəˈtaizmənt] or [ˈædvəˌtaizmənt] is a free formation on the basis of the verb.

The distinction between a formula and a free combination also affects word-order. One example may suffice: so long as *some*+*thing* is a free combination of two elements felt as such, another adjective may be inserted in the usual way: *some good thing*. But as soon as *something* has become a fixed formula, it is inseparable, and the adjective has to follow: *something good.* Compare also the difference between the old "They turned *each to other*" and the modern "they turned *to each other.*"

The coalescence of originally separate elements into a formula is not always equally complete: in *breakfast* it is shown not only by the pronunciation [brekfəst] as against [breik, fa·st], but also by forms like *he breakfasts, breakfasted* (formerly *breaks fast, broke fast*), but in *take place* the coalescence is not carried through to the same extent, and yet this must be recognized as a formula in the sense 'come to happen,' as it is impossible to treat it in the same way as *take* with another object, which in some combinations can be placed first (*a book he took*) and which can be made the subject in the passive (*the book was taken*), neither of which is possible in the case of *take place.*

Though it must be admitted that there are doubtful instances in which it is hard to tell whether we have a formula or not, the distinction here established between formulas and free combinations has been shown to pervade the whole domain of linguistic activity. A formula may be a whole sentence or a group of words, or it may be one word, or it may be only part of a word,—that is not important, but it must always be something which to the actual speech-instinct is a unit which cannot be further analyzed or decomposed in the way a free combination can. The type or pattern according to which a formula has been constructed, may be either an extinct one or a living one; but the type or pattern according to which a free expression is framed must as a matter of course be a living one; hence formulas may be regular or irregular, but free expressions always show a regular formation.

Grammatical Types.

The way in which grammatical types or patterns are created in the minds of speaking children is really very wonderful, and in many cases we see curious effects on the history of languages. In German the prefix *ge-*, which at first could be added to any form of the verb to express completed action, has come to be specially associated with the past participle. In the verb *essen* there was, however, a natural fusion of the vowel of the prefix and the initial vowel of the verb itself, thus *gessen* ; this was handed down as a formular unit and was no longer felt to contain the same prefix as *getrunken, gegangen, gesehn* and others ; in a combination like *ich habe getrunken und gessen* it was then felt as if the latter form was incomplete, and *ge-* was added : *ich habe getrunken und gegessen,* which restored parallelism.

Grammatical habits may thus lead to what from one point of view may be termed redundancy. We see something similar with regard to the use of *it* in many cases. It became an invariable custom to have a subject before the verb, and therefore a sentence which did not contain a subject was felt to be incomplete. In former times no pronoun was felt to be necessary with verbs like Latin *pluit, ningit* ' it rains, it snows,' etc. ; thus Italian still has *piove, nevica,* but on the analogy of innumerable such expressions as *I come, he comes,* etc., the pronoun *it* was added in E. *it rains it snows,* and correspondingly in French, German, Danish and other languages : *il pleut, es regnet, det regner.* It has been well remarked that the need for this pronoun was especially felt when it became the custom to express the difference between affirmation and question by means of word-order (*er kommt, kommt er ?*), for now it would be possible in the same way to mark the difference between *es regnet* and *regnet es ?*

Verbs like *rain, snow* had originally no subject, and as it would be hard even now to define logically what the subject *it* stands for and what it means, many scholars [1] look upon it as simply a grammatical device to make the sentence conform to the type most generally found. In other cases there is a real subject, yet we are led for some reason or other to insert the pronoun *it*. It is possible to say, for instance, " To find one's way in London is not easy," but more often we find it convenient not to introduce the infinitive at once ; in which cases, however, we do not begin with the verb and say " Is not easy to find one's way in London," because we are accustomed to look upon sentences beginning with a verb as interrogative ; so we say " It is not easy," etc. In the same way it is possible to say " That Newton was a great genius cannot be denied," but if we do not want to place the clause with *that* first we have to say " It cannot be denied that Newton was a great genius." In these sentences *it* represents the following infinitive construction or clause, very much as in " He is a great scoundrel,

Brugmann among others. See also below under Gender.

that husband of hers " *he* represents the words *that husband of hers*. Cf. the colloquial : " It is perfectly wonderful the way in which he remembers things." It would be awkward to say " She made that he had committed many offences appear clearly " with the various grammatical elements arranged as in the usual construction of *make appear* (" She made his guilt appear clearly ") : this awkwardness is evaded by using the representative *it* before the infinitive : *She made it appear clearly that he had committed many offences*. In this way many of the rules concerning the use of *it* are seen to be due on the one hand to the speaker's wish to conform to certain patterns of sentence construction found in innumerable sentences with other subjects or objects, and on the other hand to his wish to avoid clumsy combinations which might even sometimes lead to misunderstandings.

The rules for the use of the auxiliary *do* in interrogative sentences are to be explained in a similar way. The universal tendency is towards having the word-order Subject Verb, but there is a conflicting tendency to express a question by means of the inverted order Verb Subject, as in the obsolete " writes he ? " (cf. German " Schreibt er ? " and French " Écrit-il ?). Now many interrogative sentences had the word-order Auxiliary Subject Verb (" Can he write ? " " Will he write ? " " Has he written," etc.), in which the really significant verb came after the subject just as in ordinary affirmative sentences : through the creation of the compromise form " Does he write ? " the two conflicting tendencies were reconciled : from a formal point of view the verb, though an empty one, preceded the subject to indicate the question, and from another point of view the subject preceded the real verb. But no auxiliary is required when the sentence has an interrogative pronoun as subject (" Who writes ? ") because the interrogatory pronoun is naturally put first, and so the sentence without any *does* conforms already to the universal pattern.[1]

Building up of Sentences.

Apart from fixed formulas a sentence does not spring into a speaker's mind all at once, but is framed gradually as he goes on speaking. This is not always so conspicuous as in the following instance. I want to tell someone whom I met on a certain occasion, and I start by saying : " There I saw Tom Brown and Mrs. Hart and Miss Johnstone and Colonel Dutton. . . ." When I begin

---

[1] Cf. *Language*, 357 f. The use of *do* in negative sentences is due to a similar compromise between the universal wish to have the negative placed before the verb and the special rule which places *not* after a verb : in *I do not say* it is placed after the verb which indicates tense, number, and person, but before the really important verb ; cf. *Negation*, p. 10 f.

my enumeration I have not yet made up my mind how many I am
going to mention or in what order, so I have to use *and* in each case.
If, on the other hand, before beginning my story I know exactly
whom I am going to mention, I leave out the *and*s except before the
last name.   There is another characteristic difference between the
two modes of expression :

(1) There I saw Tom Brown, and Mrs. Hart, and Miss Johnstone,
and Colonel Dutton.

(2) There I saw Tom Brown, Mrs. Hart, Miss Johnstone, and
Colonel Dutton,—

namely that in the former I pronounce each name with a
falling tone, as if I were going to finish the sentence there, while
in the latter all the names except the last have a rising tone.
It is clear that the latter construction, which requires a comprehensive conception of the sentence as a whole, is more appropriate
in the written language, and the former in ordinary speech.   But
writers may occasionally resort to conversational style in this as
well as in other respects.   Defoe is one of the great examples of
colloquial diction in English literature, and in him I find (*Robinson
Crusoe,* 2. 178) " our God made the whole world, and you, and I,
and all things,"—where again the form " I " instead of *me* is characteristic of this style, in which sentences come into existence only
step by step.

Many irregularities in syntax can be explained on the same
principle, e.g. sentences like " Hee that rewards me, heaven reward
him " (Sh.).   When a writer uses the pronoun *thou*, he will have
no difficulty in adding the proper ending -*st* to the verb if
it follows immediately upon the pronoun ; but if it does not
he will be apt to forget it and use the form that is suitable
to the *you* which may be at the back of his mind.   Thus in
Shakespeare (Tp. I. 2. 333) " Thou *stroakst* me, and *made* much
of me."   Byron apostrophizes Sulla (Ch. H. IV. 83) : " Thou,
who *didst* subdue Thy country's foes ere thou *wouldst* pause
to feel The wrath of thy own wrongs, or reap the due Of
hoarded vengeance . . . thou who with thy frown *Annihilated*
senates . . . thou *didst* lay down," etc.   In Byron such transitions
are not uncommon.

In a similar way the power of *if* to require a subjunctive is often
exhausted when a second verb comes at some distance from the
conjunction, as in Shakespeare (Hml V. 2. 245) If Hamlet from
himselfe *be* tane away, And when he's not himselfe, *do's* wrong
Laertes, Then Hamlet does it not | (Meas. III. 2. 37) if he *be* a
whoremonger, and *comes* before him, he were as good go a mile on
his errand | Ruskin : But if the mass of good things *be* inexhaust-
ible, and there *are* horses for everybody,—why is not every beggar

on horseback ? | Mrs. Ward : A woman may chat with whomsoever she likes, provided it *be* a time of holiday, and she *is* not betraying her art.[1]

Anyone who will listen carefully to ordinary conversation will come across abundant evidence of the way in which sentences are built up gradually by the speaker, who will often in the course of the same sentence or period modify his original plan of presenting his ideas, hesitate, break off, and shunt on to a different track. In written and printed language this phenomenon, anakoluthia, is of course much rarer than in speech, though instances are well known to scholars. As an illustration I may be allowed to mention a passage in Shakespeare's *King Lear* (IV. 3. 19 ff.), which has baffled all commentators. It is given thus in the earliest quarto—the whole scene is omitted in the Folio—

> Patience and sorrow strove,
> Who should expresse her goodliest[.] You have seene,
> Sun shine and raine at once, her smiles and teares,
> Were like a better way those happie smilets,
> That playd on her ripe lip seeme[d] not to know,
> What guests were in her eyes which parted thence,
> As pearles from diamonds dropt[.] In briefe,
> Sorow would be a raritie most beloued,
> If all could so become it.[2]

Some editors give up every attempt to make sense of lines 20–1, while others think the words *like a better way* corrupt, and try to emend in various ways (" Were link'd a better way," " Were like a better day," " Were like a better May," " Were like a wetter May," " Were like an April day," " Were like a bridal day," " Were like a bettering day," etc.—see the much fuller list in the Cambridge edition). But no emendation is necessary if we notice that the speaker here is a courtier fond of an affectedly refined style of expression. It is impossible for him to speak plainly and naturally in the two small scenes where we meet with him (Act III, sc. i., and here) ; he is constantly on the look-out for new similes and delighting in unexpected words and phrases. This, then, is the way in which I should read the passage in question, changing only the punctuation :

> You have seen
> Sunshine and rain at once ; her smiles and tears
> Were like—

[pronounced in a rising tone, and with a small pause after *like* ; he is trying to find a beautiful comparison, but does not succeed to

---

[1] Other examples of this have been collected by C. Alphonso Smith, "The Short Circuit," in *Studies in Engl. Syntax*, p. 39.

[2] I have changed *streme* into the obvious *strove*, and *seeme* into *seemed*, besides putting full stops after *goodliest* and *dropt*. On these points there is a general consensus among editors.

his own satisfaction, and therefore says to himself, ' No, I will put
it differently.']

—a better way:

[I have now found the best way beautifully to paint in words
what I saw in Cordelia's face :]

those happy smilets
That play'd on her ripe lip seem'd not to know
What guests were in her eyes [1]——

My chief object in writing this chapter has been to make the
reader realize that language is not exactly what a one-sided occupa-
tion with dictionaries and the usual grammars might lead us to think,
but a set of habits, of habitual actions, and that each word and each
sentence spoken is a complex action on the part of the speaker.
The greater part of these actions are determined by what he has
done previously in similar situations, and that again was determined chiefly by what he had habitually heard from others. But
in each individual instance, apart from mere formulas, the speaker
has to turn these habits to account to meet a new situation, to
express what has not been expressed previously in every minute
detail; therefore he cannot be a mere slave to habits, but has to
vary them to suit varying needs—and this in course of time may
lead to new turns and new habits; in other words, to new grammatical forms and usages. Grammar thus becomes a part of
linguistic psychology or psychological linguistics ; this, however,
is not the only way in which the study of grammar stands in need
of reshaping and supplementing if it is to avoid the besetting sins
of so many grammarians, pedantry and dogmatism—but that will
form the subject-matter of the following chapters.

[1] Abridged from my article in *A Book of Homage to Shakespeare*, 1916,
p. 481 ff.

CHAPTER II

SYSTEMATIC GRAMMAR

Descriptive and Historical Linguistics. Grammar and Dictionary. Sounds.
Usual Division of Grammar. New System. Morphology.

Descriptive and Historical Linguistics.

THERE are two ways of treating linguistic phenomena which may be
called the descriptive and the historical. They correspond to what
in physics are called statics and dynamics (or kinetics) and differ
in that the one views phenomena as being in equilibrium, and the
other views them as being in motion. It is the pride of the linguistic
science of the last hundred years or so that it has superseded older
methods by historical grammar, in which phenomena are not only
described, but explained, and it cannot be denied that the new
point of view, by showing the inter-connexion of grammatical
phenomena previously isolated, has obtained many new and important results. Where formerly we saw only arbitrary rules and
inexplicable exceptions, we now in very many cases see the reasons.
The plural *feet* from *foot* was formerly only mentioned as one of
a few exceptions to the rule that plurals in English substantives
were formed in -*s* : now we know that the long [i·] of the plural is
the regular development of Proto-English [œ·], and that this
[œ·], wherever it was found, through [e·] (still represented in the
E spelling) became [i·] in Present English (cp. *feed, green, sweet*, etc.).
Further, the [œ·] of *fœ·t* has been shown to be a mutation of the
original vowel [o·], which was preserved in the singular *fo·t*, where
it has now through a regular raising become [u] in the spoken
language, though the spelling still keeps *oo*. The mutation in
question was caused by an *i* in the following syllable ; now the
ending in a number of plurals was -*iz* in Proto-Gothonic (urgerman-
isch). Finally this ending, which was dropped after leaving a
trace in the mutated vowel, is seen to be the regular development
of the plural ending found, for instance, in Latin -*es*. Accordingly
what from the one-sided (static) Modern English point of view is
an isolated fact, is seen to be (dynamically) related to a great
number of other facts in the older stages of the same language
and in other languages of the same family. Irregularities in one
stage are in many instances recognized as survivals of regularities

in older stages, and a flood of light has been thrown over very much that had hitherto been veiled in obscurity. This is true not only of historical linguistics in the stricter sense, but also of comparative linguistics, which is only another branch of the same science, supplementing by analogous methods the evidence that is accessible to us in historical sources, by connecting languages whose common " ancestor " is lost to tradition.

But, great as have been the triumphs of these new methods, it should not be forgotten that everything is not said when the facts of a language are interpreted in the terms of linguistic history. Even when many irregularities have been traced back to former regularities, others still remain irregular, however far we dive into the past ; in any case, the earliest accessible stage remains unexplained and must be taken as it is, for we have now shaken off the superstition of the first generation of comparative linguists who imagined that the Aryan (Indo-Germanic) language which is the basis of our family of languages (grundsprache) was a fair representative of the primeval language of our earliest ancestors (ursprache). We can explain many irregularities, but we cannot explain them away : to the speakers of our modern language they are just as irregular as if their origin had not been made clear to us. The distinction between regular and irregular always must be important to the psychological life of language, for regular forms are those which speakers use as the basis of new formations, and irregular forms are those which they will often tend to replace by new forms created on the principle of analogy.

At any rate, descriptive linguistics can never be rendered superfluous by historical linguistics, which must always be based on the description of those stages of the development of a language which are directly accessible to us. And in the case of a great many languages only one definite stage is known and can be made the subject of scientific treatment. On the other hand, in treating such languages the student will do well never to lose sight of the lesson taught by those languages which can be investigated historically, namely that languages are always in a state of flux, that they are never fixed in every detail, but that in each of them there are necessarily points that are liable to change even in the course of a single generation. This is an inevitable consequence of the very essence of language and of the way in which it is handed down from one generation to the next.

Grammar and Dictionary.

When we come to consider the best way in which to arrange linguistic facts, we are at once confronted with the very important division between grammar and dictionary (lexicology). Grammar deals with the general facts of language, and lexicology with special facts (cf. Sweet, CP 31).[1] That *cat* denotes that particular animal is a special fact which concerns that word alone, but the formation of the plural by adding the sound -*s* is a general fact because it concerns a great many other words as well : *rats, hats, works, books, caps, chiefs*, etc.

It might be objected that if this be the proper distinction between grammar and dictionary, the formation of the plural *oxen* from *ox* should form no part of English grammar and should be mentioned in dictionaries only. This is partly true as shown by the fact that all dictionaries mention such irregularities under the word concerned, while they do not trouble to indicate the plural of such words as *cat* and the others just mentioned. Similarly with irregular and regular verbs. Yet such irregularities should not be excluded from the grammar of a language, as they are necessary to indicate the limits within which the " general facts " or rules hold good : if we did not mention *oxen*, a student might think that *oxes* was the real plural of *ox*. Grammar and dictionary thus in some respects overlap and deal with the same facts.

We see now that the usual enumeration in grammars of numerals is really out of place there, but that, on the other hand, such facts as the formation of ordinals by means of the ending -*th* and of 20, 30, etc., by means of -*ty* unquestionably belong to the province of grammar.

With regard to prepositions, it is quite right that dictionaries should account for the various uses of *at, for, in*, etc., just as they deal fully with the various meanings of the verbs *put* and *set*. But on the other hand prepositions find their proper place in grammars in so far as there are " general facts " to be mentioned in connexion with them. I shall mention a few : while prepositions may sometimes govern dependent interrogatory clauses (" they disagree *as to how* he works," " that depends *on what* answer she will give "), they cannot generally govern a clause introduced by *that* (as they can in Danish : " der er ingen tvivl *om at* han er dræbt," literally : there is no doubt of that he has been killed) ; the chief exception is *in that* (" they differ in that he is generous and she is miserly "). Therefore *sure* is treated in two ways in Goldsmith's " Are you sure *of* all this, are you sure *that* nothing ill has befallen my boy ? " Other general facts concern the combination of two prepositions as in " *from behind* the bush " (note that *to behind* is impossible), the relations between preposition and adverb (as in " climb *up* a

---

[1] I do not understand how Schuchardt can say (Br. 127) : Es gibt nur eine grammatik, und die heisst bedeutungslehre oder wohl richtiger bezeichnungslehre. . . . Das wörterbuch stellt keinen anderen stoff dar als die grammatik ; es liefert die alphabetische inhaltsangabe zu ihr.

tree," " he is *in*," cf. " *in* his study," " he steps *in*," cf. " he steps *into* his study "). Grammar also has to deal with general facts concerning the ways in which prepositions express rest at a place and movement to or from a place, as also the relation between the local and temporal significations of the same preposition ; even more strictly within the province of grammar are those uses of some prepositions in which they lose their local or temporal signification and descend into the category of empty or colourless (" pale ") words or auxiliaries ; this is the case with *of* in " the father of the boy " (cf. the genitive case in " the boy's father "), " all of them," " the City of London," " that scoundrel of a servant," etc., and similarly with *to* before an infinitive and when it is what many grammars term a dative equivalent (" I gave a shilling to the boy " = " I gave the boy a shilling "). But in some cases it may remain doubtful and to some extent arbitrary what to include in the grammar and what to reserve for exclusive treatment in the dictionary.

Now any linguistic phenomenon may be regarded either from without or from within, either from the outward form or from the inner meaning. In the first case we take the sound (of a word or of some other part of a linguistic expression) and then inquire into the meaning attached to it ; in the second case we start from the signification and ask ourselves what formal expression it has found in the particular language we are dealing with. If we denote the outward form by the letter O, and the inner meaning by the letter I, we may represent the two ways as $O \longrightarrow I$ and $I \longrightarrow O$ respectively.

In the dictionary we may thus in the first place ($O \longrightarrow I$) take a word, say English *cat*, and then explain what it means, either by a paraphrase or definition in English, as in a one-language dictionary, or else by the French translation ' chat,' as in a two-language dictionary. The various meanings of the same word are given, and in some instances these may in course of time have become so far differentiated as to constitute practically two or more words, thus *cheer* (1) face, (2) food, (3) good humour, (4) applause. In this part we have to place together words that have the same sound (homophones or homonyms), e.g. *sound* (1) what may be heard, (2) examine, probe, (3) healthy, sane (4) part of the sea.[1]

In the second place, by starting from within ($I \longrightarrow O$) we shall have a totally different arrangement. We may here try to arrange all the things and relations signified in a systematic or logical order. This is easy enough in some few cases, thus in that of the numerals,

---

[1] In our ordinary dictionaries are also placed together homographs or words of identical spelling, but different sounds *e.g. bow* (1) [bou] weapon ; (2) [bau] bend forward, fore-end of a boat.

whose place, as we have seen above, is in the dictionary rather than in the grammar : one, two, three. . . . But what would be the best logical arrangement of the words *image, picture, photo, portrait, painting, drawing, sketch* ? On account of the utter complexity of the world around us and of the things and thoughts which language has to express, it is an extremely difficult thing to make a satisfactory arrangement of the whole vocabulary on a logical basis ; a well-known attempt is made in Roget's *Thesaurus of English Words and Phrases* ; Bally's arrangement in *Traité de stylistique française* Vol. II seems an improvement on Roget's arrangement, but is far less complete. If in the O —> I part all homophones were placed together, here on the other hand we have to place synonyms together ; thus *dog* will go with *hound, pup, whelp, cur, mastiff, spaniel, terrier,* etc. ; *way* in one signification with *road, path, trail, passage,* etc., in another with *manner, method, mode.* So again, *cheer* will be found in one place with *repast, food, provision, meal,* etc., in another with *approval, sanction, applause, acclamation,* etc. These remarks apply to a one-language dictionary of the class I —> O ; in a two-language dictionary we simply start from some word in the foreign language and give the corresponding word or words in our own.

As a natural consequence of the difficulty of a systematic arrangement of all these special facts most dictionaries content themselves with an arrangement in alphabetical order which is completely unscientific, but practically convenient. If our alphabet had been like the Sanskrit alphabet, in which sounds formed by the same organ are placed together, the result would, of course, have been better than with the purely accidental arrangement of the Latin alphabet, which separates *b* and *p, d* and *t* and throws together sounds which have no phonetic similarity at all, consonants and vowels in complete disorder. It would also be possible to imagine other arrangements, by which words were placed together if their sounds were so similar that they might easily be misheard for one another, thus *bag* and *beg* in one place, *bag* and *back* in another. But on the whole no thoroughly satisfactory system is conceivable in the dictionary part of language.

Anyone accepting, as I have done here, Sweet's dictum that grammar deals with the general, and the dictionary with the special facts of language will readily admit that the two fields may sometimes overlap, and that there are certain things which it will be necessary or convenient to treat both in the grammar and in the dictionary. But there exists a whole domain for which it is difficult to find a place in the twofold system established by that dictum, namely the theory of the significations of words. No generally accepted name has been invented for this branch of linguistic science : Bréal, one of the pioneers in this field, uses the word "semantics" (sémantique) from Gr. *sēmaino*, while others speak of "semasiology," and others again (Sayce, J. A. H. Murray) of "sematology"; Noreen says "semology," which is rather a barbarous formation from Gr. *sēma, sēmatos*, which, by the way, does not mean ' signification,' but ' sign '; and finally Lady Welby has an equally objectionable name " significs." I shall use Bréal's word *semantics* for this study, which has of late years attracted a good deal of attention. It is a natural consequence of the historical trend of modern linguistics that much less has been written on static than on dynamic semantics, i.e. on the way in which the meanings of words have changed in course of time, but that static semantics also may present considerable interest, is seen, for instance, in K. O. Erdmann's book *Die bedeutung des wortes*. In spite of the fact that the subject-matter of semantics is the way in which meanings and changes of meanings may be classified and brought into a general system, and that this branch of linguistic science thus deals with " general " and not with " special " facts, it is not customary to include semantics in grammar (though this is done in Nyrop's great *Grammaire historique*), and I may therefore be excused if I leave semantics out of consideration in this volume.

Sounds.

If next we proceed to grammar, the first part of nearly all scientific treatises consists of a theory of sounds without regard to the meanings that may be attached to them. It is a simple consequence of the nature of the spoken language that it is possible to have a theory of human speech-sounds in general, the way in which they are produced by the organs of speech, and the way in which they are combined to form syllables and higher units. By the side of this we have the theory of what is peculiar to the one particular language with which the grammarian is concerned. For the general theory of sounds the word *phonetics* is in common use, though the same term is often used of the theory of the sounds of a particular language, as when we speak of " English Phonetics," etc. It would, perhaps, be advisable to restrict the word " phonetics " to universal or general phonetics and to use the word *phonology* of the phenomena peculiar to a particular language (e.g. " English Phonology "), but this question of terminology is not very important. Some writers would discriminate between the two words by using " phonetics " of descriptive (static), and " phonology " of historical (dynamic) " lautlehre," but this terminology is reversed by some (de Saussure, Sechehaye).

It lies outside the scope of this work to say much about phonetics or phonology ; a few remarks may, however, find their place here. The arrangement followed in most books on this subject seems to me very unsystematic ; the learner is bewildered at the outset by a variety of details from many different spheres. In contrast to this, in my own *Fonetik* (Danish edition, 1897–99, German edition *Lehrbuch der Phonetik*, an English edition in preparation) I have tried to build up the whole theory more systematically, thereby also making the subject easier for learners, as I find from many years' practice in teaching phonetics. My method is to start first with the smallest units, the elements of sounds, iss what is produced in one organ of speech, beginning from the lips and proceeding gradually to the interior speech-organs, and in each organ taking first the closed position and afterwards the more open ones ; when all the organs have thus been dealt with, I proceed to the sounds themselves as built up by the simultaneous action of all the speech-organs, and finally deal with the combination of sounds.

In treating the phonology of one of our civilized languages it is necessary to say something about the way in which sounds are represented in the traditional spelling ; especially in historical phonology sounds and spellings cannot be separately treated, however important it is never to confound the two things. The subject may, of course, be viewed from two opposite points of view : we may start from the spelling and ask what sound is connected with such and such a spelling, or, inversely, we may take the sound and ask how it is represented. The former is the point of view of the reader, the latter that of the writer.

The definition of Phonetics given above, " the theory of sounds without regard to meaning " is not strictly correct, for in dealing with the sounds of any language it is impossible to disregard meaning altogether. It is important to observe what sounds are used in a language to distinguish words, i.e. meanings. Two sounds which are discriminated in one language, because otherwise words denoting different things would be confounded together, in another language may not play that rôle, with the result that speakers of that language are quite indifferent to distinctions which in the first language were very important. Much of what is usually treated in phonology might just as well, or even better, find its place in some other part of the grammar. Grammarians are very seldom quite consistent in this respect, and I must myself plead guilty to inconsistency, having in Vol. I of my MEG given some pages to the difference in stress between substantives and verbs, as in *present, object,* etc. But it must be admitted that there are many things in grammar which may equally well or nearly so be placed at different places in the system.

Usual Division of Grammar.

After thus limiting our field we come to what is by common consent reckoned as the central part of grammar, by some even as the whole of the province of grammar. The main division of the subject, as given in grammars with little or no deviation, is into the three parts :

1. Accidence or Morphology.
2. Word-formation.
3. Syntax.

This division with its subdivisions as commonly treated offers many points for attack. The following survey of the traditional scheme will show that a consistent system of grammar cannot be built up on that basis.

In the traditional scheme Morphology is generally divided into chapters, each dealing with one of the usually recognized " parts of speech." Substantives, as the most noble class, are placed first, then adjectives, etc., prepositions and conjunctions last. The grammarian has something to say about each of these classes. In the case of substantives, we get their flexion (inflexion), i.e. the changes undergone by these words, but nothing is said about the significance of these changes or the functions of any given form except what is implied in such names as genitive, plural, etc. The arrangement is paradigmatic, all the forms of some single word being placed together ; thus there is no attempt to bring together the same ending if it is found in various paradigms ; in OE, for instance, the dative plural is given separately in each of the several classes in spite of the fact that it ends in -um in all words.

Next we come to adjectives, where the arrangement is the same, apart from the fact that (in languages of the same type as Latin, OE, etc.) many adjectives have separate forms for the three genders and the paradigms are therefore fuller than those of the substantives. As the endings, on the other hand, are generally the same as in the corresponding classes of substantives, much of what is said in this chapter is necessarily a repetition of what the reader knows from the first chapter.

If we next proceed to the chapter dealing with numerals, we shall find a similar treatment of their flexion in so far as numerals are subject to changes, as is often the case with the early ones. Irregular flexion is given in full, otherwise we are referred to the chapter on adjectives. Besides this, however, the grammarian in this chapter on numerals does what he never dreamed of doing in the two previous chapters, he gives a complete and orderly enumeration of all the words belonging to this class. The next chapter deals with pronouns ; these are treated in very much the same way as substantives, only with the significant modification that as in the case of the numerals all pronouns are enumerated, even if there is nothing peculiar to be told about their forms. Moreover, these words are classified not according to the method of their flexion (different " stems," etc.), as substantives are, but according to their signification : personal, possessive, demonstrative pronouns, etc. In many grammars, a list of pronominal adverbs is given in this chapter, though they have nothing to do with " morphology " proper, as they are not subject to flexional changes.

Verbs, again, are treated in the same manner as substantives, with no regard either to the signification of the verbs themselves or to that of the flexional forms, apart from what is implied in the simple mention of such and such a form as being the first person singular, or in such names as indicative, subjunctive, etc.

In the adverbs we have only one kind of flexion, comparison. This, of course, is given, but besides that many grammars here include a division according to signification, adverbs of time, of place, of degree, of manner, etc., very much as if in the first chapter we had had a division of substantives into nouns of time (year, month, week . . .), nouns of place (country, town, village . . .), etc. Often, too, we have here a division into immediate adverbs and derived adverbs with rules for the manner in which adverbs are formed from adjectives, but this evidently belongs to part 2, Word-formation.

The next class comprises prepositions : as they are unchanged, and as many grammarians want, nevertheless, to say something about this class of words, they will in this place give lists of those prepositions which govern one case and those that govern another, though it would seem obvious that this should really form part of one subdivision of the syntax of cases. Finally we have conjunctions and interjections, and in order to have something to say about these flexionless words many writers here too will enumerate all of them, and sometimes arrange them in classes like those of the adverbs.

Next comes the section dealing with word-formation (G. wortbildung, Fr. dérivation). Here it is well worth noticing that in this section the meaning of each derivative element (prefix, suffix) is generally given with its form. As for the arrangement, various systems prevail, some based on the form (first prefixes, then suffixes, each of these treated separately), some on the signification (formation of abstract nouns, of agent-nouns, causative verbs, etc.), and some jumbling together both points of view in the most perplexing manner. The usual division according to the parts of speech is not always beneficial : thus in one very good book on English grammar I find under the substantives the ending -ics (politics, etc.) totally separated from the adjectives in -ic ; while in a third place comes a discussion on the substantivizing of adjectives (shown by a plural in -s) the three things being consequently treated as if they had nothing to do with one another.

The third part, Syntax, to a very great extent is taken up with detailing the signification (i.e. function) of those flexional forms which were dealt with from another point of view in the first part (cases of nouns, tenses, and moods of verbs, etc.), but not of those treated in the section Word-formation. In some chapters on syntax, on the other hand, we find that the formal and functional sides of each phenomenon are treated in one and the same place (the construction of sentences, word-order).

It needs no more than this short synopsis of the various chapters of ordinary grammars to show how inconsistent and confused they really are ; the whole system, if system it can be called, is a survival from the days when grammatical science was in its infancy, and only the fact that we have all of us been accustomed to it from our childhood can account for the vogue it still enjoys. Many grammarians have modified the system here and there, improving the arrangement in many details, but as a whole it has not yet been superseded by a more scientific one. Nor is the task an easy one, as seen perhaps best by the failure of the two best thought-out attempts at establishing a consistent system of arrangement of grammatical facts, those by John Ries (*Was ist syntax ?* Marburg, 1894) and Adolf Noreen (*Vårt språk*, Stockholm, 1903 ff., not yet finished). Both books contain many highly ingenious remarks and much sound criticism of earlier grammarians, but their systems do not appear to me satisfactory or natural. Instead, however, of criticizing them, I prefer here to give my own ideas of the subject and to leave it to others to find out where I agree and where I disagree with my predecessors.[1]

New System.

A consistent system can be arrived at if we take as our main division what we have already found to constitute the two parts of the lexicology of a language. In grammar, too, we may start either from without or from within ;[2] in the first part (O —⟩ I) we

---

[1] I have criticized Ries (indirectly) in my review of Holthausen's *Altis-ländisches elementarbuch* (*Nord. tidsskrift f. filologi, tredie række,* IV, 171), and Noreen in *Danske studier,* 1908, 208 ff.

[2] This division is found already in my *Studier over engelske kasus,* Copenhagen, 1891, p. 69, repeated in *Progress in Language,* 1894, p. 141 (now *Chapters on Engl.,* p. 4), probably under the influence of v. d. Gabelentz, in whose *Chinesische Grammatik* there is a similar division ; in Chinese, however, with its total lack of flexion, everything is so different from our European languages, rules for word-order and for the employment of 'empty' words forming the whole of grammar, that his system cannot be transferred without change to our languages.

take a form as given and then inquire into its meaning or function ; in the second part (I ⟶ O) we invert the process and take the meaning or function and ask how that is expressed in form. The facts of grammar are the same in the two parts, only the point of view being different : the treatment is different, and the two parts supplement each other and together give a complete and perspicuous survey of the general facts of a language.

Morphology.

In the first part, then, (O ⟶ I) we proceed from the form to the meaning ; this part I propose to call Morphology, though the word thus acquires a somewhat different sense from that usually given to it. Here things are treated together that are expressed externally by the same means ; in one place we have, for instance, the ending -*s*, in another the ending -*ed*, in a third, mutation, etc. But it is very important to notice that this does not mean that we leave the meaning out of account ; at each point we have also to investigate the function or use of such and such an ending or whatever it may be, which, of course, amounts to the same thing as answering the question " What does it signify ? " In many instances this can be done simply by giving the name : under -*s* in *cats* we say that it turns the singular *cat* into a plural ; in dealing with the ending -*ed* we say that in *added*, etc., it denotes the second (passive) participle and the preterit, etc. These may be called syntactic definitions, and in very simple instances everything necessary can be said under this head in a few words, while generally a more detailed analysis must be reserved for the second part of our grammar. Though Sweet makes practically the same distinction as I do between the two parts of grammar, I cannot agree with him when he says (NEG I, 204) that it is " not only possible, but desirable, to treat form and meaning separately—at least, to some extent. That part of grammar which concerns itself specially with forms, and ignores their meaning as much as possible, is called accidence. That part of grammar which ignores distinction of form as much as possible, and concentrates itself on their meaning, is called syntax." Here I must take exception to the words " ignore . . . as much as possible." It should be the grammarian's task always to keep the two things in his mind, for sound and signification, form and function, are inseparable in the life of language, and it has been the detriment of linguistic science that it has ignored one side while speaking of the other, and so lost sight of the constant interplay of sound and sense (see *Language*, passim).

In an ideal language, combining the greatest expressiveness with perfect ease and complete freedom from exceptions and irregularities as well as from ambiguity, the arrangement of the grammar would be an easy thing, because the same sound or the same modification of sounds would always have the same meaning, and the same signification or function would always be expressed in the same formal way.   This is the case already to a great extent in the grammar of such artificial languages as Ido, where it is only necessary once and for all to state the rule that plurality in substantives is expressed by the ending *-i* (I $\longrightarrow$ O), or that the ending *-i* denotes the plural in substantives (O $\longrightarrow$ I) : there is thus perfect harmony between the morphological and the syntactic way of expressing the same fact.   But our natural languages are otherwise constructed, they cannot be mapped out by means of straight lines intersecting one another at right angles like most of the United States, but are more like Europe with its irregularly curved and crooked boundaries.   Even that comparison does not do justice to the phenomena of speech, because we have here innumerable overlappings as if one district belonged at the same time to two or three different states.   We must never lose sight of the fact that one form may have two or more significations, or no signification at all, and that one and the same signification or function may be denoted now by this and now by that formal means, and sometimes by no form at all.   In both parts of the system, therefore, we are obliged to class together things which are really different, and to separate things which would seem to belong naturally to the same class.   But it must be our endeavour to frame our divisions and subdivisions in the most natural manner possible and to avoid unnecessary repetitions by means of cross-references.

Let me attempt to give a short synopsis of the various subdivisions of Morphology as I have worked them out in one of the parts of my Modern English Grammar which have not yet been printed.   Just as in my phonetic books I take first sound elements, then sounds, and finally sound combinations, I here propose to take first word elements, then words, and finally word combinations. It must, however, be conceded that the boundaries between these divisions are not always clear and indisputable : *not* in *could not* is a separate word, and Americans print *can not* as two words, but in England *cannot* is written in one word ; now we cannot, of course, accept typographical custom as decisive, but the phonetic fusion with consequent vowel change in *can't, don't, won't* shows that *nt* in these combinations has to be reckoned as a word element and no longer as a separate word.   Inversely the genitive *s* tends to become more and more independent of the preceding word, as shown in the " group genitive " (the King of England's power, somebody else's hat, Bill Stumps *his* mark, see ChE Ch. III).

In the part headed Word Elements we have to speak of each affix (whether prefix, suffix, or infix) separately, state its form or forms and define its function or functions. We do not take the several word classes (parts of speech) and finish one before passing on to the next, but in speaking of the ending *-s*, for instance (with its three phonetically distinct forms [s, z, iz]), we mention first its function as a sign of the plural in substantives, then as a genitive sign, then as a mark of the third person singular in the present tense of verbs, then in the non-adjunct form of possessive pronouns, e.g. in *ours*. The ending *-n* (*-en*) in a similar way serves to form a plural in *oxen*, a non-adjunct possessive in *mine*, a participle in *beaten*, a derived adjective in *silken*, a derived verb in *weaken*, etc. In separate chapters we have to deal with such less conspicuous word elements as are shown by modifications of the kernel of the word, thus the voicing of the final consonant to form verbs (*halve, breathe, use* from *half, breath, use*), the mutation (umlaut) to form the plural (*feet* from *foot*) and a verb (*feed* from *food*), the apophony (ablaut) to form the preterit *sang* and the participle *sung* from *sing*, the change of stress which distinguishes the verb *object* from the substantive *object* ; here we may also speak of the change from the full word *that* [ðæt] to the empty or pale word spelt in the same way but pronounced [ðət].

It will probably be objected that by this arrangement we mix together things from the two distinct provinces of accidence and word-formation. But on closer inspection it will be seen that it is hard, not to say impossible, to tell exactly where the boundary has to be drawn between flexion and word-formation : the formation of feminine nouns in English (*shepherdess*) is always taken to belong to the latter, thus also to some extent in French (*maîtresse*), but what are we to say of *paysanne* from *paysan* ?—is that to be torn away from *bon, bonne*, which is counted as flexion and placed under Accidence ? The arrangement here advocated has the advantage that it brings together what to the naïve speech instinct is identical or similar, and that it opens the eyes of the grammarian to things which he would otherwise have probably overlooked. Take, for instance, the various *-en*-endings, in adjectives, in verbal derivatives, and in participles : in all these cases *-en* is found (whether this means that it is historically preserved or is a later addition) after the same consonants, while after other consonants it is not found (i.e. it is in some cases dropped, in others it has never been added). Note also the parallelism between the adjunct form in *-en* and another form without *-en* : *a drunken boy* : *he is drunk* | *ill-gotten wealth* : *I've got* | *silken dalliance* : *clad in silk* | *in olden days* : *the man is old* | *hidden treasures* : *it was hid* (the original form, now also *hidden*) | *the maiden queen* : *an old maid*. Now all this can be shown to have a curious connexion with the extension of a great many verbs by means of *-en* which took place from about 1400 and gave rise not only to the forms *happen, listen, frighten,* but also to verbs like *broaden, blacken, moisten,* which now are apprehended as formed from adjectives, while originally they were simply phonetic expansions of existing *verbs* that had the same form as the adjectives. (I have not yet published the account of these phenomena which I promised in MEG I, p. 34.) The new arrangement brings into focus things which had previously escaped our attention.

Speaking of word-formation it may not be superfluous here to enter a protest against the practice prevalent in English grammars of treating the formatives of Latin words adopted into English as if they were English formatives. Thus the prefix *pre-* is given with such examples as *precept, prefer, present,* and *re-* with such examples as *repeat, resist, redeem, redolent,* etc., although the part of the words which remains when we take off the prefix has no existence as such in English (*cept, fer,* etc.). This shows that all these words (although originally formed with the prefixes *præ, re*) are in English indivisible " formulas." Note that in such the first syllable is pronounced with the short [i] or [e] vowel (cf. *prepare, preparation, repair, reparation*), but by the side of such words we have others with the same *written* beginning, but pronounced in a different way, with long [iˑ], and here we have a genuine English prefix with a signification of its own : *presuppose, predetermine, re-enter, re-open.* Only this *pre-* and this *re-* deserve a place in English grammars : the other words belong to the dictionary. Similar considerations hold good with regard to suffixes : although there is really an English suffix *-ty,* we should not include among the examples of it such a word as *beauty* [bjuˑti], because there is no such thing as [bjuˑ] in English (*beau* [bou] has now nothing to do with *beauty*). That *beauty* is a unit, a formula, is seen by the fact that the corresponding adjective is *beautiful* ; we may establish the proportion *beautiful : beauty* = Fr. *beau : beauté* (for in the French word *-té* is a living suffix). An English grammar would have to mention the suffix *-ty* in *safety, certainty,* etc., and the change in the kernel wrought in such instances as *reality* from *real, liability* from *liable,* etc.

The next part deals with words, mainly the so-called grammatical words or auxiliaries, whether pronouns, auxiliary verbs, prepositions, or conjunctions, but only in so far as they are really parts of grammar, that is " general expressions." Under *will* (and the shorter form *'ll* in *he'll,* etc.) we shall thus mention its use to express (1) volition, (2) futurity, (3) habit. But, as stated above, there can be here no hard and fast line between grammar and dictionary

Finally, in the part devoted to Combination of Words we shall have to describe each type of word-order and indicate the rôle it plays in speech. Thus the combination substantive + substantive, apart from such collocations as *Captain Hall*, is used in various kinds of compound substantives, such as *mankind, wineglass, stone wall, cotton dress, bosom friend, womanhater, woman author*; the relations between the two components will have to be specified both as regards form (stress, also secondarily orthography) and as regards meaning. Adjective + substantive is chiefly used in such adjunct groups as *red coat*, whence compounds of the type *blackbird*; but a special kind of compounds is seen in *redcoat* ' one who wears a red coat.' The combination substantive + verb forms a finite sentence in *father came*, where *father* is the subject. In the inverse order the substantive may according to circumstances be the subject (as in the inserted " said Tom " or in the question " Did Tom ? " or after certain adverbs " and so did Tom " or in a conditional clause without a conjunction " had Tom said that, I should have believed it "); or the substantive may be the object (as in " I saw Tom "), etc. All, of course, that I can do here is to sketch out the bare outlines of the system, leaving the details to be worked out in future instalments of my Grammar.

Many people probably will wonder at the inclusion of such things in Morphology, but I venture to think that this is the only consistent way of dealing with grammatical facts, for word-order is certainly as much a formal element in building up sentences as the forms of the words themselves. And with these remarks I shall leave the first main division of grammar, in which things were to be looked at from without, from the sound or form. It will be seen that in our scheme there is no room for the usual paradigms giving in one place all the forms of the same word, like Latin *servus serve servum servo servi, amo amas amat amamus*, etc. Such paradigms may be useful for learners,[1] and in my system may be given in an appendix to Morphology, but it should not be overlooked that from a purely scientific point of view the paradigmatic arrangement is not one of grammatical form, as it brings together, not the same forms, but different forms of the same word, which only belong to one another from a lexical point of view. The arrangement here advocated is purely grammatical, treating together, in its first part what may be called grammatical homophones (homomorphs) and in its second part grammatical synonyms. It will be remembered that we had the corresponding two classes in the two divisions of the dictionary.

[1] Though it is impossible to see the use of such paradigms as are found in many English grammars for foreigners : *I got, you got, he got, we got, you got, they got—I shall get, you will get, he will get, we shall get, you will get, they will get*, etc.

CHAPTER III

SYSTEMATIC GRAMMAR—*continued*

Syntax. Universal Grammar? Differences of Languages. What Categories to Recognize. Syntactic Categories. Syntax and Logic. Notional Categories.

Syntax.

THE second main division of grammar, as we have said, is occupied with the same phenomena as the first, but from a different point of view, from the interior or meaning (I—➤O). We call this syntax. The subdivisions will be according to the grammatical categories, whose rôle and employment in speech is here defined.

One chapter of syntax will deal with Number; it will have first to recount the several methods of forming the plural (*dogs, oxen, feet, we, those,* etc.); this will be done most easily and sum- marily by a reference to those paragraphs in our Morphology in which each ending or other formative is dealt with. Next will follow an account of everything that is common to all singulars and to all plurals, no matter how these latter happen to be formed; thus the plural in "a thousand and one nights" (where Danish and German have the singular on account of *one*), the singular in "more than one *man*" (= more *men* than one), cases of attraction, the 'generic' use of singular and plural to denote the whole class (*a cat* is a four-footed animal, *cats* are four-footed animals), and many other things that could not find their place in the morphological part.

Under the heading of Case we must deal, among other things, with the genitive and its synonym the *of*-phrase (which is often wrongly called a genitive): *Queen Victoria's death = the death of Queen Victoria.* Those cases must be specified in which it is not possible to substitute one of these forms for the other ("I bought it at *the butcher's*" on the one hand, and "the date of her death" on the other). In the chapter on Comparison we shall bring together such forms as *sweetest, best,* and *most evident,* which in our Morphology are dealt with under different heads, and shall examine the use of the comparative and superlative in speaking of two persons or things. Another chapter will be given to the different ways of expressing Futurity (I *start* to-morrow; I *shall start* to-morrow ; he *will start* to-morrow ; I *am to start* to-morrow ; I *may start* to-morrow ; I *am going to start* to-morrow). These indications may suffice to show the nature of the syntactic treatment of grammatical phenomena. The same things that were described in the morphological part are here considered from a different point of view, and we are faced with new problems of a more comprehensive character. Our double method of approach will leave us with a clearer picture of the intricate grammatical network of such a language as English than was possible to those who approached it by the old path. To make this more obvious, we will try to tabulate one part of this network with its manifold cross-strands of form and function :

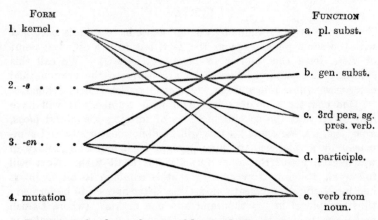

FORM
1. kernel

2. -s

3. -en

4. mutation

FUNCTION
a. pl. subst.

b. gen. subst.

c. 3rd pers. sg. pres. verb.

d. participle.

e. verb from noun.

Examples. 1a *sheep.*—1c *can.*—1d *put.*—1e *hand.*—2a *cats.*—2b *John's.*—2c *eats.*—3a *oxen.*—3d *eaten.*—3e *frighten.*—4a *feet.*—4e *feed*

If we compare these two parts of grammar and remember what was said above of the two parts of a dictionary, we discover that the two points of view are really those of the hearer and of the speaker respectively. In a duologue the hearer encounters certain sounds and forms, and has to find out their meaning—he moves from without to within (O → I). The speaker, on the other hand, starts from certain ideas which he tries to communicate ; to him the meaning is the given thing, and he has to find out how to express it : he moves from within to without (I → O).

Universal Grammar ?

With regard to the categories we have to establish in the syntactic part of our grammatical system, we must first raise an extremely important question, namely, are these categories purely logical categories, or are they merely linguistic categories ? If the former, then it is evident that they are universal, i.e. belong to all languages in common ; if the latter, then they, or at any rate some of them, are peculiar to one or more languages as distinct from the rest. Our question thus is the old one : Can there be such a thing as a universal (or general) grammar ?

The attitude of grammarians with regard to this question has varied a good deal at different times. Some centuries ago it was the common belief that grammar was but applied logic, and that it would therefore be possible to find out the principles underlying all the various grammars of existing languages ; people conse- quently tried to eliminate from a language everything that was not strictly conformable to the rules of logic, and to measure every- thing by the canon of their so-called general or philosophical grammar. Unfortunately they were too often under the delusion that Latin grammar was the perfect model of logical consistency, and they therefore laboured to find in every language the distinctions recognized in Latin. Not unfrequently *a priori* speculation and pure logic led them to find in a language what they would never have dreamt of if it had not been for the Latin grammar in which they had been steeped from their earliest school-days. This confusion of logic and Latin grammar with its consequence, a Procrustean method of dealing with all languages, has been the most fruitful source of mistakes in the province of grammar. What Sayce wrote long ago in the article " Grammar " in the ninth edition of the *Encyclopædia Britannica,* " The endeavour to find the dis- tinctions of Latin grammar in that of English has only resulted in grotesque errors, and a total misapprehension of the usage of the English language "—these words are still worth taking to heart, and should never be forgotten by any grammarian, no matter what language he is studying.

In the nineteenth century, with the rise of comparative and historical linguistics, and with the wider outlook that came from an increased interest in various exotic languages, the earlier attempts at a philosophical grammar were discountenanced, and it is rare to find utterances like this of Stuart Mill :

" Consider for a moment what Grammar is. It is the most elementary part of Logic. It is the beginning of the analysis of the thinking process. The principles and rules of grammar are the means by which the forms of language are made to correspond with the universal forms of thought. The distinctions between the various parts of speech, between the cases of nouns, the moods and tenses of verbs, the functions of particles, are distinctions in thought, not merely in words. . . . The structure of every sentence is a lesson in logic " (Rectorial Address at St. Andrews. 1867).

Such ideas are least to be expected from philologists and linguists ; the latest occurrence I have come across is in Bally (St 156) : " la grammaire qui n'est que la logique appliquée au langage."

Much more frequently found are such views as the following : " A universal grammar is no more conceivable than a universal form of political Constitution or of religion, or than a universal plant or animal form ; the only thing, therefore, that we have to do is to notice what categories the actually existing languages offer us, without starting from a ready-made system of categories " (Steinthal, *Charakteristik*, 104 f.). Similarly, Benfey says that after the results achieved by modern linguistics universal and philosophical grammars have suddenly disappeared so completely that their methods and views are now only to be traced in such books as are unaffected by real science (*Gesch. d. sprachwiss.* 306). And according to Madvig (1856, p. 20, Kl p. 121), grammatical categories have nothing to do with the real relations of things in themselves.

In spite of the aversion thus felt by most modern linguists to the idea of a grammar arrived at by a process of deductive reasoning and applicable to all languages, the belief that there are grammatical notions or categories of a universal character will crop up here and there in linguistic literature. Thus C. Alphonso Smith, in his interesting *Studies in English Syntax*, says (p. 10) that there is a kind of uniformity of linguistic processes which is not in individual words, or sounds, or inflexions, but in word relations ; that is, in syntax. " Polynesian words, for example, are not our words, but the Polynesians have their subjunctive mood, their passive voice, their array of tenses and cases, because the principles of syntax are psychical and therefore universal." And on p. 20 : " One comes almost to believe that the norms of syntax are indestructible, so persistently do they reappear in unexpected places."

I am afraid that what is here said about Polynesians is not the result of a comprehensive study of their languages, but is rather based on the *a priori* supposition that no one can dispense with the syntactic devices mentioned, exactly as the Danish philosopher Kroman, after establishing a system of nine tenses on a logical basis, says that " as a matter of course the language of every thinking nation must have expressions " for all these tenses. A survey of actually existing languages will show that these have in some cases much less, in other cases much more, than we should expect, and that what in one language is expressed in every sentence with painstaking precision, is in another language left unexpressed as if it were of no importance whatever. This is especially true if we come to speak of such things as " the subjunctive mood "— those languages which have a separate form for it by no means apply it to the same purposes, so that even if this mood is known by the same name in English, German, Danish, French, and Latin, it is not strictly speaking one and the same thing ; it would be perfectly impossible to give such a definition of the subjunctive in any of these languages as would assist us in deciding where to use it and where to use the indicative, still less such a definition as would at the same time cover its employment in all the languages mentioned. No wonder, therefore, that there are a great many languages which have nothing that could be termed a subjunctive mood, however widely the sense of the word should be stretched. As a matter of fact, the history of English and Danish shows how the once flourishing subjunctive has withered more and more, until it can now be compared only with those rudimentary organs whose use is problematic or very subordinate indeed.

Differences of Languages.

In comparative lexicology we constantly see how the things to be represented by words are grouped differently according to the whims of different languages, what is fused together in one being separated in another : where English distinguishes between *clock* and *watch*, and French between *horloge, pendule*, and *montre*, German has only one word, *uhr* (but compensates through being able by means of compounds to express many more shades : *turmuhr, schlaguhr, wanduhr, stubenuhr, standuhr, stutzuhr, taschen-uhr*) ; where English has *prince*, German distinguishes between *prinz* and *fürst* ; French has *café* for *coffee* and *café* ; French *temps* corresponds to E. *time* and *weather*, and E. *time* to Fr. *temps* and *fois*—to take only a few obvious examples. It is the same in grammar, where no two languages have the same groupings and make the same distinctions. In dealing with the grammar of a particular language it is therefore important to inquire as carefully as possible into the distinctions actually made by that language, without establishing any single category that is not shown by actual linguistic facts to be recognized by the speech-instinct of that community or nation. However much the logician may insist that the superlative is a necessary category which every thinking nation must be able to express in its language, French has no superlative, for though *le plus pur, le plus fin, le meilleur* serve to render the genuine English superlative *the purest, the finest, the best*, these forms are nothing but the comparative made definite by the addition of the article, and we cannot even say that French has a superlative consisting of the comparative with the definite article preposed, for very often we have no definite article, but another determining word which then has the same effect : *mon meilleur ami*, etc.

4

On the other hand, while French has a real future tense (*je donnerai*, etc.), it would be wrong to include a separate future in the tense system of the English language. Futurity is often either not expressed at all in the verb (*I start to-morrow at six;* cf. also " If he comes "), or it is expressed by means of phrases which do not signify mere futurity, but something else besides ; in *will* (he will start at six) there is an element of volition, in *am to* (the congress is to be held next year) an element of destiny, in *may* (he may come yet) an element of uncertainty, and in *shall* (I shall write to him to-morrow) an element of obligation. It is true that the original meanings are often nearly obliterated, though not to the extent to which the original meaning of infinitive + *ai* (have to . . .) is totally forgotten in French futures. The oblitera- tion is especially strong in *shall*, as there is no sense of obligation in " I shall be glad if you can come," and as *shall* is hardly ever used now in the original sense (compare the biblical " thou shalt not kill " with the modern " you mustn't walk there "), *shall* forms the nearest approach in English to a real auxiliary of the future, and if it were used in all persons, we should have no hesi- tation in saying that English had a future tense. But if we were to recognize " he will come " as a future tense, we might just as well recognize as future tenses " he may come," " he is coming," " he is going to come," and other combinations. Thus the objection is not that *will* is a separate " word " and that to recognize a " tense " we must always have a form of a verb in which the kernel and the flexional ending make up one inseparable unit ; nothing would hinder us from saying that a language had a future tense if it had an auxiliary (verb or adverb) that really served to indicate future time, only this would be placed in that part of Morphology which treats of words, and not, as the French future, in the part that treats of word elements,—in the Syntax as viewed in this book that would make no difference.

What Categories to Recognize.

The principle here advocated is that we should recognize in the syntax of any language only such categories as have found in that language formal expression, but it will be remembered that " form " is taken in a very wide sense, including form-words and word-position. In thus making form the supreme criterion one should beware, however, of a mistaken notion which might appear to be the natural outcome of the same principle. We say *one sheep, many sheep* : are we then to say that *sheep* is not a singular in the first phrase, and not a plural in the second, because it has the same form, and that this form is rather to be called ' common

'number' or 'no-number' or something equivalent? It might
be said that *cut* in " I cut my finger every day " is not in the present
tense, and *cut* in " I cut my finger yesterday " is not in the past
tense (or preterit), because the form in both sentences is identical.
Further, if we compare " our *king's love* for his subjects " and
" our *kings love* their subjects," we see that the two forms are the
same (apart from the purely conventional distinction made in
writing, but not in speaking, by means of the apostrophe), and a
strict formalist thus would not be entitled to state anything with
regard to the case and number of *kings*. And what about *love*?
There is nothing in the form to show us that it is a substantive in
the singular in one phrase and a verb in the plural in the other, and
we should have to invent a separate name for the strange category
thus created. The true moral to be drawn from such examples
is, however, I think, that it is wrong to treat each separate linguistic
item on its own merits ; we should rather look at the language as
a whole. *Sheep* in *many sheep* is a plural, because in *many lambs*
and hundreds of other similar cases the English language recognizes
a plural in its substantives ; *cut* in one sentence is in the present
and in the other in the past tense, because a difference at once
arises if we substitute *he* for *I* (*he cuts, he cut*), or another verb for
cut (*I tear, I tore*) ; *kings* in one instance is a genitive singular
and in the other a nominative plural, as seen in " the *man's* love
for his subjects " and " the *men* love their subjects," and finally
love is a substantive and a verb respectively as shown by the form
in such collocations as " our king's *admiration* for his subjects "
and " our kings *admire* their subjects." In other words, while we
should be careful to keep out of the grammar of any language
such distinctions or categories as are found in other languages,
but are not formally expressed in the language in question, we should
be no less averse to deny in a particular case the existence of distinctions elsewhere made in the same language, because they happen
there to have no outward sign. The question, *how many* and *what*
grammatical categories a language distinguishes, must be settled
for the whole of that language, or at any rate for whole classes
of words, by considering what grammatical functions find expression
in form, even if they do not find such expression in all and every
case where it might be expected : the categories thus established
are then to be applied to the more or less exceptional cases
where there is no external form to guide us. In English, for
instance, we shall have to recognize a plural in substantives,
pronouns, and verbs, but not in adjectives any more than in
adverbs; in Danish, on the other hand, a plural in substantives,
adjectives, and pronouns, but no longer in verbs. There will
be a special reason to remember this principle when we come

to consider the question how many cases we are to admit in English.

The principle laid down in the last few paragraphs is not unfrequently sinned against in grammatical literature. Many writers will discourse on the facility with which English can turn substantives into verbs, and vice versa—but English never confounds the two classes of words, even if it uses the same form now as a substantive, and now as a verb : *a finger* and *a find* are substantives, and *finger* and *find* in *you finger this and find that* are verbs, in flexion and in function and everything. An annotator on the passage in *Hamlet*, where the ghost is said to go " slow and stately " says with regard to *slow* : " Adjectives are often used for adverbs "—no, *slow* really is an adverb, just as *long* in " he stayed long " is an adverb, even if the form is the same as in " a long stay," where it is an adjective. The substantive in *five snipe* or *a few antelope* or *twenty sail* is often called a singular (sometimes a " collective singular "), although it is no more a singular than *sheep* in *five sheep* : a form which is always recognized as a plural, probably because grammarians know that this word has had an unchanged plural from Old English times. But history really has nothing to do with our question. *Snipe* is now one form of the plural of that word (" the unchanged plural "), and the fact that there exists another form, *snipes*, should not make us blind to the real value of the form *snipe*.

Syntactic Categories.

We are now in a position to return to the problem of the possibility of a Universal Grammar. No one ever dreamed of a universal morphology, for it is clear that all actually found formatives, as well as their functions and importance, vary from language to language to such an extent that everything about them must be reserved for special grammars, with the possible exception of a few generalities on the rôle of sentence-stress and intonation. It is only with regard to syntax that people have been inclined to think that there must be something in common to all human speech, something immediately based on the nature of human thought, in other words on logic, and therefore exalted above the accidental forms of expression found in this or that particular language. We have already seen that this logical basis is at any rate not coextensive with the whole province of actual syntax, for many languages do without a subjunctive mood, or a dative case, some even without a plural number in their substantives. How far, then, does this basic logic extend, and what does it mean exactly ?

In the system sketched above we found, corresponding to each separate form, an indication of its syntactic value or function.

thus for the ending E. -*s* on the one hand " plural of substantive," on the other hand " third person singular present of verb," etc. Each of these indications comprised two or more elements, one of which concerned the " part of speech " or word-class, one denoted singular or plural number, one the third person, and finally one the present tense. In English these indications contained comparatively few elements, but if we take Latin, we shall find that matters are often more complicated : the ending of *bonarum*, for instance, denotes plural, feminine gender, and genitive case, that of *tegerentur* plural, third person, imperfect tense, subjunctive mood, passive voice, and so with other forms. Now it is clear that though it is impossible, or not always possible, to isolate these elements from a formal point of view (in *animalium*, where is the sign of the plural, and where of the genitive ? in *feci*, where the indication of the person, of the perfect, of the indicative mood, of the active voice, etc. ?), on the other hand from the syntactic point of view it is not only possible, but also natural to isolate them, and to bring together all substantives, all verbs, all singulars, all genitives, all subjunctives, all first persons, etc. We thus get a series of isolated syntactic ideas, and we must even go one step further, for some of these isolated syntactic ideas naturally go together, forming higher groups or more comprehensive syntactic classes.

In this way substantives, adjectives, verbs, pronouns, etc., together constitute the division of words into parts of speech or word-classes.

The singular and plural (with the dual) form the category of number.

The nominative, accusative, dative, genitive, etc., form the category of cases.

The present, preterit (imperfect, perfect), future, etc., form the category of tenses.

The indicative, subjunctive, optative, imperative, etc., form the category of moods.

The active, passive, and middle voice (medium) form the category of ' voices ' or ' turns.'

The first, second, and third persons form, as the name indicates, the category of persons.

The masculine, feminine, and neuter form the category of genders.

Syntax and Logic.

We are able to establish all these syntactic ideas and categories without for one moment stepping outside the province of grammar, but as soon as we ask the question, what do they stand for, we at once pass from the sphere of language to the outside world [1]

[1] Of course, as this ' outside world ' is mirrored in the human mind.

or to the sphere of thought. Now, some of the categories enumerated above bear evident relations to something that is found in the sphere of things : thus the grammatical category of number evidently corresponds to the distinction found in the outside world between " one " and " more than one " ; to account for the various grammatical tenses, present, imperfect, etc., one must refer to the outside notion of " time " ; the difference between the three grammatical persons corresponds to the natural distinction between the speaker, the person spoken to, and something outside of both. In some of the other categories the correspondence with something outside the sphere of speech is not so obvious, and it may be that those writers who want to establish such correspondence, who think, for instance, that the grammatical distinction between substantive and adjective corresponds to an external distinction between substance and quality, or who try to establish a " logical " system of cases or moods, are under a fundamental delusion. This will be examined in some of the following chapters, where we shall see that such questions involve some very intricate problems.

The outside world, as reflected in the human mind, is extremely complicated, and it is not to be expected that men should always have stumbled upon the simplest or the most precise way of denoting the myriads of phenomena and the manifold relations between them that call for communication. The correspondence between external and grammatical categories is therefore never complete, and we find the most curious and unexpected overlappings and intersections everywhere. From a sphere which would seem to be comparatively simple I shall here give one concrete illustration which appears to me highly characteristic of the way in which actual language may sometimes fall short of logical exigencies and yet be understood. Take a commonplace truth and one of Shakespeare's bits of proverbial wisdom :

(1) Man is mortal.

(2) Men were deceivers ever.

If we analyze these grammatically, we see that (apart from the different predicatives) they differ in that one is in the singular, and the other in the plural number, and that one is in the present tense, the other in the preterit or past tense. Yet both sentences predicate something about a whole class, only the class is different in the two sentences : in the former it is mankind without regard to sex, in the latter the male part of mankind only, a sex-distinction being thus implied in what is grammatically a numerical distinction. And though the tenses are different, no real distinction of time is meant, for the former truth is not meant to be confined to the present moment, nor the second to some time in the past. What is intended in both is a statement that pays no regard to the distinction between now and then, something meant to be true for all time. A logician would have preferred a construction of language in which both sentences were in the same universal number (" omnial," as Bréal calls it) and in the same universal or generic tense, but the subject of the former in the common gender and that of the latter in the masculine gender, for then the meaning would have been unmistakable : " all human beings have been, are, and always will be mortal," and " all male human beings have been, are, and always will be deceitful." But as a matter of fact, this is not the way of the English language, and grammar has to state facts, not desires.

Notional Categories.

We are thus led to recognize that beside, or above, or behind, the syntactic categories which depend on the structure of each language as it is actually found, there are some extralingual categories which are independent of the more or less accidental facts of existing languages ; they are universal in so far as they are applicable to all languages, though rarely expressed in them in a clear and unmistakable way. Some of them relate to such facts of the world without as sex, others to mental states or to logic, but for want of a better common name for these extralingual categories I shall use the adjective *notional* and the substantive *notion*. It will be the grammarian's task in each case to investigate the relation between the notional and the syntactic categories.

This is by no means an easy task, and one of the great difficulties that stand in the way of performing it satisfactorily is the want of adequate terms, for very often the same words are used for things belonging to the two spheres that we wish to distinguish. How a separate set of terms serves to facilitate the comprehension of a difficult subject may be shown by one illustration, in which we briefly anticipate the contents of a subsequent section of this book. *Gender* is a syntactic category in such languages as Latin, French, and German ; the corresponding natural or notional category is *sex* : sex exists in the world of reality, but is not always expressed in language, not even in those languages which, like Latin, French, or German, have a system of grammatical genders which agrees in many ways with the natural distinction of sexes. Hence we may distinguish :

GRAMMAR.	NATURE.
Gender (syntactic) :	Sex (notional) :
(1) masculine ⎫	(1) male ⎫
(2) feminine ⎬ words	(2) female ⎬ beings
(3) neuter ⎭	(3) sexless things

Let us take a few French and German examples. *Der soldat, le soldat :* male beings, masculine gender ; *die tochter, la fille :* female beings, feminine gender ; *der sperling, le cheval :* beings of both sexes, masculine gender ; *die maus, la souris :* beings of both sexes, feminine gender ; *das pferd :* both sexes, neuter gender ; *die schildwache, la sentinelle :* male sex, feminine gender ; *das weib :* female sex, neuter gender ; *der tisch, le fruit :* non-sexual, masculine gender ; *die frucht, la table :* non-sexual, feminine gender ; *das buch :* non-sexual, neuter gender.[1] In other departments it is not possible as here to formulate two sets of terms, one for the world of reality or universal logic, and one for the world of grammar, but it should be our endeavour always to keep the two worlds apart.

Our examples of gender and sex will make it clear that the relations between the syntactic and notional categories will often present a similar kind of network to that noticed between formal and syntactic categories (above, p. 46). We have thus in reality arrived at a threefold division, three stages of grammatical treatment of the same phenomena, or three points of view from which grammatical facts may be considered, which may briefly be described as (A) form, (B) function, (C) notion. Let us take one functional (syntactic) class and see its relation on the one hand to form, on the other hand to notion. The English preterit is formed in various ways, and though it is one definite syntactic category, it has not always the same logical purport, as seen in the following scheme :

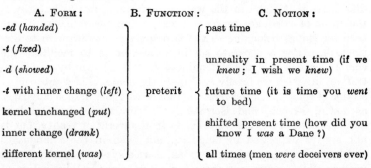

A. Form :	B. Function :	C. Notion :
-ed (*handed*)		past time
-t (*fixed*)		
-d (*showed*)		unreality in present time (if we *knew* ; I wish we *knew*)
-t with inner change (*left*)	preterit	future time (it is time you *went* to bed)
kernel unchanged (*put*)		
inner change (*drank*)		shifted present time (how did you know I *was* a Dane ?)
different kernel (*was*)		all times (men *were* deceivers ever)

Syntactic categories thus, Janus-like, face both ways, towards form, and towards notion. They stand midway and form the

---

[1] This terminology is clearer than Sweet's (NEG § 146). He speaks of natural gender when gender agrees with sex, and of grammatical gender when gender diverges from sex ; thus OE *wifmann* is a grammatical masculine, while OE *mann* is a natural masculine. In my terminology both words are masculines, while *wifmann* 'woman' denotes a female being and *mann* denotes either a male being or, in many instances, a human being irrespective of sex.

connecting link between the world of sounds and the world of ideas. In speaking (or writing) we start from the right side (C) of this scheme, and move through syntax (B) to the formal expression (A) : in hearing (or reading) the movement is in the opposite direction, from A through B to C.

The movement thus is the following :

	C	B	A	B	C
Speaker :	Notion →	Function →	Form		
Hearer :			Form →	Function →	Notion

In finding out what categories to recognize in the third division (C) it is important always to remember that these are to have a linguistic significance ; we want to understand linguistic (grammatical) phenomena, and consequently it would not do to set to work as if language did not exist, classifying things or ideas without regard to their linguistic expression. On the contrary, we should rather do, *mutatis mutandis*, what we did above when establishing our syntactic categories : there we paid the strictest attention to what had found expression in the forms of the language examined, and here we must again pay the strictest attention to the already discovered syntactic categories. It will be the task of the greater part of this work to attempt a systematic review of the chief notional categories in so far as they find grammatical expression, and to investigate the mutual relation of these two " worlds " in various languages. Often enough we shall find that grammatical categories are at best symptoms, foreshadowings of notional categories, and sometimes the ' notion ' behind a grammatical phenomenon is as elusive as Kant's *ding an sich* ; and on the whole we must not expect to arrive at a " universal grammar " in the sense of the old philosophical grammarians. What we obtain is the nearest approach to it that modern linguistic science will allow.

POSTSCRIPT TO CHAPTER III.

The eminent historian of the French language, Ferdinand Brunot, proposes to revolutionize the teaching of (French) grammar by starting from within, from the thoughts to be expressed, instead of from the forms. His great book, *La Pensée et la Langue*, extremely fertile in new observations and methodical remarks, was published (Paris, Masson et Cie, 1922) when more than two-thirds of this volume was written either in its final shape or in nearly the same shape in which it appears now. It is possible, though I cannot at present feel it, that my book would have taken a different shape, had M. Brunot's work appeared before my own convictions had become settled ; as it is now, though I hail him as a powerful ally, I disagree with him on at least two important points. First, what he advocates as the proper method (starting from within, from ' la pensée ') should according to my view be one of two ways of approaching the facts of language, one from without to within, and another from within to without. And secondly, grammar should be kept distinct from dictionary, while M. Brunot in his lists of synonymous terms too often mixes up the two domains. Nor can I share his utter contempt for the old theory of " parts of speech," however wrong it is in many details.

CHAPTER IV

PARTS OF SPEECH

Old Systems. Definitions. The Basis of Classification. Language **and**
Real Life. Proper Names. Actual Meaning of Proper Names.

Old Systems.

I⊤ is customary to begin the teaching of grammar by dividing
words into certain classes, generally called " parts of speech "
—substantives, adjectives, verbs, etc.—and by giving definitions
of these classes. The division in the main goes back to the Greek
and Latin grammarians with a few additions and modifications,
but the definitions are very far from having attained the degree
of exactitude found in Euclidean geometry. Most of the definitions
given even in recent books are little better than sham definitions
in which it is extremely easy to pick holes ; nor has it been possible
to come to a general arrangement as to what the distinction is to
be based on—whether on form (and form-changes) or on meaning
or on function in the sentence, or on all of these combined.

The most ingenious system in this respect is certainly that of
Varro, who distinguishes four parts of speech, one which has cases
(nouns, nomina), one which has tenses (verbs), one which has both
cases and tenses (participles), and one which has neither (particles).
If this scheme is now generally abandoned, the reason evidently
is that it is so manifestly made to fit Latin (and Greek) only and
that it is not suitable either to modern languages evolved out of
a linguistic structure similar to Latin (English, for instance) or to
languages of a totally different type, such as Eskimo.

A mathematical regularity similar to that in Varro's scheme
is found in the following system : some nouns distinguish tense
like verbs and distinguish gender like ordinary nouns (participles),
others distinguish neither gender nor tense (personal pronouns).
Verbs are the only words combining tense distinction with lack
of genders. Thus we have :

nouns
  - ordinary :   with gender, without tense
  - personal pronouns : without gender, without tense
  - participles :   with gender and with tense

verbs :   without gender, with tense. [1]

[1] Schroeder, *Die formelle unterscheidung der redetheile im griech. u. lat.*
Leipzig, 1874.

This system, again, fits only the ancient languages of our family, and differs mainly from Varro's scheme in being based on gender instead of case distinction. Both are equally arbitrary. In both tense is made the really distinctive feature of verbs, a conception which has found expression in the German rendering of *verb* by *zeitwort* : but on that showing Chinese has no verbs, while on the other hand we shall see later that nouns sometimes distinguish tenses. Other grammarians think that the distinctive feature of verbs is the personal endings (Steinthal, etc.). But this criterion would also exclude the Chinese verb from that denomination ; in Danish, again, verbs do not distinguish persons, and it is no help out of the difficulty to say, as Schleicher does (NV 509) that " verbs are words which have or have had personal endings," for it should not be necessary to know linguistic history to determine what part of speech a word belongs to.

Definitions.

Let us now cast a glance at some of the definitions found in J. Hall and E. A. Sonnenschein's *Grammar* (London, 1902). " Nouns name. Pronouns identify without naming." I cannot see that *who* in *Who killed Cock Robin?* identifies ; it rather asks some one else to identify. And *none* in *Then none was for a party*—whose identity is established by that pronoun ? " Adjectives are used with Nouns, to describe, identify or enumerate." [1] But cannot adjectives be used without nouns ? (*the absent* are always at fault. He was *angry*). On the other hand, is *poet* in *Browning the poet* an adjective ? " By means of Verbs something is said about something or somebody " : *You scoundrel*—here something is said about " you " just as much as in *You are a scoundrel*, and in the latter sentence it is not the verb *are*, but the predicative that says something. " Conjunctions connect groups of words or single words "—but so does *of* in *a man of honour* without being on that account a conjunction. Not a single one of these definitions is either exhaustive or cogent. [2]

---

[1] " Enumerate " seems to be used here in a sense unknown to dictionaries. If we take it in the usual signification, then, according to the definition *coat*, etc., would be adjectives in " All his garments, coat, waistcoat, shirt and trousers, were wet."

[2] Long after this was written in the first draft of my book, I became acquainted with Sonnenschein's *New English Grammar* (Oxford, 1921—in many ways an excellent book, though I shall sometimes have occasion to take exception to it). Here some of the definitions have been improved " A pronoun is a word used in place of a noun, to indicate or enumerate persons or things, without naming them." *Indicate* is much better than *identify*, but the difficulty about *none* and *who* persists. " A co-ordinating conjunction is a word used to connect parts of a sentence which are of equal rank. A subordinating conjunction is a word used to connect an adverb-

The Basis of Classification.

Some grammarians, feeling the failure of such definitions as those just given have been led to despair of solving the difficulty by the method of examining the meaning of words belonging to the various classes : and therefore maintain that the only criterion should be the *form* of words. This is the line taken, for instance, by J. Zeitlin ("On the Parts of Speech. The Noun," in *The English Journal*, March 1914), though unfortunately he deals only with nouns. He takes "form" in rather a wide sense, and says that "in English the noun does still possess certain formal characteristics which attach to no other class of words. These are the prefixing of an article or demonstrative, the use of an inflexional sign to denote possession and plurality, and union with prepositions to mark relations originally indicated by inflexional endings." He is careful to add that the absence of all the features enumerated should not exclude a word from being a noun, for this should be described "as a word which has, or in any given usage may have" those formal signs.

If form in the strictest sense were taken as the sole test, we should arrive at the absurd result that *must* in English, being indeclinable, belonged to the same class as *the, then, for, as, enough,* etc. Our only justification for classing *must* as a verb is that we recognize its use in combinations like *I must (go), must we (go)* ? as parallel to that of *I shall (go), shall we (go)* ?—in other words, that we take into consideration its meaning and function in the sentence. And if Zeitlin were to say that the use of *must* with a nominative like *I* is "formal" (in the same way as "union with prepositions" was one of the "formal" tests by which he recognized a noun), I should not quarrel with him for taking such things into account, but perhaps for calling them formal considerations.

In my opinion everything should be kept in view, form, function, and meaning, but it should be particularly emphasized that form, which is the most obvious test, may lead to our recognizing some word-classes in one language which are not distinct classes in other languages, and that meaning, though very important, is most difficult to deal with, and especially that it is not possible to base a classification on short and easily applicable definitions.

We may imagine two extreme types of language structure, one in which there is always one definite formal criterion in each word-class, and one in which there are no such outward signs in

clause or a noun-clause with the rest of a complex sentence." A co-ordinating conjunction may also be used to connect whole sentences (Sonnenschein, § 59). The definition is rather complicated, and pre supposes many other grammatical terms ; it really gives no answer to the question, what is a conjunction ? What is common to the two classes ?

any class. The nearest approach to the former state is found, not in any of our natural languages, but in an artificial language such as Esperanto or, still better, Ido, where every common substantive ends in -o (in the plural in -i), every adjective in -a, every (derived) adverb in -e, every verb in -r, -s, or -z according to its mood. The opposite state in which there are no formal signs to show word-classes is found in Chinese, in which some words can only be used in certain applications, while others without any outward change may function now as substantives, now as verbs, now as adverbs, etc., the value in each case being shown by syntactic rules and the context.

English here steers a middle course though inclining more and more to the Chinese system. Take the form *round* : this is a substantive in " a round of a ladder," " he took his daily round," an adjective in " a round table," a verb in " he failed to round the lamp-post," an adverb in " come round to-morrow," and a preposition in " he walked round the house." *While* similarly may be a substantive (he stayed here for a while), a verb (to while away time), and a conjunction (while he was away). *Move* may be a substantive or a verb, *after* a preposition, an adverb, or a conjunction,[1] etc.

On the other hand, we have a great many words which can belong to one word-class only ; *admiration, society, life* can only be substantives, *polite* only an adjective, *was, comprehend* only verbs, *at* only a preposition.

To find out what particular class a given word belongs to, it is generally of little avail to look at one isolated form. Nor is there any flexional ending that is the exclusive property of any single part of speech. The ending -ed (-d) is chiefly found in verbs (*ended, opened*, etc.), but it may be also added to substantives to form adjectives (*blue-eyed, moneyed, talented*, etc.). Some endings may be used as tests if we take the meaning of the ending also into account ; thus if an added -s changes the word into a plural, the word is a substantive, and if it is found in the third person singular, the word is a verb : this, then, is one of the tests for keeping the substantive and the verb *round* apart (many rounds of the ladder ; he rounds the lamp-post). In other cases the use of certain words in combinations is decisive, thus *my* and *the* in " my love for her " and " the love I bear her," as against " I love her," show that *love* is a substantive and not a verb as in the last combination (cf. *my admiration, the admiration* as against *I admire*, where *admiration* and *admire* are unambiguous).[2]

---

[1] We shall discuss later whether these are really different parts of speech.
[2] See the detailed discussion in MEG II, Chs. VIII and IX, on the question whether we have real substantives in combinations like "Motion requires

It is, however, very important to remark that even if *round* and *love* and a great many other English words belong to more than one word-class, this is true of the isolated form only : in each separate case in which the word is used in actual speech it belongs definitely to one class and to no other. But this is often overlooked by writers who will say that in the sentence " we tead at the vicarage " we have a case of a substantive used as a verb. The truth is that we have a real verb, just as real as *dine* or *eat,* though derived from the substantive *tea*—and derived without any distinctive ending in the infinitive (cf. above, p. 52). To form a verb from another word is not the same thing as using a substantive as a verb, which is impossible. Dictionaries therefore must recognize *love* sb. and *love* v. as two words, and in the same way *tea* sb. and *tea* v. In such a case as *wire* they should even recognize three words, (1) sb. ' metallic thread,' (2) ' to send a message by wire, to telegraph '—a verb formed from the first word without any derivative ending, (3) ' message, telegram '—a sb. formed from the verb without any ending.

In teaching elementary grammar I should not begin with defining the several parts of speech, least of all by means of the ordinary definitions, which say so little though seeming to say so much, but in a more practical way. As a matter of fact the trained grammarian knows whether a given word is an adjective or a verb not by referring to such definitions, but in practically the same way in which we all on seeing an animal know whether it is a cow or a cat, and children can learn it much as they learn to distinguish familiar animals, by practice, being shown a sufficient number of specimens and having their attention drawn successively now to this and now to that distinguishing feature. I should take a piece of connected text, a short story for instance, and first give it with all the substantives printed in italics. After these have been pointed out and briefly discussed the pupil will probably have little difficulty in recognizing a certain number of substantives of similar meaning and form in another piece in which they are not marked as such, and may now turn his attention to adjectives, using the same text as before, this time with the adjectives italicised. By proceeding in this way through the various classes he will gradually acquire enough of the " grammatical instinct " to be

a *here* and a *there*," " a *he*," " a *pick-pocket*," "my *Spanish* is not very good," etc. A specially interesting case in which one may be in doubt as to the class of words is dealt with in MEG II, Ch. XIII : have first-words in English compounds become adjectives ? (See there instances like : intimate and *bosom* friends | the *London* and American publishers | a *Boston* young lady | his own umbrella—the *cotton* one | much purely *class* legislation | the most *everyday* occurrences | the roads which are all *turnpike* | her *chiefest* friend | *matter-of-factly, matter-of-factness.*)

able to understand further lessons in accidence and syntax in his own and foreign languages.

It is not, however, my purpose here to give advice on elementary grammatical teaching, but to try to arrive at some scientific understanding of the logical basis of grammar. This will be best attained, I think, if we consider what it is that really happens when we talk of something, and if we examine the relation between the real world and the way in which we are able to express its phenomena in language.

Language and Real Life.

Real life everywhere offers us only *concretissima* : you see this definite apple, definitely red in one part and yellowish in that other part, of this definite size and shape and weight and degree of ripeness, with these definite spots and ruggednesses, in one definite light and place at this definite moment of this particular day, etc. As language is totally unable to express all this in corresponding concreteness, we are obliged for the purpose of communication to ignore many of these individual and concrete characteristics : the word " apple " is not only applied to the same apple under other circumstances, at another time and in another light, but to a great many other objects as well, which it is convenient to comprise under the same name because otherwise we should have an infinite number of individual names and should have to invent particular names for new objects at every moment of the day. The world is in constant flux around us and in us, but in order to grapple with the fleeting reality we create in our thought, or at any rate in our language, certain more or less fixed points, certain averages. Reality never presents us with an average object, but language does, for instead of denoting one actually given thing a word like *apple* represents the average of a great many objects that have something, but of course not everything, in common. It is, in other words, absolutely necessary for us, if we want to communicate our impressions and ideas, to have more or less abstract [1] denominations for class-concepts : *apple* is abstract in comparison with any individual apple that comes within our ken, and so is *fruit* to an even higher degree, and the same is still more true of such words as *red* or *yellow* and so on : language everywhere moves in abstract words, only the degree of abstraction varies infinitely.

Now, if you want to call up a very definite idea in the mind of your interlocutor you will find that the idea is in itself very complex, and consists of a great many traits, really more than you

---

[1] " Abstract " is used here in a more popular sense than in the logico-grammatical terminology to be considered below in Ch. X.

would be able to enumerate, even if you were to continue to the end of time. You have to make a selection, and you naturally select those traits that according to the best of your belief will be best fitted to call up exactly the same idea in the other man's mind. More than that, you select also those that will do it in the easiest way to yourself and to your hearer, and will spare both of you the trouble of long circuitous expressions. Therefore instead of *a timid gregarious woolly ruminant mammal* you say *sheep,* instead of *male ruler of independent state* you say *king,* etc. Thus wherever you can, you use single special terms instead of composite ones. But as special terms are not available for all composite ideas, you often have to piece together expressions by means of words each of which renders one of the component traits of the idea in your mind. Even so, the designation is never exhaustive. Hence the same man may under various circumstances be spoken of in totally different ways, and yet the speaker is in each case understood to refer to the same individual : as " James Armitage " or simply " Armitage " or " James," or else as " the little man in a suit of grey whom we met on the bridge," or as " the principal physician at the hospital for women's diseases," as " the old Doctor," as " the Doctor," as " Her husband," as " Uncle James," as " Uncle," or simply as " he." In each case the hearer supplies from the situation (or context), i.e. from his previous knowledge, a great many distinctive traits that find no linguistic expression—most of all in the last-mentioned case, where the pronoun " he " is the only designation.

Among these designations for the same individual there are some which are easily seen to have a character of their own, and we at once single out *James* and *Armitage* (and, of course, the combination *James Armitage*) as *proper names,* while we call such words as *man, physician, doctor, husband, uncle,* which enter into some of the other designations, *common names,* because they are common to many individuals, or at least to many more, than are the proper names. Let us now try to consider more closely what is the essence of proper names.

Proper Names.

A proper name would naturally seem to be a name that can only be used in speaking of one individual. It is no objection to this definition that *the Pyrenees* or *the United States* are proper names, for in spite of the plural form by which they are designated this range of mountains and this political body are looked upon as units, as individuals : it is not possible to speak of *one Pyrenee* or of *one United State,* but only of *one of the Pyrenees, one of the United States.*

A more serious difficulty encounters us when we reflect that *John* and *Smith* by common consent are reckoned among proper names, and yet it is indubitable that there are many individuals that are called *John*, and many that are called *Smith*, and even a considerable number that are called *John Smith*. *Rome* similarly is a proper name, yet there are at least five towns of that name in North America besides the original Rome in Italy. How then are we to keep up the distinction between proper and common names?

A well-known attempt at a solution is that of John Stuart Mill (*System of Logic*, I, Ch. II). According to him proper names are not *connotative*; they *denote* the individuals who are called by them; but they do not indicate or imply any attributes as belonging to those individuals, they answer the purpose of showing what thing it is we are talking about, but not of telling anything about it. On the other hand, such a name as *man*, besides *denoting* Peter, James, John, and an indefinite number of other individuals, *connotes* certain attributes, corporeity, animal life, rationality, and a certain external form, which for distinction we call the human. Whenever, therefore, the names given to objects convey any information, that is, whenever they have any meaning, the meaning resides not in what whey *denote*, but in what they *connote*. The only names of objects which connote nothing are proper names; and these have, strictly speaking, no signification.

Similarly a recent Danish writer (H. Bertelsen, *Fællesnavne og egennavne*, 1911) says that John is a proper name, because there is nothing else besides the name that is common to all John's in contradistinction to Henry's and Richard's, and that while a common name indicates by singling out something that is peculiar to the individual persons or things to whom the name is applied, the opposite is true of a proper name. Accordingly, the distinction has nothing to do with, or at any rate has no definite relation to, the number of individuals to whom a name is given. I do not think, however, that this view gets to the bottom of the problem.

Actual Meaning of Proper Names.

What in my view is of prime importance is the way in which names are actually employed by speakers and understood by hearers. Now, every time a proper name is used in actual speech its value to both speaker and hearer is that of denoting one individual only, and being restricted to that one definite being. To-day, in talking to one group of my friends, I may use the name John about a particular man of that name, but that does not prevent me from using it to-morrow in different company of a totally different individual; in both cases, however, the name fulfils its purpose of calling up in the mind of the hearer the exact meaning which I intend.   Mill and his followers lay too much stress on what might be called the dictionary value of the name, and too little on its contexual value in the particular situation in which it is spoken or written.   It is true that it is quite impossible to tell the meaning of *John* when nothing but the name is before us, but much the same thing may be said of a great many " common names."   If I am asked to give the meaning of *jar* or *sound* or *palm* or *tract*, the only honest answer is, Show me the context, and I will tell you the meaning.   In one connexion *pipe* is understood to mean a tobacco-pipe, in another a water-pipe, in a third a boatswain's whistle, in another one of the tubes of an organ, and in the same way John, in each separate sentence in which it is used, has one distinct meaning, which is shown by the context and situation ; and if this meaning is more special in each case than that of *pipe* or the other words mentioned, this is only another side of the important fact that the number of characteristic traits is greater in the case of a proper name than in the case of a common name.   In Mill's terminology, but in absolute contrast to his view, I should venture to say that proper names (as actually used) " connote " the greatest number of attributes.

The first time you hear of a person or read his name in a newspaper, he is " a mere name " to you, but the more you hear and see of him the more will the name mean to you.   Observe also the way in which your familiarity with a person in a novel grows the farther you read.   But exactly the same thing happens with a " common name " that is new to you, say *ichneumon* : here again, the meaning or connotation grows along with the growth of your knowledge.   This can only be denied on the assumption that the connotation of a name is something inherent in the name, something with an existence independent of any human mind knowing and using the name : but that is surely absurd and contrary to all right ideas of the essence of language and human psychology.

If proper names as actually understood did not connote many attributes, we should be at a loss to understand or explain the everyday phenomenon of a proper name becoming a common name.   A young Danish girl was asked by a Frenchman what her father was, and in her ignorance of the French word for ' sculptor ' got out of the difficulty by saying : " Il est un *Thorvaldsen* en miniature."   Oscar Wilde writes : " Every great man nowadays has his disciples, and it is always *Judas* who writes the biography " (*Intentions*, 81)—a transition to speaking of *a Judas*.   Walter Pater says that France was about to become *an Italy* more Italian than Italy itself (*Renaissance*, 133).   In this way *Cæsar* became the general name for Roman emperors, German Kaisers and

Russian tsars (in Shakespeare's tragedy III. 2. 55, the rabble shouts: " Liue Brutus, liue, liue. . . . Let him be Cæsar ")—to mention only a few examples.[1]

Logicians, of course, see this, but they dismiss it with some remark like this (Keynes FL 45) : " Proper names, of course, become connotative when they are used to designate a certain type of person ; for example, a Diogenes, a Thomas, a Don Quixote, a Paul Pry, a Benedick, a Socrates. But, when so used, such names have really ceased to be proper names at all ; they have come to possess all the characteristics of general names." The logician as such with his predilection for water-tight compartments in the realm of ideas, is not concerned with what to me as a linguist seems a most important question, viz. how is it to be explained that a sequence of sounds with no meaning at all suddenly from non-connotative becomes connotative, and that this new full meaning is at once accepted by the whole speaking community ?

If we take the view suggested above, this difficulty vanishes at once. For what has happened is simply this, that out of the complex of qualities characteristic of the bearer of the name concerned (and, as I should say, really connoted by the name) one quality is selected as the best known, and used to characterize some other being or thing possessed of the same quality. But this is exactly the same process that we see so very often in common names, as when a bell-shaped flower is called a bell, however different it is in other respects from a real bell, or when some politician is called an old *fox*, or when we say that *pearl*, or *jewel*, of a woman. The transference in the case of original proper names is due to the same cause as in the case of common names, viz. their connotativeness, and the difference between the two classes is thus seen to be one of degree only.

The difference between *Crœsus* as applied to the one individual and as used for a very rich man may be compared to that between *human* (connoting everything belonging to man) and *humane* (selecting one particular quality).

With our modern European system of composite personal names we have a transference of names of a somewhat different kind, when a child through the mere fact of his birth acquires his father's family name. Here it would be rash to assert that Tymperleys, for instance, of the same family have nothing in common but their name ; they may sometimes be recognized by their nose or by their gait, but their common inheritance, physical and psychical, may be much more extensive, and so the name Tymperley may get a sense not essentially different from that of such " common

[1] The Lithuanian word for ' king,' *karalius*, is derived from *Carolus* (Charlemagne) ; so also Russ. *korol*, Pol. *król*, Magy. *király*.

names " as *Yorkshireman,* or *Frenchman,* or *negro,* or *dog.* In some of the latter cases it is difficult to define exactly what the name " connotes " or by what characteristics we are able to tell that a person belongs to this or the other class, yet logicians agree that all these names are connotative. Then why not *Tymperley* ?

It is different, of course, with Christian names, which are given in a much more arbitrary way. One Maud may have been so called " after " a rich aunt, and another simply because her parents thought the name pretty, and the two thus have nothing but the name in common. The *temple* of worship and the *temple* of the head are in much the same case. (The two Mauds have really more in common than the two temples, for they are both female human beings.[1]) But that does not affect the main point in my argument, which is that whenever the name Maud is naturally used it makes the hearer think of a whole complex of distinctive qualities or characteristics.

Now it will be said against this view that " the connotation of a name is not the quality or qualities by which I or anyone else may happen to recognize the class which it denotes. For example, I may recognize an Englishman abroad by the cut of his clothes, or a Frenchman by his pronunciation, or a proctor by his bands, or a barrister by his wig ; but I do not *mean* any of these things by these names, nor do they (in Mill's sense) form any part of the connotation of the names " (Keynes FL 43). This seems to establish a distinction between essential characteristics comprised in the " connotation " [2] and unessential or accidental qualities. But surely no sharp line can be drawn. If I want to know what is connoted by the names *salt* and *sugar* respectively, is it necessary to apply chemical tests and give the chemical formula of these two substances, or am I permitted to apply the popular criterion of tasting them ? What qualities are connoted by the word " dog " ? In this and in a great many other cases we apply class-names without hesitation, though very often we should be embarrassed if asked what we " mean " by this or that name or why we apply it in particular instances. Sometimes we recognize a dog by this, and sometimes by that characteristic, or group of characteristics, and if we apply the name " dog " to a particular animal, it means that we feel confident that it possesses the rest of that complex of traits which together make up dog-nature.[3]

---

[1] A further method of transference of proper names is seen in the case of married women, when Mary Brown by marrying Henry Taylor becomes Mrs. Taylor, Mrs. Mary Taylor, or even Mrs. Henry Taylor.

[2] Cf. ib. 24, " we include in the connotation of a class-name only those attributes upon which the classification is based."

[3] The best definition of a dog probably is the humorous one that a dog is that animal which another dog will instinctively recognize as such.

The use of proper names in the plural (cf. MEG II, 4. 4) is made intelligible by the theory we have here defended. In the strictest sense no proper name can have a plural, it is just as unthinkable as a plural of the pronoun " I " : there is only one " I " in existence, and there is only one " John " and one " Rome," if by these names we understand the individual person or city that we are speaking of at the moment. But in the above-mentioned modified senses it is possible for proper names to form a plural in the usual way. Take the following classes :

(1) individuals which have more or less arbitrarily been designated by the same name : in the party there were three *Johns* and four *Marys* | I have not visited any of the *Romes* in America ;

(2) members of the same family : all the *Tymperleys* have long noses | in the days of the *Stuarts* | the *Henry Spinkers* (cf. Ch. XIV, plural of approximation) ;

(3) people or things like the individual denoted by the name : *Edisons* and *Marconis* may thrill the world with astounding novelties | *Judases* | *King-Henrys*,   *Queen-Elizabeths*   go   their way (Carlyle) | the Canadian Rockies are advertised as " fifty *Switzerlands* in one " ;

(4) by metonymy, a proper name may stand for a work of the individual denoted by the name : there are two *Rembrandts* in this gallery.

It should also be remembered that what we designate by an individual name is, if we look very closely into it, merely an abstraction. Each individual is constantly changing from moment to moment, and the name serves to comprehend and fix the permanent elements of the fleeting apparitions, or as it were, reduce them to a common denominator. Thus we understand sentences like the following, which are very hard to account for under the assumption that proper names are strictly non-connotative : he felt convinced that Jonas was again the Jonas he had known a week ago, and not the Jonas of the intervening time (Dickens) | there were days when Sophia was the old Sophia—the forbidding, difficult Sophia (Bennett) | Anna was astounded by the contrast between the Titus of Sunday and the Titus of Monday (id.) | The Grasmere before and after this outrage were two different vales (de Quincey). In this way, too, we may have a plural of a proper name : Darius had known England before and after the repeal of the Corn Laws, and the difference between the two *Englands* was so strikingly dramatic . . . (Bennett).

Linguistically it is utterly impossible to draw a sharp line of demarcation between proper names and common names. We have seen transitions from the former to the latter, but the opposite transition is equally frequent. Only very few proper names have always been such (e.g. *Rasselas*), most of them have originated, totally or partially, in common names specialized. Is " the Union " as applied to one particular students' union at Oxford or Cambridge a proper name ? Or the " British Academy " or the " Royal Insurance Company," or—from another sphere—" Men and Women " or " Outspoken Essays " or " Essays and Reviews " as book-titles ? The more arbitrary the name is, the more inclined we are to recognize it at once as a proper name, but it is no indispensable condition. The Dover road (meaning ' the road that leads to Dover ') is not originally a proper name, while *Dover Street* which has no connexion with Dover and might just as well have been baptized *Lincoln Street*, is a proper name from the first. But the *Dover Road* may in course of time become a proper name, if the original reason for the name is forgotten and the road has become an ordinary street ; and the transition may to some extent be marked linguistically by the dropping of the definite article. One of the London parks is still by many called " the Green Park," but others omit the article, and then *Green Park* is frankly a proper name ; compare also *Central Park* in New York, *New College, Newcastle*. Thus, the absence of the article in English (though not in Italian or German) becomes one of the exterior marks by which we may know proper from common names.

In the familiar use of such words as *father, mother, cook, nurse* without the article we accordingly have an approximation to proper names ; no doubt they are felt as such by children up to a certain age, and this is justified if the mother or an aunt in speaking to the child says *father* not of her own, but of the child's father.

The specialization which takes place when a common name becomes a proper name is not different in kind, but only in degree, from specializations to be observed within the world of common names. Thus when *the Black Forest* (or, still more distinctly, the German name *Schwarzwald*) has become the name of a particular mountain range, the relation between this name and the combination " the black forest " which might be applied as a common name to some other forest is similar to that between *the blackbird* and *the black bird*.[1]

Our inquiry, therefore, has reached this conclusion, that no sharp line can be drawn between proper and common names, the

[1] One final example may be given to illustrate the continual oscillations between common and proper names. When musicians speak of the Ninth Symphony they always mean Beethoven's famous work. It thus becomes a proper name ; but Romain Rolland makes that again into a common name by using it in the plural (marked by the article, while the singular form of the noun and the capital letters show it to be apprehended as a proper name) when writing about some French composers : ils faisaient des *Neuvième Symphonie* et des *Quatuor* de Franck, mais beaucoup plus difficiles (Jean Chr. 5. 83).

difference being one of degree rather than of kind.   A name always connotes the quality or qualities by which the bearer or bearers of the name are known, i.e. distinguished from other beings or things.   The more special or specific the thing denoted is, the more probable is it that the name is chosen arbitrarily, and so much the more does it approach to, or become, a proper name.   If a speaker wants to call up the idea of some person or thing, he has at his command in some cases a name specially applied to the individual concerned, that is, a name which in this particular situation will be understood as referring to it, or else he has to piece together by means of other words a composite denomination which is sufficiently precise for his purpose.   The way in which this is done will be the subject of our consideration in the next chapter.

CHAPTER V

SUBSTANTIVES AND ADJECTIVES

Survey of Forms.   Substance and Quality.   Specialization.   Interchange of
the Two Classes.   Other Combinations.

Survey of Forms.

AMONG the designations for the same individual which we found
above, p. 64, there were some which contained two elements
that evidently stood in the same relation to each other, viz. *little
man, principal physician, old Doctor*. Here we call the words
little, principal, and *old* adjectives, and *man, physician*, and *Doctor*
substantives.   Adjectives and substantives have much in common,
and there are cases in which it is difficult to tell whether a word
belongs to one or the other class ; therefore it is convenient to
have a name that comprises both, and in accordance with the old
Latin terminology which is frequently found also in recent continental works on grammar, I shall use the word *noun* (Lat. *nomen*)
for the larger class of which substantives and adjectives are subdivisions.   English scholars generally use the word noun for what
is here called substantive ; but the terminology here adopted
gives us on the one hand the adjective *nominal* for both classes,
and on the other hand the verb *substantivize* when we speak, for
instance, of a substantivized adjective.

While in some languages, e.g. Finnish, it seems impossible to
find any criteria in flexion that distinguish substantives from
adjectives, a word like *suomalainen* being thus simply a noun,
whether we translate it in some connexions as a substantive (Finn,
Finlander) or in others as adjective (Finnish), our own family of
languages distinguishes the two classes of nouns, though with
different degrees of explicitness.   In the older languages, Greek,
Latin, etc., the chief formal difference has reference to gender
and is shown by the concord of adjectives with their substantives.
While every substantive is of one definite gender, the adjective
varies, and it is the fact that we say *bonus dominus, bona mensa,
bonum templum*, that obliges us to recognize substantives and
adjectives as two distinct classes of nouns.   Now it is interesting
to note that adjectives are as it were more " orthodox " in their
gender flexions than substantives : we have masculine substantives

in -*a* and feminine substantives in -*us*, but only *bonus* in the masculine and *bona* in the feminine (*bonus poeta, bona fagus*). On the
whole substantives present many more irregularities in their flexion
(indeclinable or defective words, words in which one stem supple-
ments another) than adjectives. The same characteristic difference
is still found in German grammar : substantives are more indivi-
dualistic and conservative, while adjectives are more subject to
the influence of analogy.

In the Romanic languages, apart from the disappearance of
the neuter gender, the same relations obtain between the two
classes as in Latin, though in spoken French the distinctions
between the masculine and feminine forms have largely been
obliterated—*donné* and *donnée, poli* and *polie, menu* and *menue,
grec* and *grecque* being pronounced the same. It is also noteworthy
that there is no invariable rule for the position of adjectives, which
are in some cases placed before, and in others after their substantives. As a consequence of this, one may here and there be in
doubt which of two collocated words is the substantive and which
the adjective, thus in *un savant aveugle, un philosophe grec* (see
below) ; such combinations as *un peuple ami, une nation amie*
(also *une maîtresse femme*) may be taken either as a substantive
(*peuple, nation, femme*) with an adjective, or else as two substantives joined very much like English *boy messenger, woman writer*.

In the Gothonic (Germanic) languages similar doubts cannot,
as a rule, exist. At a very early date, adjectives took over some
endings from the pronouns, and then they developed the peculiar
distinction between a strong and a weak declension, the latter
originally an -*n*-flexion transferred from one class of substantives
and gradually extended to all adjectives and chiefly used after
a defining word, such as the definite article. This state of things
is preserved with some degree of fidelity in German, where we
still have such distinctly adjectival forms as *ein alter mann, der
alte mann, alte männer, die alten männer*, etc. Icelandic still keeps
the old complicated system of adjective flexion, but the other
Scandinavian languages have greatly simplified it, though retain-
ing the distinction between strong and weak forms, e.g. Dan. *en
gammel mand, den gamle mand* ' an old man, the old man.'

In Old English things were pretty much the same as in German.
But in course of time, phonetic and othe. developments have
brought about a system that is radically different from the older
one. Some endings, such as those containing *r*, have completely
disappeared ; this has also happened to the endings -*e* and -*en*,
which formerly played a very important rôle in both substantives
and adjectives. While -*s* was formerly used in the genitive of
adjectives in the sg. (m. and n.), it has now been completely

discarded from the adjectives, which consequently have now only one form for all cases in both numbers, no matter whether they are preceded or not by the definite article. On the other hand, the simplification of substantive flexions, though very radical, has not been quite so thorough as that of the adjectives. Here the -s-endings have been especially vigorous, and now form the chief distinctive feature of substantives, while every trace of the old Aryan concord has disappeared. Thus we must say that in *the old boy's* (gen.) and *the old boys'* (pl.), we see that *old* is an adjective, from its having no ending, and that *boys* is a substantive, from the ending -s. When we have *the blacks* used of the negro race, the adjective *black* has become completely substantivized ; similarly *the heathens* is a substantive, while *the heathen* continues to be an adjective, even if it stands alone without any following substantive, employed in what many grammarians call a " substantival function." Accordingly, in Shakespeare, H5 III. 5. 10 " Normans, but bastard Normans, Norman bastards " we have first the adj. *bastard* and the subst. *Normans,* and then the adj. *Norman* and the subst. *bastards.*

Substance and Quality.

This brief survey has shown us that though the formal distinction between substantive and adjective is not marked with equal clearnesss in all the languages considered, there is still a tendency to make such a distinction. It is also easy to show that where the two classes are distinguished, the distribution of the words is always essentially the same : words denoting such ideas as *stone, tree, knife, woman* are everywhere substantives, and words for *big, old, bright, grey* are everywhere adjectives. This agreement makes it highly probable that the distinction cannot be purely accidental : it must have some intrinsic reason, some logical or psychological (" notional ") foundation, and we shall now proceed to examine what that foundation is.

An answer very often given is that substantives denote substances (persons and things), and adjectives qualities found in these things. This definition is evidently at the root of the name substantive, but it cannot be said to be completely satisfactory. The names of many " substances " are so patently derived from some one quality that the two ideas cannot possibly be separated : *the blacks, eatables, desert, a plain* must be called substantives and are in every respect treated as such in the language. And no doubt a great many other substantives the origin of which is now forgotten were at first names of one quality singled out among others by the speakers. So, linguistically the distinction between

" substance " and " quality " cannot have any great value. And from a philosophical point of view it may be said that we know substances only through their qualities ; the essence of any substance is the sum of all those qualities that we are able to perceive (or conceive) as in some way connected. While formerly substances were thought of as realities *per se* and qualities were considered as having no existence in themselves, there is perhaps now a strong tendency in the opposite direction, to look upon the substance or " substratum " of various qualities as a fiction, rendered more or less necessary by our habits of thought, and to say that it is the " qualities " that ultimately constitute the real world, i.e. everything that can be perceived by us and is of value to us.[1]

Whether the reader may be inclined to attach much or little importance to the arguments just presented, he must acknowledge that the old definition is powerless to solve the riddle of the so-called " abstracts " like *wisdom, kindness,* for though these words are to all intents and purposes substantives and are treated as such in all languages, yet they evidently denote the same qualities as the adjectives *wise* and *kind,* and there is nothing substantial about them. Whatever notional definition one gives of a substantive, these words make difficulties, and it will be best at the present moment to leave them out of consideration altogether—we shall return to them in a following chapter (X).

Specialization.

Apart from " abstracts," then, I find the solution of our problem in the view that on the whole substantives are more special than adjectives, they are applicable to fewer objects than adjectives, in the parlance of logicians, the extension of a substantive is less, and its intension is greater than that of an adjective. The adjective indicates and singles out one quality, one distinguishing mark, but each substantive suggests, to whoever understands it, many distinguishing features by which he recognizes the person or thing in question. What these features are, is not as a rule indicated in the name itself ; even in the case of a descriptive name one or two salient features only are selected, and the others are understood : a botanist easily recognizes a *bluebell* or a *blackberry* bush even at a season when the one has no blue flowers and the others no black berries.[2]

---

[1] The three words *substance* (with *substantive*), *substratum,* and *subject* are differentiations of the Aristotelian *to hupokeimenon* ' the underlying.'

[2] My definition is similar to that given by Paul (P § 251 :)" Das adj. bezeichnet eine einfache oder als einfach vorgestellte eigenschaft, das subst. schliesst einen komplex von eigenschaften in sich "—but in the lines immediately following Paul seems to disavow his own definition. It may not be

The difference between the two classes is seen very clearly when the same word may be used in both capacities. We have a great many substantivized adjectives, but their meaning is always more special than that of the corresponding adjectives, compare e.g. *a cathedral* (*une cathédrale*, Sp. *un catedral*), *the blacks* (= negroes), *natives* (both = ' inhabitants ' and ' oysters '), *sweets, evergreens,* etc. The same is true of those cases where the adjectival use has disappeared, as in *tithe* (orig. a numeral, ' tenth '), *friend* (an old participle of a verb ' to love '), and of such old Latin or Greek participles as *fact, secret, serpent, Orient, horizon.*

Inversely, when a substantive is made into an adjective, we find that its meaning has become less special. Thus the French *rose, mauve, puce,* etc., are more general when they stand as colour-indicating adjectives than as substantives : they can be applied to more different things, as they now " connote " only one of the characteristics that go to make up the things they stand for in their original signification.[1] English examples of the transition are *chief, choice, dainty* (orig. ' a delicacy '), *level, kindred* (orig. ' relationship ').

The Latin adjective *ridiculus* according to Bréal (MSL 6. 171) is evolved from a neuter substantive *ridiculum* ' objet de risée,' formed in the same way as *curriculum, cubiculum, vehiculum.* When applied to persons it took masculine and feminine endings, *ridiculus, ridicula,* and it is this formal trait which made it into an adjective ; but at the same time its signification became slightly more general and eliminated the element of ' thing.'

A gradual transition from substantive to adjective is seen in the so-called weak adjectives in Gothonic. As Osthoff has pointed out, these go back to an old substantive-formation parallel to that found in Gr. *strabōn* ' the squint-eyed man ' corresponding to the adj. *strabos* ' squinting,' or Lat. *Cato Catonis* ' the sly one,' cp. adj. *catus, Macro* cp. adj. *macer.* In Gothonic this was gradually extended, but at first these forms, like the Greek and Latin words mentioned, were nicknames or distinguishing names, thus individual in their application. As Osthoff says, Latin *M. Porcius Cato, Abudius Rufo,* transferred into German, meant something like *M. Porcius der Kluge, Abudius der Rote,* just as in OHG we have

amiss expressly to state what will appear from the following disquisitions and exemplifications, that I do not mean to say that the "extension" of *any* substantive is always and under all circumstances less than that of *any* adjective : very often a numerical comparison of the instances in which two words are applicable is excluded by the very nature of the case.

[1] " Elle avait un visage plus rose que les roses " (Andoux, Marie Claire, 234). The difference made in writing between *des doigts roses* and *des gants paille* is artificial. Note the recent adjective *peuple* ' plebeian ' as in " Ses manières affables . . . un peu trop expansives, un peu peuple " (Rolland JChr 6. 7) and " Christophe, beaucoup plus peuple que lui " (ib. 9. 48).

with the same ending *Ludowig ther snello,* and as we still in German
have the weak form of the adjective in *Karl der Grosse, Friederich
der Weise, August der Starke.* The definite article was not at first
required, cf. ON *Brage Gamle* ('the old one') and only later *Are
enn (hinn) gamle.* Thus also in Beowulf *beahsele beorhta,* originally
to be interpreted as two substantives in apposition, 'ringhall—the
bright one'; *hrefen blaca* 'raven, the black being.' A combina-
tion like " þær se goda sæt | Beowulf " is at first like " there the
good one sat, (namely) Beowulf," parallel to " þær se cyning sæt,
Beowulf," but later *se goda* was connected more directly with
Beowulf or some other substantive; this formation was extended
to neuters (not yet in the oldest English epic) and finally became
the regular way of making an adjective definite before its substantive. The number of words that require the weak form of
an adjective has been constantly growing, especially in German.
By this gradual development, which has made these forms just
as much real adjectives as the old " strong " forms, the old indi-
vidualizing force has been lost, and the words have become more
general in their meaning than they were once, though it may be said
still that *(der) gute (mann)* is more special than *(ein) guter (mann).*

Bally (*Traité de stylistique française,* 305) calls attention to
another effect of substantivizing an adjective : " Vous êtes un
impertinent " est plus familier et plus énergique que " Vous êtes
impertinent." Here the substantivizing is effected simply by
adding the indefinite article. The same effect is observed in other
languages, compare " He is a bore " with " He is tedious "; " Er
ist ein prahlhans " with " Er ist prahlerisch," etc. It is the same
with terms of endearment : " You are a dear " is more affectionate
than " You are dear," which is hardly ever said. The explanation
is obvious : these substantives are more vigorous because they
are more special than the adjectives, though seemingly embodying
the same idea.

It is a simple corollary of our definition that the most special
of substantives, proper names, cannot be turned into adjectives
(or adjuncts, see below) without really losing their character of
proper names and becoming more general. We see this in such
a combination as *the Gladstone ministry,* which means the ministry
headed by Gladstone, and stands in the same relation to the real
proper name Gladstone as *Roman* to *Rome* or *English* to *England.*
The general signification is seen even more clearly in such examples
as *Brussels sprouts* (which may be grown anywhere) or a *Japan
table* (which means a table lacquered in the way invented in Japan).[1]

---

[1] The use of capital letters in words derived from proper names varies
from language to language, e.g. E. *French* in all cases, *Frenchify,* Fr. *français*
as an adj. and of the language, *Français* 'Frenchman,' *franciser.*

Interchange of the Two Classes.

Let us now turn to those cases in which an adjectival and a substantival element of the same group can more or less naturally be made to exchange places. Couturat, who is on the whole inclined to make light of the difference between the two classes of words, possibly on account of the slight formal difference found in his own mother-tongue, adduces such examples as : " *un sage sceptique* est un *sceptique sage, un philosophe grec* est un *Grec philosophe,*" and says that the difference is only a nuance, according as one of the qualities is looked upon as more essential or simply as more important or interesting under the circumstances : for it is evident that one is a Greek before being a philosopher, " et néanmoins nous parlons plutôt des philosophes gres que des Grecs philosophes " (*Revue de Métaphysique et de Morale,* 1912, 9).

Now it may be difficult to say which of these two ideas is the more important or interesting, but if we apply the above-mentioned criterion we shall easily see why in choosing between the two ways of designating the Greeks who are philosophers (= the philosophers who are Greeks), we naturally make philosopher (the more special idea) the substantive and Greek (the more general one) the adjective and say *the Greek philosophers* (*les philosophes grecs*) rather than *les Grecs philosophes* (in English the conversion is not so complete and *the philosophical Greeks* does not exactly cover the French expression). A famous German book is called " Griechische denker." " Denkende griechen " would be a much weaker title, because the adjective *denkend* is much more vague in its application than the substantive *denker*, which at once singles out those who think more deeply and more professionally than ordinary " thinking " people.

Another example : Mr. Galsworthy somewhere writes : " Having been a Conservative Liberal in politics till well past sixty, it was not until Disraeli's time that he became a Liberal Conservative." The words *conservative* and *liberal* are made into substantives (and then take -*s* in the plural) when they mean members of two political parties ; evidently this is a more special idea than that which is attached to the same words as general adjectives.[1]

If we compare the two expressions *a poor Russian* and *a Russian pauper*, we see first that the substantive *Russian* is more special than the corresponding adjective in that it implies the idea ' man or woman,' and that on the other hand *pauper* is more special than *poor*, which may be applied to many things besides human beings : *pauper* is even more specialized than ' a poor

---

[1] Further examples (such as Chesterton's "most official Liberals wish to become Liberal officials ") in MEG II, 8. 14.

person ' as implying one that is entitled to or receives public charity.[1]

Other Combinations.

The rule of the greater complexity and specialization of substantives thus holds good wherever we are able directly to compare two words of closely similar signification ; but can it be applied to other cases—can we say that in any collocation of an adjective and a substantive the former is always less special than the latter ? In a great many cases we can undoubtedly apply the criterion, even in its most arithmetical form, by counting how many individuals each word may be applied to. *Napoleon the third* : there are only few Napoleons, but many persons and things that are third in a series. *A new book* : there are more new things than books in existence. *An Icelandic peasant* : it is true that there are more peasants in the world than Icelanders, but then the adjective *Icelandic* can be applied to a great many things as well as to persons : Icelandic mountains and waterfalls and sheep and horses and sweaters, etc., etc. Some of my critics objected to my example *a poor widow*, saying that if we substitute *rich* it was unfortunately very doubtful whether there were more rich persons in existence than widows—thus overlooking the fact that *rich* may be said of towns, villages, countries, mines, spoils, stores, rewards, attire, experience, sculpture, repast, cakes, cream, rimes and so forth. *The Atlantic Ocean* : the adjective is found, for instance in Shelley's poems, with the substantives clouds, waves, and islets. The adjective *rare*, though meaning ' not often met with ' may be used in speaking of innumerable objects, men, stones, trees, stamps, mental qualities, etc., and thus falls within the definition. But it must, of course, be conceded that the numerical test cannot always be applied, as adjectives and substantives which may be put together are very often by the nature of the case incommensurable : we speak of *a grey stone*, but who shall say whether the word *grey* or *stone* is applicable to the greater number of objects. But applicability to a greater or lesser number is only one side of what is implied in the words special and general, and I am inclined to lay more stress on the greater complexity of qualities denoted by substantives, as against the singling out of one quality in the case of an adjective. This complexity is so essential that only in rare cases will it be possible by heaping

---

[1] Mill (*Logic*, 15) says that " there is no difference of meaning between *round*, and *a round object*." This is to some extent true when *round* is found as a predicative (" the ball is round " = " is a round object "), but not elsewhere : this definition, applied to " a round ball," would imply a meaningless tautology. It is only when the adj. becomes really substantivized that we can say that it implies the notion of ' object.'

adjective upon ad'ective to arrive at a complete definition of the notion evoked by the naming of a substantive : there will always, as Bertelsen remarks, remain an indefinable x, a kernel which may be thought of as " bearer " of the qualities which we may have specified. This again is what underlies the old definition by means of " substance," which is thus seen to contain one element of truth though not the whole truth. If one wants a metaphorical figure, substantives may be compared to crystallizations of qualities which in adjectives are found only in the liquid state.

It must also be mentioned here that our languages contain a certain number of substantives of a highly general signification, *thing, body, being.* But their " general " signification is not of the same order as that of adjectives : they very often serve as comprehensive terms for a number of undoubtedly substantival ideas (*all these things,* said instead of enumerating books, paper, garments, etc.)—this use is very frequent in philosophic and abstract scientific thinking. In everyday speech they may be loosely used instead of a special substantive which is either not found in the language or else is momentarily forgotten (cp. such words as *thingummybob,* G. *dingsda*). Otherwise they rarely occur except in combination with an adjective, and then they are often little more than a kind of grammatical device for substantivizing the adjective like the E. *one.* (*Ones,* in *the new ones,* is a substitute for the substantive mentioned a few moments before ; in *her young ones,* said of a bird, it supplies the want of a substantive corresponding to *children*). This leads to their use in compound pronouns : *something, nothing, quelquechose, ingenting, somebody,* etc. On the other hand, when once a language has a certain way of forming adjectives, it may extend the type to highly specialized adjectives, e.g. in *a pink-eyed cat, a ten-roomed house,* which combinations have been advanced against my whole theory : there are more cats than pink-eyed beings, etc. This, however, does not seem to me to invalidate the general truth of the theory as here explained : it must be remembered also that the real adjectival part of such combinations is *pink* or *ten,* respectively.

It will be easily understood from what has been said above that the so-called degrees of comparison (*greater, greatest*) are as a rule found only with adjectives : such comparisons necessarily deal with one quality at a time. The more special an idea is, the less use will there be for degrees of comparison. And where we do find in actual usage comparatives or superlatives of substantive forms they will be seen on closer inspection to single out one quality and thus to mean the same thing as if they were formed from real adjectives. Thus Gr. *basileuteros, basileutatos* ' more (most) of a king, kinglier, kingliest' (other examples Delbrück, Synt. 1. 415), Magyar *szamár* ' ass,' *szamarabb* ' sillier,' *róka* ' fox,' *rókább* ' slyer.' Finnish *ranta* ' strand,' *rannempi* ' nearer to the strand,' *syksy* ' autumn,' *syksymänä* ' later in the autumn.' Cf. also Paul P § 250.

One final remark : we cannot make the complexity of qualities or specialization of signification a criterion by which to decide whether a certain word is a substantive or an adjective : that must be settled in each case by formal criteria varying from language to language. What has been attempted in this chapter is to find whether or no there is anything in the nature of things or of our thinking that justifies the classification found in so many languages by which substantives are kept distinct from adjectives. We cannot, of course, expect to find any sharp or rigid line of demarcation separating the two classes in the way beloved by logicians : language-makers, that is ordinary speakers, are not very accurate thinkers. But neither are they devoid of a certain natural logic, and however blurred the outlines may sometimes be, the main general classifications expressed by grammatical forms will always be found to have some logical foundation. It is so in the case before us : substantives are broadly distinguished as having a more special signification, and adjectives as having a more general signification, because the former connote the possession of a complexity of qualities, and the latter the possession of one single quality.[1]

---

[1] This chapter is rearranged and somewhat modified from *Sprogets logik* (Copenhagen, 1913). I have here, without essentially altering my view, tried to meet the criticisms of S. Ehrlich (*Språk och stil*, 1914), H. Bertelsen (*Nordisk tidskrift*, 1914), H. Schuchardt (*Anthropos*, 1914), N. Beckman (*Arkiv för psykologi och pedagogik*, 1922), cf. also Vendryes L 153 ff.

CHAPTER VI

PARTS OF SPEECH—*concluded*

Pronouns. Verbs. Particles. Summary. Word.

Pronouns.

PRONOUNS are everywhere recognized as one of the word-classes, but what constitutes their distinctive peculiarity ? The old definition is embodied in the term itself : pronouns stand instead of the name of a person or thing. This is expanded by Sweet (NEG § 196) : a pronoun is a substitute for a noun and is used partly for the sake of brevity, partly to avoid the repetition of a noun, and partly to avoid the necessity of definite statement. But this does not suit all cases, and the definition breaks down in the very first pronoun ; it is very unnatural to the unsophisticated mind to say that " I see you " stands instead of " Otto Jespersen sees Mary Brown," on the contrary most people will say that in *Bellum Gallicum* the writer uses the word *Cæsar* instead of " I." We may also say " I, Otto Jespersen, hereby declare . . .," which would be preposterous if " I " were simply a substitute for the name. And grammatically it is very important that " I " is the first person, and the name is in the third, as shown in many languages by the form of the verb. Further : no one doubts that *nobody* and the interrogative *who* are pronouns, but it is not easy to see what nouns they can be said to be substitutes for.

It is true that *he, she,* and *it* are most often used instead of naming the person or thing mentioned, and it would indeed be possible to establish a class of words used for similar purposes, but then not all of them are reckoned among pronouns, viz. :

(1) *he, she, it, they* used instead of a substantive.

(2) *that, those* similarly ; cf. " his house is bigger than *that* of his neighbour."

(3) *one, ones* : " a grey horse and two black *ones*," " I like this cake better than the *one* you gave me yesterday."

(4) *so* : " he is rich, but his brother is still more *so* " ; " Is he rich ? I believe *so*."

(5) *to* : " Will you come ? I should like *to*."

(6) *do* : " He will never love his second wife as he *did* his first.'

In this way we should get a class of substitute words which might be subdivided into pro-nouns, pro-adjectives, pro-adverbs, pro-infinitives, pro-verbs (and pro-sentences as *so* in the second instance above), but it could hardly be called a real grammatical class.

Noreen's treatment of pronouns (VS 5. 63 ff.) is very original and instructive. He contrasts pronouns with "expressive sememes" the signification of which is fixed in so far as it is essentially contained in the linguistic expression itself ; pronouns then are characterized by their signification being variable and essentially contained in a reference to some circumstance which is found outside of the linguistic expression itself and is determined by the whole of the situation. "I" is a pronoun because it signifies one person when John Brown, and another when Mary Smith speaks. The consequence is that a great many words and groups of words are pronouns, according to Noreen, for instance *the undersigned* ; *today* ; (there were three boys), *the biggest one*, etc. No two words could be more pronominal than *yes* and *no* (but what about *On the contrary* as a reply instead of *no ?*) ; *here* is the pronominal adverb of place of the first person, and *there* the corresponding adverb for the second and third persons, and *now* and *then* are the corresponding pronominal adverbs of time (but the combinations *here and there*, *now and then*, meaning ' in various not defined places ' and ' occasionally ' cannot be pronouns according to Noreen's definition). Further *right*, *left*, *on Sunday*, *the horse* (not only *the*, but both words together), *my horse*, are all of them pronouns. Noreen is at some pains (not very successfully) to prove that such a common " proper name " as *John* is not a pronoun though its proper signification wherever it occurs is determined by the whole situation. And what about *father* as used by the child for ' my father ' ?

Noreen's class is too comprehensive and too heterogeneous, and yet it is not easy to see how words like the interrogative *who* and *what* or like *some*, *nothing* can fall within the definition. But the main defect in his treatment of this and of other points to my mind is due to his building up categories entirely from the " semological " or what I should call the notional point of view without regard to the way in which the meaning is expressed in actual language, that is, without any consideration of formal elements. If we keep both sides in view we shall find that there is really some sense in comprising a certain number of shifters (to use the term I employ in *Language*, p. 123), reminders (ib. 353), representative and relational words under one class with the old-established name of pronouns. It may not be easy to say what is common to all of them from the notional point of view, but if we take each of the traditional sub-classes by itself its notional unity is manifest : personal pronouns with the corresponding possessives —demonstrative pronouns—relative pronouns—interrogative pronouns—indefinite pronouns, though with regard to this last class the boundaries between a few of them, such as *some*, and such adjectives as *many*, are rather vague ; consequently grammarians disagree as to what words they should include in this sub-class. This, however, is not essentially different from what we find in any other grammatical classification : there will always be some borderline cases. And when we investigate the forms and functions of these pronouns in various languages we discover that they present certain features by which they are distinguished from other words. But these features are not the same in all languages, nor are they exactly the same with all the pronouns found within the same one language. Formal and functional anomalies abound in pronouns. In English we have the distinction between two cases as in *he : him, they : them*, and between an adjunct and a non-adjunct form in *my : mine*, the sex-distinction in *he : she* and the similar distinction *who : what*, the irregular plural in *he, she : they, that : those*, combinations of the type of *somebody, something*, which are not found with ordinary adjectives, the use of *each* without any accompanying substantive or article, etc.[1] Similar peculiarities are found in the pronouns of other languages ; in French we have, for instance, the special forms *je, me, tu, te*, etc., which are only found in close conjunction with verbal forms.

The term pronoun is sometimes restricted (generally in French books, but also in the Report of the Joint Committee on Terminology) to those words which function as what in Ch. VII I shall call " primary words," while *my* is called a ' possessive adjective " and *this* in *this book* a " demonstrative adjective." There is, however, not the slightest reason for thus tearing asunder *my* and *mine*, or, even worse, *his* in " his cap was new " and " his was a new cap " or *this* in " this book is old " and " this is an old book " [2] and assigning the same form to two different " parts of speech," especially as it then becomes necessary to establish the same sub-classes of adjectives (possessive, demonstrative) as are found in pronouns. I should even go so far as to include among pronouns the so-called pronominal adverbs *then, there, thence,*

---

[1] It is also worth noticing that the voiced sound of written *th* [ð] is found initially in pronouns only : *thou, the, that*, etc., including under pronominal words the adverbs *then, there, thus.*

[2] The difference in function (" rank ") is parallel to that between *poor* in " the poor people loved her " and " the poor loved her," and between " there were only *two* men " and " there were only *two*." Sonnenschein (§ 118) says that *both* in " both boys " is an adjective, but in " both the boys " a pronoun standing in apposition—surely a most unnatural distinction.

when, where, whence, etc., which share some of the peculiarities of pronouns and are evidently formed from them (note also such formations as *whenever,* cf. *whoever,* and *somewhere,* etc.).

Numerals are often given as a separate part of speech ; it would probably be better to treat them as a separate sub-class under the pronouns, with which they have some points in common. *One* besides being a numeral is, in English as well as in some other languages, an indefinite pronoun (" one never knows "), cf. also the combination *oneself.* Its weak form is the so-called " indefinite article," and if its counterpart the " definite article " is justly reckoned among pronouns, the same should be the case with *a, an,* Fr. *un,* etc. To establish a separate " part of speech " for the two " articles," as is done in some grammars, is irrational. E. *other* was originally an ordinal meaning ' second ' as *anden* still does in Danish ; now it is generally classed among pronouns, and this is justified by its use in *each other, one another.* Most numerals are indeclinable, but in languages where some of them are declined, these often present anomalies comparable to those found in other pronouns. If we include numerals among pronouns, we might include also the indefinite numerals *many, few* : logically these stand in the same series as *all, some* and the negative *none, no,* which are always reckoned among indefinite pronouns. But then we must also include *much, little* as in *much harm, little gold* (with mass-words, cf. Ch. XIV).[1] All these quantifiers, as they might be called, differ from ordinary qualifying adjectives in being capable of standing alone (without articles) as " primaries " as when we say " some (many, all, both, two) were absent," " all (much, little) is true " ; they are always placed before qualifiers and cannot be transcribed in the form of a predicative : " a nice young lady " is the same as " a lady who is nice and young," but such a transposition is impossible with " many ladies," " much wine," etc., just as it is impossible with " no ladies," " what ladies," " that wine," and other pronouns.

A final word may be added about the names of some of the sub-classes. *Relative* pronouns : in these days when everything has been shown to be relative, it would perhaps be possible to introduce a more pertinent name, e.g. *connective* or *conjunctive* pronouns, as their business is to join sentences in pretty much the same way as conjunctions do : indeed it may be questioned whether E. *that* is not the conjunction rather than a pronoun ; compare the possibility of omitting *that* : " I know the man (that) you mentioned " and " I know (that) you mentioned the man," and the impossibility of having a preposition before *that* : " the man that you spoke about " as against " the man about whom

---

[1] In a different sense *little* is an ordinary adjective, e.g. in *my little girl.*

you spoke."—*Personal* pronouns : if this refers to *person* in the sense of 'human being,' it is improper in cases like G. *er*, Fr. *elle* or E. *it* applied to a table (*der tisch, la table*), and even more to the "impersonal" *it, es, il* in *it rains, es regnet, il pleut*. If on the other hand the name *personal* is taken to refer to the three grammatical persons (see Ch. XVI), it may be justly said that only the two first persons strictly belong here, for all the other pronouns (*this, who, nothing*, etc.) are of the third person just as much as *he* or *she*. But it will be difficult to find a better name to substitute for "personal" pronouns, and the question is not very important. The delimitation of personal and demonstrative pronouns sometimes offers difficulties; thus in Dan., where *de, dem* formally go with the demonstrative *den, det*, but functionally are the plural both of *den, det* and of *han, hun* 'he, she.'

Verbs.

Verbs in most languages, at any rate those of the Aryan, Semitic, and Ugro-finnic types, have so many distinctive features that it is quite necessary to recognize them as a separate class of words, even if here and there one or more of those distinguishing traits that are generally given as characteristic of verbs may be found wanting. Such traits are the distinctions of persons (first, second, third), of tense, of mood, and of voice (cf. above, p. 58). As for their meaning, verbs are what Sweet calls phenomenon words and may be broadly divided into those that denote action (he *eats, breathes, kills, speaks*, etc.), those that denote some process (he *becomes, grows, loses, dies*, etc.), and those that denote some state or condition (he *sleeps, remains, waits, lives, suffers*, etc.), though there are some verbs which it is difficult to include in any one of these classes (he *resists, scorns, pleases*). It is nearly always easy to see whether a given idea is verbal or no, and if we combine a verb with a pronoun as in the examples given (or with a noun : *the man eats*, etc.) we discover that the verb imparts to the combination a special character of finish and makes it a (more or less) complete piece of communication—a character which is wanting if we combine a noun or pronoun with an adjective or adverb. The verb is a life-giving element, which makes it particularly valuable in building up sentences : a sentence nearly always contains a verb, and only exceptionally do we find combinations without a verb which might be called complete sentences. Some grammarians even go so far as to require the presence of a verb in order to call a given piece of communication a sentence. We shall discuss this question in a later chapter.

If now we compare the two combinations *the dog barks* and *the barking dog*, we see that though *barks* and *barking* are evidently closely related and may be called different forms of the same word, it is only the former combination which is rounded off as a complete piece of communication, while *the barking dog* lacks that peculiar finish and makes us ask : What about that dog ? The sentence-building power is found in all those forms which are often called " finite " verb forms, but not in such forms as *barking* or *eaten* (participles), nor in infinitives like *to bark, to eat*. Participles are really a kind of adjectives formed from verbs, and infinitives have something in common with substantives, though syntactically both participles and infinitives retain many of the characteristics of a verb. From one point of view, therefore, we should be justified in restricting the name verb to those forms (the finite forms) that have the eminently verbal power of forming sentences, and in treating the " verbids " (participles and infinitives) as a separate class intermediate between nouns and verbs (cf. the old name *participium,* i.e. what participates in the character of noun and verb). Still it must be admitted that it would be somewhat unnatural to dissociate *eat* and *eaten* in such sentences as *he is eating the apple, he will eat the apple, he has eaten the apple* from *he eats the apple, he ate the apple* ; [1] and it is, therefore, preferable to recognize non-finite forms of verbs by the side of finite forms, as is done in most grammars.

Particles.

In nearly all grammars adverbs, prepositions, conjunctions, and interjections are treated as four distinct " parts of speech," the difference between them being thus put on a par with that between substantives, adjectives, pronouns, and verbs. But in this way the dissimilarities between these words are grossly exaggerated, and their evident similarities correspondingly obscured, and I therefore propose to revert to the old terminology by which these four classes are treated as one called " particles."

As regards form they are all invariable—apart from the power that some adverbs possess of forming comparatives and superlatives in the same way as the adjectives to which they are related. But in order to estimate the differences in meaning or function that have led most grammarians to consider them as different parts of speech, it will be necessary to cast a glance at some words outside these classes.

Many words are subject to a distinction which is designated

[1] Note also the Russian past tenses, like *kazal* 'showed,' orig. a past participle 'having showed.'

by different names and therefore not perceived as essentially the
same wherever found, namely that between a word complete in
itself (or used for the moment as such) and one completed by some
addition, generally of a restrictive nature. Thus we have the
complete verb in *he sings, he plays, he begins* ; and the same verb
followed by a complement in *he sings a song, he plays the piano,
he begins work*. In this case it is usual to call the verb intransitive
in one case and transitive in the other, while the complement is
termed its object. In other verbs where these names are not
generally used, the distinction is really the same : *he can* is complete ; in *he can sing* the verb *can* is completed by the addition
of an infinitive. For this latter distinction we have no settled
term, and the terms used by some, independent and auxiliary
verb, are not quite adequate ; for while on the one hand we have
an antiquated use of *can* with a different kind of complement in
" He could the Bible in the holy tongue," we have on the other
hand such combinations as " He is able," " he is able to sing,"
and " he wants to sing." A further case in point is seen in *he
grows*, where the verb is complete, and *he grows bigger*, where it
is complemented by a " predicative " ; cp. *Troy was* and *Troy
was a town*. Yet in spite of these differences in verbs no one thinks
of assigning them to different parts of speech : *sing, play, begin,
can, grow, be* are always verbs, whether in a particular combination
they are complete or incomplete.

If now we turn to such words as *on* or *in*, we find what is to
my mind an exact parallel to the instances just mentioned in
their employment in combinations like " put your cap on " and
" put your cap on your head," " he was in " and " he was in the
house " ; yet *on* and *in* in the former sentences are termed adverbs,
and in the latter prepositions, and these are reckoned as two
different parts of speech. Would it not be more natural to include
them in one class and to say that *on* and *in* are sometimes complete
in themselves and sometimes followed by a complement (or object) ?
Take other examples : " he climbs *up* " and " he climbs up a
tree," " he falls *down* " and " he falls down the steps " (cf. " he
ascends, or descends " with or without the complement " the
steps " expressed) ; " he had been there *before* " and " he had
been there before breakfast." [1] Is *near* in " it was near one
o'clock " a preposition or an adverb according to the usual system ?
(Cf. the two synonyms *almost* and *about*, the former called an adverb,
the latter a preposition.) The close correspondence between the
object of a transitive verb and that of a " preposition " is seen in
those cases in which a preposition is nothing but a verbal form
in a special use, as for example *concerning* (G. *betreffend*) and *past*

[1] Cf. also " the house *opposite* ours " and " the house opposite."

in " he walked past the door at half-past one," which is simply
the participle *passed* written in a different way; in " he walked
past " it has no complement.

Nor is there any reason for making conjunctions a separate
word-class. Compare such instances as " *after* his arrival " and
" after he had arrived," " *before* his breakfast " and " before he
had breakfasted," " she spread the table *against* his arrival " and
(the antiquated) " she spread the table against he arrived," " he
laughed *for* joy " and " he laughed for he was glad." The only
difference is that the complement in one case is a substantive,
and in the other a sentence (or a clause). The so-called conjunction is really, therefore, a sentence preposition : the difference
between the two uses of the same word consists in the nature of the
complement and in nothing else ; and just as we need no separate
term for a verb completed by a whole sentence (clause) as distinct
from one completed by a substantive, so it is really superfluous
to have a separate name for a " conjunction "; if we retain the
name, it is merely due to tradition, not to any scientific necessity,
and should not make us recognize conjunctions as a " part of
speech." Note the parallelism in

(1) I *believe* in God.   They have lived happily ever
                                   since.
(2) I *believe* your words.   They have lived happily *since*
                                   their marriage.
(3) I *believe* (that) you are right. They have lived happily *since*
                                   they were married.

We may even find the same word used in two ways in the same
sentence, thus " *After* the Baden business, and he had [= after
he had] dragged off his wife to Champagne, the Duke became
greatly broken " (Thackeray) ; if this is rare it must be remembered that it is similarly rare to find one and the same verb in the
same sentence construed first transitively and then intransitively,
or first with a substantive and then with a clause as object.

The examples given above show the same word used now as
a preposition and now as a conjunction , in other cases we have
slight differences as in " *because of* his absence " and " *because* he
was absent," which is historically explained by the origin of *because*
from *by cause* (people once said " because that he was absent ").
In other cases, again, a particular word has only one use, either
with an ordinary object or with a clause as its complement :
" *during* his absence," " *while* he was absent." But this should
not make us hesitate to affirm the essential identity of prepositions
and conjunctions, just as we put all verbs in one class in spite of
the fact that they cannot all take a complementary clause.

The definition of a conjunction as a sentence-preposition does not apply to some words which are always reckoned among conjunctions, such as *and* in " he and I are great friends," " she sang and danced," and *or* in " was it blue or green ? " etc. The same words may be used to connect sentences, as in " she sang, and he danced," " he is mad, or I am much mistaken." In both cases they are coordinating connectives, while prepositions and the conjunctions hitherto considered are subordinating connectives, but though this is an important distinction there is no reason on that account to separate them into two word-classes. *And* and *with* mean nearly the same thing, the chief difference between them being that the former coordinates and the latter subordinates ; this has some grammatical consequences—notice for example the form of the verb in " he and his wife *are* coming " as against " he with his wife *is* coming " (" he is coming with his wife ") and the possessive pronoun in Danish : " han og *hans* kone kommer," but " han kommer med *sin* kone." But the slightness of the notional difference makes people apt to infringe the strict rule, as in Shakespeare's " Don Alphonso, With other gentlemen of good esteeme Are journying " (see MEG II, 6.53 ff.).[1] *Both, either* and *neither* are so far peculiar in that they ' anticipate ' an *and, or, nor,* following, but they need not, of course, be considered as a class apart.

As the last " part of speech " the usual lists give interjections, under which name are comprised both words which are never used otherwise (some containing sounds not found in ordinary words, e.g. an inhaled *f* produced by sudden pain, or the suction-stop inadequately written *tut*, and others formed by means of ordinary sounds, e.g. *hullo, oh*), and on the other hand words from the ordinary language, e.g. *Well ! Why ! Fiddlesticks ! Nonsense ! Come !* and the Elizabethan *Go to !* The only thing that these elements have in common is their ability to stand alone as a complete " utterance," otherwise they may be assigned to various word-classes. They should not therefore be isolated from their ordinary uses. Those interjections which cannot be used except as interjections may most conveniently be classed with other ' particles.'

---

[1] *As* and *than* in comparisons are coordinating : "I like you nearly as well as (better than) *her* " (i.e. as, or than, I do her). " I like you nearly as well as (better than) *she* (i.e. as, or than, she does). But on account of such instances as " I never saw anybody stronger than *he* " (scil. is), and " than *him* " (agreeing with anybody), the feeling for the correct use of the cases is easily obscured, and *he* is used for *him*, and conversely. Many examples ChE p. 60 ff. The use of nom. after *as* even induces some people to say *like I* instead of *like me*, ibid. 62.

Summary.

The net result of our inquiry is that the following word-classes, and only these, are grammatically distinct enough for us to recognize them as separate " parts of speech," viz. :

(1) Substantives (including proper names).
(2) Adjectives.
    In some respects (1) and (2) may be classed together as " Nouns."
(3) Pronouns (including numerals and pronominal adverbs).
(4) Verbs (with doubts as to the inclusion of " Verbids ").
(5) Particles (comprising what are generally called adverbs, prepositions, conjunctions—coordinating and subordinating—and interjections). This fifth class may be negatively characterized as made up of all those words that cannot find any place in any of the first four classes.

I have finished my survey of the various word-classes or parts of speech. It will be seen that while making many criticisms, especially of the definitions often given, I have still been able to retain much of the traditional scheme. I cannot go so far as, for instance, E. Sapir, who says (L 125) that " no logical scheme of the parts of speech—their number, nature, and necessary confines —is of the slightest interest to the linguist " because " each language has its own scheme. Everything depends on the formal demarcations which it recognizes."

It is quite true that what in one language is expressed by a verb may in another be expressed by an adjective or adverb : we need not even step outside of English to find that the same idea may be rendered by *he happened to fall* and *he fell accidentally*. We may even draw up a list of synonymous expressions, in which substantive, adjective, adverb, and verb seem to change places quite arbitrarily. For example :

He moved astonishingly fast.
He moved with astonishing rapidity.
His movements were astonishingly rapid.
His rapid movements astonished us.
His movements astonished us by their rapidity.
The rapidity of his movements was astonishing.
The rapidity with which he moved astonished us.
He astonished us by moving rapidly.
He astonished us by his rapid movements.
He astonished us by the rapidity of his movements.

But this is an extreme example, which is only made possible by the use of " nexus-words " (verbal substantives and so-called

" abstracts "), which are specially devised for the purpose of trans-posing words from one word-class to another, as will be shown in Ch. X. In the vast majority of instances such jugglery is impossible. Take a simple sentence like

This little boy picked up a green apple and immediately ate it.

Here the word-classes are quite fixed and allow of no trans-position : substantives (*boy, apple*), adjectives (*little, green*), pronouns (*this, it*), verbs (*picked, ate*), particles (*up, and, immediately*).

I therefore venture to maintain that the demarcation of these five classes is consonant with reason, though we are unable to define them so rigidly as to be left with no doubtful or borderline cases. Only we must beware of imagining that these classes are absolutely notional : they are *grammatical* classes and as such will vary to some extent—but only to some extent—from language to language. They may not fit such languages as Eskimo and Chinese (two extremes) in the same way as they fit Latin or English, but in these and the other languages which form the chief subject of this book the old terms substantive, adjective, etc., are indispensable : they will therefore be retained in the senses and with the provisos indicated in these chapters.

Word.

What is a word ? and what is one word (not two or more) ? These are very difficult problems, which cannot be left untouched in this volume.[1]

Words are linguistic units, but they are not phonetic units : no merely phonetic analysis of a string of spoken sounds can reveal to us the number of words it is made up of, or the division between word and word. This has long been recognized by phoneticians and is indisputable : *a maze* sounds exactly like *amaze, in sight* like *incite, a sister* like *assist her,* Fr. *a semblé* like *assemblé, il l'emporte* like *il en porte,* etc. Nor can the spelling be decisive, because spelling is often perfectly arbitrary and dependent on fashion or, in some countries, on ministerial decrees not always well advised. Does *at any rate* change its character, if written, as it now is occasionally, *at anyrate* ? Or *any one, some one* if written *anyone, someone* ? (*No one* is parallel, but the spelling *noone* could never become popular, because it would be read as *noon.*) There is hardly sufficient reason for German official spellings

[1] The proper definition of *word* has been discussed in innumerable places in linguistic literature. Let me mention a few : Noreen VS 7. 13 ff. ; H. Pedersen, *Gött. gel. Anz.* 1907, 898 ; Wechssler, *Giebt es Lautgesetze,* 19 ; Boas, *Handbook of Amer. Indian Languages,* 1. 28 ; Sapir L 34 ; Vendryes L 85. 103 ; A. Gardiner, *British Journal of Psychology,* April 1922.

like *miteinander, infolgedessen, zurzeit,* etc. In his first books Barrie wrote the Scottish phrase *I suppaud,* probably because he thought it a verb like *suppose,* but later he was told its origin and now, if I am not mistaken, writes *I'se uphauld* (= I shall uphold). All this shows the difficulty of deciding whether certain combinations are to be considered two un-amalgamated words or one amalgamated word.

On the other hand, words are not notional units, for, as Noreen remarks, the word *triangle* and the combination *three-sided rectilinear figure* have exactly the same meaning, just as " Armitage " and " the old doctor in the grey suit whom we met on the bridge " may designate the same man. As, consequently, neither sound nor meaning in itself shows us what is one word and what is more than one word, we must look out for grammatical (syntactic) criteria to decide the question.

In the following cases purely linguistic criteria show that what was originally two words has become one. G. *grossmacht* and Dan. *stormagt* differ from E. *great power* as shown by their flexion : *die europäischen grossmächte, de europœiske stormagter,* but in English with a different word-order we say *the great European Powers.*[1] The numerals 5 + 10 both in Lat. *quindecim* and E. *fifteen* differ in sound from the uncompounded numerals ; Lat. *duodecim* also in not having a dative form *duobusdecim,* etc. Fr. *quinze, douze* must, of course, be considered units, even in a higher degree, because they have lost all similarity with *cinq, deux* and *dix.* Dan. *een og tyve* ' one and twenty ' is one word in spite of the spelling, because the same form is used before a neuter : *een og tyve år* (but *et år*). E. *breakfast, vouchsafe* were two words until people began saying *he breakfasted, he vouchsafes* instead of the earlier *he broke fast, he vouches safe* ; cp. p. 24. *Each other* might claim to be spelt as one word, because it takes a preposition before the whole combination (*with each other*) instead of the old construction *each with other.* In French *je m'en fuis* has become *je m'enfuis,* and is now rightly so written because the perfect is *je me suis enfui* ; but the parallel expression *je m'en vais* is always written separately : it is true that colloquially *je me suis en-allé* is often said instead of the orthodox *je m'en suis allé,* but the amalgamation cannot be complete as with *enfuis,* because the use of different stems (*vais, allé, irai*) prevents the fusion into one form. Fr. *république,* E. *republic,* are units, which Lat. *res publica* cannot be on account of its flexion : *rem publicam.* The absence of inner flexion in G. *jedermann, jedermanns, die mitternacht* (*jeder* is originally nom.,

---

[1] It may perhaps be said that Lat. *forsitan* is more of a unit when it is followed by an indicative than when it is followed by a subjunctive in consequence of its origin : *fors sit an.* Fr. *peut-être* is now one word, as seen by the possibility of saying *il est peut-être riche.*

mitter dat.) shows completed unification, as does also the flexion
in Lat. *ipsum* instead of *eumpse* (*ipse* from *is-pse*).

In all these cases a complete amalgamation of what was at
first two words must be recognized, because we have unmistakable
linguistic criteria by which to show that native instinct really
treats the combination as a unity ; but this is not the case in
E. *he loves*, which has sometimes been thought to be as much a
unit as Lat. *amat* (*ama-t*) : in English we can separate the
elements (*he never loves*) and isolate each of them, while in *amat*
this is impossible ; similarly, Fr. *il a aimé* is not a unit in the same
way as Lat. *amavit*, because we can say *il n'a pas aimé, a-t-il aimé*,
etc. (see my criticism of various scholars, *Language*, p. 422 ff.).

Sometimes we have the opposite movement, from word-units
to looser combinations. The cohesion between the two elements
of English compound substantives is looser than it was formerly
(and than it is in German and Danish). While G. *steinmauer* and
Dan. *stenmur* are in every respect one word, E. *stone wall* and
similar combinations are now rather to be considered two, *stone*
being an adjunct and *wall* a primary. This is shown not only by
the equal (or varying) stress, but also in other ways : by coordina-
tion with adjectives : his personal and *party* interests | among the
evening and weekly papers | a *Yorkshire* young lady ; by the use
of *one* : five gold watches, and seven *silver* ones ; by the use of
adverbs : a purely *family* gathering ; by isolation : any position,
whether *State* or national | things that are dead, *second-hand*, and
pointless. Some of these first elements have in this way become
so completely adjectival, that they can take the superlative ending
-est (*chiefest, choicest*), and adverbs can be formed from them
(*chiefly, choicely*), see MEG II, Ch. XIII (above, 62 note). In
Shakespeare's " so new a fashioned robe " we see how another type
of compound (*new-fashioned*) is also felt as loosely coherent.

All these considerations, as well as the changes of initial sounds
frequent, for instance, in Keltic languages, and such phenomena
as ON " hann kvaðsk eigi vita " (he said-himself not know, i.e.
he said that he did not know) and many others [1] show how difficult
it is in many cases to say what is one and what is two words.
Isolability in many cases assists us, but it should not be forgotten
that there are words, which we must recognize as such, and which
yet for one reason or another cannot be isolated ; thus the Russian
prepositions consisting of a consonant alone, *s, v,* or French words
like *je, tu, le*, which never occur alone, although there is, indeed,
no purely phonetic reason against their being isolated. If these
are words, it is because they can be placed in various positions

---

[1] Cf. Metanalysis (*a naddre* > *an adder*, etc.), *Language*, 173. 132 ; Fr.
interrogative *ti* from *est-il, fait-il*, ib. 358.

with other words, which are undoubtedly complete words ; consequently *je, tu,* etc., are not themselves parts of words, but whole
words.   In the same way *an, bei, statt* in G. " ich nehme es an,
wir wohnten der versammlung bei, es findet nur selten statt "
are words, and a consistent orthography would have to write
" an zu nehmen, bei zu wohnen, es hat statt gefunden " instead
of the usual forms in one word : the position of the words is the
same as in " gern zu nehmen, dort zu wohnen, er hat etwas gefunden," etc.[1]

We should never forget that words are nearly always used in
connected speech, where they are more or less closely linked with
other words : these are generally helpful, and often quite indispensable, to show the particular meaning in which the given word
is to be understood. Isolated words, as we find them in dictionaries and philological treatises, are abstractions, which in that
form have little to do with real living speech. It is true that in
answers and retorts words occur isolated, even words which cannot
otherwise stand by themselves, e.g. *if* : " If I were rich enough . . ."
" Yes, if ! "—but then the meaning is understood from what precedes, exactly as " Yesterday " when said as an answer to the
question " When did she arrive ? " means " She arrived yesterday."
But such isolation must always be considered an exception, not
the rule.

A term is wanted for a combination of words which together
form a sense unit, though they need not always come in immediate
juxtaposition and thus are shown to form not one word but two
or more words. This may be called a *phrase,* though that term
is used in a different way by other writers. The words *puts off*
form a phrase, the meaning of which (' postpones ') cannot be
inferred from that of the words separately ; the words may be
separated, e.g. *he puts it off.* G. *wenn auch* forms a phrase, e.g. in
wenn er auch reich ist.

---

[1] Recent grammarians sometimes indulge in curious exaggerations and
misconceptions connected with the problem here discussed, e.g. when one
says that the plural in modern French is formed by a preposed *z* : (*le*)*z-arbres,*
etc. : but what about *beaucoup d'arbres* and *les pommes* ? Or when it
is said that substantives in French are now declined through the article
(Brunot PL 162) : *le cheval, du cheval, au cheval* : but in *Pierre, de Pierre,
à Pierre* there is no article. (Besides, this cannot properly be called declension.) Or, finally, when a German writer speaks of *der mann, dem mann,*
etc., as forming one word, so that we have " flexion am anfang oder genauer
im innern des wortes an stelle der früheren am ende."

CHAPTER VII

THE THREE RANKS

Subordination. Substantives. Adjectives. Pronouns. Verbs. Adverbs.
Word Groups. Clauses. Final Remarks.

Subordination.

THE question of the class into which a word should be put—whether
that of substantives or adjectives, or some other—is one that
concerns the word in itself. Some answer to that question will
therefore be found in dictionaries.[1] We have now to consider
combinations of words, and here we shall find that though a substantive always remains a substantive and an adjective an adjective,
there is a certain scheme of subordination in connected speech
which is analogous to the distribution of words into ' parts of
speech,' without being entirely dependent on it.

In any composite denomination of a thing or person (such as
those to which I referred on p. 64), we always find that there is
one word of supreme importance to which the others are joined
as subordinates. This chief word is defined (qualified, modified)
by another word, which in its turn may be defined (qualified,
modified) by a third word, etc. We are thus led to establish different
" ranks " of words according to their mutual relations as defined
or defining. In the combination *extremely hot weather* the last
word *weather*, which is evidently the chief idea, may be called
primary ; *hot*, which defines *weather*, secondary, and *extremely*,
which defines *hot*, tertiary. Though a tertiary word may be further
defined by a (quaternary) word, and this again by a (quinary)
word, and so forth, it is needless to distinguish more than three
ranks, as there are no formal or other traits that distinguish words
of these lower orders from tertiary words. Thus, in the phrase
a certainly not very cleverly worded remark, no one of the words
certainly, *not*, and *very*, though defining the following word, is in
any way grammatically different from what it would be as a
tertiary word, as it is in *certainly a clever remark, not a clever
remark, a very clever remark.*

---

[1] Note, however, that any word, or group of words, or part of a word,
may be turned into a substantive when treated as a *quotation word* (MEG II,
8. 2.), e.g. your *late* was misheard as *light* | his speech abounded in *I think
so's* | there should be two *l*'s in his name.

If now we compare the combination *a furiously barking dog* (*a dog barking furiously*), in which *dog* is primary, *barking* secondary, and *furiously* tertiary, with *the dog barks furiously*, it is evident that the same subordination obtains in the latter as in the former combination. Yet there is a fundamental difference between them, which calls for separate terms for the two kinds of combination : we shall call the former kind *junction*, and the latter *nexus*. The difference has already been mentioned on p. 87, and there will be occasion for a fuller discussion of it in Ch. VIII, where we shall see that there are other types of nexus besides the one seen in *the dog barks*. It should be noted that *the dog* is a primary not only when it is the subject, as in *the dog barks*, but also when it is the object of a verb, as in *I see the dog*, or of a preposition, as in *he runs after the dog*.

As regards terminology, the words *primary*, *secondary*, and *tertiary* are applicable to nexus as well as to junction, but it will be useful to have the special names *adjunct* for a secondary word in a junction, and *adnex* for a secondary word in a nexus. For tertiary we may use the term *subjunct*, and quaternary words, in the rare cases in which a special name is needed, may be termed *sub-subjuncts*.[1]

Just as we may have two (or more) coordinate primaries, e.g. in *the dog and the cat ran away*, we may, of course, have two or more coordinate adjuncts to the same primary : thus, in *a nice young lady* the words *a*, *nice*, and *young* equally define *lady* ; compare also *much* (*II*) *good* (*II*) *white* (*II*) *wine* (*I*) with *very* (*III*) *good* (*II*) *wine* (*I*). Coordinate adjuncts are often joined by means of connectives, as in *a rainy and stormy afternoon* | *a brilliant, though lengthy novel*. Where there is no connective the last adjunct often stands in a specially close connexion with the primary as forming one idea, one compound primary (*young-lady*), especially in some fixed combinations (*in high good humour, by great good fortune*, MEG II, 15. 15; *extreme old age*, ib. 12. 47). Sometimes the first of two adjuncts tends to be subordinate to the second and thus nearly becomes a subjunct, as in *burning hot soup, a shocking bad nurse*. In this way *very*, which was an adjective (as it still is in *the very day*) in Chaucer's *a verray parfit gentil knight*, has become first an intermediate between an adjunct and a subjunct, and then a subjunct which must be classed among adverbs ; other examples MEG II, 15. 2. A somewhat related instance is *nice* (*and*) in *nice and warm* (15. 29), to which there is a curious parallel in It. *bell'e* : Giacosa, Foglie 136 il concerto. . . . On ci ho bell'e rinunziato |

[1] I now prefer the word *primary* to the term *principal* used in MEG Vol. II. One might invent the terms *superjunct* and *supernex* for a primary in a junction and in a nexus respectively, and *subnex* for a tertiary in a nexus but these cumbersome terms are really superfluous.

ib : 117 Tu l'hai bell'e trovato. Other instances of adjuncts, where subjuncts might be expected, are Fr. *elle est toute surprise | les fenêtres grandes ouvertes.*

Coordinated subjuncts are seen, e.g. in *a logically and grammatically unjustifiable construction | a seldom or never seen form.*

In the examples hitherto chosen we have had substantives as primaries, adjectives as adjuncts, and adverbs as subjuncts ; and there is certainly some degree of correspondence between the three parts of speech and the three ranks here established. We might even define substantives as words standing habitually as primaries, adjectives as words standing habitually as adjuncts, and adverbs as words standing habitually as subjuncts. But the correspondence is far from complete, as will be evident from the following survey : the two things, word-classes and ranks, really move in two different spheres.

Substantives.

Substantives as Primaries. No further examples are needed.

Substantives as Adjuncts. The old-established way of using a substantive as an adjunct is by putting it in the genitive case, e.g. *Shelley's* poems | the *butcher's* shop | *St. Paul's* Cathedral. But it should be noted that a genitive case may also be a primary (through what is often called ellipsis), as in " I prefer Keats's poems to *Shelley's* | I bought it at the *butcher's* | *St. Paul's* is a fine building." In English what was the first element of a compound is now often to be considered an independent word, standing as an adjunct, thus in *stone* wall | a *silk* dress and a *cotton* one ; on the way in which these words tend to be treated as adjectives, see p. 94, above. Other examples of substantives as adjuncts are *women* writers | a *queen* bee | *boy* messengers, and (why not ?) *Captain* Smith | *Doctor* Johnson—cf. the non-inflexion in G. *Kaiser* Wilhelms Erinnerungen (though with much fluctuation with compound titles).

In some cases when we want to join two substantival ideas it is found impossible or impracticable to make one of them into an adjunct of the other by simple juxtaposition ; here languages often have recourse to the ' definitive genitive ' or a corresponding prepositional combination, as in Lat. *urbs Romæ* (cf. the juxtaposition in Dan. *byen Rom*, and on the other hand combinations like *Captain Smith*), Fr. *la cité de Rome*, E. *the city of Rome*, etc., and further the interesting expressions E. *a devil of a fellow | that scoundrel of a servant | his ghost of a voice | G. ein alter schelm von lohnbediener* (with the exceptional use of the nominative after *von*) | Dan. *den skurk av en tjener | et vidunder av et barn | det fæ*

til Nielsen | Fr. *ce fripon de valet* | *un amour d'enfant* | *celui qui
avait un si drôle de nom* | It. *quel ciarlatano d'un dottore* | *quel pover
uomo di tuo padre*, etc. This is connected with the Scandinavian
use of a possessive pronoun *dit fœ* ' you fool ' and to the Spanish
Pobrecitos de nosotros ! | *Desdichada de mi !* Cf. on this and similar
phenomena Grimm, *Personenwechsel*, Schuchardt Br. 197, Tegnér
G. 115 ff., Sandfeld in Dania VII.

Substantives as Subjuncts (subnexes). The use is rare, except
in word groups, where it is extremely frequent (see p. 102). Ex-
amples : emotions, *part* religious . . . but *part* human (Stevenson) |
the sea went *mountains* high. In " Come *home* | I bought it *cheap* "
home and *cheap* were originally substantives, but are now generally
called adverbs ; cf. also go *South*.

Adjectives.

Adjectives as Primaries : you had better bow to the *impossible*
(sg.) | ye have the *poor* (pl.) always with you (MEG II, Ch. XI)—
but in *savages, regulars, Christians, the moderns*, etc., we have
real substantives, as shown by the plural ending ; so also in
" the child is *a dear*," as shown by the article (MEG Ch. IX).
G. *beamter* is generally reckoned a substantive, but is rather
an adjective primary, as seen from the flexion : *der beamte, ein
beamter*.

Adjectives as Adjuncts : no examples are here necessary.

Adjectives as Subjuncts. In " a *fast* moving engine | a *long*
delayed punishment | a *clean* shaven face " and similar instances
it is historically more correct to call the italicized words adverbs
(in which the old adverbial ending -*e* has become mute in the same
way as other weak -*e*'s) rather than adjective subjuncts. On
new-laid eggs, *cheerful* tempered men, etc., see MEG II, 15. 3, on
burning hot, see p. 97, above.

Pronouns.

Pronouns as Primaries : *I* am well | *this* is *mine* | *who* said
that ? | *what* happened ? | *nobody* knows, etc. (But in *a mere
nobody* we have a real substantive, cf. the pl. *nobodies*.)

Pronouns as Adjuncts : *this* hat | *my* hat | *what* hat ? | *no*
hat, etc.

In some cases there is no formal distinction between pronouns
in these two employments, but in others there is, cf. *mine* : *my* |
none : *no ;* thus also in G. *mein* hut : *der meine*. Note also " Hier
ist *éin* umstand (*éin* ding) richtig genannt, aber nur *éiner* (*éines*)."

In Fr. we have formal differences in several cases :　*mon* chapeau :
le mien | *ce* chapeau : *celui*-ci | *quel* chapeau : *lequel ?* | *chaque* :
chacun | *quelque* : *quelqu'un.*

Pronouns as Subjuncts.　Besides " pronominal adverbs," which
need no exemplification, we have such instances as " I am *that*
sleepy (vg.) | *the* more, *the* merrier | *none* too able | I won't stay
any longer | *nothing* loth | *somewhat* paler than usual." [1]

Verbs.

Finite forms of verbs can only stand as secondary words
(adnexes), never either as primaries or as tertiaries.　But participles, like adjectives, can stand as primaries (the *living* are more
valuable than the *dead*) and as adjuncts (the *living* dog).　Infinitives,
according to circumstances, may belong to each of the three ranks ;
in some positions they require in English *to* (cf. G. *zu*, Dan. *at*).　I
ought strictly to have entered such combinations as *to go*, etc.,
under the heading " rank of word groups."

Infinitives as Primaries : *to see* is *to believe* (cf. *seeing* is *believing*) |
she wants *to rest* (cf. she wants *some rest*, with the corresponding
substantive).　Fr. *espérer*, c'est *jouir* | il est défendu *de fumer* ici |
sans *courir* | au lieu de *courir.*　G. *denken* ist schwer | er verspricht
zu kommen | ohne *zu laufen* | anstatt *zu laufen*, etc.

Infinitives as Adjuncts :　in times *to come* | there isn't a girl *to
touch* her | the correct thing *to do* | in a way not *to be forgotten* |
the never *to be forgotten* look (MEG II, 14. 4 and 15. 8).　Fr. la
chose *à faire* | du tabac *à fumer*.　(In G. a special passive participle
has developed from the corresponding use of the infinitive :　das
zu lesende buch.)　Spanish :　todas las academias existentes y
por existir (Galdós).　This use of the infinitive in some way
makes up for the want of a complete set of participles (future,
passive, etc.).

Infinitives as Subjuncts :　*to see* him, one would think | I shudder
to think of it | he came here *to see* you.

Adverbs.

Adverbs as Primaries.　This use is rare ; as an instance may
be mentioned " he did not stay for *long* | he's only just back from

---

[1] There are some combinations of pronominal and numeral adverbs
with adjuncts that are not easily " parsed," e.g. *this once* | we should have
gone to Venice, or *somewhere not half so nice* (Masefield) | Are we going *any-
where particular* ?　They are psychologically explained from the fact that
once = ' one time,' *somewhere* and *anywhere* = (to) some, any place ;　the
adjunct thus belongs to the implied substantive.

abroad." With pronominal adverbs it is more frequent : from
here | till *now.* Another instance is " he left *there* at two o'clock " :
there is taken as the object of *left. Here* and *there* may also be
real substantives in philosophical parlance : " Motion requires *a
here and a there* | in the Space-field lie innumerable other *theres* "
(NED, see MEG II, 8. 12).

Adverbs as Adjuncts. This, too, is somewhat rare : the *off*
side | in *after* years | the few *nearby* trees (US) | all the *well* pas-
sengers (US) | a *so-so* matron (Byron). In most instances the
adjunct use of an adverb is unnecessary, as there is a corresponding
adjective available. (Pronominal adverbs : the *then* government |
the *hither* shore) MEG II, 14. 9.

Adverbs as Subjuncts. No examples needed, as this is the
ordinary employment of this word-class.

When a substantive is formed from an adjective or verb, a
defining word is, as it were, lifted up to a higher plane, becoming
secondary instead of tertiary, and wherever possible, this is shown
by the use of an adjective instead of an adverb form.

absolutely novel	absolute novelty
utterly dark	utter darkness
perfectly strange	perfect stranger
describes accurately	accurate description
I firmly believe	my firm belief, a firm believer
judges severely	severe judges
reads carefully	careful reader
II + III	I + II

It is worth noting that adjectives indicating size (*great, small*)
are used as shifted equivalents of adverbs of degree (*much, little*) :
a great admirer of Tennyson, Fr. *un grand admirateur de Tennyson.*
On these shifted subjunct-adjuncts, cf. MEG II, 12. 2, and on nexus-
words, p. 137, below. Curme (GG 136) mentions G. *die geistig
armen, etwas längst bekanntes,* where *geistig* and *längst* remain
uninflected like adverbs " though modifying a substantive " :
the explanation is that *armen* and *bekanntes* are not substantives,
but merely adjective primaries, as indicated by their flexion.
Some English words may be used in two ways : " these are *full
equivalents* (*for*) " or " *fully equivalent* (*to*)," " *the direct opposites*
(*of*) " or " *directly opposite* (*to*) " ; Macaulay writes : " The government of the Tudors was *the direct opposite to* the government of
Augustus" (E 2. 99), where *to* seems to fit better with the adjective
opposite than with the substantive, while *direct* presupposes the
latter. In Dan. people hesitate between *den indbildt syge* and *den
indbildte syge* as a translation of *le malade imaginaire.*

Word Groups.

Word groups consisting of two or more words, the mutual relation of which may be of the most different character, in many instances occupy the same rank as a single word. In some cases it is indeed difficult to decide whether we have one word or two words, cf. p. 93 f. *To-day* was originally two words, now there is a growing tendency to spell it without the hyphen *today*, and as a matter of fact the possibility of saying *from today* shows that *to* is no longer felt to have its original signification. *Tomorrow*, too, is now one word, and it is even possible to say "I look forward *to tomorrow*." For our purpose in this chapter it is, however, of no consequence at all whether we reckon these and other doubtful cases as one word or two words, for we see that a word group (just as much as a single word) may be either a primary or an adjunct or a subjunct.

Word groups of various kinds as Primaries : *Sunday afternoon* was fine | I spent *Sunday afternoon* at home | we met *the kind old Archbishop of York* | it had taken him *ever since* to get used to the idea | You have *till ten to-night* | *From infancy to manhood* is rather a tedious period (Cowper). Cf. Fr. *jusqu'au roi* l'a cru ; nous avons assez pour *jusqu'à samedi* ; Sp. *hasta los malvados* creen en él (Galdós).

Word groups as Adjuncts : a *Sunday afternoon* concert | the Archbishop *of York* | the party *in power* | *the kind old Archbishop of York's* daughter | a *Saturday to Monday* excursion | the time *between two and four* | his *after dinner* pipe.

Word groups as Subjuncts (tertiaries) : he slept *all Sunday afternoon* | he smokes *after dinner* | he went *to all the principal cities of Europe* | he lives *next door to Captain Strong* | the canal ran *north and south* | he used to laugh *a good deal* | *five feet* high | he wants things *his own way* | things shall go *man-of-war fashion* | he ran upstairs *three steps at a time*. Cf. the "absolute construction" in the chapter on Nexus (IX).

As will have been seen already by these examples, the group, whether primary, secondary, or tertiary, may itself contain elements standing to one another in the relation of subordination indicated by the three ranks. The rank of the group is one thing, the rank within the group another. In this way more or less complicated relations may come into existence, which, however, are always easy to analyze from the point of view developed in this chapter. Some illustrations will make this clear "We met the kind old Archbishop of York " : the last six words together form one group primary, the object of *met* ; but the group itself consists of a primary *Archbishop* and four adjuncts, *the, kind, old, of York*, or, we should rather say that *Archbishop of York*, consisting of the primary *Archbishop* and the adjunct *of York*, is a group primary qualified by the three adjuncts *the, kind*, and *old*. But the adjunct *of York* in its turn consists of the particle (preposition) *of* and its object, the primary *York*. Now, the whole of this group may be turned into a group adjunct by being put in the genitive : We met *the kind old Archbishop of York's* daughter.

He lives on this side the river : here the whole group consisting of the last five words is tertiary to *lives* ; *on this side*, which consists of the particle (preposition) *on* with its object *this* (adjunct) *side* (primary), forms itself a group preposition, which here takes as an object the group *the* (adjunct) *river* (primary). But in the sentence *the buildings on this side the river are ancient*, the same five-word group is an adjunct to *buildings*. In this way we may arrive at a natural and consistent analysis even of the most complicated combinations found in actual language.[1]

Clauses.

A special case of great importance is presented by those groups that are generally called clauses. We may define a clause as a member of a sentence which has in itself the form of a sentence (as a rule it contains a finite verb). A clause then, according to circumstances, may be either primary, secondary, or tertiary.

I. Clauses as Primaries (clause primaries).

That he will come is certain (cp. His coming is c.).
Who steals my purse steals trash (cp. He steals trash).
What you say is quite true (cp. Your assertion is . . .).
I believe *whatever he says* (cp. . . . all his words).
I do not know *where I was born* (cp. . . . my own birthplace).
I expect *(that) he will arrive at six* (cp. . . . his arrival).
We talked of *what he would do* (cp. . . . of his plans).
Our ignorance of *who the murderer was* (cp. . . . of the name of the murderer).

In the first three sentences the clause is the subject, in the rest it is the object, either of the verb or of the preposition *of*. But there is a kind of pseudo-grammatical analysis against which I must specially warn the reader : it says that in sentences like the

---

[1] A friend once told me the following story about a seven years old boy. He asked his father if babies could speak when they were born. ' No ! ' said his father. ' Well,' said the boy, ' it's very funny then that, in the story of Job, the Bible says Job cursed the day that he was born.' The boy had mistaken a group primary (object) for a group tertiary.

second the subject of *steals trash* is a *he* which is said to be implied in *who*, and to which the relative clause stands in the same relation as it does to *the man* in *the man who steals*—one of the numerous uncalled-for fictions which have vitiated and complicated grammar without contributing to a real understanding of the facts of language.[1]

II. Clauses as Adjuncts (clause adjuncts).

I like a boy *who speaks the truth* (cp. . . . . a truthful boy).
This is the land *where I was born* (cp. my native land).

[1] Sweet (NEG § 112 and 220) says that in *what you say is true* there is condensation, the word *what* doing duty for two words at once, it is the object of *say* in the relative clause and at the same time the subject of the verb *is* in the principal clause ; in *what I say I mean* it is the object in both clauses, and in *what is done cannot be undone* it is the subject in both clauses. He says that the clause introduced by a condensed relative precedes, instead of following, the principal clause, and that if we alter the construction of such sentences, the missing antecedent is often restored : *it is quite true what you say ; if I say a thing, I mean it.* But the last sentence is not at all the grammatical equivalent of *what I say I mean*, and there is neither antecedent nor relative in it ; in *it is quite true what you say* we cannot call *it* the antecedent of *what*, as it is not possible to say *it what you say* ; for its true character see p. 25, above. *What* can have no antecedent. The position before, instead of after, the principal clause is by no means characteristic of clauses with "condensed" pronouns : in some of Sweet's sentences we have the normal order with the subject first, and in *what I say I mean* we have the emphatic front-position of the object, as shown by the perfectly natural sentence *I mean what I say*, in which *what* is the relative pronoun, though Sweet does not recognize it as the "condensed relative." (In the following paragraphs he creates unnecessary difficulties by failing to see the difference between a relative and a dependent interrogative clause.) The chief objection to Sweet's view, however, is that it is unnatural to say that *what* does duty for two words at once. *What* is not in itself the subject of *is true*, for if we ask "What is true ? " the answer can never be *what* but only *what you say*, and similarly in the other sentences. *What* is the object of *say*, and nothing else, in exactly the same way as *which* is in *the words which you say are true* ; but in the latter sentence also in my view the subject of *are* is *the words which you say*, and not merely *the words*. It is only in this way that grammatical analysis is made conformable to ordinary common sense. Onions (AS § 64) speaks of omission of the antecedent in Pope's " To help *who want*, to forward *who excel*," i.e. *those who* ; he does not see that this does not help him in *I heard what you said*, for nothing can be inserted before *what* ; Onions does not treat *what* as a relative, and it would be difficult to make it fit into his system. Neither he nor Sweet in this connexion mentions the "indefinite relatives" *whoever, whatever*, though they evidently differ from the "condensed relatives" only by the addition of *ever*. Sentences like " Whoever steals my purse steals trash " or " Whatever you say is true " or " I mean whatever I say " should be analyzed in every respect like the corresponding sentences with *who* or *what*. When Dickens writes " Peggotty always volunteered this information to whomsoever would receive it " (DC 456), *whom* is wrong, for *whosoever* is the subject of *would receive*, though the whole clause is the object of *to* ; but *whomsoever* would be correct if the clause had run (*to*) *whomsoever it concerned*. Cp. also " he was angry with *whoever crossed his path*," and Kingsley's   Be good, sweet maid, and let *who can* be clever." Ruskin writes, " I had been writing of what I knew nothing about " : here *what* is governed by the preposition *about*, while *of* governs the whole clause consisting of the words *what I knew nothing about*.

It is worth remarking that often when we have seemingly two relative clauses belonging to the same antecedent (i.e. primary) the second really qualifies the antecedent as already qualified by the first, thus is adjunct to a group primary consisting of a primary and the first relative clause as adjunct. I print this group primary in italics in the following examples : they murdered *all they met* whom they thought gentlemen | there is *no one who knows him* that does not like him | it is not *the hen who cackles the most* that lays the largest eggs.

III. Clauses as Subjuncts or tertiaries (clause subjuncts).

Whoever said this, it is true (cp. anyhow).

It is a custom *where I was born* (cp. there).

When he comes, I must go (cp. then).

If he comes I must go (cp. In that case).

As this is so, there is no harm done (cp. accordingly).

Lend me your knife, *that I may cut this string* (cp. to cut it with).

Note here especially the first example, in which the clause introduced by *whoever* is neither subject nor object as the clauses considered above were, but stands in a looser relation to *it is true*.

The definition of the term " clause " necessitates some remarks on the usual terminology, according to which the clauses here mentioned would be termed 'dependent' or 'subordinate' clauses as opposed to 'the principal clause' (or 'principal proposition ') ; corresponding terms are used in other languages, e.g. G. 'nebensatz, hauptsatz.' But it is not at all necessary to have a special term for what is usually called a principal clause. It should first be remarked that the principal idea is not always expressed in the 'principal clause,' for instance not in " *This was* because he was ill." The idea which is expressed in the 'principal clause' in " *It is true* that he is very learned," may be rendered by a simple adverb in " *Certainly* he is very learned "—does that change his being learned from a subordinate to a principal idea ? Compare also the two expressions " I tell you that he is mad " and " He is mad, as I tell you." Further, if the 'principal clause' is defined as what remains after the subordinate clauses have been peeled off, we often obtain curious results. It must be admitted that in some cases the subordinate clauses may be left out without any material detriment to the meaning, which is to some extent complete in itself, as in " *I shall go to London* (if I can) " or " (When he got back) *he dined with his brother.*" But even here it does not seem necessary to have a special term for what remains after the whole combination has been stripped of those elements, any more than if the same result had followed from the omission of some synonymous expressions of another form, e.g. "*I shall go to London* (in that case)" or "(After his return) *he dined with his brother.*" If we take away the clause *where I was born* from the three sentences quoted above, what remains is (1) I do not know, (2) This is the land, (3) It is a custom ; but there is just as little reason for treating these as a separate grammatical category as if they had originated by the omission of the underlined parts of the sentences (1) I do not know *my birth-place*, (2) This is my *native* land, (3) It is a custom *at home*. Worse still, what is left after deduction of the dependent clauses very often gives no meaning at all, as in "(Who steals my purse) *steals trash*" and even more absurdly in "(What surprises me) *is* (that he should get angry)." Can it really be said here that the little word *is* contains the principal idea ? The grammatical unit is the whole sentence including all that the speaker or writer has brought together to express his thought ; this should be taken as a whole, and then it will be seen to be of little importance whether the subject or some other part of it is in the form of a sentence and can thus be termed a clause or whether it is a single word or a word group of some other form.

Final Remarks.

The grammatical terminology here advocated, by which the distinction **of the three ranks** is treated as different from the distinction between substantives, adjectives, and adverbs, is in many ways preferable to the often confused and self-contradictory terminology found in many grammatical works. Corresponding to my three ranks we often find the words substantival, adjectival, and adverbial, or a word is said to be "used adverbially," etc. (Thus NED, for instance, in speaking of *a sight* too clever.) Others will frankly call *what* or *several* in one connexion substantives, in another adjectives, though giving both under the heading pronouns (Wendt.) Falk and Torp call Norw. *sig* the substantival reflexive pronoun, and *sin* the adjectival reflexive pronoun, but the latter is substantival in "hver tog sin, så tog jeg min." Many scholars speak of the 'adnominal genitive' (= adjunct) as opposed to the 'adverbial genitive,' but the latter expression is by some, though not by all, restricted to the use with verbs. In "The King's English" the term 'adverbials' is used for subjunct groups and clauses, but I do not think I have seen "adjectivals" or "substantivals" used for the corresponding adjuncts and primaries. For my own 'adjective primary' the following terms are in use : substantival adjective, substantivized adjective, absolute adjective, adjective used absolutely (but "absolute" is also used in totally different applications, e.g. in absolute ablative), quasi-substantive (e.g. NED *the great*), a free adjective (Sweet NEG § 178 on G. *die gute*), an adjective partially converted into a noun (ib. § 179 about E. *the good*), a substantive-equivalent, a noun-equivalent. Onions (AS § 9) uses the last expression ; he applies the term 'adjective-equivalent' among other things to "a noun in apposition," e.g. 'Simon Lee, the old *huntsman*' and 'a noun or verb-noun forming part of a compound noun,' e.g. "*cannon* balls." In *a lunatic asylum* he says that *lunatic* is a noun (this is correct, as shown by the pl. *lunatics*), but this noun is called 'an adjective-equivalent'; consequently he must say that in *sick room* the word *sick* is an adjective which is a noun-equivalent (§ 9. 3), but this noun-equivalent at the same time must be an adjective-equivalent according to his § 10 6 ! This is an example of the "simplified" uniform terminology used in Sonnenschein's series. Cf. MEG II, 12. 41. *London* in *the London papers* is called an adjective-equivalent, and *the poor*, when standing by itself, a noun-equivalent; thus in *the London poor* the substantive must be an adjective-equivalent, and the adjective a noun-equivalent. Some say that in *the top one* the substantive is first adjectivized and then again substantivized, and both these conversions are effected by the word *one*. Cf. MEG II, 10. 86 : *top* in my system always remains a substantive, but is here adjunct to the primary *one*. My terminology is also much simpler than that found, for instance, in Poutsma's Gr., where we find such expressions as 'an attributive adnominal adjunct consisting of a (pro)noun preceded by a preposition' for my 'prepositional (group) adjunct' (Poutsma using the word *adjunct* in a wider sense than mine).

We are now in a position rightly to appreciate what Sweet said in 1876 (CP 24) : "It is a curious fact, hitherto overlooked by grammarians and logicians, that the definition of the noun applies strictly only to the nominative case. The oblique cases are really attribute-words, and inflexion is practically nothing but a device for turning a noun into an adjective or adverb. This is perfectly clear as regards the genitive. . . . It is also clear that *noctem* in *flet noctem* is a pure adverb of time." Sweet did not, however, in his own Anglo-Saxon Grammar place the genitive of nouns under adjectives, and he was right in not doing so, for what he says is only half true : the oblique cases are devices for turning the substantive, which in the nominative is a primary, into a secondary word (adjunct) or tertiary word, but it remains a substantive all the same. There is a certain correspondence between the tripartition substantive, adjective, adverb, and the three ranks, and in course of time we often see adjunct forms of substantives pass into real adjectives, and subjunct forms into adverbs (prepositions, etc.), but the correspondence is only partial, not complete. *The 'part of speech' classification and the 'rank' classification represent different angles from which the same word or form may be viewed, first as it is in itself, and then as it is in combination with other words.*

CHAPTER VIII

JUNCTION AND NEXUS

Adjuncts. Nexus.

Adjuncts.

It will be our task now to inquire into the function of adjuncts : for what purpose or purposes are adjuncts added to primary words ? Various classes of adjuncts may here be distinguished.

The most important of these undoubtedly is the one composed of what may be called *restrictive or qualifying adjuncts* : their function is to restrict the primary, to limit the number of objects to which it may be applied; in other words, to specialize or define it. Thus *red* in *a red rose* restricts the applicability of the word *rose* to one particular sub-class of the whole class of roses, it specializes and defines the rose of which I am speaking by excluding white and yellow roses ; and so in most other instances : *Napoleon the third | a new book | Icelandic peasants | a poor widow*, etc.

Now it may be remembered that these identical examples were given above as illustrations of the thesis that substantives are more special than adjectives, and it may be asked : is not there a contradiction between what was said there and what has just been asserted here ?   But on closer inspection it will be seen that it is really most natural that a less special term is used in order further to specialize what is already to some extent special : the method of attaining a high degree of specialization is analogous to that of reaching the roof of a building by means of ladders : if one ladder will not do, you first take the tallest ladder you have and tie the second tallest to the top of it, and if that is not enough, you tie on the next in length, etc.   In the same way, if *widow* is not special enough, you add *poor*, which is less special than *widow*, and yet, if it is added, enables you to reach farther in specialization ; if that does not suffice, you add the subjunct *very*, which in itself is much more general than *poor*.   *Widow* is special, *poor widow* more special, and *very poor widow* still more special, but *very* is less special than *poor*, and that again than *widow*.

Though proper names are highly specialized, yet it is possible to specialize them still more by adjuncts   *Young Burns* means

either a different person from *old Burns,* or if there is only one
person of that name in the mind of the actual speaker (and hearer)
it mentions him with some emphasis laid on the fact that he is
still young (in which case it falls outside the restrictive adjuncts,
see below, p. 111).

Among restrictive adjuncts, some of a pronominal character
should be noticed. *This* and *that,* in *this rose, that rose* differ from
most other adjuncts in not being in any way descriptive : what
they do, whether accompanied by some pointing gesture or not,
is to *specify.* The same is true of the so-called definite article
the, which would be better called the defining or determining
article ; this is the least special of adjuncts and yet specializes
more than most other words and just as much as *this* or *that* (of
which latter it is phonetically a weakened form). In *the rose, rose*
is restricted to that one definite rose which is at this very moment
in my thought and must be in yours, too, because we have just
mentioned it, or because everything in the situation points towards
that particular rose. Cf. " Shut *the* door, please." While *king* in
itself may be applied to hundreds of individuals, *the king* is as
definite as a proper ame : if we are in the middle of a story or a
conversation about some particular king, then it is he that is meant,
otherwise it means ' our king,' the present king of the country
in which we are living. But the situation may change, and then
the value of the definition contained in the article changes automatically. " The King is dead. Long live the King ! " (Le
roi est mort. Vive le roi !) In the first sentence mention is made
of one king, the king whom the audience thinks to be still king
here ; in the second sentence the same two words necessarily
refer to another man, the legal successor of the former. It is
exactly the same with cases like " *the Doctor* said that *the patient*
was likely to die soon," and again with those cases in which Sweet
(NEG § 2031) finds the " unique article " : *the Devil* [why does he
say that *a devil* has a different sense ?], the *sun, the moon, the earth,*
etc. (similarly Deutschbein SNS 245). There is, really, no reason
for singling out a class of " persons or things which are unique in
themselves."

This, however, is not the only function of the definite article.
In cases like the *English* King | the King *of England* | the *eldest*
boy | the boy *who stole the apples,* etc., the adjuncts here printed
in italics are in themselves quite sufficient to individualize, and
the article may be said so far to be logically superfluous though
required by usage, not only in English but in other languages.
We may perhaps call this the article of supplementary determination. The relation between *the King* and *the English King* is
parallel to that between *he, they,* standing alone as sufficient to

denote the person or persons pointed out by the situation (*he can afford it* | *they can afford it*) and the same pronouns as determined by an adjunct relative clause (*he that is rich can afford it* | *they that are rich can afford it*). Cf. also the two uses of *the same*, first by itself, meaning 'the identical person or thing that has just been mentioned,' and second supplemented with a relative clause : *the same boy as* (or, *that*) *stole the apples*. But, as remarked in NED, the definite article with *same* often denotes an indeterminate object, as in "all the planets travel round the sun in the same direction," in which sense French may employ the indefinite article (deux mots qui signifient *une même* chose) and English often says *one and the same*, where *one* may be said to neutralize the definite article ; so in other languages, Lat. *unus et idem*, Gr. (*ho*) *heis kai ho autos*, G. *ein und derselbe*, Dan. *een og samme*. (N.B. without the definite article.[1])

An adjunct consisting of a genitive or a possessive pronoun always restricts, though not always to the same extent as the definite article. *My father* and *John's head* are as definite and individualized as possible, because a man can only have one father and one head ; but what about *my brother* and *John's hat* ? I may have several brothers, and John may possess more than one hat, and yet in most connexions these expressions will be understood as perfectly definite : *My brother arrived yesterday* | *Did you see my brother this morning ?* | *John's hat blew off his head*—the situation and context will show in each case which of my brothers is meant, and in the last sentence the allusion, of course, is to the particular hat which John was wearing on the occasion mentioned. But when these expressions are used in the predicative the same degree of definiteness is not found : when a man is introduced with the words "This is my brother" or when I say "That is not John's hat," these words may mean indefinitely 'one of my

---

[1] This is not the place for a detailed account of the often perplexing uses of the definite article, which vary idiomatically from language to language and even from century to century within one and the same language. Sometimes the use is determined by pure accidents, as when in E. *at bottom* represents an earlier *at the* (*atte*) *bottom*, in which the article has disappeared through a well-known phonetic process. There are some interesting, though far from convincing, theories on the rise and diffusion of the article in many languages in G. Schütte, *Jysk og østdansk artikelbrug* (Videnskabernes selskab, Copenhagen, 1922). It would be interesting to examine the various ways in which languages which have no definite article express determination. In Finnish, for instance, the difference between the nominative and the partitive often corresponds to the difference between the definite article and the indefinite (or no article) : *linnut* (nom.) *ovat* (pl.) *puussa* 'the birds are in the tree,' *lintuja* (part.) *on* (sg., always used with a subject in the part.) *puussa* 'there are birds in the tree,' *ammuin linnut* 'I shot the birds,' *ammuin lintuja* 'I shot some birds' (Eliot FG 131. 126). The partitive, however, resembles the Fr. "partitive article" more than the use of the Finnish nominative does our definite article.

brothers ' and ' one of John's hats.' In German a preposed genitive renders definite (*Schiller's gedichte*) but a postposed genitive does not, whence the possibility of saying *einige gedichte Schiller's* and the necessity of adding the definite article (*die gedichte Schiller's*) if the same degree of definiteness is wanted as in the preposed genitive. Where a prepositional group is used instead of the genitive, the article is similarly required : *die gedichte von Schiller*, so in other languages : *the poems of Schiller, les poèmes de Schiller, i poemi dello Schiller.*

In some languages it is possible to use a possessive pronoun in the incompletely restricted sense. MHG had *ein sîn bruoder*, where now *ein bruder von ihm* is said. In Italian, possessives are not definite, hence the possibility of saying *un mio amico | alcuni suoi amici | con due o tre amici suoi | si comunicarono certe loro idee di gastronomia* (Serao, Cap. Sans. 304). Consequently the article is needed to make the expression definite : *il mio amico*. But there is an interesting exception to this rule : with names indicating close relationship no article is used : *mio fratello, suo zio.* If I am not mistaken this must have originated with *mio padre, mia madre,* where definiteness is a natural consequence of one's having only one father and one mother, and have been analogically extended to the other terms of kinship. It is perfectly natural that the article should be required with a plural : *i miei fratelli,* and on the other hand that it should not be used with a predicative : *questo libro è mio.* In French the possessives are definite, as shown through their combination with a comparative as in *mon meilleur ami* ' my best friend,' where the pronoun has the same effect as the article in *le meilleur ami.*[1] But a different form is used in (the obsolete) *un mien ami* = It. *un mio amico,* now usually *un de mes amis* (*un ami à moi*). In English indefiniteness of a possessive is expressed by means of combinations with *of : a friend of mine | some friends of hers,* cf. also *any friend of Brown's,* a combination which is also used to avoid the collocation of a possessive (or genitive) and some other determining pronoun : *that noble heart of hers | this great America of yours,* etc. As a partitive explanation [2] is excluded here, we may call this construction " pseudo-partitive."

Next we come to *non-restrictive adjuncts* as in *my dear little Ann !* As the adjuncts here are used not to tell which among several Anns I am speaking of (or to), but simply to characterize

---

[1] Cf., however, the partitive article in " J'ai eu *de ses* nouvelles."

[2] The only explanation recognized by Sonnenschein (§ 184), who says : In sentences like ' He is a friend of John's ' there is a noun understood : ' of John's ' means ' of John's friends,' so that the sentence is equivalent to ' He is one of John's friends.' Here ' of ' means ' out of the number of.' But is " a friend of John's friends " = one of John's friends ?

her, they may be termed ornamental ("epitheta ornantia") or from another point of view parenthetical adjuncts. Their use is generally of an emotional or even sentimental, though not always complimentary, character, while restrictive adjuncts are purely intellectual. They are very often added to proper names : *Rare Ben Jonson* | *Beautiful Evelyn Hope is dead* (Browning) | *poor, hearty, honest, little Miss La Creevy* (Dickens) | *dear, dirty Dublin* | *le bon Dieu*. In *this extremely sagacious little man*, *this* alone defines, the other adjuncts merely describe parenthetically, but in *he is an extremely sagacious man* the adjunct is restrictive.

It may sometimes be doubtful whether an adjunct is of one or the other kind. *His first important poem* generally means 'the first among his important poems' (after he had written others of no importance), but it may also mean the first he ever wrote and add the information that it was important (this may be made clear in the spoken sentence by the tone, and in the written by a comma). *The industrious Japanese will conquer in the long run :* does this mean that the J. as a nation will conquer, because they are industrious, or that the industrious among the Japanese nation will conquer ?

I take a good illustration of the difference between the two kinds of adjuncts from Bernhard Schmitz's French Grammar : *Arabia Felix* is one part of Arabia, but the well-known epigram about (the whole of) Austria, which extends her frontiers by marriages, while other countries can only extend theirs by war, says : "Tu, *felix Austria*, nube." The same difference between a preposed non-restrictive and a postposed restrictive adjunct is seen in the well-known rules of French Grammar, according to which *ses pauvres parents* comprises all his relatives in sympathetic compassion, while *ses parents pauvres* means those of his relatives that are poor—a distinction which is not, however, carried through consistently with all adjectives.

The distinction between the two kinds of adjuncts is important with regard to relative clauses. In English, while the pronouns *who* and *which* may be found in both, only restrictive clauses can be introduced by *that* or without any pronoun : *the soldiers that were brave ran forward* | *the soldiers, who were brave, ran forward* | *everybody I saw there worked very hard*. The difference between the first two sentences can be made still more evident by the insertion of *all* : *all the soldiers that* were brave . . . | *the soldiers, who were all of them brave. . . .* It will be noticed that there is also a marked difference in tone, a non-restrictive clause beginning on a deeper tone than a restrictive one ; besides, a pause is permissible before a non-restrictive, but hardly before a restrictive clause ; cf. the use of a comma in writing. In Danish the difference is shown by the article of the antecedent : *(alle) de soldater som var modige løb frem | soldaterne, som (alle) var modige, løb frem.* But this criterion is not always available ; if the antecedent has another adjunct the only difference is in the stress of the preposed article : *ᶦde franske ɣoldater som . . . | de ᶦfranske soldater, som. . . .* A so-called continuative relative clause is, of course, non-restrictive : *he gave the letter to the clerk, who then copied it,* Dan. *han gav brevet til kontoristen, som så skrev det av* (but : *. . . to the clerk who was to copy it . . . til den kontorist som skulde skrive det av*).

The following examples will serve further to illustrate the two kinds of relative clause adjuncts : *there were few passengers that escaped without serious injuries | there were few passengers, who escaped without serious injuries | they divide women into two classes :* those they want to kiss, and those they want to kick, who are those they don't want to kiss.

The distinction between restrictive and non-restrictive adjuncts (which are both in a certain sense qualifiers) does not affect quantifying adjuncts, such as *many, much, some, few, little, more, less, no, one* and the other numerals. Whenever these are found with adjectives as adjuncts to the same primary they are always placed first : *many small boys | much good wine | two young girls.* There is a curious relation between such quantifiers and combinations of substantives denoting number or quantity followed by an *of-*group (or in languages with a more complicated form-system, a partitive genitive or a partitive case) : *hundred* was originally a substantive and in the plural is treated as such : *hundreds of soldiers,* but in the singular, in spite of the preposed *one* or *a,* it is treated like the other numerals : *a hundred soldiers* ; thus also *three hundred soldiers* ; cp. *dozens of bottles, a dozen bottles.* Where E. has *a couple of days, a pair of lovers,* G. has *ein paar tage,* Dan. *et par dage,* even *die paar tage, de par dage* exactly as *die zwei tage, de to dage.* To E. *much wine, many bottles, no friends,* corresponds Fr. *beaucoup de vin, beaucoup de bouteilles, pas d'amis* ; to E. *a pound of meat, a bottle of wine* corresponds G. *ein pfund fleisch, eine flasche wein,* Dan. *et pund kød, en flaske vin,* etc.

Wherever an indefinite article is developed, it seems always to be an unemphatic form of the numeral *one : uno, un, ein, en, an (a),* Chinese *i,* a weak form of *yit* (Russ. *odin* is often used like an indefinite article). In English *a* has in some cases the value of the numeral, as in *four at a time, birds of a feather,* and in some cases the full and the weakened forms are synonymous, as in *one Mr. Brown = a Mr. Brown,* where we may also say *a certain Mr. Brown.* This use of the word *certain* reminds us that in most cases where we use the " indefinite " article we have really something very definite in our mind, and " indefinite " in the grammatical sense practically

means nothing but " what shall not (not yet) be named," as in the
beginning of a story : " In a certain town there once lived a tailor
who had a young daughter "—when we go on we use the definite
form about the same man and say : " The tailor was known in
that town under the name of, etc."   (On the " generic " use of the
indefinite article see p. 152 and Ch. XV.)

As the indefinite article is a weakened numeral, it is not used
with " uncountables " (mass-words, Ch. XIV). And as *one*—and consequently *a(n)*—has no plural, there is no plural indefinite article,
unless you count the curious Sp. *unos* as one. But in a different
way French has developed what may be called an indefinite article
to be used with mass-words and plurals in its " partitive article,"
as in *du vin, de l'or, des amis*. This, of course, originated in a prepositional group, but is now hardly felt as such and at any rate
can be used after another preposition : *avec du vin | j'en ai parlé à
des amis*. It is now just as good an adjunct as any numeral or as
the synonym *quelque(s)* or E. *some*.

Nexus.

We now proceed to what was above (p. 97) termed nexus.
The example there given was *the dog barks furiously* as contrasted
with the junction *a furiously barking dog*. The tertiary element
furiously is the same in both combinations, and may therefore
here be left out of account. The relation between *the dog barks*
and *a barking dog* is evidently the same as that between *the rose
is red* and *a red rose*. In *the dog barks* and *the rose is red* we have
complete meanings, complete sentences, in which it is usual to
speak of *the dog* and *the rose* as the subject, and of *barks* and
is red as the predicate, while the combination is spoken of as
predication. But what is the difference between these and the
other combinations ?

Paul thinks that an adjunct is a weakened predicate (ein degra-
diertes prädikat, P 140 ff.), and in the same way Sheffield says that
an adjunct " involves a latent copula " (GTh 56). If this means
that *a red rose* is equivalent to (or had its origin in) *a rose which is red*,
and that therefore *red* is always a kind of predicative, it should
not be overlooked that the relative pronoun is here smuggled into
the combination, but the function of the relative is precisely that
of making the whole thing into an adjunct (an attribute, an epithet).
Barking is not a degraded *barks*, though *a barking dog* is *a dog who
barks*. Peano is much more right when he says that the relative
pronoun and the copula are like a positive and a negative addition
of the same quantity which thus annul one another (*which* $= -$ *is*,
or $-$ *which* $= +$ *is*), thus *which is* $= 0$.

While Paul thinks that junction (attributivverhältnis) has developed from a predicate relation, and therefore ultimately from a sentence, Sweet does not say anything about the relative priority of the two combinations, when he says that " assumption " (his name for what is here called junction) is implied or latent predication, and on the other hand, that predication is a kind of strengthened or developed assumption (NEG § 44). But this way of looking at the question really leads nowhere.

Wundt and Sütterlin distinguish the two kinds as open and closed combinations (offene und geschlossene wortverbindungen). It would probably be better to say that one is unfinished and makes one expect a continuation (*a red rose,—well, what about that rose ?*) and the other is rounded off so as to form a connected whole (*the rose is red*). The former is a lifeless, stiff combination, the latter has life in it. This is generally ascribed to the presence of a finite verb (the rose *is* red ; the dog *barks*), and there is certainly much truth in the name given to a verb by Chinese grammarians, " the living word " as opposed to a noun which is lifeless. Still, it is not the words themselves so much as their combinations that impart life or are deprived of life and, as we shall see presently, we have combinations without any finite verb which are in every respect to be ranged with combinations like *the rose is red*, or *the dog barks*. These form complete sentences, i.e. complete communications, and this, of course, is very important, even from the grammarian's point of view. But exactly the same relation between a primary and a secondary word that is found in such complete sentences is also found in a great many other combinations which are not so rounded off and complete in themselves as to form real sentences. We need not look beyond ordinary subordinate clauses to see this, e.g. in (I see) *that the rose is red*, or (she is alarmed) *when the dog barks*. Further, the relation between the last two words in *he painted the door red* is evidently parallel to that in *the door is red* and different from that in *the red door*, and the two ideas " the Doctor " and " arrive " are connected in essentially the same way in the four combinations (1) the Doctor arrived, (2) I saw that the Doctor arrived, (3) I saw the Doctor arrive, (4) I saw the Doctor's arrival. What is common to these, and to some more combinations to be considered in the next chapter, is what I term a nexus, and I shall now try to determine what constitutes the difference between a nexus and a junction, asking the reader to bear in mind that on the one hand the presence of a finite verb is not required in a nexus, and that on the other hand a nexus may, but does not always, form a complete sentence.

In a junction a secondary element (an adjunct) is joined to a primary word as a label or distinguishing mark : a house is characterized by being mentioned as *the next house* or *the Doctor's house.* Adjunct and primary together form *one* denomination, a composite name for what conceivably might just as well have been called by a single name. As a matter of fact, instead of *new-born dog* we often say *puppy,* instead of *silly person* we may say *fool ;* compare also the composite expressions *a female horse, the warm season, an unnaturally small person, an offensive smell* with the single-word expressions *a mare, the summer, a dwarf, a stench,* etc. What in one language is expressed by one word, must often in another be rendered by means of a primary with an adjunct : E. *claret,* Fr. *vin rouge,* and on the other hand, Fr. *patrie,* E. *native country.* A junction is therefore a unit or single idea, expressed more or less accidentally by means of two elements.[1]

A nexus, on the contrary, always contains two ideas which must necessarily remain separate : the secondary term adds something new to what has already been named. Whereas the junction is more stiff or rigid, the nexus is more pliable ; it is, as it were, animate or articulated. Comparisons, of course, are always to some extent inadequate, still as these things are very hard to express in a completely logical or scientific way, we may be allowed to say that the way in which the adjunct is joined to its primary is like the way in which the nose and the ears are fixed on the head, while an adnex rests on its primary as the head on the trunk or a door on a wall. A junction is like a picture, a nexus like a process or a drama. The distinction between a composite name for one idea and the connexion of one concept with another concept is most easily seen if we contrast two such sentences as *the blue dress is the oldest* and *the oldest dress is blue ;* the fresh information imparted about the dress is, in the first sentence that it is the oldest, and in the second that it is blue ; cf. also *a dancing woman charms* and *a charming woman dances.*

We shall now consider more in detail the various grammatical combinations characterized by nexus. Some of these are well known to grammarians, but the collocation of them all from this point of view, so far as I know, is new.

---

[1] Similarly a secondary and a tertiary word may sometimes denote an idea which can also be rendered by a single secondary term : *very small = tiny, extremely big = enormous, smells foully = stinks.*

CHAPTER IX

VARIOUS KINDS OF NEXUS

Finite Verb. Infinitival Nexus. Nexus without a Verb. Nexus-Object, etc. Nexus Subjunct. Nexus of Deprecation. Summary. Copula. Predicative.

Finite Verb.

IN attempting to classify the various kinds of nexus we shall first very briefly mention the three kinds which contain a finite verb : first the ordinary complete sentences, as in " the dog barks " | " the rose is red." Second, the same combinations in subordinate clauses, that is, as parts of a sentence, as in " she is afraid when *the dog barks* | I see that *the rose is red.*" Third, the very interesting phenomenon seen in " Arthur *whom* they say *is kill'd* to-night " (Shakesp., John IV, 2. 165). The nexus *whom is kill'd* is the object of *they say*, whence the use of the accusative *whom*. In the Appendix I shall give other examples of this construction as well as my reasons for defending the form *whom*, which is generally considered as a gross error.

Infinitival Nexus.

Next we have a series of constructions containing an infinitive. The accusative with the infinitive. Examples of this well-known construction : I heard *her sing* | I made *her sing* | I caused *her to sing*—thus in some combinations with, and in others without, *to*. Similarly in other languages. Sweet, § 124, notices the difference between *I like quiet boys* and *I like boys to be quiet*, the latter sentence implying not even the slightest liking for boys, as the former does, but he does not see the real reason for this difference, as according to him " the only word that *I like* governs grammatically is *boys*, *to be quiet* being only a grammatical adjunct to *boys*." It would be more correct to say that it is not *boys* that is the object, but the whole nexus consisting of the primary *boys* and the infinitive, exactly as it is the whole clause and not only the subject of it that would be the object, if we were to translate it into " I like that boys are quiet." (This construction is rare with this verb, though NED has a quotation from Scott ; with other verbs which also take the acc. with the inf., such as *see, believe*, it is

117

in common use.)   Sonnenschein § 487, here speaks of " two direct objects " and places the sentence on the same footing as " he asked *me a question*," but this is misleading, for without change of sense we may say " he asked *a question*," while " I like *to be quiet* " is totally different from the sentence with *boys* inserted.   The relation between *boys* and the infinitive is not at all the same as that between *me* and *a question*, but is exactly the same as between the two parts of any other nexus, e.g. between the subject and the predicate of a complete sentence.

The same construction is frequently found in English in cases where the nexus is the object not of a verb, but of a preposition, or perhaps rather of a phrase consisting of a verb and a preposition, which is often synonymous with a single verb (*look on* = *consider*, *prevail on* = *induce*, etc.).   Examples : I looked upon *myself to be fully settled* (Swift) | she can hardly prevail upon *him to eat* | you may count on *him to come.*

While " I long *for you to come* " can be analyzed in the same way, this is not true of some other combinations with *for* and an infinitive that have developed in modern English.   The original division of a sentence like " It is good for a man not to touch a woman " was " It is good for a man | not to touch a woman," but it came to be apprehended as " It is good | for a man not to touch a woman," where *for a man* was taken to belong more closely to the infinitive.   This led to the possibility of placing *for* and the word it governs first, as in : for a man to tell how human life began is hard (Milton) | for you to call would be the best thing, and to the further use after *than* : Nothing was more frequent than for a bailiff to seize Jack (Swift) | nothing could be better than for you to call : *for* and its object are now nothing but the primary (subject) of the nexus, whose secondary part is the infinitive ; combinations like " it might seem disrespectful to his memory for me to be on good terms with [his enemy] " (Miss Austen) show how far the construction has wandered from its original use, as *to his memory* here serves the same purpose as the *for*-phrase did at first.   (See my paper on this shifting in " Festschrift W. Viëtor." Die neueren Sprachen, 1910.)

There is a close parallel to this English development in Slavic, where a dative with an infinitive is frequent in places where Greek and Latin would have an acc. with inf., see Miklosich, Synt. 619, Vondrák, SG 2. 366 and especially C. W. Smith in Opuscula philol. ad I. N. Madvigium, 1876, 21 ff.   From such sentences as OSl. *dobro jestĭ namŭ sĭde byti* ' it is good for us to be here,' where the dative originally belonged to ' is good ' it was extended to cases like *ne dobro jestĭ mnogomŭ bogomŭ byti* ' it is not good for many gods to be, i.e. that there are many gods ' ; the construction is used even with verbs which cannot naturally take a dative. In the early Gothonic languages there was a similar construction, and Grimm and others speak of a dative-with-infinitive construction in Gothic *jah wairþ þairhgaggan imma þairh atisk* (Mark 2. 23 'and it happened for him to go through the field') and similar instances in the related languages ; they can, however, scarcely be considered as more than the first abortive beginnings of the development that proved so fruitful in Slavic (see the able discussion in Morgan Callaway, *The Infin. in Anglo-Saxon*, Washington, 1913, p. 127 and 248 ff., where earlier writers on the subject are quoted).

We have seen the primary, or what is virtually the subject of an infinitive, put in the accusative, and in the dative, and with the preposition *for* ; but in some languages it may also be put in the nominative. In ME the common case of substantives, which represents the earlier nominative and accusative alike, was used in combinations like : Lo ! swich it is *a millere to be fals* (Chaucer) | And verelye *one man to lyue in pleasure*, whyles all other wepe . . . that is the parte of a iayler (More). In pronouns we find the nominative : *Thow to lye* by our moder is to muche shame for vs to suffre (Malory). In Spanish we have a nominative : Es causa bastante Para *tener hambre yo* ? 'Is that reason enough for me to be hungry ? ' | Qué importará, si está muerto Mi honor, el *quedar yo vivo* ! 'What matters it that I remain alive, if my honour is dead ? ' (both from Calderon, Alc. de Zal. 1. 308 and 2. 840). In the same way in Italian, and in Portuguese also with *eu* 'I.'[1] An Italian combination like " prima di narrarci il poeta la favola," in which the infinitive has both a subject and two objects, reminds one strongly of a subordinate clause (" before the poet tells us the story "), from which it differs only in not having a finite verb. Similarly in Arabic, according to Steinthal, *Charakteristik*, 267, I transcribe his translation of one example : ' es ist gemeldet-mir die tödtung (nominat.) Mahmud (nominat.) seinen-bruder, d. h. dass Mahmud seinen bruder getödtet hat.'

The following instances show another way in which a nominative may be the notional subject of an infinitive. If the object of *he believes* in " he believes me to be guilty " is the whole nexus consisting of the four last words, it is necessary to say that in the passive construction " I am believed to be guilty " the subject is not " I " alone, but the nexus *I to be guilty*, although these words

---

[1] In the second person singular and in the plural Portuguese has developed another way of indicating what is the notional subject of an infinitive, in its " inflected infinitive " : *ter-es* ' for thee to have,' pl. *ter-mos, ter-des, ter-em* (Diez, *Gramm*. 2. 187, 3. 220 ; according to some, this is not historically to be explained by the infinitive adopting analogically the personal endings of the finite verb, but directly from finite forms, but this does not alter the character of the forms from the point of view of actual usage).

do not stand together, and though the person of the verb is determined by the first word alone. What is believed is my guilt. In
the same way *he is said* (*expected, supposed*) *to come at five* (his arrival
at five is expected) | *I am made* (*caused*) *to work hard* (what is
caused is not " I," but my working) and correspondingly in other
languages.[1]

The same consideration holds good in active constructions, e.g.
he seems *to work hard* | *er* scheint *hart zu arbeiten* | *il* semble (paraît)
travailler durement (where Dan. has the passive form just as in the
above-mentioned sentences : *han* synes *at arbejde hårdt*) : the real
subject is the whole underlined nexus.[2] This analysis must con-
sistently be extended to instances like E. *he* is sure (likely) *to come* |
she happened *to look up*, etc., though these latter constructions are
historically developed from older ones in which what is now in the
nominative was put in the dative case.

While all the infinitive-combinations hitherto mentioned are
primary members of the main sentence, we have now to deal with
the rare cases in which similar combinations are subjuncts, e.g.
the caul was put up in a raffle to fifty members at half-a-crown a
head, *the winner to spend* five shillings (Dickens) | we divided it :
he to speak to the Spaniards and I to the English (Defoe). The
infinitive here has the same signification of what is destined or
enjoined as in *he is to spend*, and the whole nexus may be said to
be used instead of the clumsy *the winner being to spend*, which
would belong in a following paragraph.

A further kind of nexus is found, as already noted (p. 115),
in combinations like " I heard of *the Doctor's arrival*." But these
verbal substantives will require a separate chapter (Ch. X). The
only thing to be mentioned here is that the similarity between such
combinations and sentences like " the Doctor arrived " is recognized
in the traditional term " subjective genitive " as contrasted with
the " possessive genitive " in " the Doctor's house, the Doctor's
father."

Nexus without a Verb.

A final series of nexuses consists of those which contain neither
a finite verb nor an infinitive nor a verbal substantive.

Here we first encounter the so-called nominal sentences, con-

---

[1] Sonnenschein, § 301, says that in " He is believed by me to be guilty "
the infinitive *to be* is a retained object, like the accusative in " He was awarded
the prize " (passive form of " They awarded him the prize "). Surely the
parallel is far from striking.

[2] It is not clear whether Sonnenschein, loc. cit., would also use the term
" retained object " for the infinitive in " He seems *to be* guilty."

taining a subject and a predicative, which may be either a substantive or an adjective. These sentences are extremely frequent both in such languages as have not developed a " copula," i.e. a verb meaning ' to be,' and in those languages which have a copula, but do not use it as extensively as e.g. English. Among the latter are some of the oldest languages of our family—for instance, old Greek ; see especially Meillet, *La phrase nominale en indo-européen*, MSL 14, 1906, p. 1 ff. In Russian this is the ordinary construction where *we* use the present tense of *be* : ' I am ill ' is *ja bolen*, ' he is a soldier ' *on soldat* ; a difference is made in the form of an adjective according as it is used as a predicative or as an adjunct, e.g. *dom nov* ' the house is new,' *dom novyj* ' a new house, the new house.' The verb ' be,' however, has to be expressed in other tenses, as well as in sentences meaning ' there is, or are.'

It is generally said that such " nominal " sentences are no longer found in our West-European languages, but as a matter of fact there is one particular form in which they are extremely common. Under the influence of strong feeling there seems to be everywhere a tendency to place the predicative first, to which the subject is added as a kind of afterthought, but without the verb *is*. In this way we get sentences which are analogous in every respect to the Greek as " Ouk agathon polukoiraniē " (Not a good thing, government by the many), for instance : Nice goings on, those in the Balkans ! | Quite serious all this, though it reads like a joke (Ruskin) | Amazing the things that Russians will gather together and keep (H. Walpole) | what a beastly and pitiful wretch that Wordsworth (Shelley ; such *that*-phrases are frequent.[1]) | Fr. Charmante, la petite Pauline ! | Dan. Et skrækkeligt bæst, den Christensen ! | Godt det samme !

This construction is frequent with expressions for " happy " : Gr. Trismakares Danaoi kai tetrakis, hoi tot' olonto Troiēi en eureiēi ' thrice and four times happy the Danaans who perished then in broad Troy (Odyss. 5. 306) | felix qui potuit rerum cognoscere causas (Virg.) | Beati possidentes | Happy the man, whose wish and care A few paternal acres bound (Pope) | Thrice blest whose lives are faithful prayers (Tennyson) | Dan. Lykkelig den, hvis lykke folk foragter ! (Rørdam) ; cf. also Gothic Hails þiudans iudaie (Joh. 19. 3) | ON. Heill þū nū Vafþrūþner | All haile Macbeth ! [2] Another frequent form is : Now I am in Arden, *the more fool I !* (Sh.).

[1] Is *witness the way in which he behaved* to be classed here, *witness* being taken as a substantive ? One might perhaps take *witness* as a verb in the subjunctive.

[2] *Hail* in this construction was originally an adjective, but was later taken as a substantive, whence the addition of *to* : " hail to thee, thane of Cawdor ! "

Very often the subject that follows the predicative is an infinitive or a whole clause : Gr. Argaleon, basileia, diēnekeōs agoreusai ' difficult, your Majesty, to speak at length ' (Od. 7. 241) | Needless to say, his case is irrefutable | Fr. Inutile d'insister davantage | What a pity that he should die so young | Wie schade dass er so früh sterben sollte | Quel dommage qu'il soit mort si tôt | Skade at han døde så ung | Small wonder that we all loved him exceedingly | How true, that there is nothing dead in this Universe (Carlyle) | true, she had not dared to stick to them.

In a special French form we have *que* before the subject : Singulier homme qu'Aristote ! | Mauvais prétexte que tout cela !

I have given all these examples, because grammarians generally fail to appreciate these constructions. It is no use saying that we have here ellipsis of *is* ; it would only weaken the idiomatic force of such sentences if we were to add the verb, though it would be required if the subject were placed first.

Corresponding verbless combinations are also found in clauses : Russian *govorjat čto on bolen* ' they say that he is ill ' | *However great the loss*, he is always happy | *the greater his losses*, the more will he sing | his patrimony was so small that *no wonder* he worked now and then for a living wage (Locke).

Nexus-Object, etc.

A nexus-object is often found : " I found *the cage empty*," which is easily distinguished from " I found *the empty cage* " where *empty* is an adjunct. It is usual here to say that *the cage* is the object and that *empty* is used predicatively of, or with, the object, but it is more correct to look upon the whole combination *the cage empty* as the object. (Cf. " I found that the cage was empty " and " I found the cage to be empty.") This is particularly clear in sentences like " I found her gone " (thus did not find her !), cf. also the contrast between " I found Fanny not at home," where the negative belongs to the subordinate nexus, and " I did not find Fanny at home," where *not* negatives *find*.

Other examples : they made him President (*him President* is the object of result) | he made (rendered) her unhappy | does that prove me wrong ? | he gets things done | she had something the matter with her spine | what makes you in such a hurry ? | she only wishes the dinner at an end. The predicate-part of the nexus may be any word or group that can be a predicative after the verb *to be*.

The most interesting thing here is that a verb may take a nexus-object which is quite different from its usual objects, as in *he drank himself drunk* | the gentleman had drunke *himselfe out of his five senses* (Sh.; *he drank himself* is absurd) and that verbs otherwise intransitive may have a nexus-object of result : he slept *himself sober* | A louer's eyes will gaze *an eagle blind* (Sh.) | Lily was nearly screaming *herself into a fit.*

Other languages present similar phenomena, e.g. Dan. de drak Jeppe fuld | de drak Jeppe under bordet | ON. þeir biðja hana gráta Baldr ór helju ' they ask her to weep B. out of Hades.' Paul P. 154 mentions combinations like : die augen rot weinen | die füsse wund laufen | er schwatzt das blaue vom himmel herunter | denke dich in meine lage hinein ; but his remarks do not show clearly how he apprehends this " freie verwendung des akkusativs." In Finnish we have here the characteristic case called " translative," as in : äiti makasi lapsensa kuoliaaksi ' the mother slept her child (into) dead (overlay it) ' | hän joi itsensä siaksi ' he drank himself (into) a swine ' ; the examples taken from Eliot FG 128, others in Setälä, *Finska språkets satslära* § 29.

The close analogy between the accusative with infinitive and this nexus-object makes it easy to understand that we sometimes find the same verb taking both constructions in the same sentence : a winning frankness of manner which made most people fond of her, and pity her (Thackeray) | a crowd round me only made me proud, and try to draw as well as I could (Ruskin) | he felt himself dishonored, and his son to be an evil in the tribe (Wister).

In the passive turn corresponding to sentences with nexus-objects, we must consistently (as in the infinitive-constructions, p. 119) look upon the whole nexus as the (notional) subject, thus *he . . . President* in " he was made President," etc., though, of course, the person of the verb is dependent on the primary part of the nexus only : if *I am* made President. In Danish we have constructions like " han blev drukket under bordet | pakken ønskes (bedes) bragt til mit kontor, literally, ' the parcel is wished (asked) brought to my office.' Cf. ON. at biðja, at *Baldr* væri grátinn *ór Helju* ' to ask that Baldr should be wept out of Hades.'

Analogous constructions are sometimes found with active verbs, as in Greek : allous men pantas elanthane dakrua leibōn (Od. 8. 532) ' he escaped the attention of the others shedding tears, i.e. the fact that he shed . . .' | hōs de epausato lalōn (Luk. 5. 4 ; the E. translation " when he had left off speaking " is only seemingly in accordance with the Greek text, for *speaking* is the verbal substantive as object of *left*, not a participle in the nom. as *lalōn*).[1]

A nexus may be the object of a preposition. In English this is particularly frequent after *with* as in : I sat at work in the school-

---

[1] This can hardly be distinguished from instances in which a verb takes a predicative, e.g. *she seems happy.*

room *with the window open* (different from : near the open window) |
you sneak back *with her kisses hot on your lips* (Kipl.) | he fell asleep
with his candle lit | let him dye, *With euery ioynt a wound* (Sh.) | he
kept standing *with his hat on.* The character of the construction
and the peculiar signification of *with* (different from that in " he
stood with his brother on the steps ") is particularly clear when
the adnex neutralizes the usual meaning of *with* : *with both of us
absent* | wailed the little Chartist, *with nerve utterly gone* | I hope
I'm not the same now, *with all the prettiness and youth removed.*

Without also is found governing a nexus : like a rose, full-blown,
but without one petal yet fallen.

In Danish *med* often takes a nexus : *med hænderne tomme* ' with
the hands empty,' different from *med de tomme hænder* ' with the
empty hands,' which presupposes some action by means of the
hands, while the former combination implies nothing more than a
clause (while, or as, his hands are, or were, empty). Similarly also
in other languages.

With other prepositions we have the well-known Latin con-
structions *post urbem conditam* | *ante Christum natum.* When
Madvig here says that the idea is not so much of the person or thing
in a certain condition, as of the action as a *substantival conception*
he is thinking of the (Danish, etc.) translation by means of a substantive, but this, of course, is of the class described below as
nexus-substantive ('after the *construction* of the town, before the
birth of Christ '), which is different from ordinary substantival
conceptions, and calls for a separate elucidation, so that Madvig's
explanation leaves us just where we were. Nor do we get much
further with Allen and Greenough's comment that " a noun and a
passive participle are often so united that the participle and not
the noun contains the main idea." Brugmann (IF 5. 145 ff.)
characterizes the explanation by means of an abbreviated clause
as " sterile linguistic philosophy " [1] and thinks himself that the
construction took its origin in a shifting of the syntactic structure
(verschiebung der syntaktischen gliederung) in combinations like
post hoc factum, which at first meant ' after this fact ' (*hoc* adjunct
to the primary *factum,* if I may use my own terms), but was afterwards apprehended with *hoc* as primary and *factum* as secondary,

---

[1] Brugmann, of course, is quite right in opposing this as an account of
the *origin* of the construction, the only question that interests him and his
school. But the historic (or dynamic) way of looking at linguistic phenomena is not the only one, and, besides asking what something has come
from, it is also important to know what it has come to be. In the same
way the etymology of a word is only one part, and not always the most
important part of the information we look for in a dictionary. As a matter
of fact the construction in question means the same thing as a subordinate
clause and that justifies us in treating it in this chapter.

this being subsequently extended to other cases. The whole explanation seems rather far-fetched. None of these grammarians thinks of classing the phenomenon with the rest of the constructions which I mention in this chapter (absolute ablative, etc.), though it is only through a collective treatment that they can be fully understood as illustrating one another.

In Italian the same construction is pretty frequent after *dopo* : dopo vuotato il suo bicchiere, Fileno disse | Cercava di rilegger posatamente, dopo fatta la correzione (Serao) | Dopo letta questa risposta, gli esperti francesi hanno dichiarato che . . . (Newspaper).

Milton's " after Eve seduc'd " and Dryden's " the royal feast for Persia won " are no doubt due to conscious imitation of Latin syntax, but that does not account for similar constructions found here and there in less learned writers : before one dewty done (Heywood) | they had heard of a world ransom'd, or one destroyed (Sh., may be adjunct) | after light and mercy received (Bunyan) | he wished her joy on a rival gone (Anthony Hope)—to pick out only a few of the examples I have collected.

Similar nexuses may be found also in other positions, where they are not the object either of a verb or of a preposition, thus in Lat. : dubitabat nemo quin violati hospites, legati necati, pacati atque socii nefario bello lacessiti, fana vexata hanc tantam efficerent vastitatem (Cicero, translated by Brugmann ' dass die mishandlung der gastfreunde, die ermorderung der gesandten, die ruchlosen angriffe auf friedliche und verbündete völker, die schändung der heiligtümer ').

A similar example is found in Shakespeare : Prouided that my banishment repeal'd, And lands restor'd againe be freely graunted (R2 III. 3. 40 = the repealing of my b. and restoration of my l.). But in cases like the following it may be doubtful whether we have a participle or a verbal substantive : the 'Squire's portrait being found united with ours, was a honour too great to escape envy (Goldsmith) | And is a wench having a bastard all your news ? (Fielding).

French examples have been collected by Sandfeld Jensen (*Bisœtningerne i moderne fransk*, 1909, p. 120) and E. Lerch (*Prädikative partizipia für verbalsubstantiva im französ.*, 1912), e.g. le verrou poussé l'avait surprise ' the fact that the door was bolted ' | c'était son rêve accompli ' das war die erfüllung ihres traumes.' The adnex need not be a participle, as is seen by some relative clauses analyzed by Sandfeld Jensen : Deux jurys qui condamnent un homme, ça vous impressionne, in which *ça* (singular) clearly shows the character of the combination. Cf. now Brunot PL 208.

I am inclined to include here some combinations with " quantifiers," which are not to be taken in the usual way, e.g. the proverb *too many cooks spoil the broth* = the circumstance that the cooks are too numerous spoils. Thus also : trop de cuisiniers gâtent la sauce | viele köche verderben den brei | mange kokke fordærver maden | many hands make quick work | mange hunde er harens død | no news is good news | you must put up with no hot dinner. This is evidently quite different from the adjuncts in " too many people are poor " or " no news arrived on that day."

Nexus Subjunct.

We next come to nexus subjuncts. None of the usual names (duo ablativi, ablativi consequentiæ, ablativi absoluti, absolute participles) get at the essence of the phenomenon : " absolute " must mean ' standing out of the syntactic connexion,' but do these words stand more outside than other subjuncts ? Participle should not be mentioned in the name, for no participle is required, e.g. *dinner over* | *Scipione autore*, etc. Brugmann (KG. § 815) makes an attempt at explaining the various cases employed (gen. in Gr., and Sanskrit, abl. in Lat., dat. in Gothic, O.H.G., OE., ON., etc.) ; he thinks that the participle to begin with was an ordinary adjunct, which later through a " verschiebung der syntaktischen gliederung " was felt together with some other word to be " eine art von (temporalem oder dgl.) nebensatz." In my view what is characteristic of the construction is contained in two things : (1) that there are two members standing to another in the peculiar relation here termed nexus, thus parallel to the relation between subject and verb in " the dog barks," and (2) that this combination plays the part of a subjunct in the sentence. I am not here concerned with the question how the Latin ablative is to be explained, whether as originally local or temporal or instrumental ; in the language as we know it the temporal *Tarquinio rege* only differs from *hoc tempore* in this, that *rege* stands in another relation to its primary *Tarquinio* than *hoc* (adjunct) to its primary *tempore*. The same difference is seen in *me invito* as against *hoc modo*, both combinations denoting manner.[1]

---

[1] The subject-part (primary) of a Latin nexus-subjunct may be an accusative-with-infinitive or a clause, in which case it cannot be put in the ablative, thus in the following examples, which I take from Madvig, italicizing the primary : Alexander, audito *Dareum movisse ab Ecbatanis*, fugientem insequi pergit | consul . . . edicto *ut quicunque ad vallum tenderet pro hoste haberetur*, fugientibus obstitit | additur dolus, missis *qui magnam vim lignorum ardentem in flumen conjicerent*. As in other cases mentioned above, I cannot approve of the analysis according to which the subject of *missis* in the last sentence is an imaginary pronoun in the ablative case " understood " before *qui*. In the first sentence the subject-part of the nexus subjunct is in itself a nexus with *Dareum* as its subject-part. Madvig here and in the second sentence unnecesarily takes the participle as an " impersonal expression " taking an object.

In the Romanic languages, the nexus-subjunct is still so common that a few examples will suffice : It. *morto mio padre, dovei andare a Roma* | *sonate le cinque, non è più permesso a nessuno d'entrare* | Fr. *Ces dispositions faites, il s'est retiré* | *Dieu aidant, nous y parviendrons.*[1] Sp. *concluídos los estudios . . . pues no hube clase . . . Examinadas imparcialmente las cualidades de aquel niño, era imposible desconocer su mérito* (Galdós, D. Perf. 83).

In English the construction is frequent, though apart from certain restricted applications it is more literary than popular : we shall go, *weather permitting* | *everything considered*, we may feel quite easy | *this done*, he shut the window | she sat, *her hands crossed on her lap, her eyes absently bent upon them* [2] | he stood, *pipe in mouth* [2] | *dinner over*, we left the hotel. Thus very often with one of the other words or groups that can be predicatives besides adjectives and participles.

There is in certain cases a tendency to introduce the nexus-subjunct by some word like *once* : *Once the murderer found*, the rest was easy enough | Fr. *Une fois l'action terminée, nous rentrâmes chez nous* (*sitôt achevée cette tâche*).

In German nexus-subjuncts are pretty common now, though comparatively young in the language ; I select a few of Paul's examples (Gr. 3. 278) : *Louise kommt zurück, einen mantel umgeworfen* | *alle hände vol*[1], wollen Sie noch immer mehr greifen | *einen kritischen freund an der seite* kommt man schneller vom fleck. Paul is not explicit as to how this " art des freien akkusativs " is to be apprehended, but his remark (after examples with a passive participle) " In allen diesen fällen könnte man statt des passiven ein aktives attributives partizipium einsetzen " and his mention (on p. 284) of the accusative as an acc. of object leave us in the lurch with regard to those combinations that contain no participles. Curme (GG 266, 553) also takes the participle in an active sense and thinks that *habend* is understood : *Dies vorausgeschickt [habend], fahre ich in meiner erzählung fort* | *Solche hindernis alle ungeachtet [habend], richtet gott diesen zug aus.* I am very sceptical with regard to this explanation of the origin of the construction through sub-audition ; anyhow, it does not explain how (in Curme's own words) " the construction has become productive, so that we now find as predicate of the clause [what I call the nexus] not only a perfect participle of a transitive verb, but also the perfect participle of an intransitive verb, an adjective, adverb, or a prepositional phrase."

---

[1] In the proverb " Morte la bête, mort le venin " we have first a nexus subjunct, then an independent nexus of the kind described, p. 121.

[2] In these combinations, it would be possible to add the preposition *with*, and the close similarity with the construction mentioned above, pp. 123–4, thus is obvious.

As nexus-subjuncts we may also consider the genitives in *unverrichteter dinge kam er zurück* | *wankenden schrittes . . . erscheint der alte mann* (Raabe, quoted by Curme).

The " absolute dative " in the old Gothonic languages is often explained as an imitation of the Latin construction. In Dan. the construction plays only a subordinate rôle, apart from a few fixed combinations like " *Alt vel overvejet,* rejser jeg imorgen | *alt iberegnet* | *dine ord i œre,* tror jeg dog . . ." as in G. *dein wort in ehren,* literally ' your words in honour,' i.e. with due deference to your words.

To begin with, the subject-part of this nexus-subjunct was everywhere put in some oblique case, though, as we have seen, this case was different in different languages. But independently of one another, various languages began to use the nominative case as more conformable to the rôle as subject. This is the rule now in Modern Greek (Thumb, Handb. 2 ed. 161), and goes far back, as Sandfeld tells me, e.g. in the apocryphal Evang. Thomæ 10. 1 Met' oligas hēmeras *skhizōn tis* xula . . . epesen hē axinē. To the same friend I am indebted for an early mediæval Latin example : Peregrinatio Silviæ 16. 7 *benedicens nos episcopus* profecti sumus. In Romanic languages the case is not shown in substantives, but with pronouns we have the nominative, e.g. It. essendo *egli* Cristiano, *io* Saracina (Ariosto), Sp. Rosario no se opondrá, *queriendolo yo* (Galdós, D. Perf. 121). In English the nominative has prevailed in the standard language : For, *he being dead,* with him is beautie slaine (Sh. Ven. 1019). In G. the nominative is found now and then, see Paul Gr. 3. 281 and 283, who gives the following example from Grillparzer : *der wurf geworfen,* fliegt der stein, and Curme GG 554, who has examples from Schiller, Auerbach, Hauptmann, etc.

In *this notwithstanding* (*notwithstanding this*) and *notwiths.anding all our efforts* we have properly a nexus-subjunct with *this* and *all our efforts* as primaries and the negative participle as adnex, but the construction is now practically to be considered as containing a preposition and its object ; thus also G. *ungeachtet unserer bemühungen,* Dan. *uagtet vore anstrengelser.* In the same way Fr. *pendant ce temps,* E. *during that time* (orig. ' while that time dures or lasts '). German here goes still further in metanalysis : the old genitive nexus-subjunct *währendes krieges,* pl. *währender kriege,* is dissolved into *während des krieges, während der kriege* : in this way *während* has become a preposition governing the genitive.

In Spanish nexus-subjuncts we witness a shifting which can be explained from the natural relation between subject and object ; I take facts and examples from Hanssen § 39. 3, but the interpretation is my own :

(1) subject-part + participle : *estas cosas puestas,* as in French and other languages.

(2) the same with inverse word-order : *visto que no quieres hacerlo | oídos los reos* ' the defendants (being) heard ' (thus also in the examples quoted above, p. 127). The primary here follows after the participle as the object does in a finite sentence. It is therefore apprehended as an object, and as objects denoting living beings are in Spanish provided with the preposition *á,* this peculiarity is extended to the noun in these combinations, the result being :

(3) *oído á los reos.* It is noteworthy here that the participle is no longer in the plural : the construction is thus parallel to that in an active sentence like *he oído á los reos* ' I have heard the defendants,' and may to a certain extent be looked upon as a preterit of the active participle *oyendo á los reos* ; in other words, the participle is used in an active sense and with no subject expressed. Popular instinct in Spanish has thus finally led to a form which shows the same conception as that which according to Curme (and possibly Paul, above, p. 127) was the starting-point for the German construction.

A nexus is very often expressed by means of a genitive and an " abstract substantive " as in *I doubt the Doctor's cleverness,* which means the same thing as ' I doubt that the Doctor is clever.' The parallelism with verbal substantives, as in *the Doctor's arrival,* is obvious, but nevertheless traditional grammatical terminology restricts the use of the name ' subjective genitive ' to the latter combination, though it might just as well be applied to cases like *the Doctor's cleverness.*[1] On both kinds of substantives see the next chapter.

Nexus of Deprecation.

In all the various kinds of nexus thus far considered the connexion between the two members is to be taken in a direct or positive sense. But we now come to what might be termed the nexus of deprecation in which the connexion is as it were brushed aside at once as impossible ; the meaning is thus negative, and this is expressed in speech by the intonation, which is the same as in questions, often in an exaggerated form and not infrequently given to

---

[1] If *the Doctor's* is called a possessive genitive, it is because we say that the Doctor *possesses,* or *has* (the quality of) cleverness, but this evidently is merely a figure of speech.

the two members separately : we shall see in a later chapter that question and negation are often closely akin.

There are two forms of deprecating nexus : first with an infinitive, e.g. What ? I loue ! I sue ! I seeke a wife ! (Sh.) | "Did you dance with her ? " "Me dance ! " says Mr. Barnes (Thackeray) | I say anything disrespectful of Dr. Kenn ? Heaven forbid ! (G. Eliot).[1] In the last example, the words "Heaven forbid" show how the idea of the nexus is rejected ; the following example from Browning shows how the construction, if continued so as to form a whole sentence of the regular pattern, conforms to the type mentioned above, p. 121 : She to be his, were hardly less absurd Than that he took her name into his mouth. It is not, however, common to complete the sentence in this way, the emotion having found sufficient vent in the subject and the infinitive in the particular tone of voice to which I have referred.

Other languages use the same trick, e.g. Er ! so was sagen ! | Han gifte sig ! | Toi faire ça ! | Io far questo ! | Mene incepto desistere victam ?—in Latin with the accusative with infinitive that would be required if a proper predicate were added.[2]

Second, a subject and a predicative may be placed together with the same interrogative tone and the same effect of brushing aside the idea of their combination as real or possible : Why, his grandfather was a tradesman ! *he a gentleman !* (Defoe) | The denunciation rang in his head day and night. *He arrogant, uncharitable, cruel !* (Locke).—It is, of course, possible to add a negative in the form of an answer so as to make the meaning perfectly clear : He arrogant ? *No, never !* or, *Not he !*

In the same way in other languages : Hun, utaknemlig ! | Er ! in Paris ! | Lui avare ? etc. In G. also with *und* : er sagte, er wolle landvogt werden. *Der und landvogt !* Aus dem ist nie was geworden (Frenssen).

These sentences with nexus of deprecation may be added to those mentioned above, in which we had complete (independent) sentences without a verb in one of the finite forms. From another point of view they may be given as instances of aposiopesis : under the influence of a strong emotion the speaker does not trouble to finish his sentence, and not infrequently it would be difficult to go on so as to produce a regularly constructed sentence.

---

[1] Further examples, *Negation*, p. 23 f.

[2] There is a related idiom, generally introduced by *and*, in which the connexion of the two ideas is not so emphatically rejected as here, but simply surprise is expressed, e.g. What ? A beggar ! a slave ! and he to deprave and abuse the virtue of tobacco ! (Ben Jonson) | One of the ladies could not refrain from expressing her astonishment—"A philosopher, and give a picnic ! " (Spencer). Cf. ChE, p. 70 ff.

Summary.

We may end this chapter by giving a tabulated survey of the principal instances of nexus, using characteristic examples instead of descriptive class-names. In the first column I place instances in which a verb (finite or infinitive) or a verbal substantive is found, in the second instances without such a form.

1.	*the dog barks*	*Happy the man, whose* . . .
2.	when *the dog barks*	*However great the loss*
3.	Arthur, *whom* they say *is kill'd*	
4.	I hear *the dog bark*	he makes *her happy*
5.	count on *him to come*	with *the window open*
6.	*for you to call*	*violati hospites*
7.	*he is believed to be guilty*	*she* was made *happy*
8.	*the winner to spend*	*everything considered*
9.	*the doctor's arrival*	*the doctor's cleverness*
10.	*I dance !*	*He a gentleman !*

In 1 and 10 the nexus forms a complete sentence, in all the other instances it forms only part of a sentence, either the subject, the object or a subjunct.

APPENDIX TO CHAPTER IX.

Copula.   Predicative.

This may be the proper place to insert a few remarks on what is often termed the copula, i.e. the verb *is* as the sign of a completed combination (nexus) of two ideas which stand in the relation of subject and predicate. Logicians are fond of analyzing all sentences into the three elements, subject, copula, and predicate ; *the man walks* is taken to contain the subject *the man*, the copula *is*, and the predicate *walking*. A linguist must find this analysis unsatisfactory, not only from the point of view of English grammar, where *is walking* means something different from *walks*, but also from a general point of view. The analysis presents some difficulties when the present tense is not used : *the man walked* cannot be dissolved into anything containing the form *is*, but only into *the man was walking*—but then logicians move always in the present of eternal truths ! The copula is so far from being the typical verb, that many languages have never developed any copula at all, and others dispense with it in many cases, as we have seen above. The verb *be* has become what it is through a long process of wearing down a more concrete signification ('grow'); it took a predicative in exactly the same way as many other verbs with a fuller signification still do : he grows old | goes mad | the dream will come true | my blood runs cold | he fell silent | he looks healthy | it looms large | it seems important | she blushed red | it tastes delicious | this sounds correct, etc. It may be remarked also that a predicative is found not only after verbs, but also after some particles, in English especially *for, to, into, as* : I take it for granted | you will be hanged for a pirate (Defoe) | he set himself down for an ass | he took her to wife (obsolete) | she grew into a tall, handsome girl | I look upon him as a fool, etc. This is particularly interesting in the combinations mentioned above (p. 124) : with his brother as protector | the Committee, with the Bishop and the Mayor for its presidents, had already held several meetings. Similarly in other languages : Goth. ei tawidedeina ina du þiudana ' that they might make him (to) king ' | G. das wasser wurde zu wein | Dan. blive til nar, holde een for nar. Note the nominative in G. Was für ein mensch, so also in Dutch *wat voor een* and Russian after čto za (cf. Shakespeare's What is he for a foole ?). It is interesting that in this way the preposition *for* may govern an adjective (participle), which is not otherwise possible : I gave myself over for lost ; cp. Lat. sublatus pro occiso | quum pro damnato mortuoque esset | pro certo habere aliquid ; It. Giovanni non si diede por vinto ; Fr. Ainsi vous n'êtes pas assassiné, car pur volé nous savons que vous l'êtes.—The parallel with a predicative after a verb is also seen in the E. rules for the use of the indefinite article, which are the same in both cases : in his capacity as a Bishop | in his capacity as Bishop of Durham.

CHAPTER X

NEXUS-SUBSTANTIVES. FINAL WORDS ON NEXUS

"Abstracts." Infinitives and Gerunds. Final Words on Nexus.

" Abstracts."

THOSE who define substantives as names of substances or things encounter difficulties with such words as *beauty, wisdom, whiteness,* which evidently are substantives and in all languages are treated as such, yet cannot be said to be names of substances or things. On the strength of this consideration it is habitual to distinguish two classes of substantives, concrete and abstract. The former are also called reality nouns (dingnamen, substanzbezeichnende substantiva), they comprise names of persons and of " objects," to which are also reckoned such more or less " intangible " phenomena as *sound, echo, poem, lightning, month,* etc. " Abstracts " are also called thought-names (begriffsnamen, verdinglichungen). The distinction of the two classes seems easy enough, for we hardly ever hesitate to which class we are to assign any given noun ; yet it is by no means easy to find a satisfactory definition of " abstract substantives."

Let us first look at the question as treated by a distinguished logician.

J. N. Keynes (FL, p. 16) expands the definition that a concrete name is the name of a thing, whilst an abstract name is the name of an attribute, by saying that " a *concrete* name is the name of anything which is regarded as possessing attributes, i.e. as a *subject of attributes* ; while an *abstract* name is the name of anything which is regarded as an attribute of something else, i.e. as an *attribute of subjects*." But on p. 18 he mentions that attributes may themselves be the subjects of attributes, as in the sentence " unpunctuality is irritating," and says that " *Unpunctuality*, therefore, although primarily an abstract name, can also be used in such a way that it is, according to our definition, concrete." But when " names which are primarily formed as abstracts and continue to be used as such are apt also to be used as concretes, that is to say, they are names of attributes which can themselves be regarded as possessing

attributes," Keynes has to admit that " this result is paradoxical "
He sees two ways of avoiding this difficulty, but rejects the first
as logically of no value.   This consists in defining an abstract name
as the name of anything which *can* be regarded as an attribute of
something else, and a concrete name as the name of that which
cannot be regarded as an attribute of something else.   He therefore
prefers the second way out, that is, he gives up for logical purposes
the distinction between concrete and abstract names, and substitutes for it a distinction between the concrete and the abstract
use of names, adding that " as logicians we have very little to do
with the abstract use of names," for " when a name appears either
as the subject or as the predicate of a non-verbal proposition [1]
its use is always concrete."

This is really tantamount to brushing away the whole distinction,
and yet there is no denying that such a word as *hardness* is on a
different plane altogether from *stone*, etc.   I think Dr. Keynes's
result has been arrived at on account of the unhappy term
" abstract " and especially of its contrast " concrete," because
these words in ordinary language are often applied to differences
which have no connexion with the distinction occupying us here.
This is seen with particular clearness in V. Dahlerup's article
" Abstrakter og konkreter " (*Dania* 10. 65 ff.), in which he says
that the distinction between abstract and concrete is a relative
one and applies not only to substantives, but to all other word-
classes as well.   *Hard* is concrete in " a hard stone," but abstract
in " hard work," *towards* in concrete in " he moved towards the
town," but abstract in " his behaviour towards her," *turn* is concrete
in " he turned round," but abstract in " he turned pale," etc.
This usage, according to which " concrete " stands chiefly for what
is found in the exterior world as something palpable, space-filling,
perceptible to the senses, and " abstract " refers to something only
found in the mind, evidently agrees with popular language, but
it does not assist us in understanding what is peculiar to such
words as " whiteness " in contradistinction to other substantives.

W. Hazlitt (*New and Improved Grammar*, 1810, Preface viii)
says : " a substantive is neither the name of a thing, nor the name
of a substance, but the name of a substance or of any other thing
or idea, considered as it is in itself, or as a distinct individual.
That is, it is not the name of a thing really subsisting by itself
(according to the old definition), but of a thing *considered* as subsisting by itself.   So if we speak of *white* as a circumstance or
quality of snow, it is an adjective ; but if we abstract the idea of

---

[1] A " verbal proposition " is defined on p. 49 as " one which gives information only in regard to the meaning or application of the term which
constitutes its subject."

white from the substance to which it belongs, and consider this colour as it really is in itself, or as a distinct subject of discourse, it then becomes a substantive, as in the sentence, White or whiteness is hurtful to the sight."

Essentially the same idea is found in many recent writers, who define substantives like " whiteness " with slight variations as " fictitiously substantival words," " names of only imaginary substances," " vorstellungen, welche als selbständige gegenstände gedacht werden," " gegenständlich gedachte begriffe," etc., " mere names, thought of, and consequently grammatically treated as if they were independent things " (Noreen VS 5. 256 f.[1]). In spite of this consensus I must confess that when I speak of a young girl's *beauty* or of an old man's *wisdom*, I do not think of these qualities as " things " or " real objects " ; these are to me only other ways of expressing the thought that she is beautiful and he is wise. When Wundt says that *humanity* (*menschlichkeit*) denotes a quality just as much as *human* does, he is perfectly right, but not so when he adds that the substantival form makes it easier to treat this quality in our thoughts as an *object* (gegenstand). Misteli avoids this fiction and lays stress exclusively on the grammatical treatment, but no one really explains how and why all languages come to have such substantives for adjectival notions.

Sweet long before Wundt and Misteli had expressed similar ideas (1876, CP 18, cf. NEG § 80, 99) : " The change of *white* into *whiteness* is a purely formal device to enable us to place an attribute-word as the subject of a proposition . . . *Whiteness* is correctly described as an " abstract " name, as signifying an attribute without reference to the things that possess the attribute. *White*, however, is held to be connotative. . . . The truth is, of course, that *white* is as much an abstract name as *whiteness* is, the two being absolutely identical in meaning." To Sweet, therefore, " the only satisfactory definition of a part of speech must be a purely formal one : *snow*, for instance, is not a noun because it stands for a thing, but because it can stand as the subject of a proposition, because it can form its plural by adding *s*, because it has a definite prefix [i.e. the definite article], etc., and *whiteness* is a noun for precisely the same reasons." [2]

Sweet is right in saying that *white* and *whiteness* are equally abstract (in the sense ' separated from individual things '), but not in maintaining that the two are absolutely identical in meaning.

---

[1] Finck, KZ 41. 265 says that we still [!] speak of *death, war, time, night,* etc., as if they were things like stones and trees.

[2] What Sweet says in the later work, NEG 61, on Abstract Nouns does not contribute to clarity ; he counts as such not only words like *redness, reading*, but also *lightning, shadow, day* and many others ; *north* and *south* are abstract from one point of view, concrete from another

The difference may be slight, but it is nevertheless a real one, else why should all nations have separate words for the two ideas ? Observe that we use different verbs in the two cases : *being* white = *having* whiteness ; the minister is (becomes) wise, he possesses (acquires) wisdom. In Ido Couturat ingeniously created the ending *-eso* for these nouns, which is the root of the verb *es-ar* ' to be ' with the substantive ending *-o* : *blind-es-o* ' the being blind,' i.e. ' blindness,' *superbeso* ' pride,' etc. Here we might perhaps say that the idea of ' being ' is smuggled into the word, exactly as our linguistic habits incline us to smuggle a (neither expressed nor necessary) ' is ' into such Russian sentences as *dom nov* ' the house (is) new ' ; but Couturat rightly perceived the cardinal truth that in such substantives the adjectival element enters as a predica-tive. This then is what is really characteristic of these formations : they are *predicative-substantives*.[1]

There is evidently great similarity between the substantives here considered, which are formed from adjectives, and verbal substantives (nouns of action, nomina actionis) like *coming, arrival, movement, change, existence, repose, sleep, love*, etc.[2] But the examples show that the name "noun of action" is not adequate, unless we count such states as *rest* and *sleep* as actions. My own view has already been indicated : starting from the fact that "I saw the Doctor's arrival " = " I saw the Doctor arrive, I saw that the Doctor arrived " and that " I doubt the Doctor's cleverness " = " I doubt that the Doctor is clever " we have to recognize a separate class of words which we shall term nexus-substantives and subdivide into verbal nexus-words (*arrival*) and predicative nexus-words (*cleverness*).

The task then remains of investigating the use of this class, or the purpose for which these words are employed in actual speech. So far as I can see, their use lies in the power they afford us of avoiding many clumsy expressions, because subordinate clauses would otherwise be necessary to render the same idea. Try, for instance, to express without the italicized substantives the following passage from a recent novel : " His *display* of *anger* was equivalent to an *admission* of *belief* in the other's boasted *power* of *divination*."

---

[1] Most of them are derived from adjectives (*kindness* from *kind*, etc.) or have natural affinity to adjectives (*ease, beauty* to *easy, beautiful*) ; this is quite natural in consideration of the frequency with which adjectives are used as predicatives, but other words of the same class are derived from substantives (*scholarship, professorship, professorate, chaplaincy*).—It is sometimes given as one of the chief grammatical characteristics of " ab-stracts " that they do not admit of any plural ; but this is not quite correct, see the chapter on number.

[2] The kinship between the two classes accounts for the fact that Danish which has no verbal substantive corresponding to the verb *elske* ' love, uses instead the word *kærlighed* from the adjective *kærlig* 'affectionate, kind.

The value of this power of creating handy expressions for complex thoughts is greatly increased by the fact that when a verb or a predicative is thus raised into a substantive, subordinate members are also in consequence raised to a higher plane : tertiary members are made secondary, and quaternary, tertiary. In other words, subjuncts become adjuncts, and sub-subjuncts become subjuncts, and we are able to construct sentences with a facility which more than makes up for the concomitant change of a primary member (the subject or object) into a secondary member (an adjunct, " subjective " or " objective " genitive).

This must be illustrated by a few examples. " The Doctor's extremely quick arrival and uncommonly careful examination of the patient brought about her very speedy recovery "—if we compare this with the sentences " the Doctor arrived extremely quickly and examined the patient uncommonly carefully ; she recovered very speedily," we shall see that (giving the rank of the word in Roman numbers) the verbs *arrived, examined, recovered* (II) have been turned into the substantives *arrival, examination, recovery* (I), the subjuncts (adverbs) *quickly, carefully, speedily* (III) have become the adjuncts (adjectives) *quick, careful, speedy* (II), while the change from sub-subjuncts (IV) into subjuncts (III) has entailed no formal change in *extremely, uncommonly, very.* On the other hand, the primary words (subject and object) *the Doctor, the patient, she* (I) have been turned into the secondary members (adjuncts) *the Doctor's, of the patient, her* (II).

Similar shiftings are observed in the sentence " we noticed the Doctor's (II) really (III) astonishing (II) cleverness (I)," as compared with " the Doctor (I) was really (IV) astonishingly (III) clever (II)." (If *really* is here referred to the verb *was*, it has the rank III.)

Predicative-nouns are also very handy in the frequent combinations in which they are made the object of the preposition *with*, as they enable us to get rid of long-winded subjunct combinations : " He worked with positively surprising rapidity " (instead of " positively surprisingly rapidly "), " with absolute freedom," " with approximate accuracy," etc. Cf. the shiftings mentioned above, p. 91.

We are now in a position to get a clearer view of a grammatical phenomenon which is generally termed " the cognate object." [1]

---

[1] Other names are "inner object," "object of content," "factitive object " ; an older name is "figura etymologica." Many examples from the early stages of Aryan languages in Delbrück, Synt. 1. 366 ff., Brugmann VG II, 2. 621 ff., Willmanns DG 3. 485 ; cf. also Paul Gr. 3. 226, Curme GG 491, Falk & Torp DNS 26, M. Cahen, *Et. sur le Vocabulaire religieux*, 97, 236, where other works are quoted. Many of these grammarians, however, mix this phenomenon up with other kinds of object with which, in my opinion, it has nothing to do. The phenomenon is known outside our family of languages ; see, for instance, Setälä, *Finska språkets satslära*, § 30.

Its purpose cannot be fully understood if we start from such examples as " I dreamed a dream " (Onions, AS 35) or " servitutem servire," for such combinations are, to say the least, extremely rare in actual speech, for the simple reason that such an object is inane and adds nothing to the verbal notion. In actual speech we meet with such sentences as : I would faine dye a dry death (Sh.) | I never saw a man die a violent death (Ruskin) | she smiled a little smile and bowed a little bow (Trollope) | Mowgli laughed a little short ugly laugh (Kipling) | he laughed his usual careless laugh (Locke) | he lived the life, and died the death of a Christian (Cowper), etc.

These examples make it clear that the nexus-substantive is simply introduced to give us an easy means of adding some descriptive trait in the form of an adjunct which it would be difficult or impossible to tack on to the verb in the form of a subjunct (cf. also " fight the good fight," which is different from " fight well "). Sometimes this extra description is added as a kind of " appositum," marked off by means of a comma or dash, as in : The dog sighed, the insincere and pity-seeking sigh of a spoilt animal (Bennett) | Kitty laughed—a laugh musical but malicious (Mrs. H. Ward). We see the same device employed in other cases, where some special addition to a secondary word cannot conveniently be expressed by means of a subjunct ; a predicative-word is consequently loosely attached to the sentence as the bearer of the specialization in the form of an adjunct, thus in : her face was very pale, a greyish pallor (Mrs. Ward) | he had been too proud to ask—the terrible pride of the benefactor (Bennett). Not infrequently the addition is introduced by the preposition *with* : she was pretty, with the prettiness of twenty | I am sick with a sickness more than of body, a sickness of mind and my own shame (Carlyle).

If I add that nexus-substantives are also often convenient in cases where idiomatic usage does not allow a dependent clause, as after *upon* in " Close upon his resignation followed his last illness and death," I hope I have accounted sufficiently for the rôle played in the economy of speech by these formations.[1] But like most good things in this world substantives of this type can

---

[1] Outside their proper sphere these words are by a frequent semantic change used to denote ("concretely") the possessor of such and such a quality : *a beauty* = a thing of beauty (frequently a beautiful woman), *realities* = real things, *a truth* = a true saying, etc. Contrast the two meanings in " I do not believe in the personality of God " (that He is a person) and " The Premier is a strong personality." The transition is parallel to that of verbal substantives, as in *building, construction* = 'a thing built, constructed.' Sometimes the concrete signification becomes so habitual that a new " abstract " is formed : *relationship, acquaintanceship.*—Note also the frequent figure of speech found, e.g., in " He was all kindness and attention on our journey home."

be abused. This is well brought out in an interesting paper by
Hermann Jacobi on the Nominal Style in Sanskrit (IF 14. 236 ff.).
When languages begin to grow old (alternde sprachen ! !) they
tend, he says, to nominal expressions, especially when they have
for a long time served as vehicles for scientific thinking. It seems
possible to express ideas with greater precision and adequacy by
means of nouns than by means of the more pictorial verbs (die
mehr der sphäre der anschauung sich nähernden verba).   " Sanskrit had become the privileged vehicle for the higher education in
India ; it had become unintelligible to the lower classes of the
people and had ceased to be used for all purposes of human life.
While Sanskrit was increasingly diverted from the practical details
of everyday life and was simultaneously used more and more to
serve the interests of the higher life of the intellect, abstract methods
of diction were more and more needed as the sphere of ideas to be
expressed became narrower and narrower," and that led naturally
to the preference for substantives, i.e. our nexus-substantives.

I think the difference between the two kinds of style can be
illustrated by comparing my English translation of the last sentence
with the German original : " Mit der zunehmenden abkehr von der
gemeinen alltäglichkeit des daseins und der damit hand in hand
gehenden zuwendung zum höheren geistigen leben stieg in dem sich
also einengenden ideenkreise, welchem das Sanskrit als ausdrucks-
mittel diente, das bedürfnis begrifflicher darstellung." German
scientific prose sometimes approaches the Sanskrit style described
by Jacobi.   When we express by means of nouns what is generally
expressed by finite verbs, our language becomes not only more
abstract, but more abstruse, owing among other things to the
fact that in the verbal substantive some of the life-giving elements
of the verb (time, mood, person) disappear.   While the nominal
style may therefore serve the purposes of philosophy, where, however, it now and then does nothing but disguise simple thoughts
in the garb of profound wisdom, it does not lend itself so well to
the purposes of everyday life.

Infinitives and Gerunds.

It is interesting to note in the history of language how verbal
substantives sometimes tend to discard some of the characteristics
of substantives and to assume some of those verbal characteristics
which were above alluded to as " life-giving," or in other words
how speakers have here and there treated them as they were accustomed to treat finite verbs.

This is the case with our infinitives, which are now universally
admitted to be fossilized case-forms of old verbal substantives

They have approached the finite verbs morphologically and syntactically, though not to the same extent in all languages : they can take their object in the same case as the ordinary verb (accusative, dative, etc.), they admit the usual combinations with negatives and other subjuncts, they develop tense-distinctions (perfect infinitive like Lat. *amavisse*, E. *to have loved*, in some languages also future infinitive), and the distinction between active and passive (the latter in Lat. *amari*, E. *to be loved*, etc.). All these traits are alien to such words as *movement, construction,* or *belief.* A further assimilation of the infinitive to finite verbs is seen in those languages which admit of its being combined with a subject in the nominative ; see p. 119.

In some languages the infinitive can be used with the definite article. This substantival trait has the advantage that the case-form of the article shows the function of the infinitive in the sentence. Where this can be applied to a combination like the Greek accusative with the infinitive, it is of greater value than where it is only the " naked " infinitive that can take the article, as in German.[1]

A development corresponding to what we have here observed in the infinitive is found in some other verbal substantives. An object in the accusative is seen in rare cases in Sanskrit, Greek and Latin as in the often-quoted Plautine sentence " Quid tibi *hanc curatiost rem* ? " (Delbrück, Synt. 1. 386). In some Slavic languages, for instance Bulgarian, it has become quite a common thing to add an object in the accusative to the verbal substantive in *-anije* and corresponding endings. In Danish the verbal substantive in *-en* can take an object, though only if verb and object enter into a close semantic union which is shown by unity-stress on the latter : *denne skiften tilstand, tagen del i lykken,* etc., examples in my *Fonetik,* 565.

The most interesting case in point is the English form in *-ing,* where we witness a long historical development by which what was originally a pure substantive formed only from some particular verbs comes to be formed from any verb and acquires more and more of the characteristics of the finite verb (GS § 197 ff.). It can take an object in the accusative (*on seeing him*) and an adverb (*he proposed our immediately drinking a bottle together*), it develops a perfect (*happy in having found a friend*) and a passive (*for fear of*

---

[1] The combination with *to* (*to do,* etc.) originally was an ordinary prepositional group (OE *to dōnne,* the latter word in the dative), which was properly used with the ordinary meaning of *to,* e.g. in sentences corresponding to the modern " I went to see the Duke," or " he was forced to go " ; *to see* and *to go* were thus subjuncts. But gradually the use of these combinations was extended, and their grammatical import changed in many cases : in " I wish to see the Duke " *to see* is now a primary, the object of *wish* ; in " to see is to believe " the two groups are also primaries, etc.

being killed). As for the subject, which originally had always to be put in the genitive and is still often found so, it is now often put in the common case (*he insisted on the Chamber carrying out his policy | without one blow being struck*) and may even exceptionally in colloquial speech be put in the nominative (*Instead of he converting the Zulus, the Zulu chief converted him*, with strong stress on *he*). When an Englishman now says " There is some possibility of the place having never been inspected by the police," he deviates in four grammatical points from the construction that would have been possible to one of his ancestors six hundred years ago (common case, perfect, passive, adverb).

Here we may mention also the Latin Gerund. The development of this form is rather interesting. Latin had a passive participle in -*ndus* (the " gerundive ") which might be used in the same way as other participles and adjectives so as to imply a nexus (cf. above, p. 125), thus in " elegantia augetur *legendis oratoribus et poetis*," ' elegance is increased through read orators and poets,' i.e. through the fact that they are read, through reading them. By the side of *cupiditas libri legendi*, which is to be interpreted in this way, it became possible to say *cupiditas legendi* without any substantive as primary ; this further led to *legendi* being felt as a kind of genitive of the infinitive and admitting an object in the accusative. Thus was created what is now given as a separate form of the verbs, inflected in the various cases (except the nominative) of the singular like an ordinary neuter substantive and termed the " gerund " (see, e.g., Sommer, *Handb. d. lat. laut- u. formenlehre* 631). The original and the derived constructions are found side by side in Cæsar's " neque *consilii habendi neque arma capiendi* spatio dato." [1]

Final Words on Nexus.

As I have emphasized the existence of two notions in a nexus (as opposed to junctions, where the two members together formed one notion), the reader may be surprised to find that I am here putting the question whether it is not possible to have a nexus consisting of only one member, and still more to find that I am answering that question in the affirmative. We do find cases in which we have either a primary alone or a secondary alone, and which nevertheless offer so close an analogy to an ordinary nexus that it is impossible to separate them from undoubted instances of nexus. But an accurate analysis will show that the usual two

[1] Agent-nouns (e.g. *believer*) and participles (e.g. a *believing* Christian; *believed*), presuppose a nexus, but do not signify the nexus itself in the same way as action-nouns (e.g. *belief*) or infinitives (e.g. *to believe*).

members are everywhere present to the mind, and that it is only in the linguistic expression that one of them may now and then be absent.

First we may have a primary alone or, in other words, a nexus without an adnex. This is seen in such an English sentence as (Did they run ?) *Yes, I made them* : this means the same thing as *I made them run*, and thus, however paradoxical it may sound, it is an accusative-with-infinitive without the infinitive ; *them* implies a real nexus and is different from the object in (Who made these frames ?) *I made them*. In the same way in colloquial English we may have an isolated *to* standing as a representative of an infinitive with *to* : *I told them to* (= I told them to run). Psychologically these are cases of aposiopesis ('stop-short sentences' or 'pull-up sentences,' as I have called them, *Language*, 251) : the infinitive is left out as in (Will you play ?) *Yes, I will*, or *Yes, I am going to* (*I am willing to, anxious to*).

Next we have the secondary part of a nexus alone, without any primary. This is extremely frequent in exclamations, where it is not necessary to tell the hearer what one is speaking about ; they form complete pieces of communication and should unhesitatingly be termed " sentences." Thus, for instance, *Beautiful* | *How nice !* | *What an extraordinary piece of good luck !* These are really predicatives, cf. *This is beautiful*, etc. : the predicative comes first to the mind of the speaker ; if afterwards he thinks of adding the subject, the result is a sentence of the form considered above, p. 121 : *Beautiful this view !* Or he may choose another form by adding a question : *Beautiful, isn't it ?* (just as in *This view is beautiful, isn't it ?* [1])

I think we may speak also of a nexus with the primary unexpressed in all those cases in which a finite verbal form is sufficient in itself without a noun or pronoun as subject, e.g. Lat. *dico, dicis, dicunt*, etc. In many cases a verb in the third person in various languages is expressive of the " generic person " (Fr. *on*) ; see the interesting collections by H. Pedersen and J. Zubatý in KZ 40. 134 and 478 ff.

In our modern languages, the subject must generally be expressed, and those few cases in which it is omitted, may be explained through prosiopesis, which sometimes becomes habitual in certain stock exclamations like *Thank you* | G. *danke* | | G. *bitte* | *Bless you* | *Confound it !* Cf. also *Hope I'm not boring you*.

---

[1] Wundt calls *Welch eine wendung durch gottes fügung !* an attributive sentence, in which *welch eine wendung* is the subject and *durch gottes fügung* an attribute (corresponding to my " adjunct "). But this is very unnatural : the whole is the predicative (adnex) of a nexus, the unexpressed primary of which appears if we add : *dies ist*.

In all the cases so far considered a one-member nexus has been an independent sentence. It may also be merely a part of a sentence. There is no primary in the nexus which forms the object of *makes* in the E. proverb "practice makes perfect," i.e. makes one perfect; this is very frequent in Danish, e.g. "penge alene gør ikke lykkelig" (money alone does not make [a man] happy) | jeg skal gøre opmærksom på at . . ., G. ich mache darauf aufmerksam, dass . . .

An accusative-with-infinitive without the accusative is not at all rare, e.g. live and *let live* | *make believe* | *I have heard say* | *Lat see* now who shal telle another tale (Chaucer; this is obsolete). In Dan. frequent : han lod *lyse* til brylluppet | jeg har hørt *sige at* . . ., etc. Thus also in German and Fr. The unexpressed primary is the 'generic person.' In G. *ich bitte zu bedenken* it may be the second person.

Nor are these the only instances in which the primary of a nexus is left unexpressed, for in the great majority of cases in which we use either an infinitive or a nexus-substantive there is no necessity expressly to indicate who or what is the subject of the nexus. This may be either definite, as shown by the actual context, as in : I like *to travel*, or I like *travelling* (the unexpressed primary is *I*) | it amused her *to tease him* (the primary is *she*) | he found *happiness* in *activity* and *temperance* (the primary is *he*), etc. Or else it may be the indefinite 'generic person' (Fr. *on*): *to travel* (*travelling*) is not easy nowadays | *activity* leads to *happiness* | *poverty* is no disgrace, etc. That the primary, though not expressed, is present to the mind is shown by the possibility of using a "reflexive" pronoun, i.e. one indicating identity of subject and object, etc., with infinitives and nexus-substantives : to deceive *oneself* | control of *oneself* (self-control) | contentment with *oneself* | Dan. at elske *sin* næste som *sig* selv er vanskeligt | glæde over *sit* eget hjem | G. *sich* mitzuteilen ist natur | Lat. contentum rebus *suis* esse maximæ sunt divitiæ (Cic.), and similarly in other languages.

I think that by laying stress on the notion of nexus and the inherent necessity of a "primary" or subject-part I have attained a better understanding of "abstracts," of "nomina actionis," and of infinitives, and especially of the rôle these forms play in the economy of speech than by the usual definitions. Nothing is really gained by defining the infinitive as "that form of a verb which expresses simply the notion of the verb without predicating it of any subject" (NED) or as "the form that expresses the notion of a verb in general without indicating it as predicated of any definite subject, with which it might form a sentence" (Madvig)—to which it might be objected that as a matter of fact there is very often a definite subject, sometimes expressed and sometimes to be gathered from the context, and that on the other hand the subject of a finite verb is very often just as indefinite as that of an isolated infinitive. I venture to hope that the reader will find that the numerous phenomena brought together in this and the preceding chapter throw so much light on one another that it warrants my grouping of these constructions in a separate class, for which the term " nexus " may not be found inappropriate.

CHAPTER XI

SUBJECT AND PREDICATE

Various Definitions. Psychological and Logical Subject. Grammatical Subject. There is.

Various Definitions.

THE discussion of the two members of a nexus has already to some extent anticipated the question of the relation of subject and predicate, for in those nexuses which constitute complete sentences, the " primary " has been shown to be identical with the subject, and the adnex (secondary member) identical with the predicate ; in other forms of nexus, we might also use the terms " subject-part " and " predicate-part " instead of " primary " and " adnex."

We have now to discuss various definitions given of the terms " subject " and " predicate " by previous writers, who have not as a rule taken into consideration anything but " sentences " or even the more restricted class called " judgments." An exhaustive critical examination of everything that has been said by grammarians and logicians on this question would require a whole volume, but I hope the following remarks will be found comprehensive enough.

The subject is sometimes said to be the relatively familiar element, to which the predicate is added as something new. " The utterer throws into his subject all that he knows the receiver is already willing to grant him, and to this he adds in the predicate what constitutes the new information to be conveyed by the sentence . . . In ' A is B ' we say, ' I know that you know who A is, perhaps you don't know also know that he is the same person as B ' " (Baldwin's Dict. of Philosophy and Psychol. 1902, vol. 2. 364). This may be true of most sentences, but not of all, for if in answer to the question " Who said that ? " we say " Peter said it," *Peter* is the new element, and yet it is undoubtedly the subject. The " new information " is not always contained in the predicate, but it is always inherent in the *connexion* of the two elements,—in the fact that these two elements are put together, i.e. in the " nexus," cf. what was said about the difference between junction and nexus on pp. 114–117.

Others say that the rôle of the predicate is to specify or determine what was at the outset indefinite and indeterminate, that the subject is thus a determinandum which only by means of the predicate becomes a determinatum (Keynes FL 96, Noreen VS 5. 153, Stout AP 2. 213). But this description is far more true of an adjunct as *blushing* in *the blushing girl* than of *blushes* in *the girl blushes*. What is here made determinate is not the girl but the whole situation.

Another definition that is frequently given is that the subject is what you talk about, and the predicate is what is said about this subject. This is true about many, perhaps most, sentences, though the man in the street would probably be inclined to say that it does not help him very much, for in such a sentence as " John promised Mary a gold ring " he would say that there are four things of which something is said, and which might therefore all of them be said to be " subjects," namely (1) John, (2) a promise, (3) Mary, and (4) a ring. This popular definition, according to which subject is identified with subject-matter or topic, is really unsatisfactory, as may perhaps be best appreciated if we see where it leads a distinguished psychologist like Stout, who in a famous passage (AP 2. 212 ff.) starts from it and then lands us at a point which is admittedly very far from the grammarian's conception of subject and predicate : " The predicate of a sentence is the determination of what was previously indeterminate. The subject is the previous qualification of the general topic to which the new qualification is attached. The subject is that product of previous thinking which forms the immediate basis and starting-point of further development. The further development is the predicate. Sentences are in the process of thinking what steps are in the process of walking. The foot on which the weight of the body rests corresponds to the subject. The foot which is moved forward in order to occupy new ground corresponds to the predicate. . . . All answers to questions are, as such, predicates, and all predicates may be regarded as answers to possible questions. If the statement " I am hungry " be a reply to the question, " Who is hungry ? " then " I " is the predicate. If it be an answer to the question, " Is there anything amiss with you ? " then " hungry " is the predicate. If the question is, " Are you really hungry ? " then " am " is the predicate. Every fresh step in a train of thought may be regarded as an answer to a question. The subject is, so to speak, the formulation of the question ; the predication is the answer."

If this is the logical consequence of the popular definition of ' subject,' then the grammarian cannot use that definition, for it does not assist him in the least. It is, indeed, unfortunate that the grammarian has to use the word "subject," which in ordinary language means, among other things, also 'topic' ('subject-matter ').

Psychological and Logical Subject.

The confusion arising from the ambiguity of the word "subject " is also responsible for much of what linguists and logicians have written on the so-called *psychological and logical subject and predicate*. As a matter of fact, these terms are by various writers used of totally different concepts, as will be seen from the following survey, which is probably not by any means exhaustive.

(1) Sequence in time. Thus G. v. d. Gabelentz (Zeitschr. f. völkerpsychologie u. sprachwissensch. VI and VIII and shorter in Spr. 348 ff.) : the hearer first apprehends a word A and asks full of expectation : What about this A ? Then he receives the next word or idea B, adds together these two and asks : Now, what about this (A + B) ? The answer is the next idea C, and so forth. Each successive word is the predicate of the subject contained in what he has already heard. It is as with the two rolls of paper in a telegraphic apparatus, on the one side there is the roll filled with writing, which is continually expanding, on the other side the blank roll, which is continually gliding over and swelling the other. The speaker knows beforehand both what is contained in one roll and what is to fill the empty paper. What now makes him mention A first, and then B, etc. ? Evidently he will place first what makes him think : his 'psychological subject,' and next what he thinks about it ; his 'psychological predicate '; after that both together may be made the subject of further thinking and speech. (Similarly, Mauthner, *Kritik der sprache*, 3. 217 ff.)

This is interesting, and Gabelentz's clever analysis from this point of view of the sentence "Habemus senatusconsultum in te vehemens et grave " might be quoted in any study of the psychological effect of word-order ; but the analogy between this and the subject-predicate relation is far too loose for the same name to be applied to both. Wegener's name "exposition " for what Gabelentz calls psychological subject is much more to the point. But it should always be remembered that word-order in actual language is not exclusively determined by psychological reasons, but is often purely conventional and determined by idiomatic rules peculiar to the language in question and independent of the will of the individual speaker.

(2) Novelty and importance. Paul (Gr. 3. 12) seems first to agree with Gabelentz when defining the psychological subject as the idea or group of ideas that is first present in the mind of the

speaker, and the psychological predicate as what is then joined (neu angeknüpft) to it. But he neutralizes that definition when he adds that even if the subject-idea is the first in the mind of the speaker, it is sometimes placed later, because in the moment when he begins to speak, the predicate-idea presses for utterance as the new and more important one, especially under the influence of strong emotion. In his former work (P 283) he says that the psychological predicate is the most important element, that which it is the aim of the sentence to communicate and which therefore carries the strongest tone. If in " Karl fährt morgen nach Berlin " everything is equally new to the hearer, then *Karl* is the subject to which the predicate *fährt* is added ; to the latter as subject comes as a first predicate *morgen*, and as a second predicate *nach Berlin*. If on the other hand the hearer knows about Karl's trip to-morrow but is ignorant of his destination, then *nach Berlin* is the predicate ; if he knows that he is going to Berlin, but does not know when, then *morgen* is the predicate, etc. Paul even goes so far as to say that if the only thing he is ignorant of is the manner of getting there (whether on horseback, or in a carriage, or on foot), then *fährt* " ist gewissermassen in zwei bestandteile zu zerlegen, ein allgemeines verbum der bewegung und eine bestimmung dazu, welche die art der bewegung bezeichnet, und nur die letzere ist prädikat." It would be difficult to imagine greater or more unnecessary subtlety. Why not avoid the terms subject and predicate in this sense and simply say that what is new to the hearer in any piece of communication may be found according to circumstances in any part of the sentence ?

(3) Stress (or tone). This view is hardly to be kept distinct from the former. Høffding (*Den menneskelige tanke*, 88) says that the logical predicate is often the grammatical subject or an adjective belonging to it : " *You* are the man " | " *All* the guests have arrived." It is recognized everywhere by the stress : " The king will *not* come " | " He *has* gone." In sentences of descriptive contents nearly every word may express a logical predicate because it may receive stress as containing new information. What is here termed logical predicate is nearly identical with what Paul calls psychological predicate, but it would be better to recognize that it has very little to do with logic proper : in the same writer's textbook of formal logic he continually uses the words subject and predicate, for instance in the rules he gives for syllogisms, but there the words will be always found to be taken not in their logical, but in their *grammatical* signification without any regard to stress. As this is generally determined less by strictly logical considerations than by emotion (the interest felt in an idea or the value ascribed to it at the moment), Bloomfield (SL 114) rightly

prefers the term *the emotionally dominant element* [1] for what Paul calls the logical and Høffding the psychological predicate.

(4) Any primary word in a sentence is the logical subject. Thus according to Couturat (*Revue de Métaphysique*, Janvier 1912, 5) in the sentence " Pierre donne un livre à Paul," which means the same thing as " Paul reçoit un livre de Pierre," the three words *Pierre, livre, Paul* (by him called *termes*) are all of them " les sujets du verbe qui exprime leur relation."

(5) " In *guter vater* ist *gut*, logisch betrachtet, eben so wohl prädicat zum subject *vater*, wie in *der vater ist gut* ; in *einen brief schreiben, schön schrieben*, hat, logisch genommen, das subject *schreiben* sein prädicat *einen brief, schön* " (Steinthal, *Charakteristik* 101).

(6) Wegener (U 138) analyzes the G. verb *satteln* as consisting of *sattel* + the suffix which makes it into a verb, and says that the two elements are respectively the logical predicate (*sattel*) and the logical subject (*-n*).

(7) Sweet (NEG, p. 48) says that in a sentence like " I came home yesterday morning " the word *came* by itself is the grammatical predicate, but *came-home-yesterday-morning* the logical predicate. And in another place (HL 49) he says that in *gold is a metal*, the strictly grammatical predicate is *is*, but the logical predicate is *metal*.

(8) Many grammarians use the term " logical subject " for that part of a passive sentence which would be the subject if the same idea had been expressed in the active turn, thus *his father* in " he was loved by his father " (called ' converted subject ' below, Ch. XII).

(9) Others will say that in " It is difficult to find one's way in London," " it cannot be denied that Newton was a genius," *it* is the formal subject, and the infinitive or the clause the logical subject.

(10) Still other grammarians will say that in such a " subjectless " sentence as G. *mich friert* the logical subject is " I." [2]

(11) A final use of the same term (closely related to 10) is seen when the transition from the old construction " Me dreamed a strange dream " to the modern " I dreamed a strange dream " is described by saying that the psychological (or logical) subject has become also the grammatical subject.

It is no wonder that after all this purposeless talking about logical and psychological subjects some writers have tried to avoid

---

[1] Cf. already Wundt S 2. 259 ff.

[2] A reflexive pronoun generally refers to the subject of the sentence, but sometimes to what would according to this paragraph be termed the logical subject, thus in ON. (Laxd. saga, 44. 17), Gúðrún mælti nú vid Bolla, at *henni* þótti hann eigi hafa *sér* allt satt til sagt ' that he seemed to her not to have told her the full truth ' ; cf. Lat. " sunt et *sua* fata sepulchris."

the term subject altogether. Thus Schuchardt (Br 243) would substitute the word *agens*, but that does not seem appropriate in *he suffers, he broke his leg*, etc., and in *A loves B* we should rather say that B acts on A than inversely. The only two linguists, so far as I know, who have seriously tried to dispense with the term *subject* in their grammatical analysis are the Swedes Svedelius and Noreen. Nothing, however, is gained by this. It is much better to retain the traditional terms, but to restrict them to domains where everybody knows what they import, i.e. to use subject and predicate exclusively in the sense of grammatical subject and predicate, and to discountenance any proposals to attach to these words the adjuncts 'logical' and 'psychological.'

Grammatical Subject.

Clearly to understand what the word subject means in its grammatical application, it will be well to recur to what was said in the chapter on the three ranks. In every sentence there are some elements (secondary words) which are comparatively fluid or liquid, and others (primary words) that are more firmly fixed and resemble rocks rising out of the sea. The subject is always a primary, though not necessarily the only primary in the sentence ; this amounts to saying that the subject is comparatively definite and special, while the predicate is less definite, and thus applicable to a greater number of things.

Doubt as to which word is the subject may sometimes arise when the colourless verb *be* is followed by a predicative,[1] though even here there is generally no difficulty in seeing which is the subject if we keep in mind what has been said about the more specialized nature of a subject as contrasted with a predicate.

After the results attained by our inquiry in Chapter V we are prepared to find that adjectives are extremely frequent as predicatives, because they are less special than substantives and applicable to a greater number of different things ; thus in *my father* is old | *the dress* was blue, no one doubts that the words printed in italics are the subjects, and the two adjectives the predicatives.

Where two substantives are connected by means of *is*, we can formulate some rules in accordance with our principle.

If one of the substantives is perfectly definite, and the other not, the former is the subject ; this is the case with a proper name :

Tom is a scoundrel.

---

[1] Note the difference between the terms predicate and predicative : in "the man paints flowers," *paints* (or, according to others, better *paints flowers*) is the predicate, in "the man is a painter," *is a painter* is the predicate, which in this case consists of the verb *is* and the predicative *a painter*. On predicatives after other verbs, see p. 131.

Thus also if one substantive is rendered definite by the definite article or a word of similar effect :

the thief was a coward | *my father* is a judge.

It will be well to point out that word-order is not always decisive, though in many languages there is a strong tendency, and in English a very strong tendency, to place the subject first. We find exceptions when adjectives are placed first, though undoubtedly used as predicatives (Great was *his astonishment* when he saw the result) and also with substantive predicatives (A scoundrel is *Tom*) ; this is very frequent in German, where all will agree that in Heine's line " König ist *der hirtenknabe* " the latter is the subject. In Danish the subject need not be placed first, but on the other hand, if it is not, it must be placed immediately after the (first) verb, while infinitives and such words as *ikke* ' not ' are placed before the predicative. Now we have two words spelt alike *Møller*, but if it is a proper name it is pronounced with the glottal stop in the *l*, while as a common name ' a miller ' it has no glottal stop. The curious result is that Danes will never hesitate about the pronunciation of the four sentences :

(1) Møller skal være Møller.
(2) Møller skal Møller være.
(3) Møller er ikke Møller.
(4) Møller er Møller ikke.

In (1) and (3) they will give the first Møller the glottal stop and thereby mark it out as the proper name, because the word-order shows it to be the subject ; inversely in (2) and (4). The English meaning of (1) and (2) is (Mr.) Miller is to be a miller, and of (3) and (4) Miller is not a miller, where the difference is shown by the indefinite article.

If the two substantives connected by *is* are equally indefinite in form, it depends on the extension of each which is the subject :

a *lieutenant* is an officer | *a cat* is a mammal |
a *mammal* is an animal,

and thus evidently everywhere where we have a hierarchy (class, order, family, genus, species).

It is possible to say

a *spiritualist* is a man,

but not

a *man* is a spiritualist (with *a man* as the subject),

though of course it is possible to say

this man is a spiritualist.

It is no exception to the rule that it is perfectly natural to say

> *a man* is a spiritualist, if he believes in the possibility of communication with the spirits of the dead,

because the conditional clause is equivalent to a specification, for the sentence means ' *a man who believes . . . is* a spiritualist.' In the same way we may say

> if *a man* is a spiritualist, etc.,

for that means ' I am talking only of those men who are spiritualists.'

Here we may make a curious observation, namely that if the subject and predicative are seemingly equally indefinite, there is nevertheless a difference, for the subject is taken in the generic sense, and the predicative in an individual sense. Thus in the plural : the sentence

> *thieves* are cowards

means ' all thieves are cowards, i.e. are some of the cowards in existence.' The same idea can be expressed in the singular number :

> *a thief* is a coward.

In saying this, I am not speaking of one particular thief, but of any thief (though of course I do not mean that any thief is any coward, that the two are co-extensive). In the same way :

> *a cat* is a mammal, etc.

It is worth noticing how the value of the indefinite article shifts automatically. Take a conversation like the following : A says : " The sailor shot an albatross," i.e. one individual of that species. B asks : " What is an albatross ? " The question is not about that one albatross, but about the whole species, and accordingly A's reply " An albatross is a big sea-bird " relates to the whole species, and says that all albatrosses belong to the wider class of sea-birds.

This will make us understand why it is that predicatives are often used either without any article or with the indefinite article, though the rules are somewhat different in different languages. In English one says :

> *John* was a tailor, and
> *John* was a liar,

where German and Danish would have the indefinite article in the latter sentence, but not in the former, where the predicative denotes a profession : *Hans* war schneider, *Hans* war ein lügner ; *Jens* var skrædder, *Jens* var en lögnhals. In English the predicative stands without an article if its sense is limited : Mr. X is

Bishop of Durham, but requires an article where its sense is not limited : He is a bishop. Thus also : He was made President— because there is only one president at a time. (In the same way in a nexus-object : They made him President.)

Now, take the two sentences :

My brother was captain of the vessel, and
The captain of the vessel was my brother.

In the former the words *my brother* are more definite (my only brother, or the brother whom we are talking about) than in the second (one of my brothers, or leaving the question open whether I have more than one). Cf. on the meaning of possessives, p. 110 above.

It has been disputed (by Noreen and others) which is the subject, and which the predicative, in some sentences in which it is possible to transpose the two members, e.g.

Miss Castlewood was the prettiest girl at the ball.
The prettiest girl at the ball was Miss Castlewood.

The question is not very important, and if we look at it from the point of view here advocated, we may say that one term is just as special as the other. Yet it seems natural in such cases to take the proper name as the more special and therefore as the subject. We see this if we formulate the corresponding questions, for the neuter *what* always takes the place of the predicative ; now both sentences are natural answers to either of the questions : What was Miss C. ? and Who was the prettiest girl ? [1] but What was the prettiest girl at the ball ? would be a question about something else. We obtain the same result by noticing that it is possible to say " I look on Miss C. as the prettiest girl at the ball," but not " I look on the prettiest girl at the ball as Miss C." [2]

Where there is perfect identity (coextension) of the two terms connected by *is*, they may change places as subject and predicative ; this is what Keats implied in his line : " Beauty is truth ; truth, beauty." But as we have seen, perfect identity is rare, and it is important to remark that the linguistic " copula " *is*

---

[1] Here *Who* evidently is the subject. But curiously enough Sweet, NEG § 215, says that " an interrogative pronoun is always the predicate of the sentence it introduces." This is correct for the sentence he gives as his instance *Who is he ?* simply because *he* is more definite than *who*, but in *Who is ill ? Who said it ? who* is the subject ; note also the word-order in the indirect question : *I asked who he was* | *I asked who was ill* ; in Dan. with *der* after the subject : *jeg spurgte hvem han var* | *jeg spurgte hvem der var syg.*

[2] If we apply the Danish test with the position of *ikke*, we see that in " Frk. C. var den smukkeste pige på ballet " it is impossible to place *ikke* last, it must come after *var*, though in " Den smukkeste pige på ballet var frk. C." either position would be allowable.

does not mean or imply identity, but subsumption in the sense of the old Aristotelian logic, which is thus in closer accordance with grammar than the so-called logic of identity (Leibniz, Jevons, Høffding). According to the latter the sentence " Peter is stupid " should be analyzed as " Peter is a stupid Peter," or, as it is also maintained that the substance of the predicate influences that of the subject, we obtain perfect identity only by saying " Stupid Peter is stupid Peter." In this way, however, the character of communication from speaker to hearer is lost ; by the words " is stupid Peter " the hearer is told nothing more than he had heard at the beginning, and the sentence has no value whatever. Ordinary mortals, therefore, will always prefer the formula " Peter is stupid," by which Peter is ranged among those beings (and things) that can be called " stupid."

In the mathematical formula $A = B$ we should not take the sign $=$ as the copula and B as predicative, but insert the copula *is* before the predicative *equal to* B, and thus read it as meaning : A is comprised among the (possibly several) objects that are equal to B (whether ' equal ' connotes only quantitative equality or perfect identity).

In some idiomatic uses we may be inclined to take *is* as implying identity, e.g. " to see her is to love her." " Seeing is believing." But the identity is more apparent than real. It would be impossible to invert the terms, and the logical purport of the saying is merely this : seeing immediately leads to, or causes, love, or belief. Thus also : " To raise this question is to answer it," etc.[1]

There is.

In connexion with what has been said about the subject of a sentence being more special and more definite than the predicative, we may mention the disinclination to take as subject a word with the indefinite article, except when this is meant as the " generic " article designating the whole species, which is really a definite idea. Instead of beginning a story in this way : " A tailor was once living in a small house," etc., it is much more natural to begin : " Once upon a time there was a tailor," etc. By putting the weak *there* in the place usually occupied by the subject we as it were hide away the subject and reduce it to an inferior position, because it is indefinite.

The word *there*, which is used to introduce such a sentence, though spelt in the same way as the local *there*, has really become

---

[1] " Children are children " means ' (all) children are among the beings characterized as children.'—On " it is I (me) " and its equivalents in other languages, see Spr. L. 59.

as different from it as the indefinite is from the definite article; it has no stress and is generally pronounced with the neutral (mid-mixed) vowel [ðə] instead of [ðɛ·ə]; its indefinite signification is shown by the possibility of combining it in the same sentence with the local (stressed) *there* or with *here*. It is followed by an indefinite subject : there was *a time* when . . . | there were *many people* present | there was *no moon* | there came *a beggar*, etc. The weak *there* also takes the place of the subject in combinations like " Let there be light " and " on account of there being no money in the box." Cf. also from a modern novel : No other little girl ever fell in love with you, did there ?

The indefiniteness here spoken of is not always formally indicated, thus *those* is notionally indefinite in " there are those who believe it " (= there are some who ; sunt qui credunt) and thus different from the definite *those* with which we begin a sentence : " Those who believe it are very stupid." " In Brown's room there was the *greatest* disorder " = a very great disorder, different from " The *greatest* disorder was in Brown's room," i.e. greater than in the other rooms. Note also the different word-order in " There [ðə] was found the greatest disorder " and " There [ðɛ·ə] the greatest disorder was found," though the former sentence may also be read with stressed *there*.

Sentences corresponding to English sentences with *there is* or *there are*, in which the existence of something is asserted or denied —if we want a term for them, we may call them existential sentences—present some striking peculiarities in many languages. Whether or not a word like *there* is used to introduce them, the verb precedes the subject, and the latter is hardly treated grammatically like a real subject. In Danish it has the same form as an object, though the verb is *is* : *der er dem som tror*, even with the passive *der gives dem*. In Danish the verb was here put in the singular before a plural word, even at a time when the distinction between sg. *er* and pl. *ere* was generally observed ; in English there is the same tendency to use *there's* before plurals, though in the literary language it is not now quite so strong as it was formerly ; in Italian, too, one finds *v'è* instead of *vi sono*.

In Russian the verb 'is' is in most other sentences unexpressed, but in these sentences we have a preposed verb, e.g. *byl mal'čik* ' there was a boy,' *žila vdova* ' there lived a widow.' The form *jest'* ' there is,' originally a third person singular, is used even before a plural word, and even before pronouns of the other persons (Vondrák SG 2. 267), and finally we may mention the curious form *naèxalo gostej* ' there came driving (neuter sg.) some guests ' (gen. pl., Berneker, *Russ. Gramm.* 156).

In Ancient Greek the verb *is* was not necessarily expressed in ordinary sentences, but in these sentences we find a preposed *esti*, as in Il. 3. 45 *all' ouk esti biē phresin, oude tis alkē* ; cf. Meillet MSL 14. 9.

In German we have the well-known *es gibt*, which, of course, precedes the indication of that which is said to exist ; this latter is the object of the verb, though some West German dialects use it in the nominative and say *es geben viele äpfel*—Grimm, *Wörterbuch* IV, 1. 1704, Paul Gr 3. 28.

Many languages have expressions containing the word ' has,' followed by what was originally its object, but is now not always distinct in form from the subject-case, thus Fr. *il y a*, Sp. *hay* (from *ha* ' it has ' *y* ' there '), It. *v'ha* (in *v'hanno molti* ' there are many' *molti* is treated as subject), South German *es hat*, Serbian and Bulgarian *ima*, Mod. Gr. *ekhei*. (Cf. also H. Pedersen, KZ 40. 137.) Chinese has the otherwise invariable rule that the subject is placed before the verb, but these sentences begin with *yeù*, originally ' have ' ; see Gabelentz, *Chin. Gramm.* 144. Finck (KZ 41. 226) transcribes the same word yu^3, e.g. yu^3 ko $lang^2$ ' there once was a wolf,' orig. ' has piece wolf.'

I may here mention some peculiarities of Finnish grammar. The nominative is used only with definite subjects, among which are also reckoned generic expressions ; if, on the other hand, something indefinite is denoted, the partitive is used ; cp. thus *viini* (nom.) *on pöydällä* ' the wine is on the table,' *viini on hyvää* ' wine (the species) is good,' *viiniä* (partitive) *on pöydällä* ' there is wine on the table.' Just as in English and Dan. we do not as a rule use *there, der*, when the verb has an object, because this seems to imply a kind of definiteness, Finnish in such cases has the nom., even if ' some ' are implied : *varkaat* (or *jotkut varkaat*, nom.) *varastivat tavarani* ' thieves (some thieves) stole my things,' but *varkaita* (part.) *tuli talooni* ' there came some thieves into my house ' (Eliot FG 121 f.).

CHAPTER XII

OBJECT. ACTIVE AND PASSIVE

What is an Object ? Object of Result. Subject and Object. Reciprocity.
Two Objects. Adjectives and Adverbs with Objects. Passive. Use
of the Passive. Middle Voice. Active and Passive Adjectives. Active
and Passive Substantives. Nexus-Substantives. Infinitives.

What is an Object ?

IT is easy enough to see what is the subject of a sentence when
this contains only one primary, as in *John slept | the door opened
slowly* ; and we have seen that in sentences containing two terms
connected by means of *is* or a similar verb (and also in those sentences without a verb mentioned in Ch. IX.) the member which is
most special is the subject (primary) and the less special member
the predicative. But many sentences contain two (or three)
primaries : here one is the subject and the other (or the two
others) the object (or objects) ; thus in *John beats Paul | John shows
Paul the way*, *John* is the subject, and *Paul* and *the way* are objects.
In sentences containing a verb it is nearly always easy to find
the subject, for it is that primary that has the most immediate
relation to the verb in the form in which the latter actually occurs
in the sentence : this applies to sentences like those just mentioned as well as to sentences of the form *Peter is beaten by John*,
where we might according to other definitions feel inclined to
regard *John* as the subject because he is the agent.

Various definitions have been given of *object* ; the most popular
one is that the object denotes the person or thing on which the
action of the verb is performed. This covers a great many in-
stances, such as *John beats Paul | John frightened the children | John
burns the papers*, but it is difficult to apply the definition to countless other sentences in which, however, grammarians never hesitate
to use the term object, e.g. *John burns his fingers* (i.e. he suffers
in his fingers from burning) | *John suffers pain*, etc.

Sweet long ago saw this difficulty and said (CP 25) : " With
such verbs as *beat, carry*, etc., the accusative unmistakably denotes
the object of the action expressed by the verb, but with such
verbs as *see, hear*, it is clearly a mere metaphor to talk of an
' object.' A man cannot be beaten without feeling it, but he

can be seen without knowing anything about it, and in many cases there is no action or volition at all involved in seeing. And in such a sentence as *he fears the man*, the relations are exactly reversed, the grammatical nominative being really the object affected, while the grammatical accusative represents the cause."[1] Sweet concludes that in many cases the accusative has no meaning at all—it would be better to say that it has not the meaning implied in the narrow definition usually given, but varies according to the infinitely varying meanings of the verbs themselves, as seen in such instances as : kill the calf | kill time | the picture represents the king | he represented the University | it represents the best British tradition | run a risk | run a business | answer a letter, a question, a person | he answered not a word | pay the bill | pay six shillings | pay the cabman | I shall miss the train | I shall miss you | entertain guests | entertain the idea | fill a pipe | fill an office, etc., etc. (Cf. Spr. L. 83.)

If we compare instances in which the same verb is used "intransitively" (or "absolutely"), i.e. without an object, and "transitively," i.e. with an object,[2] as in

she sings well	she sings French songs
I wrote to him	I wrote a long letter
send for the doctor	send the boy for the doctor
he doesn't smoke	he doesn't smoke cigars
he drinks between meals	he drinks wine, etc.,

we see that the object serves to make the meaning contained in the verb more special. But however important this observation

---

[1] In 1918 Deutschbein (*Sprachpsych. Studien*, p. 37) discovered anew that part of this difficulty which concerns verbs of observation : " Denn in fällen wie *ich sehe den baum* oder *ich höre das geschrei der möwen* kann man doch kaum nach der gewöhnlichen auffassung von einem affiziertwerden des objektes reden." He himself had defined the accusative as a " causative "— that name, by the way, would apply better to the nominative than to the accusative according to his own words, " Im akkusativ kommt derjenige begriff zu stehen, der die wirkung einer ursache (= nominativus) angibt "— but he now sees that the terms cause and effect cannot be simply applied to such verbs. His solution of the difficulty is that *ich sehe das schiff* originally meant *ich nehme ein schiff als bild in mir auf*, and that later this was extended to cases of non-intentional using. Deutschbein would not have devised this theory had it not been for the narrowness of the ordinary definition of "object."

[2] It is curious that in the dialect of Somerset (see Elworthy's *Grammar*, 191) a distinction is made in the form of the verb according to these two uses, the verb ending in a short [i] when it has no object : [digi] but [dig ðə graun], [ziŋi] like a man, but [ziŋ] the song. This distinction is somewhat similar to the one found in Magyar between the ' subjective' conjugation as in *irok* ' I write ' and the ' objective' conjugation as in *irom* ' I write ' (with a definite object, *it*, etc.). Cf. also Mauritius Creole *to manzé* tu manges, *to manze pósson* tu manges du poisson, Baissac, Étude sur le Patois Créole Mauricien 42 ; in Basque there is something similar, Uhlenbeck. *Karakteristiek* 32.

is, it cannot be used to define what an object is ; for the meaning of a verb may be ' specialized ' by other means, for instance by the predicative in *Troy was great*, cp. *Troy was, he grows old*, cp. *he grows*, and by a subjunct in *he walks fast | he sings loud | he walks three miles an hour | travel third class | ride post-haste.*

In some cases it may be difficult to tell whether a word is to be called a predicative or an object. The object can in many cases be recognized by the possibility of turning it into the subject of a passive sentence. The object is more closely connected with the verb of the sentence, and the predicative with the subject (to which it might under altered circumstances be joined as an adjunct). Thus it is natural that the predicative adjective in those languages which inflect it is made to agree with the subject in number and gender, and that the predicative, whether substantive or adjective, is in many languages put in the same case as the subject (nominative). Something between an object and a predicative is seen in English after *make* (she will make a good wife) and in German dialects after *geben* (see examples in Grimm's *Wörterbuch*, 1702 : welche nit gern spinnen, die geben gute wirtin | wöttu en bildhauer gäwen = willst du ein steinmetzer werden).

Subjuncts (" substantives used adverbially ") often resemble objects, and it is not always easy to draw the line between the two categories, e.g. in *he walks three miles*. We do not hesitate to regard *stones* in *throw stones* as the object of the verb, but many languages here use the instrumental case (which in old Gothonic was merged into the dative) ; in OE. the word for ' throw ' *weorpan* may take a dative (*teoselum weorpeþ* ' throws dice '), though it more often takes an accusative ; ON has *kasta (verpa) steinum* ' throw (with) stones ' ; in Russian, *brosat'* ' throw ' takes either the acc. or the instrumental. English has, of course, no longer any instrumental case, but we might speak of an " object of instrument " in cases like : she nods her head | claps her hands | shrugs her shoulders | pointed her forefinger at me | it rained fire and brimstone.

Object of Result.

There is one class of ' object ' which stands by itself and is of considerable interest, namely the object of result, as in : he built a house | she paints flowers | he wrote a letter | the mouse gnawed a hole in the cheese. Those grammarians who pay attention to this kind of object (in G. called " ergebnisobject " or " effiziertes objekt " as contrasted with " richtungsobject " or " affiziertes objekt ") mention only such verbs as *make, produce, create, construct*, etc., where it is obvious that the object must be an object of result, and ignore the more interesting fact that one and the

same verb often takes both kinds of object without really changing
its own signification, though the relation between the verb and
the object is entirely different in the two cases ; compare, for
example,

dig the ground	dig a grave
bore the plank	bore a hole in the plank
light the lamp	light a fire
he eats an apple	the moths eat holes in curtains
hatch an egg	hatch a chicken
roll a hoop	roll pills
strike the table	strike a bargain, sparks
conclude the business	conclude a treaty.

A subdivision of 'objects of result' comprises those 'inner
objects' which I mentioned under the head of nexus-substantives
(dream a strange dream | fight the good fight, etc., p. 137 f.).
Another is seen in *grope one's way | force an entrance | he smiled
his acquiescence,* etc.

Subject and Object.

The relation between subject and object cannot be determined
once and for all by pure logic or by definition, but must in each
case be determined according to the special nature of the verb
employed.   Both subject and object are primary members, and
we may to some extent accept Madvig's dictum that the object
is as it were a hidden subject, or Schuchardt's that " jedes objekt
ist ein in den schatten gerücktes subjekt " (Sitzungsber. d. preuss.
Akad. d. wiss. 1920, 462).   In many ways we see that there is some
kinship between subject and object.

If this were not so, we should be at a loss to understand the
frequency of shiftings from one to the other in course of time,
as in ME *him* (O = object) *dreams a strange dream* (S = subject),
which has become *he* (S) *dreams a strange dream* (O), a transition
which, of course, was facilitated by the great number of sentences
in which the form did not show the first word to be an object,
as *the king dreamed.* . . . This transition causes a semantic change
in the verb *like,* which from the meaning ' please, be agreeable
to ' (*him like oysters*) came to mean ' feel pleasure in ' (*he likes
oysters*).   By this change the name of the person, which had
always been placed first because of its emotional importance,
now by becoming the subject became the foremost word of the
sentence from a grammatical point of view as well.

While, then, in English and Danish a certain number of verbs
ceased in this way to be " impersonal " and became " personal,"
a corresponding change in Italian led to the development of a

kind of pronoun for the " generic person " (see on this term the chapter on Person). *Si dice così* means literally ' (it) says itself thus,' G. ' es sagt sich so,' but that is equivalent to G. 'man sagt so,' and what was at first the object came to be regarded as the subject, and vice versa, as in *si può vederlo* ' you can see him ' ; this is shown in the change of number from *si vendono biglietti,* where *biglietti* is subject, into *si vende biglietti,* where it is object. Both constructions are now found side by side, thus in Fogazzaro, Santo, p. 291, Pregò che si togliessero le candele, but p. 290 disse che si aspettava solamente loro.[1]

The logical kinship between subject and object also accounts for the fact that there are here and there sentences without a formal subject but with an object, as G. *mich friert, mich hungert.* In the vast majority of cases, however, where a verb has only one primary, this will be felt as the subject and accordingly is, or in course of time comes to be, put in the nominative as the proper subject-case.

Reciprocity.

Some verbs by virtue of their meaning make it possible to reverse the relation between subject and object. If A meets B, B also meets A (note that where we say *I met an old man,* the Germans usually, though having the same word-order, will make *an old man* into the subject : *mir begegnete ein alter mann*). When in geometry one line cuts (intersects) another line, the second line also cuts the former. If Mary resembles Ann, Ann also resembles Mary ; and if Jack marries Jill, Jill also marries Jack. In such cases we often make the two words into one connected subject and use *each other* as object ; the old man and I met each other | the two lines cut one another | Mary and Ann resemble each other | Jack and Jill marry one another. Reciprocity may, of course, also occur without being necessarily implied in the meaning of the verb itself : A may hate B without B hating A, but if B does hate him back, we may express it in the same way : A and B hate one another. In English the verb in itself often suffices to express reciprocity : A and B meet (marry, kiss, fight) = A meets (marries, kisses, fights) B, and B meets (marries, kisses, fights) A. In some of these cases Danish has the form in *-s* (old reflexive) : A og B mødes, kysses, slåss.

Two Objects.

There may be two objects in the same sentence, e.g. He gave *his daughter a watch* | he showed *his daughter the way* | he taught

---

[1] According to one theory, which, however, has been disputed, we have the inverse shifting in the Lat. passive: the original active **amatur amicos* has given rise to *amantur amici* ; see many articles quoted by Brugmann Es 27 n.

his daughter arithmetic, etc.   (But it should be noted that in " they
made **Brown** President " we have only one object, namely the
whole nexus, as in " they made Brown laugh ".)   In languages
with separate forms for the accusative and the dative, the person
is generally put in the dative, and the thing in the accusative ;
the former is called the indirect, and the latter the direct object.
But sometimes we find the dative where there is only one object,
and in some cases both objects are in the accusative—which shows
that the difference between the dative and the accusative is not
a notional one, but purely syntactic, dependent in each language
on idiomatic rules ; on this, and on the use of other cases for the
object, see the chapter on Case (XIII).

Instead of a case-form for the indirect object we often find
a preposition, which loses its original local meaning, thus E. *to*,
Romanic *a*.   This originally indicated direction and would be
appropriately used with such verbs as *give*, but its use was extended
to cases in which any idea of direction would be out of the question, e.g. with *deny*.   In Spanish *á* is used even with the direct
object, if this denotes a person.   In English the preposition *on*
is sometimes used idiomatically : *bestow something on a person*,
confer a degree on him.

The point of view which determines whether something is the
direct or the indirect object may sometimes vary, even within
one and the same language, as in E. *present something to a person*
or *present a person with something* (Fr. *présenter quelque chose à
quelqu'un*).   Where French has *fournir qch à qqn*, English says
furnish someone with something.   Only the briefest mention can
here be made of the French inclination to treat a verb and a
dependent infinitive as one verb, and therefore to turn the person
into the indirect object : *il lui fit voir le cheval* (as *il lui montra
le cheval*), but *il le fit chanter* ; [1] and then further : *je lui ai entendu
dire que*. . . .

Where the active verb has two objects, one of them may be
made the subject in the corresponding passive turn.[2]   In most
cases it is the direct object which is treated in this way, and many
languages are strict in not allowing what in the active is in the

---

[1] Brunot says (PL 390) : " On ne peut qu'admirer l'instinct linguistique
qui, malgré une construction identique, attribue deux sens si profondément
différents à : *j'ai fait faire un vêtement à mon tailleur*, et : *j'ai fait faire un
vêtement à mon fils*."   Instead of admiration, I should rather express wonder
that so ambiguous constructions produce after all comparatively few misunderstandings.

[2] In Tagala (Philippine Islands) there are three passives, and, corresponding to the sentence " search for the book with this candle in the room,"
we may have three different formations, according as the book, the candle,
or the room is looked upon as the most important and put in the nominative
(H. C. v. d. Gabelentz, *Ueber das passivum*, 484).

dative case to be made a subject in the passive. Cf., however, Fr. *je veux être obéi*. In English there is a growing tendency to make the person into the subject of the passive verb; this is quite natural because there is now no formal difference between dative and accusative, and because for emotional reasons one always tends to place the name of the person first. Thus people will naturally say : *the girl was promised an apple* | *he was awarded a gold medal*, etc. Grammarians have opposed this tendency, chiefly because they have had in their heads the rules of Latin grammar, but the native speech-instinct cannot be put down by pedantic schoolmasters. Curiously enough the pedants seem to have had fewer objections to constructions like : *he was taken no notice of*, which find their explanation in a following paragraph.

Adjectives and Adverbs with Objects.

Verbs are not the only words that can take an object. In English there are a few adjectives which can do the same : he is not *worth his salt* | he is *like his father* ; Dan. han er *det franske sprog mægtig*, G. (with gen.) er ist *der französischen sprache mächtig* ; Lat. *avidus laudis* | *plenus timoris*. We have also English combinations like *conscious that something had happened* | *anxious to avoid a scandal*, where the clause and the infinitive are objects. These adjectives, however, cannot take a substantive as their object except with a preposition : *conscious of evil* | *anxious for our safety*, where we may say that the whole groups *of evil, for our safety* are notional objects, even if we do not acknowledge them as grammatical objects. The same remark applies to *of*-groups after such adjectives as *suggestive, indicative*, etc. In Latin we have the rule that participles in *-ns* take their object in the accusative when the verbal feeling is strong: *amans patriam*, but in the genitive (like adjectives such as *tenax*) when they denote a more constant characteristic : *amans patriæ*.

If an adverb takes an object, the adverb becomes what is commonly termed a preposition; see Ch. VI. Observe that the German preposition *nach* is nothing but a phonetic variant of the adverb *nah*.

When a verb is followed by an adverb (preposition) with its object, the latter may often be looked upon as the object of the whole combination verb + adverb ; hence we find vacillations, e.g. G. *er läuft ihr nach* (*um ihr nachzulaufen*) : *er läuft nach ihr* (*um nach ihr zu laufen*), Fr. *il lui court après* = *il court après elle*. In OE. *he him æfter rād* (*æfterrād*) ' he rode after him,' *æfter* may be taken as a postpositive preposition ; notice also that the inseparable Dan. (*at*) *efterfølge*, (*at*) *efterstræbe* = the separable G.

nach(zu)folgen, nach(zu)streben. Hence come the passive construc-
tions found in E. *he was laughed at* | *he is to be depended on,* etc.

Passive.

In a few cases our languages are provided with two verbs that
stand in a similar relation to one another as *over* and *under, before*
and *after, more* and *less, older* and *younger,* thus

A precedes B = B follows (succeeds) A.

What in the first sentence is looked at from the point of view
of A is in the second looked at from the point of view of B.[1] In
most cases this shifting is effected by means of the passive turn
(B is preceded by A). Here what was the object (or one of the
objects) in the active sentence is made into the subject, and what
was the subject in the active sentence is expressed either by means
of a prepositional group, in English with *by* (formerly *of*), in French
with *par* or *de,* in Latin with *ab,* etc., or in some languages simply
by means of some case form (instrumental, ablative).

We may express this in a formula, using the letter S for subject, O for object, V for verb, a for active, p for passive, and C
for " converted subject " :

$$\text{S} \quad \text{V}^a \qquad \text{O} \qquad\qquad \text{S} \quad \text{V}^p \qquad\qquad \text{C}$$
$$\text{Jack loves} \quad \text{Jill} \quad = \quad \text{Jill is loved} \quad \text{by Jack,}$$

thus

$$\text{Jack} : \text{S}^a = \text{C}^p$$
$$\text{Jill} : \text{O}^a = \text{S}^p.$$

It is customary in English to speak about the active and
passive *voice* (Fr. *voix*). William James, in his *Talks to Teachers,*
p. 152, relates how one of his relatives was trying to explain to
a little girl what was meant by the passive voice. " Suppose
that you kill me : you who do the killing are in the active voice,
and I, who am killed, am in the passive voice." " But how can
you speak if you're killed ? " said the child. " Oh, well, you may
suppose that I am not yet quite dead ! " The next day the child
was asked, in class, to explain the passive voice, and said, " It's
the kind of voice you speak with when you ain't quite dead."
The anecdote shows not only the bad blunders that may be committed in the teaching of grammar (absurd examples, stupid
explanations), but also the drawback of the traditional term *voice.*
Some grammarians in Germany and elsewhere use the word *genus*
(genus verbi), which has the inconvenience that it is also used of
gender (genus substantivi). It would be best, probably, to use

---

[1] Cp. A *sells* it to B = B *buys* it from A ; thus also *give : receive* ; A
has (possesses) it = it *belongs to* A.

the word *turn* : and say 'active and passive turn.' The words
active and *passive* cannot very well be dispensed with, though
they, too, may lead to misconceptions : even in works by good
scholars one may occasionally find words to the effect that such
verbs as *suffer*, *sleep*, *die* should be called passive rather than
active, or that Lat. *vapulo* 'I am thrashed' is a passive in spite
of its active form, or that there is nothing active in *A sees B, A
loves B*. These ideas start from the erroneous conception that
the distinction between active and passive in the linguistic sense
is congruent with the distinction between bodily or mental activity
and passivity—an error which is connected with the similar one
we saw above where we were speaking of the definition of the
object.

It is important here as elsewhere to distinguish between syntactic and notional categories. Whether a verb is *syntactically*
active or passive depends on its form alone ; but the same idea
may be expressed sometimes by an active, sometimes by a passive
form : A precedes B = A is followed by B ; A likes B = A is
attracted by B. The passive Lat. *nascitur* has given way to the
active Fr. *naît* in the same sense and is rendered in English sometimes by the passive *is born*, sometimes by the active, *originates,
comes into existence* ; the circumstance that Lat. *vapulo* in other
languages is translated by a passive does not alter its grammatical
character as an active ; and Gr. *apothnēskei* is just as active when
we render it 'is killed' (thus when it is followed by *hupo* 'by ')
as when we simply say 'dies.' There is thus nothing in the ideas
themselves to stamp verbs as active or passive. And yet we may
speak of 'active' and 'passive' as *notional* as well as syntactic
categories, but only as applied to the meaning of each verb separately, and—what is very important—*only in case of a transposition
of the relation of the subject (and object if there is one) to the verb
itself*. "Jill is loved by Jack" and "es wird getanzt" are
notionally as well as syntactically in the passive, because the
subjects are different from those in "Jack loves Jill" and "sie
tanzen." In other cases there is disagreement between the syntactic and the notional active or passive.

Thus, if we take the two sentences "he sells the book" and
"the book sells well" we must say that the active form *sells* in
the former is a notional active, and in the latter a notional passive,
because what in one is the object in the other is the subject. In
the same way we have other verbs (in some languages more, in
others fewer), which are used idiomatically as notional actives
and notional passives, thus

Persia began the war.

The war began.

Other English examples : he opened the door ; the door opened | he moved heaven and earth ; the earth moves round the sun | roll a stone ; the stone rolls | turn the leaf ; the tide turns | burst the boiler ; the boiler bursts | burn the wood ; the wood burns, etc.

It is rarer to find verbs with passive forms that may be used in both these ways. The Dan. *mindes* has a passive form ; it generally means ' remember ' and may then be said to be a notional active, but when it is used, as occasionally happens, in the sense ' be remembered ' (" det skal mindes længe ") it is a notional passive ; similarly we have " vi må *omgås* ham med varsomhed " ' we must deal cautiously with him,' and " han må omgås med varsomhed " ' he must be dealt with cautiously.' We shall see other instances of notional passive unexpressed in form in verbal-substantives and infinitives.

In this connexion something must be said about a grammatical feature which is found in some out-of-the-way languages and which by some writers is thought to throw some light on the primitive stages of our own family of languages, namely the distinction between a *casus activus* or *transitivus* and a *casus passivus* or *intransitivus*. In Eskimo one form ending in -*p* is used as the subject of a transitive verb (when there is an object in the same sentence), while another form is used either as the subject of an intransitive verb or as the object of a transitive verb, e.g.

nan·o(q) Pe·lip takuva· = Pele saw the bear.
nan·up Pe·le takuva·   = the bear saw Pele.
Pe·le o·mavoq   = Pele lives.
nan·o(q) o·mavoq   = the bear lives.

Cp. the use in the genitive : nan·up niaqua Pe·lip takuva. ' Pele saw the bear's head ' | nan·up niaqua angivoq ' the bear's head was large ' | Pe·lip niaqua nan·up takuva· ' the bear saw Pele's head.'

Similar rules are found in Basque, in some languages of the Caucasus, and in some Amerindian languages. On this basis it has been conjectured that the primitive Aryan language had one form, characterized by -*s*, and used as an active (energetic, subjective or possessive) case, thus only with names of animate beings (masculine and feminine), and on the other side a form with no ending or with -*m*, which was used as a passive or objective case, serving also as the subject of intransitive verbs and coming naturally to be used as a ' nominative ' of names of inanimate things (neuter). The -*s*-case later was differentiated into a nominative and a genitive, the latter being characterized in some instances by a different accent, in others by the addition of a second suffix.

But originally it denoted not so much possession proper as some intimate natural union or connexion.[1] It will be seen that these speculations help to account for some peculiarities of our gender-system as well as of our case-system, and they should be remembered when we come to speak of the " subjective " genitive, though there we shall see that this is used not only with nouns from transitive verbs, but also with intransitives and passives and cannot be distinguished from the " objective " genitive.

Use of the Passive.

We use the active or passive turn according as we shift our point of view from one to the other of the primaries contained in the sentence. " Jack loves Jill " and " Jill is loved by Jack " mean essentially the same thing, and yet they are not in every respect exactly synonymous, and it is therefore not superfluous for a language to have both turns. As a rule the person or thing that is the centre of the interest at the moment is made the subject of the sentence, and therefore the verb must in some cases be put in the active, in others in the passive. If we go through all the passives found in some connected text we shall find that in the vast majority of cases the choice of this turn is due to one of the following reasons.

(1) The active subject is unknown or cannot easily be stated, e.g. He *was killed* in the Boer war | the city *is* well *supplied* with water | I *was tempted* to go on | the murderer *was caught* yesterday : here the fact of his capture is more important than the statement what policeman it was who caught him. Very often the active subject is the ' generic person ' : *it is known* = ' on sait.' In " the doctor *was sent for* " neither the sender nor the person sent is mentioned.

(2) The active subject is self-evident from the context : His memory of these events *was lost* beyond recovery | She told me that her master had dismissed her. No reason *had been assigned* ; no objection *had been made* to her conduct. She *had been forbidden* to appeal to her mistress, etc.

(3) There may be a special reason (tact or delicacy of sentiment) for not mentioning the active subject ; thus the mention of the first person is often avoided, in writing more frequently than in speaking : " Enough *has been said* here of a subject which will *be treated* more fully in a subsequent chapter." In Swedish

---

[1] Uhlenbeck, IF 12. 170, KZ 39. 600, 41. 400, Karakt. k. bask. gramm. 28, Amsterdam Acad. Verslagen, 5e reeks, Deel 2, 1916 ; Holger Pedersen, KZ 40. 151 ff., Schuchardt, IF 18. 528, Berlin Acad. 1921, 651. Different views are expressed by Finck, Berlin Acad. 1905 and KZ 41. 209 ff., and Sapir, *International Journal of American Linguistics*, Vol. I, 85.

the passive turn is rather frequent to avoid the clumsy substitutes for the second personal pronouns : Önskas en tändstick ' do you want a match ? ' | Finns inte en tändstick ? ' Haven't you got a match ? '

In none of these cases is the active subject mentioned, and it has often been pointed out that this is the general rule with passive sentences in many languages (Arabic, Lettish, old Latin, Wackernagel VS 143). Statistical investigations made by some of my pupils showed me many years ago that between 70 and 94 per cent. of passive sentences in various English writers contained no mention of the active subject.

(4) Even if the active subject is indicated (" converted subject ") the passive turn is preferred if one takes naturally a greater interest in the passive than in the active subject : the house *was struck* by lightning | his son *was run over* by a motor car.

(5) The passive turn may facilitate the connexion of one sentence with another : he rose to speak and *was listened to* with enthusiasm by the great crowd present.

In most languages there are certain restrictions on the use of the passive turn, which are not always easy to account for. The verb *have* (*have got*) in its proper sense is seldom used in the passive (though it may be used, e.g. in " This may be had for twopence at any grocer's "). Pedants sometimes object to sentences like : " this word ought to be pronounced differently " (because a word can have no duty !) or " her name will have to be mentioned." Intransitive verbs in the passive are common in some languages : Lat. *itur, itum est, curritur,* G. *es wird getanzt,* even " Was nützte es auch, *gereist musste werden* ; man musste eben vorwärts, solange es ging " (Ch. Bischoff), Dan. *der danses, her må arbejdes*—but not in English or French.

Middle Voice.

On the " middle voice " as found, for instance, in Greek there is no necessity to say much here, as it has no separate notional character of its own : sometimes it is purely reflexive, i.e. denotes identity of subject and (unexpressed) object, sometimes a vaguer reference to the subject, sometimes it is purely passive and sometimes scarcely to be distinguished from the ordinary active ; in some verbs it has developed special semantic values not easily classified.

Active and Passive Adjectives.

The notional distinction between active and passive also applies to some adjectives derived from or connected with verbs. We

have active and passive participles (E. *knowing, known,* etc.,
though the latter is not purely passive). It is also a common
conviction among comparative linguists that the old Aryan participles in *-to* and *-no,* which are at the bottom of our weak and
strong second participles, were at first neither active nor passive
in character.[1] Besides these we have adjectives with such endings
as *-some* (*troublesome, wearisome*), *-ive* (*suggestive, talkative*), *-ous*
(*murderous, laborious*), which are all of them active, and adjectives
in *-ble,* which are generally passive (*respectable, eatable, credible,
visible*), but occasionally active (*perishable, serviceable, forcible*)
-less is active in *sleepless,* passive in *tireless.* Sometimes there are
two correlated forms for active and passive : *contemptuous* :
contemptible, desirous : *desirable* ; sometimes the same word may
have now an active, and now a passive meaning : *suspicious, curious.*
It is the same in other languages. Some of the active adjectives
may take a notional object by means of the preposition *of* : suggestive of treason, oblivious of our presence, etc.

Active and Passive Substantives.

If we ask whether substantives can be active and passive,
and whether they can take objects, we first encounter the so-called
agent-nouns, which are active, e.g. *fisher, liar, conqueror, saviour,
creator, recipient.* What would be the object of the corresponding
verb, is put in the genitive (*Ann's lover*) or more often, follows
the preposition *of* (*the owner of this house, the saviour of the world*).
We may here as above speak of notional or shifted objects.—Substantives of the form *pickpocket, breakwater* contain an active verb
with its object ; *a pickpocket* may be defined as ' a picker of
pockets.'

In English we have a curious class of passive substantives in
-ee : *lessee, referee,* etc., ' one to whom a lease is given, to whom
a question is referred,' *examinee* ' person examined ' (but with the
same ending we have the active substantives *refugee, absentee*).

Nexus-Substantives.

Next we come to nexus-substantives. These are originally
neither active nor passive, but may according to circumstances
be looked upon as one or the other. To take first a familiar Latin
example : *amor dei* may mean either the love that God feels, or
the love that someone else feels with God as its object. In the
first case we call *dei* a subjective genitive (which by some is
taken simply as a possessive genitive, inasmuch as God ' has ' or

[1] Brugmann IF 5. 117, H. Pedersen KZ 40. 157 f.

' possesses ' the feeling); in the second we call it an objective genitive. In the first *dei* is, in the symbols used above, S^a, in the second O^a, but as we have seen that O^a = S^p, we may just as well say that *dei* in both cases is a subjective genitive, but that *amor* in the first case is an active, and in the second case a passive word. In both cases we have a nexus, in which the genitive indicates the primary, and *amor* the secondary element ; the nexus in itself is neither active nor passive, the only thing expressing being a connexion between the two elements God and love, in which it is left to the hearer whether he will take it as meaning the fact that God loves, or the fact that God is loved. In the same way *odium Cæsaris, timor hostium* are ambiguous. So also in Greek, e.g. 2 Cor. 5. 14 hē gar *agapē tou Khristou* sunekhei hēmas (in A.V. : the loue of Christ constreineth vs).

English sometimes presents the same ambiguity. Hodgson (*Errors in the Use of Engl.* 91) has the following anecdote : An attorney, not celebrated for his probity, was robbed one night on his way from Wicklow to Dublin. His father, meeting Baron O'Grady the next day, said : " My lord, have you heard of my *son's* robbery ? " " No, indeed," replied the Baron, " pray whom did he rob ? "

Memory is used in two ways in Hamlet : 'Tis in *my memory* locked—this is the common usage, S^a—and : a *great mans memory* may outliue his life half a year—this is the rarer S^p. Formerly the objective genitive (S^p) was more common than now, e.g. from Shakespeare : Reuenge *his foule and most vnnaturall murther* (the fact that he has been murdered) | thou didst denie *the golds receit.* There are, however, certain definite rules for the use of the genitive (and of possessive pronouns) though they have not been recognized by grammarians. The chief ones are the following.

(1) It is obvious that with intransitive verbs there can be no question of any passive sense ; the genitive therefore is always S^a : *the doctor's arrival, existence, life, death,* etc.

The following rules apply to transitive verbs, but rules (2) to (5) concern only the combination of genitive and substantive, when this is not followed by a prepositional group.

(2) Substantives formed from such transitive verbs as cannot on account of their meaning have a person as object are taken n the active sense : *his* (S^a) *suggestion, decision, supposition,* etc.

(3) Where the meaning of the verb is such that its subject generally is a person and that it may take a person as object, the genitive or possessive is generally taken as S^a : *his attack, discovery, admiration, love, respect, approbation interruption,* etc.   Here, however, we notice a curious difference, according as the nexus-substantive is the subject of the sentence or is used after a

preposition : *His assistance* (S^a) is required | come to *his assistance* (S^p). Thus also : *his service* (*support, defence*) is valuable | *at his service* (*in his support, defence*). Cf. also the somewhat archaic : in order to *his humiliation*. The substantive has the same passive sense without a genitive after verbs like *need, want* : he needs support, asks for approbation (but *my* is S^a in : he asks for my approbation).

(4) The genitive or possessive will, however, be understood in its objective sense when more interest is taken in the person who is the object of an action than in the person who is the agent in the case. Thus in a recent number of an English paper I found, at a few lines' distance, *De Valera's capture* and *De Valera's arrest* mentioned as possibilities : it is of no importance *who* captures or arrests the Irish leader. Other examples : *a man's trial* (the fact that he is brought before a judge) | *his defeat* | *his overthrow* | *his deliverance* | *his release* | *his education*. The passive sense is also found in : *her reception* was unique | he escaped *recognition*. In " he is full of *your praises* " the person who praises naturally is *he*, and *your* therefore represents $S^p = O^a$.

(5) Where the subject of a verb is as often, or more often, a thing than a person, and where, on the other hand, the object is a person, the nexus-substantive is taken in a passive sense : *his* (S^p) *astonishment, surprise, amazement, amusement, irritation*, etc.

Next we have to consider the use of prepositions with nexus-substantives. *Of* in itself is just as ambiguous as the genitive, *the love of God*, S^a or S^p. But it is unambiguous if it is combined with a genitive, for then the latter always means S^a, and the *of*-group S^p : *my trials of thy love* (Sh.) | *his instinctive avoidance of my brother*, etc. When the genitive combinations mentioned under (4) are thus followed by *of*, they immediately change their meaning : *Luther's* (S^a) *deliverance of Germany from priestcraft* | he won praise by *his release of his prisoners* | *her reception of her guests*.

In the nineteenth century the construction with *by* began to be common as an unambiguous means of denoting S^a ; it is the same *by* that is used with the passive verb, but curiously enough this recent use is not mentioned in the NED : the purchase, *by the rich*, of power to tax the poor (Ruskin) | a plea for the education *by the State* of neglected country girls | the massacre of Christians *by Chinese*. If *by* is used, the genitive may be used for S^p : *his expulsion* from power *by the Tories* (Thackeray).

For S^p there is also a growing tendency to use other prepositions than the ambiguous *of*, thus : your love *for* my daughter | the love of Browning *for* Italy | his dislike *to* (*for*) that officer | there would have been no hatred of Protestant *to* Catholic | contempt, fear *for*, attack *on*. With certain substantives similar prepositions are common in other languages as well, Dan. *for*, *til*, Lat. *odium in Antonium*, It. *la sua ammirazione per le dieci dame più belle* (Serao).[1]

The English verbal substantive in *-ing* had also originally the same double character, though it has generally an active sense : *His* (S^a) *throwing*, etc. In former times S^p was frequent, cf. : Shall we excuse *his throwing* into the water (Sh. = his having been thrown). The passive sense is also seen in " Vse euerie man after his desart, and who should scape *whipping* ? " (Sh.), and is still found in combinations like : the roads want *mending*, but the creation in comparatively recent times of the passive combination *being thrown* (*having been thrown*) restricts the simple form in the vast majority of cases to the active use. On the case of the notional subject see p. 141.

Infinitives.

We must here also say something about that early form of verbal substantive which developed into our infinitive. This, too, at first was neither active nor passive, but in course of time passive simple forms or combinations developed : *amari*, *be loved*, etc. Traces of the (active or indifferent) form as a notional passive are still found, in English for instance in " they were not to *blame* (cf. they were not to be seen) | the reason is not far *to seek* | the reason is not *difficult to see*, where *the reason* is the subject of *is*, but at the same time may be considered a kind of object for *to see*, or subject for *to see* if this is taken in the passive sense.[2]   Cf. further : *there is a lot to see in Rome* | *there is a lot to be seen in Rome* (the two sentences are not exactly synonymous).   In the following quotation we have the three possibilities in close succession : There was no one *to ask* (active form, passive sense), no one *to guide* him (the same in active sense) ; there was nothing *to be relied upon*.

Other well-known instances of this double-sided character of the infinitive : G. er liess ihn (S^a) kommen | er liess ihn (S^p) strafen | Dan. han lod ham komme | han lod ham straffe | Fr. je l'ai vu jouer | je l'ai vu battre.   In Engl., where the passive form is now extensively used in such cases, the active form was formerly used in a passive sense, e.g. (he) leet anon his deere doghter calle (Chaucer : ' let her be called, caused her to be called ') | he made cast her in to the riuer (NED *make* 53 d).

---

[1] In Finnish the gen. has both values, e.g. *isänmaan rakkaus* 'love of the native country,' *jumalan pelko* 'fear of God.' Where both are combined, S^p + the subst. is treated as a compound subst. : *kansalaisen isänmaan-rakkaus* 'the citizens' love for their country' (Setälä, *Satslära* 31).

[2] Cf. Fr. ce vin est bon à boire.

CHAPTER XIII

CASE

Number of English Cases.   Genitive.   Nominative and Oblique.   **Vocative**
Final Words about Cases.   Prepositional Groups.

Number of English Cases.

THE subject of this chapter, which has already to some extent
been touched upon in the previous chapter, is a most difficult
one, because languages differ very much on this point, and because
the underlying ideas expressed by the various cases are not as
palpable as, e.g., the difference between one and more, or between
past, present and future, which are to form the subjects of some
other chapters.   It will, perhaps, be best to start from a concrete
example, which illustrates the fundamental difference between the
two originally related languages, Latin and English.

Where the Romans said *Petrus filio Pauli librum dat*, the English
say *Peter gives Paul's son a book*.   There can be no doubt that
the Latin substantives are in four different cases, viz.

Petrus — nominative,
filio   — dative,
Pauli — genitive,
librum — accusative,

and similarly there can be no doubt that the English word *Paul's*
is in the genitive, which roughly corresponds to the same case in
Latin ; but it can be, and has been, disputed whether we are
allowed to say that *Peter* is in the nominative, *son* in the dative,
and *book* in the accusative, as there is no difference in endings in
English, as there is in Latin, to show which of these cases is
employed.   Are we to say that we have the same three cases as
in Latin, or that we have two cases, a nominative (*Peter*) and an
oblique case (*son, book*), or finally that all three words are in the
same " common case " ?   Each of these three positions has been
defended by grammarians, and as the discussion presents considerable theoretical interest besides being of practical importance
for the teaching of English and other languages in schools, it
will be necessary to devote some pages to the arguments pro
and con.

Let us first take the question : has English a dative case as distinct from an accusative case ? It would undoubtedly be so if we could find some truly grammatical criteria, either of form or of function, by which to tell the two cases apart. As word-order was in Ch. II recognized as a formal element, we might imagine someone maintaining that we have a real dative in our sentence on the ground of fixed position, it being impossible to say " he gave a book Paul's son." A closer inspection of the facts will, however, show us that it is impossible to recognize a positional dative, for in " I gave it him " we have the inverse order. Surely it would be preposterous to say either that *it* is here a dative, or that we have a positional dative which is sometimes placed before and sometimes after the accusative object. Further, if in " the man gave his son a book " *son* is in the positional dative, we must recognize a positional dative in all the following instances in which it would be impossible to revert the order of the two substantives :

> I asked the boy a few questions.
> I heard the boy his lessons.
> I took the boy long walks.
> I painted the wall a different colour.
> I called the boy bad names.
> I called the boy a scoundrel.

If we are to speak of separate datives and accusatives in English, I for one do not know where in this list the dative goes out and the accusative comes in, and I find no guidance in those grammars that speak of these two cases.

Someone might suggest that we have a criterion in the possibility of a word's being made the subject of a passive sentence, as this is allowable with accusatives only. This would be a purely linguistic test—but it is not applicable. In the first place it is not every " accusative " that can be made the subject of a passive sentence ; witness the second " accusatives " in " they made Brown Mayor," " they appointed Kirkman professor." Secondly, a " dative " *is* made the subject of the passive sentences " he was awarded a medal " | " she was refused admittance," as has been already mentioned (p. 163). Until other more infallible tests are forthcoming, we may therefore safely assert that there is no separate dative, and no separate accusative, in modern English.

This conclusion is strengthened when we see the way in which the ablest advocate of the distinction, Professor Sonnenschein, carries it out in his grammar, where it will be difficult to find any consistent system that will guide us in other cases than those that are mentioned. Sometimes historical reasons are invoked, thus when the rule is given that the case after any preposition is the accusative (§ 169, 489) : " In OE. some prepositions took the dative . . . but a change passed over the language, so that in late Old English there was a strong tendency to use the accusative after all prepositions." This is at any rate not the whole truth, for the dative was kept very late in some instances ; see, e.g., Chaucer's *of towne, yeer by yere, by weste*, etc., with the *e* sounded. We have traces of this to this day in some forms, thus the dat. sg. in *alive* (*on life*), *Atterbury* (*æt þære byrig*), the dat. pl. in (*by*) *inchmeal, on foot*, which may be looked on as a continuation of OE. *on fotum*, ME. *on foten, on fote*, at any rate when used of more than one person, as in " they are on foot." Apart from such isolated survivals the plain historical truth is that in most pronouns it was only the dative that survived, in the plurals of substantives the accusative (= nom.), and in the singulars of substantives a form in which nominative, accusative, and dative are indistinguishably mingled—but whatever their origin, from an early period these forms (*him, kings, king*) were used indiscriminately both where formerly a dative, and where an accusative was required.[1]

To return to the way in which Professor Sonnenschein distributes the two cases in modern English. In " he asked me a question " both *me* and *question* are said to be direct objects, probably because OE. *ascian* took two accusatives ; in *teach him French* we are left at liberty to call *him* an accusative or a dative, though the former seems to be preferred, in spite of the fact that *teach* is OE. *tæcan*, which takes a dative and an accusative. We should probably never have heard of two accusatives with this verb, had it not been for the fact that Lat. *doceo* and G. *lehren* have this construction [2]—but that surely is quite irrelevant to English grammar, otherwise we may expect some day to hear that *use* takes the ablative like Lat. *utor*.

Sometimes the rules given are evidently incomplete. In § 173 the dative as indirect object seems to be recognized only where the same sentence also contains an object in the accusative, as in " Forgive us our trespasses," but if we have simply " Forgive us," are we to say that *us* is in the accusative ? Is *him* in " I

---

[1] What would English boys say if they were taught at school some such rule as this : *him* in " I saw him " and " for him " is a dative, *kings* in " I saw the kings " and " for the kings " is an accusative, but *king* is an accusative in " I saw the king " and a dative in " for the king " ? Yet from an historical point of view this is much more true than Sonnenschein's pseudo-history.

[2] With German *lehren* the dative is by no means rare in the name of the person, and in the passive both *ich wurde das gelehrt* and *das wurde mich gelehrt* are felt as awkward and therefore replaced by *das wurde mir gelehrt*.

paid him " in the accusative, because it is the only object, or is
it in the dative, because it is the indirect object in " I paid him
a shilling " ?   Such questions arise by the score as soon as you
begin to put asunder what nature has joined together into one
case, and while in German it is possible to answer them because
the form actually used guides us, we have nothing to go by in
English.   In *hit him a blow* who is to say whether *him* is the
indirect object (dative) and *a blow* the direct object (" acc."), or
else *him* the direct object (" acc.") and *a blow* a subjunct (" instrumental " or " adverbial ") ?   Most people when asked about the
simple sentence *hit him* (without the addition *a blow*) would
probably say that *him* was the direct object, and thus in the
" accusative."

Sonnenschein recognizes " adverbial " uses of both cases, but
it is not possible to discover any reasons for the distribution.
" Near *him* "—dative, why ?   If because of OE. syntax, then *him*
in *to him, from him* should also be a dative ; here, however, it is
said to be an accusative because of the fiction that all prepositions
take the accusative, but why is it not the same with *near*, which
is recognized as a preposition by the NED ?   " He blew his pipe
three times "—accusative, why ?   (In OE. it would be a dative.)
And thus we might go on, for there is nothing to justify the perfectly arbitrary assignation of words to one or the other case.
The rules have to be learned by rote by the pupils, for they cannot
be understood.

Professor Sonnenschein says that a study of the history of
English grammars has led him emphatically to deny the view held
by many scholars that progress in English grammar has actually
been due to its gradual emancipation from Latin grammar.   In
Modern Language Teaching, March 1915, he said that a straight
line led from the earliest grammarians, who did not see any analogy
between English and Latin grammar, to a gradually increasing
recognition of the same cases as in Latin, a full understanding of
the agreement of the two languages having only been made
possible after comparative grammar had cleared up the relationship between them.   But this view of a steady ' progress ' towards
the Sonnenscheinian system is far from representing the whole
truth, for it has been overlooked that Sonnenschein's system is
found full-fledged as early as 1586, when Bullokar said that English
has five cases, and that in the sentence " How, John, Robert gives
Richard a shirt," *John* is vocative, *Robert* nominative, *shirt* accusative, and *Richard* dative (or, as it is quaintly called, gainative)—
four cases being thus recognized besides the genitive.   In 1920
Professor Sonnenschein himself, in the Preface to the second volume
of his Grammar, mentions some early grammarians (Gil 1619,

Mason 1622), who based English grammar on Latin grammar, but though there seem thus at all times to have been two conflicting ways of viewing this part of English grammar, Sonnenschein thinks that " in the main " the line of direction and progress has been as indicated by him. He does not mention such excellent grammarians as William Hazlitt,[1] William Cobbett, and Henry Sweet, who were opposed to his view of the cases, but mentions with special praise Lindley Murray, who took " the momentous step of recognizing an ' objective ' case of nouns " and thus " rendered English grammar the service of liberating it from the false definition of case " and " opened the door " to the next momentous step, Sonnenschein's recognition of a dative case. What is the next step to be in this progressive series, one wonders ? Probably someone will thank Sonnenschein for thus opening the door to the admission of an ablative case, and why not proceed with an instrumental, locative, etc. ? All the Professor's arguments for admitting a dative apply to these cases with exactly the same force.

He says that cases denote categories of *meaning*, not categories of *form*, and that this is just as true of Latin grammar as it is of English grammar. The different cases of a Latin noun do not always differ from one another in form : the accusative of neuter nouns has always the same form as the nominative, all ablative plurals are the same in form as dative plurals, in some nouns the dative singular does not differ in form from the genitive singular, in others from the ablative singular. All this is perfectly true, but it does not invalidate the view that the case distinctions of Latin grammar are primarily based on formal distinctions, to which different functions are attached. No one would have dreamt of postulating a Latin ablative case if it had not in many instances been different in form from the dative. And where the two cases *are* identical in form, we are still justified in saying that we have now one, and now the other case, because other words in the same position show us which is used. We say that *Julio* is the dative in *do Julio librum*, but the ablative in *cum Julio*, because in the corresponding sentences with *Julia* we have different forms : *do Juliæ librum, cum Julia*. *Templum* in some sentences is in the nominative, in others in the accusative, because in the first we

---

[1] [Lindley Murray] " maintains that there are six cases in English nouns, that is, six various terminations without any change of termination at all, and that English verbs have all the moods, tenses, and persons that the Latin ones have. This is an extraordinary stretch of blindness and obstinacy. He very formally translates the Latin Grammar into English (as so many have done before him) and fancies he has written an English Grammar ; and divines applaud, and schoolmasters usher him into the polite world, and English scholars carry on the jest " (Hazlitt, *The Spirit of the Age*, 1825, p. 119).

should have used the form *domus*, and in the others the form
domum. And thus in all the other instances, exactly as above
(p. 51) we recognized *cut* as a preterit in *I cut my finger yesterday*,
though there is nothing in the form of that particular verb to
show that it is not the present. But with English nouns it is
impossible to argue in the same way : there is a fundamental
incongruity between the Latin system where the case-distinctions
are generally, though *not always*, expressed in form, and the
English *system* where they are *never* thus expressed. To put
the English accusative and dative, which are always identical in
form, on the same footing as these two cases in Latin, which are
different in more than ninety instances out of a hundred, is simply
turning all scientific principles upside down.

It is quite true that we should base our grammatical treatment
of English on the established facts of comparative and historical
grammar, but one of the most important truths of that science
is the differentiation which in course of time has torn asunder
languages that were at first closely akin, thereby rendering it
impossible to apply everywhere exactly the same categories. We
do not speak of a dual number in English grammar as we do in
Greek, although here the notional category is clear enough ; why
then speak of a dative case, when there is just as little foundation
from a formal point of view, and when the meaning of the dative
in those languages that possess it is vague and indistinct from a
notional point of view ?

Professor Sonnenschein says that cases " denote categories of
meaning." But he does not, and cannot, specify what the particular meaning of the dative is.[1] If we look through the rules
of any German, Latin, or Greek grammar, we shall find in each
a great variety of uses, or functions, i.e. meanings assigned to the
dative, but many of them differ from one language to another.
Nor is this strange, if we consider the way these languages have
developed out of the Proto-Aryan language which is the common
" ancestor " of all of them. As Paul says, it is really perfectly
gratuitous (es ist im grunde reine willkür) to call the case we have
in German (and Old English) a dative, for besides the functions
of the dative it fulfils the functions of the old locative, ablative,
and instrumental. Formally it corresponds to the old dative
only in the singular of part of the words, in some words it represents the old locative, while in all words the dative plural is an
old instrumental. The Greek dative in the third declension in

---

[1] It cannot even be said that the *chief* meaning of the dative in German
is that of the indirect object. I counted all the datives in some pages of
a recent German book, and found that out of 157 datives only 3 (three)
were indirect objects in sentences containing another object, and that 18
were objects of verbs having no accusative objects.

the singular is an old locative, and the dative of all words has taken over the functions of the locative and instrumental as well as those of the old dative proper. However far back we go, we nowhere find a case with only one well-defined function : in every language every case served different purposes, and the boundaries between these are far from being clear-cut. This, in connexion with irregularities and inconsistencies in the formal elements characterizing the cases, serves to explain the numerous coalescences we witness in linguistic history ("syncretism") and the chaotic rules found in individual languages—rules which even thus are to a great extent historically inexplicable. If the English language has gone farther than the others in simplifying these rules, we should be devoutly thankful and not go out of our way to force it back into the disorder and complexity of centuries ago.

But if no clear-cut meaning can be attached to the dative as actually found in any of the old languages of our family, the same is true of the accusative. Some scholars have maintained a "localistic" case-theory and have seen in the accusative primarily a case denoting movement to or towards, from which the other uses have gradually developed : *Romam ire* 'go to Rome' led to *Romam petere*, and this to the other accusatives of the object, thus finally even to *Romam linquere* 'leave Rome.' Others consider the objective use the original function, and others again think that the accusative was the maid of all work who stepped in where neither the nominative nor any of the special cases was required. The only thing certain is that the accusative combined the connotation of a (direct) object with that of movement towards a place and that of spatial and temporal extension. It may even originally have had further uses which are now lost to us.

That the meanings of the accusative and dative cannot be kept strictly distinct, is shown also by the fact that the same verb may in the same language take sometimes one case and sometimes the other. Thus in German we find vacillation between them after *rufen, gelten, nachahmen, helfen, kleiden, liebkosen, versichern* and others (many examples in Andresen, *Sprachgebrauch*, 267 ff). In OE., *folgian* and *scildan* vacillated in the same way. The object after *onfon* 'take, receive' is now in the accusative, now in the dative, and now in the genitive. If we were to go by linguistic history, we should say that of the three synonyms in English, *help* governs the dative, and *aid* and *assist* the accusative. There is, of course, no foundation in the history of language for what seems to be at the root of Sonnenschein's rule, that (apart from his "adverbial" uses) a dative is found only when the verb has also another object (which then is said to be in the accusative) : that rule is found in no language and in Sonnenschein's grammar it

is due to a decree that is just as arbitrary as the Professor's ruling
that all prepositions govern the accusative.

Professor Sonnenschein tries to prop up his views by a pedago-
gical argument (Part III, Preface) : the pupil who has mastered
the uses of the English cases, as set forth in his book, will have
little to learn when he comes to Latin, except that Latin has an
extra case—the ablative. This means that part of the difficultly
of Latin grammar is shifted on to the English lessons ; the subject
in itself is not made easier even for those pupils who are going on
with Latin afterwards, the only difference is that they have to
learn part of it now at an earlier stage, and in connexion with
a language where it is perhaps more difficult to understand because
the memory has no support in tangible forms on which to fasten
the functions. And what of all those pupils who are never to take
up Latin ? Is it really justifiable to burden every boy and girl
of them with learning distinctions which will be of no earthly use
to them in later life ?

Genitive.

Not a single one of the old Aryan cases is so well-defined in
its meaning that we can say that it has some single function or
application that marks it off from all the rest. The genitive combines two functions which are kept separate in two Finnish cases,
the genitive and the partitive. But what the former function is
cannot be indicated except in the vaguest way as belonging to,
or belonging together, appertaining to, connexion with, relation
to or association with : [1] in English the use of this case is greatly
restricted, yet we find such different relations indicated by means
of the genitive as are seen in *Peter's house, Peter's father, Peter's
son, Peter's work, Peter's books* (those he owns, and those he has
written), *Peter's servants, Peter's master, Peter's enemies, an hour's
rest, out of harm's way,* etc. Some grammarians try to classify
these various uses of the genitive, but in many cases the special
meaning depends not on the use of the genitive in itself, but on
the intrinsic meaning of each of the two words connected, and
is therefore in each case readily understood by the hearer. Here
we must also mention the " subjective " and " objective " genitives
considered above (p. 169 ff.).

English has preserved only those uses in which the genitive
serves to connect two nouns, one of which is in this way made
an adjunct to the other (" adnominal genitive "), and the derived
use in which the genitive stands by itself as a primary, e.g. *at the
grocer's.* In the older languages the genitive was also used in
other ways, thus with certain verbs, where it formed a kind of

[1] G. zugehörigkeit, zusammengehörigkeit.

object, with some adjectives, etc. The relation between this genitive and an ordinary object is seen clearly in German, where some verbs, e.g. *vergessen, wahrnehmen, schonen,* which used to take the genitive, are now followed by an accusative ; *es* in *ich kann es nicht los werden, ich bin es zufrieden* was originally a genitive, but is now apprehended as an accusative.

We next come to the second value of the old Aryan genitive, the partitive, which cannot be separated from the so-called genitivus generis. In Latin it is chiefly used with primaries (substantives, etc.), e.g. *magna pars militum, major fratrum, multum temporis.* This in so far agrees with the other value of the case, as the genitive is an adjunct either way ; but there are other applications of the partitive genitive in which it comes to fulfil more independent functions in the sentence. The genitive is often used as the object of a verb, and so comes into competition with the accusative, as in OE. *bruceþ fodres* ' partakes of food,' Gr. *phagein tou artou* ' eat (some part) of the bread,' earlier German, e.g. Luther's *wer des wassers trincken wird,* Russian, e.g. *daite mně xlěba* ' give me of bread, some bread.' In Russian this use of a genitive as the object has been extended (with loss of the partitive idea) to all masculines and plurals denoting living beings. The partitive may also be used as the subject of a sentence, and so come into competition with the nominative. This is frequent with the partitive in Finnish, and the same use is found here and there in our own family of languages, thus in negative sentences in Russian, e.g. *nět xlěba* ' there is no bread,' *ne stalo našego druga* ' there was no more of our friend, i.e. he died.' We see corresponding phenomena in the Romanic languages, in which the preposition *de* has taken the place of the old genitive even in its use as a partitive, in which it is now often called the " partitive article " ; it is noteworthy that the noun with this partitive article may be used not only as an object of a verb (j'y ai vu des amis), but also as the subject of a sentence (ce soir des amis vont arriver | il tombe de la pluie), as a predicative (ceci est du vin), and after prepositions (avec du vin | après des détours | je le donnerai à des amis). If the subject-use is comparatively rare, this is explained by the general disinclination that speakers have to indefinite subjects (see p. 154 ; in *voici du vin, il y a du vin, il faut du vin* we originally had objects).

The expression of the partitive idea ' some (indefinite) quantity of . . . ' thus as it were comes athwart the ordinary case-system, because it comes to be used in the same functions for which many languages have separate cases (nominative, accusative) ; this is true whether this partitive idea is expressed by means of a separate case, as in Finnish, or by means of the genitive, as in Greek, or finally by the French combination with the preposition *de*.

If the distinction between the different cases was really one of meaning, that is, if each case had its own distinctive notional value, it would be quite unthinkable to have for one and the same construction, namely the so-called " absolute " construction (nexus-subjunct, as I call it) such complete divergence in usage as we actually find : ablative (Latin), dative (Old English), genitive (Greek), accusative (German), nominative (Modern English). It may be possible to account for this historically, but it can never be explained logically on the ground of some supposed intrinsic meaning of these cases.

The irrationality of the old case distinctions may perhaps also be brought out by the following consideration. The dative and the genitive seem to be in some way opposites, as indicated by the fact that when the old cases are replaced by prepositional groups, the preposition chosen in the former case is *to, ad*, and in the latter one which from the first denoted the opposite movement, *of* (a weak form of *off*), *de*. And yet the dative (or its substitute) often comes to mean the same thing as a genitive, as in the popular G. *dem kerl seine mutter* ' that fellow's mother,' Fr. *ce n'est pas ma faute à moi, sa mère à lui*, and the popular *la mère à Jean* (OFr. *je te donrai le file a un roi u a un conte*, Aucass). *C'est à moi* means ' it is mine.' In Norwegian dialects, combinations with *til* and *åt* (' to, at ') and in Faeroese, combinations with *hjá* (' with, chez ') have largely supplanted the obsolete genitive.[1]

Nominative and Oblique.

If the reader will recur to the question put at the beginning of this chapter, how many cases we are to recognize in the English sentence " Peter gives Paul's son a book," he will, I hope, now agree with me that it is impossible to say that *son* and *book* are in different cases (dative and accusative) ; but so far nothing has been said against the second possibility that we have in both an oblique case to be kept distinct from the nominative, of which in our sentence *Peter* is an example. Old French had such a system in its nouns, for there ' Peter ' and ' son ' in the nominative would be *Pierres* and *fils*, and in the oblique case *Pierre* and *fil*. Though there is no such formal distinction in the English substantives, I can imagine someone saying that on the strength of my own principles I should recognize the distinction, for it is found in pronouns like *I—me, he—him*, etc., and just as I say

---

[1] Finnish has no dative proper, but the ' allative ' which expresses motion on to or into the neighbourhood of, often corresponds to the Aryan dative.

that *sheep* in *many sheep*, though not distinct in form from the
singular, is a plural, because *lambs* in *many lambs* is distinct from
the singular *lamb*, and that *cut* in some sentences must be similarly
recognized as a preterit, so I ought to say that *Peter* and *son* are
in the nominative in those combinations in which we should use
the form *he*, and in the oblique case wherever we should use the
form *him*.   This looks like a strong argument ; yet I do not think
it is decisive.   In the case of *sheep* and *cut* the parallel was with
words belonging to the same word-class, where the conditions are
practically the same, but here the argument is drawn from another
word-class, the pronouns, which present a great many peculiarities
of their own and keep up distinctions found nowhere else.   If
we were to distinguish cases on the strength of their being distinct
in some pronouns, we might just as well distinguish gender in
English substantives on account of the distinctions seen in *he*,
she, *it*, and *who*, *what*, and split up adjectives and genitives into
two " states " or whatever you would call them, according as they
corresponded to *my* (adjunct) or to *mine* (non-adjunct).   But as
a matter of fact, no grammarian thinks of making such distinctions, any more than Old English grammars speak of a dual
number in substantives, while naturally recognizing it in the
personal pronouns, where it has distinct forms.   Thus we see that
distinctions which are appropriate and unavoidable in one word-
class cannot always be transferred to other parts of speech.

  With regard to the *meaning* of the nominative as distinct from
the other cases, we are accustomed from the grammar of Latin
and other languages to look upon it as self-evident that not only
the subject of a sentence, but also the predicative, is put in the
nominative.   From a logical point of view this, however, is not
the only natural thing, for subject and predicative are not to be
regarded as notionally identical or even necessarily closely akin.
Here as elsewhere it serves to broaden one's view to see how
the same ideas are expressed in other languages.   In Finnish the
predicative is (1) in the nominative, e.g. *pojat ovat iloiset* ' the
boys are glad,' (2) in the partitive " if the subject is regarded as
referred to a class in common with which the subject shares the
quality in question " (Eliot), " to denote qualities which are found
always or habitually in the subject " (Setälä), e.g. *pojat ovat iloisia*
' boys are (naturally) glad,' (3) in the essive to denote the state
in which the subject is at a given time, e.g. *isäni on kipeänä* ' my
father is (now) ill,' [1] and (4) in the translative after verbs signifying to become (change into a state), e.g. *isäni on jo tullut vanhaksi*
' my father has grown old.' [2]

---

[1] The essive is also used in apposition, e.g. *lapsena* ' as a child.'

[2] C⁀. G. *zu etwas werden*, Dan. *blive til noget*.

Even in our West-European languages the predicative does not always stand in the nominative. In Danish for a couple of centuries it has been recognized as good grammar to use the accusative (or rather oblique case) and thus to look upon the predicative as a kind of object : *det er mig*. And in English we have colloquially the same use : *it's me*. The habitual omission of the relative pronoun in such sentences as this : " Swinburne could not have been the great poet he was without his study of the Elizabethans " (thus also in Danish) also seems to show that popular instinct classes the predicative with the object.[1]

In English and Danish this cannot be separated from the tendency to restrict the use of the nominative to its use in immediate connexion with a (finite) verb to which it serves as subject (*I do | do I*), and to use the oblique form everywhere else, thus e.g. after *than* and *as* (*he is older than me | not so old as me*) and when the pronoun stands by itself (*Who is that ?—Me !*). This tendency has prevailed in French, where we have *moi* when the word is isolated, and the nom. *je*, acc. *me* in connexion with a verbal form, and similarly with the other personal pronouns ; cf. also the isolated *lui, lei, loro* in Italian.[2] (Cf. on this development in English *Progr. in Language*, Ch. VII, reprinted ChE Ch. II.)

Vocative.

On the so-called Vocative very little need be said here. In some languages, e.g. Latin, it has a separate form, and must consequently be reckoned a separate case. In most languages, however, it is identical with the nominative, and therefore does not require a separate name. The vocative, where it is found, may be said to indicate that a noun is used as a second person and placed outside a sentence, or as a sentence in itself. It has points of contact with the imperative, and might like this be said to express a request to the hearer, viz. ' hear ' or ' be attentive.'

The close relation between the vocative and the nominative is seen with an imperative, when " You, take that chair ! " with *you* outside the sentence (exactly as in " John, take that chair ") by rapid enunciation becomes " You take that chair ! " with *you* as the subject of the imperative.

[1] Instead of the term " predicative " some grammars use the expression " predicate nominative." I could not help smiling when I read in a grammatical paper on the mistakes made by school-children in Kansas : " Predicate nominative not in nominative case. Ex. They were John and *him*. It is *me*."

[2] Cf. also " Io non sono fatta come te " (Rovetta).

Final Words about Cases.

It is customary to speak of two classes of cases, grammatical cases (nom., acc., etc.) and concrete, chiefly local cases (locative, ablative, sociative, instrumental, etc.). Wundt in much the same sense distinguishes between cases of inner determination and cases of outer determination, and Deutschbein between " kasus des begrifflichen denkens " and " kasus der anschauung." It is, however, impossible to keep these two things apart, at anyrate in the best-known languages. Not even in Finnish, with its full system of local cases, can the distinction be maintained, for the allative is used for the indirect object, and the essive, which is now chiefly a grammatical case, was originally local, as shown especially in some adverbial survivals. In Aryan languages the two categories were inextricably mingled from the first. Gradually, however, the purely concrete uses of the old cases came to be dropped, chiefly because prepositions came into use, which indicated the local and other relations with greater precision than the less numerous cases had been able to do, and thus rendered these superfluous. As time went on, the number of the old cases constantly dwindled, especially as a more regular word-order often sufficed to indicate the value of a word in the sentence. But no language of our family has at any time had a case-system based on a precise or consistent system of meanings ; in other words, case is a purely grammatical (syntactic) category and not a notional one in the true sense of the word. The chief things that cases stand for, are :

address (vocative),
subject (nominative),
predicative (no special case provided),
object (accusative and dative),
connexion (genitive),
place and time, many different relations (locative, etc.),
measure (no special case),
manner (no special case),
instrument (instrumental).

Another classification, which in some ways would be better, would be according to the three ranks considered in Ch. VII.

I. Cases standing as primaries.
Subject-case.
Object-case.
This might be divided into the case of direct, and the case of indirect object.
Predicative-case.

II. Adjunct-case. Genitive.

III. Subjunct-cases.

These might be divided into time-cases (time
when, time how long), place-cases (place where,
whither, from where), measure-case, manner-case,
instrument-case.

Many of the notions, however, are ill-defined and pass imper-
ceptibly into one another. No wonder, therefore, that languages
vary enormously, even those which go back ultimately to the
same 'parent-language.' Cases form one of the most irrational
part of language in general.[1]

Prepositional Groups.

The reader will have observed that in this chapter I speak
only of the so-called synthetic cases, not of the " analytic cases,"
which consist of a preposition and its object ; these, as I maintain,
should not be separated from any other prepositional group. In
English, *to a man* is no more a dative case than *by a man* is an
instrumental case, or *in a man* a locative case, etc. Deutschbein
is an extreme representative of the opposite view, for in his SNS,
p. 278 ff., he gives as examples of the English dative, among
others : he came *to London* | this happened *to him* | complain *to
the magistrate* | adhere *to someone* | the ancient Trojans were fools
to your father | he behaved respectfully *to her* | you are like
daughters *to me* | bring the book *to me* | I have bought a villa
for my son | What's Hecuba *to him* ? | it is not easy *for a foreigner*
to apprehend—thus both with *to* and *for*, probably because German has a dative in most of these cases. It is much sounder to
recognize these combinations as what they really are, prepositional groups, and to avoid the name " dative " except where we
have something analogous to the Latin, or Old English, or German dative. It is curious to observe that Deutschbein with his
emphasizing of " Der räumliche dativ " (" he came *to London* ")
is in direct opposition to the old theory which deduced all cases
from local relations, for according to that the dative was thought
of as the case of ' rest,' the accusative as the case of ' movement
to,' and the genitive the case of ' movement from ' ; if Deutschbein
calls *to London* a dative, why not also *into the house* ? But then

[1] My main result is the same as Paul's : " Die kasus sind nur ausdrucks-
mittel, die nicht zum notwendigen bestande jeder sprache gehören, die da,
wo sie vorhanden sind, nach den verschiedenen sprachen und entwicke-
lungsstufen mannigfach variieren, und von denen man nie erwarten darf,
dass sich ihre funktionen mit konstanten logischen oder psychologischen
verhältnissen decken " (*Zeitschr. f. psych.* 1910, 114).

the German *in das haus* would be a dative in spite of the actual use of the accusative, which here means something different from the dative in *in dem haus*. Even if the two expressions " I gave a shilling to the boy " and " I gave the boy a shilling " are synonymous, it does not follow that we should apply the same grammatical term to both constructions : *man-made institutions* and *institutions made by man* mean the same thing, but are not grammatically identical.

The local meaning of the preposition *to* is often more or less effaced, but that should not make us speak of a dative even where *to* is wholly non-local. Thus also in French, where *j'irai au ministre* and *je dirai au ministre* are analogous, though with a pronoun the dative case is used in one, but not in the other construction : *j'irai à lui* and *je lui dirai.*

With the genitive the same considerations hold good. Deutschbein speaks of a genitive, not only in *the works of Shakespeare,* but also in : participate *of the nature of satire* | smell *of brandy* | proud *of his country,* and, if I am not mistaken, the man *from Birmingham* | free *from opposition* (SNS 286 ff.). Some grammarians speak of " die trennung eines genitivs von seinem regierenden worte durch andere satzteile " and mean instances like " the arrival at Cowes of the German Emperor," where we have simply two parallel prepositional group-adjuncts ; some will even use such a term as " split genitive " (Anglia, Beibl. 1922, 207) with examples like " the celebrated picture by Gainsborough of the Duchess of Devonshire," where it would be just as reasonable to call *by Gainsborough* a genitive as to use that name of the *of*-combination. Both are prepositional groups and nothing else.

I may perhaps take this opportunity of entering a protest against a certain kind of 'national psychology' which is becoming the fashion in some German university circles, but which seems to me fundamentally unsound and unnatural. It affects case-syntax in the following passage : " Wenn nun der sächs. gen. bei zeitbestimmungen im lebendigen gebrauch ist, so deutet dies darauf hin, dass der zeit im englischen sprachbewusstsein eine bevorzugte rolle eingeräumt wird, was namentlich in gewissen berufskreisen wie bei verlegern, herausgebern, zeitungsschreibern der fall sein wird " (Deutschbein SNS 289). In the same work, p. 269, the dative in G. *ich helfe meinen freunden* is taken as a sign of "ein persönliches vertrauensverhältnis statischen charakters zwischen mir und meinen freunden," but " wenn im ne. *to help* (*I help my friend*) *mit dem akk.* konstruiert wird, so verzichtet es darauf, das persönliche verhältnis von mir zu meinen freunde auszudrücken . . . das ne. besitzt demnach einen dynamischen grundcharakter, der auch in anderen zahlreichen erscheinungen der sprache bemerkbar ist." What does *dynamic* mean in that connexion ? And how does Deutschbein know that the case after *help* is not a dative still ? In *give my friend a book* he acknowledges *friend* as a dative, why not here ? The form is the same. The function is exactly the same as in the corresponding OE. sentence *ic helpe minum freonde*, of which it forms an uninterrupted continuation, and which in its turn corresponds in every respect to G. *ich helfe meinem freunde.* Why not simply say that in Modern English it is neither accusative nor dative, and then leave out all conclusions about " personal," " dynamic," and " static " national characters ?

CHAPTER XIV

NUMBER [1]

Counting. The Normal Plural. Plural of Approximation. Higher Units. Common Number. Mass-Words.

Counting.

NUMBER might appear to be one of the simplest natural categories, as simple as ' two and two are four.' Yet on closer inspection it presents a great many difficulties, both logical and linguistic.

From a logical point of view the obvious distinction is between one and more than one, the latter class being subdivided into 2, 3, 4, etc. ; as a separate class may be recognized ' all ' ; while beyond all these there is a class of ' things ' to which words like one, two are inapplicable ; we may call them uncountables, though dictionaries do not recognize this use of the word *uncountable*, which is known to them only in the relative sense ' too numerous to be (easily) counted ' (like *innumerable, numberless, countless*).

The corresponding syntactic distinctions are singular and plural, which are found in most languages, while some besides the ordinary plural have a dual, and very few a trial.

Thus we have the following two systems :

	NOTIONAL :		SYNTACTIC :
A.	Countables		
	one	.. ..	Singular
	two	.. .. ..	(Dual)
	three	.. .. ..	(Trial)
	.. .. } more than one		.. Plural
B.	Uncountables.		

We can only speak of " more than one " in regard to things which without being identical belong to the same kind. Plurality thus presupposes difference, but on the other hand if the difference

---

[1] The substance of this chapter was read as a paper before the Copenhagen Academy of Sciences on November 17, 1911, but never printed.

is too great, it is impossible to use words like two or three. A pear and an apple are two fruits ; a brick and a castle can barely be called two things ; a brick and a musical sound are not two, a man and a truth and the taste of an apple do not make three, and so on.

What objects can be counted together, genera'ly depends on the linguistic expression. In the majority of cases the classification is so natural that it is practically identical in most languages ; but in some cases there are differences called forth by varieties of linguistic structure. Thus in English there is no difficulty in saying "Tom and Mary are cousins," as *cousin* means both a male and a female cousin ; Danish (like German and other languages) has different words, and therefore must say " T. og M. er fætter og kusine," and E. *five cousins* cannot be translated exactly into Danish. On the other hand, English has no comprehensive term for what the Germans call *geschwister*, Dan. *søskende*. Sometimes, however, a numeral is placed before such a collocation as *brothers and sisters* : " they have ten brothers and sisters," which may be = 2 brothers + 8 sisters or any other combinations ; " we have twenty *cocks and hens* " (= Dan. tyve høns). The natural need for a linguistic term which will cover male and female beings of the same kind has in some languages led to the syntactical rule that the masculine plural serves for both sexes : Italian *gli zii*, Span. *los padres* (see p. 233).

In some cases it is not possible to tell beforehand what to reckon as *one* object : with regard to some composite things different languages have different points of view ; compare *un pantalon*—a pair of trousers, et par buxer, ein paar hosen ; *eine brille*—a pair of spectacles, une paire de lunettes, et par briller ; *en sax, eine schere*—a pair of scissors, une paire de ciseaux.

English sometimes tends to use the plural form in such cases as a singular, thus *a scissors, a tongs, a tweezers*.

In modern Icelandic we have the curious plural of *einn* ' one ' in *einir sokkar* ' one pair of socks ' (to denote more than one pair the ' distributive ' numerals are used : *tvennir vetlingar* ' two pairs of gloves ').

With parts of the body there can generally be no doubt what to consider as one and what as two ; yet in English there is (or rather was) some vacillation with regard to *moustache*, which is in the NED defined as (*a*) the hair on both sides of the upper lip, (*b*) the hair covering either side of the upper lip, so that what to one is a pair of moustaches, to another is a moustache : " he twirled first one moustache and then the other."

In Magyar it is a fixed rule that those parts of the body which occur in pairs are looked upon as wholes ; where the English say "my eyes are weak " or "his hands tremble" the Hungarian will use the singular : *a szemem* (sg.) *gyenge, reszket a keze* (sg.). The natural consequence, which to us appears very unnatural, is that when one eye or hand or foot is spoken of, the word *fél* 'half' is used : *fél szemmel* 'with one eye,' literally 'with half eye(s),' *fél lábára sánta* 'lame of one foot.' This applies also to words for gloves, boots, etc. : *keztyű* (pair of) gloves, *fél keztyű* (a half . . . i.e.) one glove, *csizma* (sg.) 'boots,' *fél csizma* 'a boot.' The plural forms of such words (*keztyűk, czizmák*) are used to denote several pairs or different kinds of gloves, boots.

The Normal Plural.

The simplest and easiest use of the plural is that seen, e.g., in *horses* = (one) horse + (another) horse + (a third) horse. . . . (We might use the formula : Apl. = Aa + Ab + Ac . . .) This may be called the normal plural and calls for very few remarks, as in most languages grammar and logic here agree in the vast majority of cases.

There are, however, instances in which different languages do not agree, chiefly on account of formal peculiarities. English and French have the plural of the substantive in *the eighteenth and nineteenth centuries, les siècles dix-huitième et dix-neuvième*, while German and Danish have the singular, the reason being not that the English and French are in themselves more logical than other nations, but a purely formal one : in French the article, which shows the number, is placed before the substantive and is not in immediate contact with the adjectives ; in English the article is the same in both numbers, and can therefore be placed before the (singular) adjective as if it were in the singular itself without hindering the use of the natural plural in *centuries*. In German, on the other hand, you have to choose at once between the singular and the plural form of the article, but the latter form, *die*, would be felt as incongruous before the adjective *achzehnte*, which is in the neuter singular ; if, on the other hand, you begin with the (singular) article *das*, it would be equally odd to end with the plural of the substantive (das 18te und 19te *jahrhunderte*), whence the grammatically consistent, if logically reprehensible use of the singular throughout. It is the same in Danish. In English, too, when the indefinite article is used, the singular is preferred for the same reason : *an upper and a lower shelf*. Sometimes the singular may be used to avoid misunderstandings, as when Thackeray writes " The elder and younger *son* of the house of Crawley were never at home together " : the form *sons* might have implied the existence of more than one son in each class. (See other special cases in MEG II, p. 73 ff.[1])

The English difference between the two synonymous expressions *more weeks than one* and *more than one week* shows clearly the psychological influence of proximity (attraction). The force of this is not equally strong in all languages : where Italian has the singular in *ventun anno* on account of *un,* English says *twenty-one years* exactly as it says *one and twenty years* ; thus also a *thousand and one nights.* But German and Danish here show the influence of attraction with peculiar clearness because each language has the plural when the word for ' one ' is removed from the substantive, and the singular when it immediately precedes it : *ein und zwanzig tage, tausend und eine nacht ; een og tyve dage, tusend og een nat.*

With fractions there are some difficulties : should one and a half be connected with a substantive in the singular or in the plural ? Of course one can get out of the difficulty by saying *one mile and a half,* but this will not do in languages which have an indivisible expression like G. *anderthalb,* Dan. *halvanden ;* German seems to have the plural (*anderthalb ellen*), but Danish has the singular (*halvanden krone*) though with a curious tendency to put a preposed adjective in the plural though the substantive is in the singular : *med mine stakkels halvanden lunge* (Karl Larsen), *i disse halvandet år* (Pontoppidan). Where English has *two and a half hours* (pl.), Danish has attraction : *to og en halv time* (sg.).

Where each of several persons has only one thing, sometimes the singular, and sometimes the plural is preferred : Danish says *hjertet sad os i halsen* (sg.), while English has *our hearts leaped to our mouths,* though not always consistently (*three men came marching along, pipe in mouth and sword in hand ;* see for details MEG II, p. 76 ff.). Wackernagel (VS 1. 92) gives an example from Euripides where the mother asks the children to give her the right hand : dot' ō tekna, det' aspasasthai mētri dexian khera.

Plural of Approximation.

I next come to speak of what I have termed the plural of approximation, where several objects or individuals are comprised in the

---

[1] Besides connecting different things, the word *and* may be used to connect two qualities of the same thing or being, as in " my friend and protector, Dr. Jones." This may lead to ambiguity. There is some doubt as to Shelley's meaning in *Epipsychidion* 492, " Some wise and tender Ocean-King . . . Reared it . . . a pleasure house Made sacred to *his sister and his spouse*" (one or two persons ?). Cf. the advertisement " Wanted a clerk and copyist " (one person), " a clerk and a copyist " (two). " A secret which she, and she alone, could know." German often uses the combination *und zwar* to indicate that *und* is not additive in the usual sense : " Sie hat nur ein kind, und zwar einen sohn."

same form though not belonging exactly to the same kind. *Sixties* (a man in the sixties ; the sixties of the last century) means, not (one) sixty + (another) sixty . . ., but sixty + sixty-one + sixty-two and so forth till sixty-nine. The corresponding usage is found in Danish (*treserne*), but not, for instance, in French.

The most important instance of the plural of approximation is *we*, which means I + one or more not-I's. It follows from the definition of the first person that it is only thinkable in the singular, as it means the speaker in this particular instance. Even when a body of men, in response to " Who will join me ? " answer " We all will," it means in the mouth of each speaker nothing but " I will and all the others will (I presume)."

The word *we* is essentially vague and gives no indication whom the speaker wants to include besides himself. It has often, therefore, to be supplemented by some addition : *we doctors, we gentlemen, we Yorkshiremen, we of this city.* Numerous languages, in Africa and elsewhere, have a distinction between an " exclusive " and an " inclusive " plural, as shown by the well-known anecdote of the missionary who told the negroes " We are all of us sinners, and we all need conversion," but unhappily used the form for " we " that meant " I and mine, to the exclusion of you whom I am addressing," instead of the inclusive plural (Friedrich Müller). In several languages it is possible after *we* to add the name of the person or persons who together with " I " make up the plural, either without any connective or with " and " or " with " : OE. *wit Scilling* I and Scilling, *unc Adame* ' for me and Adam,' ON. *vit Gunnarr* ' I and Gunnarr ' (cf. *þeir Sigurðr* ' S. and his people,' *þau Hjalti* ' H. and his wife '), Frisian *wat en Ellen* ' we two, I and E,' G. pop. *wir sind heute mit ihm spazieren gegangen,* ' I and he . . .,' Fr. pop. *nous chantions avec lui* ' I and he sang,' Ital. *quando siamo giunti con mia cugina* ' when my cousin and I arrived,' Russian *my s bratom pridëm* ' we with brother, i.e. I and my brother, will come,' etc.[1]

The plural of the second person may be, according to circumstances, the normal plural (ye = thou + a different thou + a third thou, etc.), or else a plural of approximation (ye = thou + one or more other people not addressed at the moment). Hence we find in some languages similar combinations to those mentioned above with *we* : OE. *git Iohannis* ' ye two (thou and) John,' ON. *it Egill* ' thou and E.', Russ. *vy s sestroj* ' ye, (thou) with thy sister.'

The idea that " we " and " ye " imply some other person(s) besides " I " and " thou " is at the root of the Fr. combination

---

[1] See, besides the ordinary grammars, Grimm, Personenwechsel 19; Tobler, VB 3. 14 ; Ebeling, Archiv. f. neu. spr. 104. 129 ; Dania, 10. 47 ; H. Möller, Zeitschr. für deutsche Wortforsch 4. 103 ; Nyrop, Études ed gramm. française, 1920, p. 13.

nous (or *vous*) *autres Français*, i.e. ' I (or thou) and the other French-men.' In Spanish *nosotros, vosotros* have been generalized and are used instead of *nos, vos*, when isolated or emphatic.

In most grammars the rule is given that if the words composing the subject are of different persons, then the plural verb is of the first person rather than the second or third, and of the second person rather than the third. It will be seen that this rule when given in a Latin grammar (with examples like " si tu et Tullia valetis, ego et Cicero valemus ") is really superfluous, as the first person plural by definition is nothing else than the first person singular plus someone else, and the second person plural corre-spondingly. In an English grammar (with examples like " he and I are friends ; you and they would agree on that point ; he and his brother were to have come," Onions, AS 21) it is even more super-fluous, as no English verb ever distinguishes persons in the plural.

A third instance of the plural of approximation is seen in *the Vincent Crummleses*, meaning Vincent Crummles and his family, Fr. *les Paul* = Paul et sa femme ; " Et Mme de Rosen les signalait : Tiens . . . *les un tel* " (Daudet, L'Immortel 160).[1]

When a person speaks of himself as " we " instead of " I " it may in some cases be due to a modest reluctance to obtrude his own person on his hearers or readers ; he hides his own opinion or action behind that of others. But the practice may even more frequently be due to a sense of superiority, as in the " plural of majesty." This was particularly influential in the case of the Roman emperors who spoke of themselves as *nos* [2] and required to be addressed as *vos*. This in course of time led to the French way of addressing all superiors (and later through courtesy also equals, especially strangers) with the plural pronoun *vous*. In the Middle Ages this fashion spread to many countries ; in English it eventually led to the old singular *thou* being practically superseded by *you*, which is now the sole pronoun of the second person and no longer a sign of deference or respect. *You* now is a common-number form, and the same is true to some extent of It. *voi*, Russian *vy*, etc. The use of the " plural of social inequality " entails several anomalies, as the German *Sie* (and in imitation of that, Dan. *De*) in speaking to one person, Russian *oni, one* (' they,' m. and f.) in speaking of one person of superior standing ; grammatical irregularities are seen, e.g., in the singular *self* in the royal *ourself*, Fr. *vous-même*, and in the singular of the predicative in Dan. *De er så god*, Russ. *vy segodnja ne takaja kak včera* (Pedersen RG 90) ' you are not the

---

[1] On the German *Rosners* in the sense ' the Rosner family,' which is originally the genitive, but is often apprehended as a plural form, and on Dan. *de gamle Suhrs*, see MEG II, 4. 42 ; cf. Tiselius in *Språk och stil* 7. 126 ff.

[2] On Greek " we " for "I " see Wackernagel, VS 98 ff.

same (sg. fem.) to-day as yesterday.' Mention should also be made of the use of the plural of deference in German verbs, when no pronoun is used : *Was wünschen der herr general ?* 'What do you want, General ? ' Politeness and servility are not always free from a comic tinge.[1]

Higher Units.

It is very often necessary or at any rate convenient to have a linguistic expression in which several beings or things are comprehended into a unit of a higher order. We must here distinguish between various ways in which this fusion may be effected.

In the first place the plural form may be used in itself. English has a facility in this respect which appears to be unknown to the same extent in other languages ; the indefinite article or another pronoun in the singular number may be simply put before a plural combination : that delightful three weeks | another five pounds | a second United States | every three days | a Zoological Gardens, etc. There can be no doubt that this is chiefly rendered possible by the fact that the preposed adjective does not show whether it is singular or plural, for a combination like *that delightful three weeks* would be felt as incongruous in a language in which *delightful* was either definitely singular or plural in form ; but the English uninflected form can easily be connected both with the singular *that* and the plural *three weeks*.

A slightly different case is seen in *a sixpence* (*a threepence*), which has been made a new singular substantive with a new plural : *sixpences* (*threepences*). In the corresponding Danish name for the coin worth two kroner the analogy of the singular *en krone, en eenkrone* has prevailed and the form is *en tokrone*, pl. *mange tokroner*. This reminds one of the E. *a fortnight, a sennight* (fourteen nights, seven nights), in which, however, the latter element is the OE. plural *niht* (the ending *s* in *nights* is a later analogical formation) ; thus also *a twelvemonth* (OE. pl. *monaþ*).

In the second place the unification of a plural may be effected through the separate formation of a singular substantive. Thus in Greek we have from *deka* ' ten ' the sb. *dekas*, L. *decas*, whence E. *decade* ; in French we have the words in *-aine : une douzaine, vingtaine, trentaine*, etc., the first of which has passed into several other languages : *dozen, dutzend, dusin*. Corresponding to *dekas* the old Gothonic languages had a substantive (Goth. *tigus*), which as is well known, enters into the compounds E. *twenty, thirty*, etc., G. *zwanzig, dreissig*, etc. These were therefore originally sub-

---

[1] I forget where I have seen the remark that in Munda-Koh it is considered indecent to speak of a married woman except in the dual : she is, as it were, not to be imagined as being without her husband.

stantives, though now they have become adjectives. Lat. *centum,
mille,* E. (Gothonic) *hundred, thousand* were also substantives of
this kind, and reminiscences of this usage are still found, e.g. in
Fr. *deux cents* and in the E. use of *a, one : a hundred, one thousand* ;
cf. also *a million, a billion.* A peculiar type of half-disguised compounds may be seen in Lat. *biduum, triduum, biennium, triennium*
for periods of two or three days or years.

With these must be classed words like *a pair* (of gloves), *a couple*
(of friends), and this leads up to words denoting an assemblage of
things as *a set* (of tools, of volumes), *a pack* (of hounds, of cards),
a bunch (of flowers, of keys), *a herd* (of oxen, of goats), *a flock, a
bevy,* etc.

Such words are rightly termed collectives, and I think this
term should not be used in the loose way often found in grammatical
works, but only in the strict sense of words which denote a unit
made up of several things or beings which may be counted
separately ; a collective, then, is logically from one point of view
" one " and from another point of view " more than one," and this
accounts for the linguistic properties of such words which take
sometimes a singular and sometimes a plural construction. (On
the difference between collectives and mass-words see below.)

Some collectives are derivatives from the words denoting the
smaller units : *brotherhood,* from *brother,* cp. also *nobility, peasantry,
soldiery, mankind.* There is an interesting class in Gothonic languages with the prefix *ga-, ge-* and the neuter suffix *-ja* ; Gothic
had *gaskohi* ' pair of shoes ' ; these formations became especially
numerous in OHG, where we have, e.g., *gidermi* ' bowels,' *giknihti*
' body of servants,' *gibirgi* ' mountainous district,' *gifildi* ' fields,
plain.' In modern G. we have *gebirge, gepäck, gewitter, ungeziefer,*
and others, partly with changed signification or construction.
Geschwister at first meant ' sisters ' (" zwei brüder und drei
geschwister "), later it came to mean ' brothers and sisters ' and
even sometimes may be used in the singular of a single brother
or sister, when it is desirable not to specify the sex. But in ordinary
speech it is now no longer used as a collective, but as an ordinary
plural.

Latin *familia* meant at first a collection of *famuli,* i.e. ' house-
mates,' later ' servants ' ; when the word *famulus* went out of use,
familia acquired its present European meaning, and as an unanalyz-
able collective must be classed with such words as *crew, crowd,
swarm, company, army, tribe, nation, mob.*

Some words may develop a collective signification by metonymy,
as when *the parish* is said for the inhabitants of the parish, *all
the world* = ' all men,' *the sex* ' women,' *the Church, the bench,
society,* etc.

The double-sidedness of collectives is shown grammatically; they are units, and as such can be used not only with *a* or *one* preposed, but also in the plural in the same way as other countables : *two flocks, many nations*, etc. On the other hand, they denote plurality, and therefore may take the verb and the predicative in the plural (*my family are early risers ; la plupart disent*, thus in many other languages as well) and may be referred to by such a pronoun as *they*. It is, however, worthy of note that this plural construction is found with such collectives only as denote living beings, and never with others, like *library* or *train*, though they mean ' collection of books, of railway-carriages.' Sometimes a collective may show the two sides of its nature in the same sentence : *this* (sg.) *family are* (pl.) *unanimous in condemning him.* This should be thought neither illogical nor " antigrammatical " (as Sweet calls it, NEG § 116), but only a natural consequence of the twofold nature of such words.

In some instances languages go farther than this and admit combinations in which the same form which is really a singular is treated as if it were the plural of the word denoting the smaller unit : *those people* (= those men), *many people* (as distinct from *many peoples* = many nations), *a few police, twenty clergy*. In Danish we have this with *folk* (as in E. with the word spelt in the same way), which is a true collective in *et folk* (a nation, with the separate pl. *mange folkeslag*), but is now also treated as a plural : *de folk, mange folk*, though we cannot say *tyve folk* ' twenty people '; there is a curious mixture in *de godtfolk* 'those brave people,' *godt* is sg. neuter. (Quotations for E. 80,000 *cattle, six clergy, five hundred infantry, six hundred troops*, etc., are found in MEG II, p. 100 ff.[1])

The transition from a collective to a plural is also seen in the Aryan substantives in *-a*. Originally they were collectives in the feminine singular ; we have seen an instance in Lat. *familia*. In many cases these collectives corresponded to neuters, as in *opera*, gen. *operæ* ' work ': *opus* ' piece of work '; hence *-a* came finally to be used as the regular way of forming the plural of neuters, though a survival of the old value of the ending is found in the Greek rule that neuters in the plural take the verb in the singular (see the full and learned treatment in J. Schmidt, *Die Pluralbildungen der indogerm. Neutra*, 1889, a short summary in my book *Language*, p. 395). It is interesting to see the development in the Romanic languages, where the same ending still serves to form a plural in

· Note also G. *ein paar* ' a pair,' which in the more indefinite signification ' a couple ' (i.e. two or perhaps three or even a few more) is made into an uninflected adjunct (*mit ein paar freunden*, not *einem paar*) and may even take the plural article : *die paar freunde*. In Dan. also *et par venner, de par venner.*

many Italian words (*frutta, uova, paja*), but has generally again become a fem. sg., though not in a collective sense; cp. It. *foglia*, Fr. *feuille* from Lat. *folia*.

Wherever we have a plural of any of the words mentioned in this section, we may speak of a " plural raised to the second power," e.g. *decads, hundreds, two elevens* (two teams of eleven each), *sixpences, crowds*, etc. But the same term, a plural raised to the second power, may be applied to other cases as well, e.g. E. *children*, where the plural ending -*en* is added to the original pl. *childer*, possibly at first with the idea that several sets (families) of children were meant, as in the Sc. dialectal *shuins* mentioned by Murray as meaning the shoes of several people, while *shuin* means one pair only (*Dial. of the Southern Counties*, 161; see also MEG II, 5. 793). This logical meaning of a double plural (a plural of a plural) cannot, however, be supposed to have been in all cases present to the minds of those who created double plurals : often they were probably from the very first simple redundancies, and at any rate they are now felt as simple plurals in such cases as *children, kine, breeches*, etc. Breton has plurals of plurals : *bugel* child, pl. *bugale*, but *bugale-ou* ' plusieurs bandes d'enfants,' *loer* ' stocking,' pl. *lerou* ' pair of stockings,' but *lereier* ' several pairs of stockings,' *daou-lagad-ou*, ' eyes of several persons ' (H. Pedersen, GKS 2. 71). We have a double plural in form, but not in sense, in G. *tränen, zähren* ' tears.' Here the old plural form *träne* (*trehene*), *zähre* (*zähere*) has now become a singular.

In Latin the use of a separate set of numerals serves to indicate the plural of a plural. *Litera* is a letter (buchstabe), pl. *literæ* may stand for ' letters (buchstaben) ' or for the composite unit ' a letter (epistle) ' or the logical plural of this ' letters (epistles) '; now *quinque literæ* means ' fünf buchstaben,' but *quinæ literæ* ' fünf briefe.' *Castra* ' a camp ' is originally the pl. of *castrum* ' a fort '; *duo castra* ' two forts,' *bina castra* ' two camps.' Similarly, in Russian the word for ' a watch ' or ' clock ' is *časy*, formally the pl. of *čas* ' hour '; two hours is *dva časa*, but ' two watches ' is *dvoe časov* ; with higher numerals *štuk* ' pieces ' is inserted : *dvadtsat' pjat' štuk časov, sto štuk časov* ' 25, 100 watches or clocks.'

In this connexion we may also notice that when we say *my spectacles, his trousers, her scissors*, no one can tell whether one pair or more pairs are meant, thus whether the correct translation into other languages would be *meine brille, son pantalon, ihre schere*, or *meine brillen, ses pantalons, ihre scheren*. (But when we say " he deals in spectacles ; the soldiers wore khaki trousers," etc., the meaning is obviously plural.) The plural forms *spectacles, trousers, scissors*, in themselves thus from a notional point of view denote a ' common number.'

Common Number.

The want of a common number form (i.e. a form that disregards the distinction between singular and plural) is sometimes felt, but usually the only way to satisfy it is through such clumsy devices as " a star or two," " one or more stars," " some word or words missing here," " the property was left to her child or children." [1] In " Who came ? " and " Who can tell ? " we have the common number, but in " Who has come ? " we are obliged to use a definite number-form in the verb even if the question is meant to be quite indefinite. Note also " Nobody prevents you, do they ? " where the idea would have been expressed more clearly if it had been possible to avoid the singular in one, and the plural in the other sentence (cf. under Gender, p. 233).

Mass-Words.

In an ideal language constructed on purely logical principles a form which implied neither singular nor plural would be even more called for when we left the world of countables (such as houses, horses ; days, miles ; sounds, words, crimes, plans, mistakes, etc.) and got to the world of uncountables. There are a great many words which do not call up the idea of some definite thing with a certain shape or precise limits. I call these " mass-words " ; they may be either material, in which case they denote some substance in itself independent of form, such as *silver, quicksilver, water, butter, gas, air*, etc., or else immaterial, such as *leisure, music, traffic, success, tact, commonsense*, and especially many " nexus-substantives " (see Ch. X) like *satisfaction, admiration, refinement*, from verbs, or like *restlessness, justice, safety, constancy*, from adjectives.

While countables are " quantified " by means of such words as *one, two, many, few*, mass-words are quantified by means of such words as *much, little, less*. If *some* and *more* may be applied to both classes, a translation into other languages shows that the idea is really different : *some horse, some horses, more horses—some quicksilver, more quicksilver, more admiration :* G. *irgend ein pferd, einige pferde, mehr (mehrere) pferde* (Dan. *flere heste*)—*etwas quecksilber, mehr puecksilber, mehr bewunderung* (Dan. *mere beundring*).

---

[1] in French most substantives, as far as their sound is concerned, are really in the " common number," but adjuncts often have separate forms, hence such constructions as the following : il prendra *son ou ses personnages* à une certaine période de leur existence (Maupassant) | *le ou les caractères fondamentaux* (Bally) | le contraire *du ou des mots choisis* comme synonymes (ib.). Cf. from German : erst gegen ende des ganzen satzes *kommen der oder die tonsprünge*, die dem satze seinen ausdruck geben (LPh 241).

As there is no separate grammatical " common-number," languages must in the case of mass-words choose one of the two existing formal numbers ; either the singular, as in the examples hitherto adduced, or the plural, e.g. *victuals, dregs, lees—proceeds, belongings, sweepings—measles, rickets, throes* and such colloquial names of unpleasant states of mind as *the blues, creeps, sulks,* etc. In many cases there is some vacillation between the two numbers (*coal(s), brain(s),* and others), and where one language has a singular, another may have a plural. It is curious that while Southern English and Standard Danish looks upon *porridge* and *grød* as singulars, the same words are in Scotland and Jutland treated as plurals. Corresponding to the E. plurals *lees, dregs,* German and other languages have singular mass-words : *hefe.* With immaterial mass-words it is the same : *much knowledge* must be rendered in German *viele kenntnisse,* in Danish *mange kundskaber.*

The delimitation of mass-words offers some difficult problems, because many words have several meanings. Some things adapt themselves naturally to different points of view, as seen, for instance, in *fruit, hair* (*much fruit, many fruits :* " shee hath *more hair* then wit, and more faults then *haires*," Shakespeare) ; cf. also *a little more cake, a few more cakes.* In a Latin edictum dry vegetables and meat are given as singulars, i.e. as mass-words, while fresh ones are given in the plural, because they are counted (Wackernagel, VS 1. 88). Note also *verse* : " He writes both prose and verse." " I like his verses to Lesbia."

Other examples, in which the same word has to do duty now as a mass-word and now as a thing-word, are seen in :

a little more *cheese*	two big *cheeses*
it is hard as *iron*	a hot *iron* (flat-iron)
cork is lighter than water	I want three *corks* for these
some *earth* stuck to his shoes	bottles
	the *earth* is round
a parcel in brown *paper*	state-*papers*
little *talent*	few *talents*
much *experience*	many *experiences,* etc.

Sometimes the original signification may belong to one, sometimes to the other of these two classes. Sometimes a word is differentiated, thus *shade* and *shadow* are derived from different case-forms of the same word (OE. *sceadu, sceadowe*). As a rule, *shade* is used as a mass-word, and *shadow* as a countable, but in some connexions *shade* is just as much a thing-word as *shadow,* e.g. when we speak of different *shades* (= nuances) of colour. *Cloth* in one sense is a mass-word as denoting one particular kind of material, but as denoting one particular thing (as a table-cloth, or a covering for a horse) it is a thing-word and has developed the new plural *cloths*, while the old plural *clothes* is now separated from *cloth* and must be termed a distinct word : a mass-word with plural form.

A name of a tree, e.g. *oak*, may be made a mass-word, not only to denote the wood or timber obtained from the tree, but also to denote a mass of growing trees (cf. *barley, wheat*) : " oak and beech began to take the place of willow and elm." A corresponding usage is also found in other languages. A related case is seen in the use of *fish*, not only to denote the " flesh " of fish which we eat, but also the living animals as an object for fishing ; this is found in other languages besides English, thus in Danish (*fisk*), Russian (*ryba*, Asboth, Gramm. 68), Magyar (Simonyi US. 259). In English and Danish this has been one of the causes that have led to the use of the unchanged plural as in *many fish, mange fisk*.

Mass-words are often made into names for countables, though languages differ considerably in this respect. Thus in E., but not in Danish, *tin* is used for a receptacle made of tin (for sardines, etc.). In English, *bread* is only a mass-word, but the corresponding word in many languages is used for what in E. is called *a loaf : un peu de pain, un petit pain = a little bread, a small loaf.*

Immaterial mass-words undergo a similar change of signification when they come to stand for a single act or instance of the quality, as when we talk of *a stupidity = a stupid act, many follies* or *kind-nesses*, etc. This usage, however, is not so universal in English as in many other languages, and the best rendering of *eine unerhörte unverschämtheit* is *a piece of monstrous impudence*, cf. also *an in-sufferable piece of injustice, another piece of scandal, an act of perfidy*, etc. (examples MEG II, 5. 33 ff.). This construction is strictly analogous with *a piece of wood, two lumps of sugar*, etc.

In one more way mass-words may become thing-words, when a nexus-substantive like *beauty* comes to stand for a thing (or a person) possessing the quality indicated. And finally we must mention the use of a mass-word to denote one kind of the mass : *this tea is better than the one we had last week ;* and then naturally in the plural : *various sauces ; the best Italian wines come from Tuscany.*

Through the term " mass-word " and through the restriction of the term " collective " to a well-defined class of words, so that the two terms are consistently opposed to one another (the notion of number being logically inapplicable to mass-words, while it is doubly applicable to collectives) I hope to have contributed something towards clarifying a difficult subject. The necessity of a term like mass-word is seen in many places in dictionaries ; in the NED, for example, we often read definitions like the following : " *claptrap* (1) with pl. : A trick . . . (2) without *a* or pl. : Language designed to catch applause "—i.e. (1) as a thing-word, (2) as a mass-word. My own division seems preferable to the two best thought-out divisions I know, those of Sweet and Noreen.

According to Sweet (NEG, § 150 ff.) the chief division is into substance-nouns or concrete nouns and abstract nouns (that is, words like *redness*, *stupidity*, *conversation*). Concrete nouns are divided into

common nouns $\begin{cases} \text{class nouns} & \begin{cases} \text{individual } (man) \\ \text{collective } (crowd) \end{cases} \\ \text{material nouns } (iron) \end{cases}$

proper names (*Plato*).

Sweet does not see the essential similarity between his 'material nouns' and 'abstract nouns'; nor is his name 'material nouns' a fortunate one, because many names of immaterial phenomena present the same characteristics as *iron* or *glass*. Neither can I see the value of the distinction he makes between singular class-nouns (like *sun* in popular as contrasted with scientific language) and plural nouns (like *tree*): both represent 'countables,' even if there is more occasion in one case than in the other to use the word in the plural.

Noreen's division is very original (VS 5. 292 ff.), viz.—apart from "abstracts" (= words like *beauty*, *wisdom*, etc.)

I. Impartitiva, which denote objects that are not considered as capable of being divided into several homogeneous parts. Such are "individua" like *I*, *Stockholm*, *the Trossachs*, and "dividua" like *parson*, *man*, *tree*, *trousers*, *measles*. Even *horses* in the sentence "horses are quadrupeds" is an impartitive, because it means the indivisible genus horse (the sentence is synonymous with "a horse is a quadruped," p. 300).

II. Partitiva. These fall into two classes:

A. Materialia or substance-names, as in "*iron* is expensive now," "he eats *fish*," "this is made of *wood*."

B. Collectives. These are subdivided into:
(1) Totality-collectives, such as *brotherhood*, *nobility*, *army*, and (2) Plurality-collectives; here such examples are given as *many a parson*, *many parsons*, *every parson*, further ordinary plurals like *fires*, *wines*, *waves*, *cows*, etc. Plurality-collectives are further subdivided into (a) homogeneous like *horses*, etc., and (b) heterogeneous like *we*, *parents* (the corresponding sg. is *father* or *mother*). This last group nearly, though not completely, corresponds to what I call the plural of approximation: it is accidental that Swedish has no singular corresponding to *föräldrar* 'parents' and that Noreen therefore gives *father* or *mother* as the singular: other languages have a singular *a parent* (thus also colloquial Danish *en forælder*), and the case is therefore not to be compared with *We* : *I*, the less so as there is a natural plural *fathers*, as in "the fathers of the boys were invited to the school," while a normal plural of "I" is unthinkable. On the whole Noreen's system seems to me highly artificial and of very little value to a linguist, because it divorces things which naturally belong together and creates such useless classes as that of the impartitives, besides giving too wide an application to the term "collective." Our first question is surely what notions admit of having words like one and two applied to them, and not what notions or things admit of being divided into homogeneous parts; the whole notion of number, though so important in everyday life, in Noreen's system is put away, as it were, in a corner of a lumber-room. Accordingly, on p. 298, he starts from the plural, and though he is, of course, right in his shrewd remark that the proper singular of *we* is *one of us*, he does not go on to say that in the same sense the proper sg. of *the horses* is not *the horse*, but *one of the horses*, and that the pl. of *one of us* (*one of the horses*) is not always *we* (*the horses*), but *some of us* (*some of the horses*).

CHAPTER XV

NUMBER—*concluded*

Various Anomalies. The Generic Singular and Plural. Dual. Number in Secondary Words. Plural of the Verbal Idea.

Various Anomalies.

IN all languages there are words which serve the purpose of singling out the individual members of a plurality and thus in the form of a singular expressing what is common to all : *every, each.* There is only a shade of difference between " everybody was glad " and " all were glad " (cf. the neuter " everything " and *all* in " all is well that ends well " = all things). Note also Lat. *uterque vir, utraque lingua, utrumque* ' each (either) of the two men, both men, both languages, both things.' A closely related case is that seen in *many a man*, which individualizes, where *many men* generalizes ; thus also in many other languages : *manch ein mann, mangen en mand, mucha palabra loca* (Hanssen, Sp. gr. § 56. 6), Fr. obsolete *maint homme.*

Here and there we find anomalies in the use of number-forms which are difficult to explain, but which at any rate show that people are not absolutely rational beings, thus in OE. the use of the singular with the tens, as in Beowulf 3042 se wæs *fiftiges fotgemearces* lang ' it was 50 feet long,' ib. 379 *pritiges manna* mægencræft ' the strength of 30 men,' thus with some inconsistency, as *fotgemearces* is sg. and *manna* is pl.—In Middle English we find the singular *a* before a numeral, *a forty men*, meaning ' about forty,' thus very frequently in Dan. *en tyve stykker* ' about twenty (pieces),' and this may be compared with E. *a few* (in Jutland dialects *œn lile fo*) ; the sg. article here turns the plural words from a quasi-negative quantity (he has few friends) into a positive (he has a few friends). But *a few* may have been induced by *a many*, where *many* may be the collective substantive and not the adjective—the forms of these, which were at first separated, have been confounded together. Fr. *vers les une heures* (as well as *vers les midi*) with its numerical incongruity is evidently due to the analogy of other indications of time such as *vers les deux heures* ; it is as if *vers-les* had become one amalgamated preposition with denominations of the hour. The G. interrogative pronoun *wer*, like E. *who*, above 198, is independent of number,

but when one wants expressly to indicate that the question refers
to more than one person this may be achieved through the addition
of *alles*, in the singular neuter ! " Wer kommt denn alles ? " (' Who
are coming ? '—" Wer kommt ? " ' Who is coming ? ') " Wen hast
du alles gesehen ? "—implying that he has seen several people.
Cf. what is said below under Sex on *beides* and *mehreres* as neuters
to the personal *beide, mehrere* (p. 237).

The Generic Singular and Plural.

We shall here deal with the linguistic expressions for a whole
species, in cases in which words like *all* (all cats),[1] *every* (every cat)
or *any* (any cat) are not used. For this notion Bréal (M 394) coins
the word " omnial " parallel to " dual, plural," and this would be a
legitimate grammatical term in a language that possessed a separate
form for that ' number.' But I do not know of any language that
has such a form ; as a matter of fact, in order to express this notion
of a whole class or species, languages sometimes use the singular
and sometimes the plural ; sometimes they have no article, sometimes the definite article, and sometimes the indefinite article.
As there is in English no indefinite article in the plural, this gives
five combinations, which are all of them represented, as seen in
the following examples :

(1) The singular without any article. In English this is found
only with *man* and *woman* (man is mortal | woman is best when she
is at rest)—and with mass-words,[2] whether material or immaterial
(blood is thicker than water | history is often stranger than fiction).
In G. and Dan. it is used only with material mass-words, in Fr. not
even with these.[3]

(2) The singular with the indefinite article : *a cat* is not as
vigilant as *a dog* ; the article may be considered as a weaker
any, or rather, one (" a ") dog is taken as representative of the
whole class.

---

[1] " All cats have four feet " = " any cat has four feet "—but this
' generic ' use of *all* should be kept distinct from the ' distributive ' *all* :
" all his brothers are millionaires " is different from " all his brothers together possess a million." In the distributive sense ' all cats ' have (together)
an enormous number of feet. Logicians give as example of the difference :
" All the angles of a triangle are less than two right angles," " All the angles
of a triangle are equal to two right angles " ; see also MEG II, 5. 4.
[2] With mass-words the ' generic ' idea refers to quantity, not to number
proper : " lead is heavy," i.e. ' all lead,' ' lead, wherever found.'
[3] Sweet (NEG § 1) writes : " From the theoretical point of view grammar
is the science of *language*. By ' language ' we understand *languages* in
general, as opposed to one or more special languages." It is interesting
to contrast this with the way in which a Frenchman expresses the same
two notions, using not only two numbers, but two words : " *Le langage et les
langues* " (e.g. Vendryes L 273).

(3) The singular with the definite article : *the dog* is vigilant. Thus also with a (neuter) adjective in philosophic parlance : *the beautiful* = 'everything that is beautiful.' Chaucer said "*The lyf* so short, *the craft* so long to lerne," where modern English has no article (Longfellow : *Art* is long, but *life* is fleeting) ; Chaucer here agrees with Greek (Hippokrates " Ho bios brakhus, hē de tekhnē makrē "), French, Danish and German usage (Wagner in Goethe's *Faust* says : " Ach gott ! die kunst ist lang ; Und kurz ist unser leben ").

(4) The plural without any article : *dogs* are vigilant | *old people* are apt to catch cold | I like *oysters*.

(5) The plural with the definite article : Blessed are *the poor* in spirit. This usage, which in English is found with adjectives only (*the old* are apt to catch cold = *old people*, above nr. 4, *the English* = the whole English nation), is the regular expression in some languages, e.g. Fr. *les vieillards* sont bavards | j'aime *les huîtres*.

One and the same generic truth is differently expressed in the G. proverb " *Ein unglück* kommt nie allein " and E. " *Misfortunes* never come singly " (cf. Shakespeare : " When sorrows come, they come not single spies, But in battalions ").—Compare also *twice a week* with *deux fois la semaine*.

With these " generic " expressions we may class the expressions for the " indefinite " or better the " generic person " :

(1) The singular without any article. Thus in G. and Dan. *man*, differentiated from the sb. *mann, mand*, in G. through loss of stress only, in Dan. also through want of " stød " (glottal stop) ; in ME we have not only *man*, but also *men* (*me*), which is often used with the verb in the singular and thus may be a phonetically weakened form of *man*. Further we have Fr. *on*, a regular development of the Lat. nominative *homo*.

(2) The singular with the indefinite article. This is frequent in colloquial English with various substantives : " What is *a man* (*a fellow, a person, an individual, a girl*, Sc. *a body*) to do in such a situation ? " It is really the same idea that lies behind the frequent use in many languages of the word *one*, as in English, G. *ein* (especially in the oblique cases), Dan. *en* (in standard language chiefly when it is not the subject, but in dialects also as the subject), It. sometimes *uno* (Serao, Cap. Sansone 135 uno si commuove quando si toccano certe tasti ; ib. 136).

(3) The singular with the definite article. French *l'on*, which is now apprehended as a phonetic variant of the simple *on*.

(4) The plural without any article. *Fellows* and *people* are often used in such a way that they may be rendered by Fr. *on* (*fellows say, people say* = *on dit*), cf. also the ME. *men* when followed

by a plural verb. When *they* (Dan. *de*) is used in the same sense, it may be compared with the generic usage mentioned above of the plural of a substantive with the definite article.—On the use of *you* and *we* for the generic person see Ch. XVI.

The difference between this " indefinite person " and the generic use of *man* (in " man is mortal ") is not easy to define, and seems often to be emotional rather than intellectual. Hence also the frequent use of *man, one, si* as a disguised " I " when one wishes to avoid mentioning oneself, and therefore generalizes what one wants to say : a similar motive leads to the use of *you* in the same sense. But it is worth mentioning as something connected with the " generic " character of the " indefinite person " that *man* or *on* is not unfrequently followed by a plural word. Dan. " man blev *enige* " | Fr. " la femme qui vient de vous jouer un mauvais tour mais voudrait qu'on reste *amis* quand même " (Daudet, L'Immortel 151).[1] Thus also in It. with *si* : Serao, l.c. 223 si resta *liberi* per tre mesi | Rovetta, Moglie S. Ecc. 49 Si diventa ministri, ma si nasce *poeti, pittori* !

Dual.

In languages possessing a dual, two different conceptions are found. One is represented in Greenlandic, where *nuna* ' land ' forms its dual *nunak* and its plural *nunat* ; here " the dual is chiefly used when the speaker wants expressly to point out that the question is about a duality ; if, on the other hand, the duality is obvious as a matter of course, as in the case of those parts of the body which are found in pairs, the plural form is nearly always employed. Thus it is customary to say *issai*, his eyes, *siutai* his ears, *talê* his arms, etc., not *issik, siutik, tatdlik*, his two eyes, etc. Even with the numeral *mardluk* (two), which is in itself a dual, the plural is often used, e.g. *inuit mardluk* two men " (Kleinschmidt, *Gramm. d. grönländ. spr.* 13).

The other conception, according to which the dual is preferably used in names of objects naturally found in pairs, as in Gr. *osse* ' the eyes,' is represented in Aryan. In many of the older languages of this family duals were found ; they tended to disappear as time went on, and now survive only in a few isolated dialects (Lithuanian, Sorb, Slovene ; a few Bavarian dialects in the personal pronouns). The gradual disappearance of dual forms in the Aryan languages [2] presents many interesting features which cannot be here detailed.

---

[1] Norwegian, quoted Western R 451 : En blir lei *hverandre*, naar en gaar to *mennesker* og ser ikke andre dag ut og dag ind.

[2] See Cuny, *Le nombre duel en grec*, Paris, 1906 ; Brugmann VG II, 2 449 ff. ; Meillet Gr 189. 226. 303; Wackernagel VS I, 73 ff. A most interesting article by Gauthiot in *Festschrift Vilh. Thomsen*, p. 127 ff., compares the Aryan and Ugro-Finnic duals.

The existence of a dual is generally (Lévy-Bruhl, Meillet) looked upon as a mark of primitive mentality; its disappearance is therefore considered as a consequence or accompaniment of progress in civilization. (In my own view of linguistic development any simplification, any discarding of old superfluous distinctions is progressive, though a causal nexus between civilization in general and particular grammatical phenomena cannot be demonstrated in detail.)

The Greek dual was lost at an early period in the colonies, where the civilization was relatively advanced, while it was kept more tenaciously in continental Greece, e.g. in Lacedæmon, Bœotia, and Attica. In Homer duals are frequent, but they appear to be an artificial archaism used for poetical purposes, especially for the sake of the metre, while the plural is often used in speaking of two even in the same breath as the dual (cp. collocations like *amphō kheiras*, Od. 8. 135). In Gothic dual forms are found only in the pronouns of the first and second persons and in the corresponding forms of verbs, but these latter are few in number ; and in the other old Gothonic languages only the pronouns ' we ' and ' ye ' keep the old distinction, which was later generally given up. (Inversely the duals *við*, *þið* have ousted the old plurals *vér*, *þér*, in modern Icelandic, and possibly also in Dan. *vi*, *I*.) Isolated traces of the old dual have been found in the forms of a few substantives, such as *door* (originally the two leaves) and *breast*, but even in these cases from the oldest times the forms were understood not as duals, but as singulars. The only words which may now be said to be in the dual are *two* and *both*, but it should be noted that the latter when used as a "conjunction" is often applied to more than two, as in "both London, Paris, and Amsterdam "; though this is found in many good writers, some grammarians object to it.[1]

According to Gauthiot, the dual forms Sanskrit *akṣī*, Gr. *osse*, Lithuanian *akì* do not properly mean ' the two eyes,' not even ' the eye and the other eye,' but ' the eye in so far as it is double,' thus *mitrā* is ' Mitra, in so far as he is double,' i.e. Mitra and Varuna, for Varuna is the double of Mitra. Similarly we have Sanskr. *áhanī* ' the day and (the night),' *pitárāu* ' the father and (the mother),' *mātárāu* ' the mother and (the father),' and then also *pitárāu matárāu* ' father and mother ' (both in the dual), and, somewhat differently, Gr. *Aiante Teukron te* ' Aias (dual) and Teukros.' Ugro-Finnic has parallels to most of these constructions, thus both words are put in the plural in combinations like

---

[1] Another extension of the dual is seen when the substantive is put in the dual with a number like 52, as in Odyssey 8. 35 *kourō de duō kai pentēkonta* (also ib. 48, attraction).

imeŋen igeŋen 'the old man and the old woman,' *teteŋen tuŋgen* 'winter and summer.'

In some cases the lost dual left some traces behind it, the true character of which has been forgotten. Thus in Old Norse, the pronoun *þau* 'they two' is an old dual form, but as it happens to be also the neuter plural, it leads to the syntactic rule that the neuter plural is used when persons of the two sexes are spoken of together.

In Russian the old dual in some words happened to have the same form as the genitive singular ; cases like *dva mužika* 'two peasants' then led to the use of the gen. sg. in other words, and, curiously enough, after the notion of a dual had been entirely forgotten, even after the words for 3 and 4, *tri, četyre* : *četyre goda* 'four years,' etc.

Number in Secondary Words.

When Sweet (NEG, § 269) says that the only grammatical category that verbs have in common with nouns is that of number, he is right so far as actual (English) grammar is concerned ; but it should be remembered that the plural does not mean the same thing in verbs as in substantives. In the latter it means plurality of that which is denoted by the word itself, while in the verb the number refers not to the action or state denoted by the verb, but to the subject : compare *(two) sticks* or *(two) walks* with *(they) walk*, which is in the plural, but implies not more walks than one, but more walkers than one. In the same way, when in Latin and other languages adjunct adjectives are put in the plural, as in *urbes magnæ*, G. *grosse städte*, this does not indicate any plurality of the adjectival idea, the plurality referring to ' towns ' and to nothing else. In both cases we have the purely grammatical phenomenon termed " concord " which has nothing to do with logic, but pervaded all the older stages of languages of the Aryan family ; it affected not only the number forms, but also the case forms of adjectival words, which were " made to agree " with the primaries they belonged to. But this rule of concord is really superfluous (cf. *Language*, 335 ff.), and as the notion of plurality belongs logically to the primary word alone, it is no wonder that many languages more or less consistently have given up the indication of number in secondary words.

In the adjectives, Danish, like German, still keeps up the distinction between *en stor mand* (*ein grosser mann*) and *store mænd* (*grosse männer*), while English is here more progressive and makes no distinction between the singular and the plural in adjectives (*a great man, great men*), the only survivals of the old rule of concord being *that man, those men, this man, these men*.—In an ideal language neither adjuncts nor verbs would have any separate plural forms.[1]

In Magyar there is the inverse rule that number is indicated in a secondary and not in a primary word, but only when a substantive is accompanied by a numeral. It is, then, put in the singular, as if we were to say " three house." This is termed " illogical " by the eminent native linguist Simonyi : I should rather call it an instance of wise economy, as in this case any express indication of the plurality of the substantive would be superfluous. The same rule is found in other languages ; in Finnic with the curious addition that in the subject not the nominative singular, but the partitive singular is used ; in the other cases there is agreement between the numeral and the substantive. There is some approximation to the same rule in Danish (*tyve mand stærk, fem daler* ' five dollars,' the value, different from *fem dalere* ' five dollar pieces,' *to fod*), in German (*zwei fuss, drei mark*, 400 *mann*), and even in English (*five dozen, three score, five foot nine, five stone* ; details in MEG II, 57 ff.).

The first part of a compound substantive is in many respects like an adjunct of the second. It is well known that in the ancient type of Aryan compounds the stem itself is used, thus number is not shown : Gr. *hippo-damos* may be one who curbs one horse, or several horses. In E. the singular form is usually employed, even when the idea is manifestly plural ; as in *the printed book section | a three-volume novel.* But in many, chiefly recent, formations the plural is found in the first part : *a savings-bank | the Contagious Diseases Act.* In Danish there is a curious instance of both parts being inflected : *bondegård*, pl. *bøndergårde* ' peasants' farms ' ; generally the singular form of the first part is kept in the plural : *tandlæger*, etc.

In verbs, English has discarded the distinction between singular and plural in all preterits (*gave, ended, drank*, etc., with the sole exception of *was, were*) and in some present tenses as well (*can, shall, must* and others, which were originally preterits) ; where it has been preserved, it is only in the third person (*he comes, they come*), while in the first and second persons no difference is now made (*I come, we come, you come*). In Danish the numerical distinction has been totally given up in verbs, where the old singular form has become a " common number " ; it is always so in spoken Danish, and now nearly always so in the literary language.

There seems to be a strong tendency everywhere to use the singular form of the verb instead of the plural (rather than inversely)

---

[1] Esperanto has the same form in verbs irrespective of the number of the subject (*mi amas, ni amas*), but in adjectives separate forms (*la bona amiko, la bonai amikoj*, while inconsistently the article is invariable). Ido, on the contrary, is strictly logical (*la bona amiki*).

when the verb precedes the subject ; the reason may often be that at the moment of his uttering the verb the speaker has not made up his mind what words are to follow. From OE I may quote " Eac wæs gesewen on ðæm wage atifred ealle da heargas," from Shakespeare " that spirit upon whose weal depends and rests The lives of many." This is particularly frequent with *there is* (Thackeray : there's some things I can't resist). It is the same in other languages. In literary Danish it was the rule to have *der er* with a plural subject at the time when *ere* was the form otherwise always required when the subject was in the plural. Similarly very often in Italian (" in teatro c'era quattro o sei persone "). The same tendency to use the singular when the verb precedes is seen in the same language when *Evviva* is used with a plural subject (Rovetta : Evviva le bionde al potere !)

Those languages which have kept the old rule of concord in secondary words are very often thereby involved in difficulties, and grammars have to give more or less intricate rules which are not always observed in ordinary life—even by the " best writers." A few English quotations (taken from MEG II, Ch. VI) will show the nature of such difficulties with verbs : not one in ten of them write it so badly | ten is one and nine | none are wretched but by their own fault | none has more keenly felt them | neither of your heads are safe | much care and patience were needed | if the death of neither man nor gnat are designed | father and mother is man and wife ; man and wife is one flesh | his hair as well as his eyebrows was now white | the fine lady, or fine gentleman, who show me their teeth | one or two of his things are still worth your reading | his meat was locusts and wild honey | fools are my theme | both death and I am found eternal. All these sentences are taken from well-known writers, the last, for instance, from Milton. Corresponding difficulties are experienced in adjectival forms in those languages which make their adjuncts agree in number (gender and case) with primary words, and a simple comparison of Fr. *ma femme et mes enfants* or *la presse locale et les comités locaux* with E. *my wife and children, the local press and committees* shows the advantage to a language of throwing overboard such superfluous distinctions in secondary words.[1]

[1] Where the subject idea, as is often the case in Aryan languages, is not expressed except in the form of the verb, the indication in the latter of the plural is, of course, not so superfluous as it is where subject and verb are kept apart, thus in Lat. *amamus Læliam, amant Læliam* ' we (they) love L.' A special case is seen in It. *furono soli con la ragazza* ' he was alone with the girl ' (= egli e la ragazza furono soli, egli fu solo con la ragazza) ; examples from Fr., G., Slav, Albanian, etc., see Meyer-Lübke, Einführ. 88, Delbrück, Synt. 3. 255. We have a corresponding use of the plural in the predicative in " Come, Joseph, be friends with Miss Sharp," Dan. " ham er jeg gode venner med."

Plural of the Verbal Idea.

The idea of " one or more than one " is not incompatible with
the idea expressed by the verb itself.   I am not thinking here of
what R. M. Meyer (IF 24. 279 ff.) terms " verba pluralia tantum,"
for he speaks of such verbs as G. *wimmeln, sich anhäufen, sich
zusammenrotten, umzingeln* (English examples would be *swarm,
teem, crowd, assemble, conspire*), where the necessary plural idea is
not in the verb as such, but in the subject,[1] but I am thinking of
those cases in which it is really the verbal idea itself that is made
plural.   What that means is easily seen if we look first at the
corresponding verbal substantives nexus-substantives (see Ch. X).
If the plural of *one walk* or *one action* is (several) *walks, actions*, the
plural idea of the verb must be ' to undertake several walks, to
perform more than one action.'   But in English and in most
languages there is no separate form of the verb to indicate this ;
when I say *he walks* (*shoots*), *they walk* (*shoot*), it is impossible to
tell whether one or more than one walk (shot) is meant.   If
we say " they often kissed " we see that the adverb expresses
exactly the same plural idea as the plural form (and the adjective)
in (*many*) *kisses*.   In other words, the real plural of the verb is
what in some languages is expressed by the so-called frequentative
or iterative—sometimes a separate " form " of the verb which is
often classed with the tense [2] or aspect system of the language in
question, as when repetition (as well as duration, etc.) is in Semitic
languages expressed by a strengthening (doubling, lengthening)
of the middle consonant, or in Chamorro by a reduplication of the
stressed syllable of the verbal root (K. Wulff, Festschrift Vilh.
Thomsen 49).   Sometimes a separate verb is formed to express
repeated or habitual action, thus in some cases in Latin by means
of the ending *-ito* : *cantito, ventito* ' sing frequently, come often ' ;
visito is from a formal point of view a double frequentative, as
it is formed from *viso*, which is in itself a frequentative of *video*,
but the plural idea tends to disappear, and Fr. *visiter*, E. *visit*
may be used of a single coming.   In Slav this category of plural or
frequentative verbs is well developed, e.g. Russ. *strělivat'* ' to fire
several shots,' from *strěljat'* ' to fire one shot.'   In English several
verbs in *-er, -le* imply repeated or habitual action : *stutter, patter,
chatter, cackle, babble*.   Otherwise repeated action must be rendered
in various other ways : he talked and talked | he used to talk
of his mother | he was in the habit of talking | he would talk of

---

[1] *Quarrel* is another case in point, for it takes at least two to make a
quarrel, and if we find in the singular, e.g. " I quarrel with him," this is to
be classed with the instances mentioned, pp. 90, 192, 209 n.

[2] See on the imperfect, p. 277.

his mother for hours | he talked of his mother over and over again, etc.

Having mentioned the plural of such verbal substantives as *walk shot, kiss*, we may remind the reader of the other kind of "nexus substantives," those containing a predicative, such as *stupidity, kindness, folly*. These also may be put in the plural, though, as remarked above, they are then changed from mass-words into countables (as they are indeed when the singular is used with the indefinite article : *a stupidity* = 'a stupid act, an instance of being stupid').

Adverbs, of course, have no distinct number, the only exceptions being such adverbs as *twice, thrice, often*, which may be said to be plurals of *once* because logically these adverbs are equivalent to ' two times, three times, many times ' ; the plural idea thus refers to the substantival idea contained in the subjunct, just as in group subjuncts like " at two (three, many) places." Similarly the groups *now and then, here and there* may be said to contain a plural idea, as they signify the same thing as ' at various times, at various places,' but this, of course, does not affect the truth of the general assertion that the notion of number is inapplicable to adverbs.

APPENDIX TO THE CHAPTERS ON NUMBER.

To indicate place in a series most (all ?) languages have words derived from (cardinal) numerals ; these are called ordinals. Very often the first ordinals are not formed from the corresponding cardinals in the usual way : *primus, first, erst* bear no relation to *unus, one, ein*, but from the beginning denote foremost in point of place or time. Lat. *secundus* originally means ' following ' and leaves it to the imagination to infer how many precede ; frequently we have a word for 2nd which at the same time has the vague meaning ' different,' thus OE *oðer* (preserved in the indefinite sense in MnE *other*, while the cardinal has been taken from French), G. *ander*, Dan. *anden*. In French there is a new regular formation from *deux : deuxième* (at first probably used in combinations like *vingt-deuxième*, cf. *vingt-et-unième*).

In many cases cardinals are used where a stricter logic would require ordinals ; this is due to considerations of convenience, especially where high numbers are concerned, thus in 1922 = the 1922nd year after Christ's birth (Russian here uses the ordinal) ; further in reading such indications as " line 725," " page 32," " Chapter XVIII," etc., in French also in " Louis XIV," " le 14 septembre," etc.

After the word for " number " (numero, etc.) this use of the cardinal instead of the ordinal is universal : " number seven " means the seventh of a series. Cf. also the indication of the " hour " : *at two o'clock, at three-fifty.*

Note the use of the ordinal in G. *drittehalb*, Dan. *halvtredie* ' twe and a half ' (the third is only half), and the somewhat different usage in Scotch *at half three*, Dan. *klokken halv tre*, G. *um halb drei uhr* ' at half-past two.'

In many languages ordinals (with or without the word for ' part ' added) have to do duty to express fractions : *five-sevenths, cinq septièmes, fünf siebentel, fem syvendedel*, etc. For 1/2, however, there is a separate word *half, demi*, etc.

CHAPTER XVI

PERSON

Definitions. Common and Generic Person. Notional and Grammatical
   Person. Indirect Speech. Fourth Person. Reflexive and Reciprocal
   Pronouns.

Definitions.

In the NED " person " as used in grammar is defined as follows :
" Each of the three classes of personal pronouns, and corresponding
distinctions in verbs, denoting or indicating respectively the person
speaking (*first person*), the person spoken to (*second person*), and
the person or thing spoken of (*third person*)." But though the
same definition is found in other good dictionaries and in most
grammars, it is evidently wrong, for when I say " I am ill " or
" you must go " it is undoubtedly " I " and " you " that are
spoken of ; the real contrast thus is between (1) the speaker,
(2) spoken to, and (3) neither speaker nor spoken to. In the first
person one speaks of oneself, in the second of the person to whom
the speech is addressed, and in the third of neither.

Further, it is important to remember that in this use the word
" person " qualified with one of the first three ordinals means
something quite different from the ordinary signification of
" person " and does not imply " personality " as a human or rational
being ; " the horse runs " and " the sun shines " are in the third
person ; and if in a fable we make the horse say " I run " or the
sun say " I shine," both sentences are in the first person. This
use of the word " person," which goes back to Latin grammarians
and through them to Greek (prosōpon) is one of the many incon-
veniences of traditional grammatical terminology which are too
firmly rooted to be now abolished, however strange it may be to
an unsophisticated mind to be taught that " impersonal verbs "
are always put in the " third person " : *pluit, it rains.* Some people
have objected to the inclusion of a pronoun like *it* among " personal pronouns," but the inclusion is justified if we take the expression " personal pronoun " to mean pronoun indicating person in
the sense here mentioned. But when we come to speak of the
distinction between the two interrogative pronouns *who* and *what*,
and find that the former refers to persons and the latter to anything

that is not a person, we might feel inclined to call *who* a personal pronoun,—which would be decidedly awkward.

It is a simple consequence of the definition that the first person, strictly speaking, is found in the singular only ; [1] in a preceding chapter (p. 192) mention has already been made of the fact that the so-called first person plural " we " is really " I + someone else or some others," and in some works dealing with Amerindian languages the figures ½ and ⅓ are conveniently used to designate " we " according as the others that are added to " I " are of the second or third persons respectively.

For the curiosity of the matter I may quote here a sentence to illustrate the emotional value of the three persons. " With Ruskin the people are always ' You ' ; with Carlyle they are even farther away, they are ' they ' ; but with Morris the people are always ' We ' " (*William Morris*, by Bruce Glacier).

In many languages the distinction between the three persons is found not only in pronouns, but in verbs as well, thus in Latin (*amo, amas, amat*), Italian, Hebrew, Finnish, etc. In such languages many sentences have no explicit indication of the subject, and *ego amo, tu amas* is at first said only when it is necessary or desirable to lay special stress on the idea " I, thou." In course of time, however, it became more and more usual to add the pronoun even when no special emphasis was intended, and this paved the way for the gradual obscuration of the sound of the personal endings in the verbs, as these became more and more superfluous for the right understanding of the sentences. Thus in Fr. *j'aime, tu aimes, il aime, je veux, tu veux, il veut, je vis, tu vis, il vit* are identical in sound. In English we have the same form in *I can, you can, he can, I saw, you saw, he saw,* and even in the plural *we can, you can, they can, we saw, you saw, they saw*—phonetic and analogical levellings have gone hand in hand to wipe out old personal distinctions. These, however, have not disappeared entirely, survivals being found in Fr. *j'ai, tu as, il a, nous avons, vous avez, ils ont,* and in E. *I go, he goes,* and generally in the third person singular of the present tense. In modern Danish all these distinctions have disappeared : *jeg ser, du ser, han ser, vi ser, I ser, de ser,* and so in all verbs and all tenses, exactly as in Chinese and some other languages. This must be considered the ideal or logical state of language, as the distinction rightly belongs to the primary idea only and need not be repeated in secondary words.

---

[1] When " I " (or " Me " or " ego ") is made into a substantive (chiefly in philosophic parlance), it is necessarily of the third person, hence is capable of being used in the plural : " several I's " or " Me's," " Egos." There is, accordingly, something incongruous in the use of the verbal forms in the following sentence : " The I who see am as manifold as what I see " (J. L. Lowes, *Convention and Revolt in Poetry*, 6).

In English a distinction has developed in the auxiliary verbs used to express futurity : *I shall go, you will go, he will go*, and correspondingly to express conditional unreality : *I should go, you would go, he would go.*

Any imperative (and we might add, any vocative) is virtually in the second person, even in such cases as " Oh, please, someone go in and tell her " or " Go one and cal the Iew into the court " (Sh.), as seen clearly, for instance, by the addition in " And bring out my hat, somebody, *will you* " (Dickens). In English the form of the verb does not show which person is used, but other languages have a third person of the imperative, in which case we must say that there is a conflict between the grammatical third person and the notional second person. Sometimes, however, the latter prevails, even in form, as when in Greek we find " sigan nun hapas *ekhe* sigan " where *ekhe* (2nd p.) according to Wackernagel (VS 106) stands instead of *ekhetō* (3rd p.) : ' everyone now hold silence.' Where we have a first person plural in the imperative, as in It. *diamo*, Fr. *donnons*, the virtual meaning is ' you give, and I will give, too,' and so the imperative here as always refers to the second person. In English the old *give we* has been supplanted by *let us give* (as in Danish and, to some extent, also in German) ; here *let*, of course, is, grammatically as well as notionally, in the second person, and the first person pl. is only shown in the dependent nexus *us give.*

The local adverb corresponding to the first person is *here*, and where we have two adverbs for ' not-here,' as in northern English dialects *there* and *yonder* (*yon, yond*), we might say that *there* corresponds to the second, and *yonder* to the third person ; [1] but very often there is only one adverb for both ideas, as in Standard English *there* (*yonder* being obsolete). The connexion between the first person and ' here ' is seen in Italian, where the adverb *ci* ' here ' is used very extensively as a pronoun of the first person plural in the oblique cases instead of *ni* ' us.' In German we have the two adverbs of movement, *hin* for a movement towards, and *her* for a movement away from, the speaker.

In his pamphlet *Les Langues Ouralo-Altaïques* (Bruxelles, 1893), W. Bang thinks it incontestable that the human mind before having the conception of " I " and " thou " had that of " here " and " there." He therefore sets up two classes of pronominal elements, one for *here, I, now*, elements beginning with *m-, n-*, and another for *not-I, there*, elements beginning with *t-, d-, s-, n-* ; this again falls into two sub-classes :

" (*a*) la personne la plus rapprochée, là, toi, naguère, tout à l'heure,

[1] Cf. also the three demonstratives in Latin *hic* (1), *iste* (2), *ille* (3).

(*b*) la personne la plus éloignée, là-bas, lui, autrefois, plus
    tard."

I mention this as an interesting view, though in this volume
I generally keep aloof from speculations about primitive grammar
and the origin of grammatical elements.

Common and Generic Person.

We have seen above (p. 198) that it is, or would be, convenient
in some cases to have a form for a " common number " ; in the
same way the want of a " common person " is also sometimes felt.
As already remarked, *we* is really a case in point, as it stands for
" I and you " or " I and someone else," and the plural *you*, *ye*
also often stands for " thou and someone else " and thus combines
the second and third persons. But this does not cover the instances in which the two persons are not joined by means of *and*,
but separated, for instance, by a disjunctive conjunction. Here
we have considerable difficulties in those languages which distinguish
persons in their verbs : " either you or I *are* (or *am* or *is* ?) wrong " ;
see the examples given in *Language*, p. 335 f. Note also the use of
our in " Clive and I went *each to our habitation* " (Thackeray,
Newc. 297), where it would also be possible to say : " . . . each to
his home," and where Danish certainly would use its reflexive
pronoun of the third person : " C. og jeg gik hver til *sit* hjem "
(cp. " vi tog hver *sin* hat "), but a common-person form would be
more logical.

A curious case in which a common-person form would have
solved the difficulty is mentioned by Wackernagel (VS 107):
Uter meruistis culpam (Plautus) ' which of you two has deserved
blame ? '—*uter* would require the third person singular, but the
verb is put in the second person plural because two men are
addressed.

As a " common person " in a still wider sense may be considered
what I should like to call the " generic person " as in Fr. *on*. In
the chapter on number (p. 204) I have already considered the
use in this sense of the generic singular and plural with or without
the article in various languages, and in the chapter on the relation
between subject and object I have spoken of the development of
It. *si* and its construction (p. 161) ; this is the place to point out
that for this notional " all-persons " or " no-person " each of the
three grammatical persons is, as a matter of fact, found in actual
language :

(1) as *we* know = comme on sait,
(2) *you* never can tell = on ne saurait le dire,

(3) *one* would think he was mad = on dirait qu'il est fou,
   what is *a fellow* to think = qu'est-ce qu'on doit penser ?
   (. . . il faut . . .)
   they say (*people* say) that he is mad = on dit qu'il est fou.

The choice between these several expressions depends on a more or less emotional element : sometimes one wants to emphasize the fact that one is included oneself in the general assertion, sometimes one wants to make a kind of special appeal to the person addressed at the moment,[1] and sometimes one wants to keep one's own person in the background, though what is meant is really the first person more than anything else (*one*, *a fellow*). But the name "*generic person*" covers the notion underlying all these uses of various grammatical persons.

It is interesting to notice that in some languages the pronoun for 'we' is disappearing and is being replaced by the generic expression ('one'). Thus in French "Je suis prêt, est-ce qu'*on part* ?" for . . . *nous partons* (Bally, LV 59); from Benjamin, *Gaspard*, I quote "*Nous, on va s'batte, nous on va s'tuer*" (with strong emphasis of contrast on *nous*, p. 13), and "Moi, j'attends le ballet, et c'est *nous qu'on dansera* avec les petites Allemandes" and it is we who will dance, p. 18). In Italian this is quite common : Verga Eros 27 la piazzetta dove *noi si giocava* a volano | Fogazzaro Dan. Cortis 31 *noi si potrebbe* anche partire da un momento all' altro | id. Santo 139 la signora Dessalle e io *si va* stamani a visitare i Conventi | 216 *Noi si sa* che lui non vole andare.[2] The frequency of this phenomenon in Italian seems to show that the reason for it cannot be that suggested by Bally, l.c., that in the first person plural *nous chantons* the verb has preserved a special ending which is useless and does not harmonize with those of *je chante, tu chantes, il chante, ils chantent*, which have become alike in pronunciation (but then what about *vous chantez* ?). But Bally is probably right when he says that while the forms *moi je chante, toi tu chantes, lui il chante, eux ils chantent* are perfectly natural, the combination with emphatic first person pl. *nous nous chantons* is obscure and

[1] In Jack London's *Martin Eden*, p. 65, I find the following conversation which well illustrates the colloquial import of the generic *you*. Miss Ruth asks Martin : "By the way, Mr. Eden, what is *booze* ? You used it several times, you know." "Oh, booze," he laughed. "It's slang. It means whisky and beer—anything that will make you drunk." This makes her say : "Don't use *you* when you are impersonal. *You* is very personal, and your use of it just now was not precisely what you meant." "I don't just see that." "Why, you said just now to me, 'whisky and beer'— anything that will make you drunk'—make *me* drunk, don't you see ? " "Well, it would, wouldn't it ? " "Yes, of course," she smiled, "but it would be nicer not to bring me into it. Substitute *one* for *you*, and see how much better it sounds."

[2] Other examples Nyrop, *Ital. Grammatik*, 1919, p. 66.

inharmonious, and that therefore the form *nous on* has been preferred as more satisfactory to the ear and to the mind.

Notional and Grammatical Person.

In the vast majority of cases there is complete agreement
between notional and grammatical person, i.e. the pronoun " I "
and the corresponding verbal forms are used where the speaker
really speaks of himself, and so with the other persons. Still,
deviations are by no means rare ; servility, deference, or simply
politeness, may make the speaker avoid the direct mention of
his own personality, and thus we may have such third-person
substitutes for " I " as *your humble servant* ; cf. Spanish " Disponga
V., caballero, de *este su servidor*." In languages of the east this
is carried to an extreme, and words meaning originally ' slave '
or ' subject ' or ' servant ' have become the normal expressions for
" I " (see, e.g., Fr. Müller, Gr. II, 2. 121). In Western Europe,
with its greater self-assertion, such expressions are chiefly used
in jocular speech, thus E. *yours truly* (from the subscription in
letters), *this child* (vulgarly *this baby*). A distinctively self-assertive
jocular substitute for " I " is *number one*. Some writers avoid
the mention of " I " as much as possible by using passive constructions, etc., and when such devices are not possible, they say *the
author, the (present) writer,* or *the reviewer.* A famous example
of self-effacement in order to produce the impression of absolute
objectivity is Cæsar, who in his commentaries throughout uses
Cæsar instead of the first pronoun. But it is, of course, different
when the same trick of using one's own name instead of the personal
pronoun is used by Marlowe's Faustus or Shakespeare's Julius
Cæsar or Cordelia or Richard II, or Lessing's Saladin, or Oehlen-
schläger's Hakon (many examples from German, Old Norse, Greek,
etc., in Grimm's *Personenwechsel,* 7 ff.). In some cases this may
be a kind of introduction of oneself to the audience, but generally
it is the outcome of pride or haughtiness. Still another case is
found when grown-up people in talking to small children say
" papa " or " Aunt Mary " instead of " I " in order to be more
easily understood.[1]

Present company may sometimes be used instead of " we,"
" us " : " You fancy yourself above present company."

Among substitutes for notional second person I shall first
mention the paternal *we,* often used by teachers and doctors

---

[1] When a person in a soliloquy addresses himself as *you* (" There you
again acted stupidly, John ; why couldn't you behave decently ? ") it is
really an instance of (notional) second person. On " you-monologues and
I-monologues " see Grimm, *Personenwechsel,* 44 ff.

("Well, and how are we to-day ? ") and denoting kindness through identifying the interests of speaker and hearer. This seems to be common in many countries, e.g. in Denmark, in Germany (Grimm, *Personenwechsel*, 19), in France (Bourget, *Disc.* 94 "Hé bien, nous deviendrons un grand savant comme le père ? " | Maupassant, *Fort c. l. m.* 224 "Oui, nous avons de l'anémie, des troubles nerveux"—immediately followed by *vous*). The usual tinge of protection in this *we* is absent from the frequent Danish " Jeg skal sige os " (Let me tell you).

Next we have the deferential substitutes consisting of a possessive pronoun and the name of a quality : *your highness* (= you that are so high), *your excellency, your Majesty, your Lordship,* etc. It is well known that in Spanish *vuestra merced* ' your grace,' shortened into *usted*, has become the usual polite word for ' you.' In French, *Monsieur, Madame, Mademoiselle* may be used instead of *vous* (*Monsieur désire ?* etc.). In countries in which great stress is laid upon titles the simple and natural personal pronouns have often to give way to such expressions as abound in German and Swedish : "Was wünscht (wünschen) der herr lieutenant ? " " Darf ich dem gnädigen fräulein etwas wein einschenken ? " etc. In Sweden it is not easy to carry on a polite conversation with a person whose title one is ignorant of or happens to have forgotten ; and I am sorry to say that my own countrymen of late years have begun more and more to imitate their neighbours to the South and to the East in this respect, and to ask " Hvad mener professoren ? " instead of " Hvad mener De ? "

In German it was formerly usual to say *er, sie* with the verb in the third person singular instead of *du*, especially in speaking to inferiors, and the corresponding practice (*han, hun*) prevailed in Denmark until well into the nineteenth century. The third person plural *Sie* has now become the usual polite word for notional second person (sg. and pl.) in German, and this usage, which Grimm rightly calls an indelible stain on the German language,[1] has been servilely imitated in Denmark : *De.*

There is a different use of the third person for a notional second person which may be illustrated from Shaw's play, where Candida says to her husband : " *My boy* is not looking well. Has *he* been overworking ? " Similarly a lover may say *my darling* or *my own girl* instead of *you*. There is also a petting way of addressing a child as *it*, which may have originated in the habit of half mentioning, half addressing an infant that is too small to understand what is being said to it. This, too, may be exemplified from Candida,

[1] " Es bleibt ein flecke im gewand der deutschen sprache, den wir nicht mehr auswaschen können " (*Personenwechsel*, 13).

who says to Marchbanks : " Poor boy ! have I been cruel ?   Did
I make *it* slice nasty little red onions ? "

With the English possessive compounds with *self* (*myself*,
yourself) we have a conflict between the grammatical person (third)
and the notional person (first, second) ; the verb is generally made
to agree with the notional person (*myself am, yourself are*), though
occasionally the third person is used (Shakespeare sometimes has
my self hath, thy self is, etc.).

Indirect Speech.

In indirect (reported) speech a shifting of the persons is in many
cases natural, a direct first person being turned according to circumstances into an indirect second person or an indirect third
person, etc. The various possibilities may be thus tabulated :
the direct statement (A speaking to B) : " I am glad of your agreement with him " (i.e. C) may become :

(1, A speaking with C) : I said I was glad of his agreement
with you.

(2, A speaking with D) : I said I was glad of his agreement
with him.

(3, B speaking with A) : You said you were glad of my agreement with him.

(4, B speaking with C) : He said he was glad of my agreement
with you.

(5, B speaking with D) : He said he was glad of my agreement
with him.

(6, C speaking with A) : You said you were glad of his agreement
with me.

(7, C speaking with B) : He said he was glad of your agreement
with me.

(8, C speaking with D) : He said he was glad of his agreement
with me.

(9, D speaking with E) : He said he was glad of his agreement
with him.

It should be remarked, however, that in the cases 2, 5, 8, and
9 clearness would certainly gain by the use of the name instead
of one or more of the ambiguous *he*'s.

It is a simple consequence of the nature of the plural *we*, that
it frequently remains unshifted, as in : " He said that he still
believed in *our* glorious future as a nation."

In English the auxiliary *shall* (*should*) is often used in reported
speech to show that the second or third person is a shifted first
person : " Do you think you shall soon recover ? "   " He thought

he should soon recover "—contrast with this the continuation
" but the Doctor knew that he would die."

There is a rather unusual case of a shifted personal (possessive)
pronoun in the *Merchant of Venice* (II. 8. 23) : Shylock exclaims
" My stones, my daughter, my ducats," and when the street-boys
mimic him, this is reported : " Why all the boyes in Venice follow
him, Crying his stones, his daughter, and his ducats." Here the
direct speech would be more natural. In Icelandic sagas it is
quite usual to find that the beginning of a reported speech only is
shifted, and that after one sentence the rest is given in the exact
form in which the speech had been made.

Fourth Person.

Should we recognize a fourth person by the side of the third ?
This was the opinion of Rask (Vejledning 1811, 96, Prisskr. 1818,
241), who said that in " he beats him " *him* is in the fourth, while in
" he beats himself " *himself* is in the third person like the subject.
(Inversely, Thalbitzer, in *Handbook of American Ind. Lang.* 1021,
denotes by " fourth person " the reflexive.) Yet it is easy to see
that if we accept the definition of " person " given above, both
these are in the third person, and that no fourth " person " is
thinkable, however true it is that the same pronoun or verbal
form (in the third person) may refer to different beings or things,
in the same or in successive sentences.

Some Amerindian languages have very subtle distinctions, see
Uhlenbeck, *Grammatische onderscheidingen in het Algonkinsch*
(Akad. van Wetensch., Amsterdam, 1909) : in Chippeway the first
time a third person is mentioned this is not especially marked,
but the subordinate second *tertia persona*, also called *obviativus*,
is marked by a suffix *-n*, and the third *tertia persona* (called *super-
obviativus*, by Uhlenbeck *subobviativus*) by the suffix *-ini*. In
" Joseph took the boy and his mother " *the boy* is the second, and
his mother the third *tertia persona*, and it is exactly indicated whether
his refers to Joseph or to the boy. This makes Brinton (*Essays
of an Americanist*, Philadelphia, 1890, 324) regret the poverty
of English, where the sentence " John told Robert's son that he
must help him " is capable of six different meanings which in
Chippeway would be carefully distinguished. Nevertheless, it
must be said that nearly always the meaning of such pronouns
as *he* and *his* will be made sufficiently clear by the situation and
context, even in such sentences as these (Alford) : " Jack was very
respectful to Tom, and always took off his hat when he met him."
" Jack was very rude to Tom, and always knocked off his hat
when he met him." Sully relates how a little girl of five was much

puzzled by the old hymn : " And Satan trembles when he sees
The weakest saint upon his knees."—" Whatever, she asked, did
they want to sit on Satan's knees for ? "

Note also the fun that was made of the Kaiser's telegram (1914)
to the Crown Princess : " Freue mich mit dir über Wilhelm's
ersten sieg. Wie herrlich hat Gott ihm zu seite gestanden. Ihm
sei dank und ehre. Ich habe ihm eisernes kreuz zweiter und
erster klasse verliehen."

In the spoken language extra stress serves in many cases to
remove any ambiguity and to show who is meant. In John Stuart
Mill's *Essay on Poetry* we read : " Shelley is the very reverse of
all this. Where Wordsworth is strong, he is weak ; where Wordsworth is weak, he is strong." This makes nonsense if read with
unstressed *he*, for that would mean Wordsworth, but it gives perfect
sense if read with stressed *he*, which then comes to mean Shelley ;
it might even be readily understood if after stressing the first *he*
we substitute a weak *he* for the second *Wordsworth*. This clarifying
stress is indicated by the italicizing of *they* in Lamb's sentence :
" Children love to listen to stories about their elders, when *they*
were children." In Somersetshire dialect *Bill cut's vinger* means
' his own,' *Bill cut ees vinger* means ' the other person's.'

Reflexive and Reciprocal Pronouns.

Many languages have developed reflexive pronouns, by means
of which many ambiguities are obviated. Their function is to
indicate identity with what has been mentioned before, in most
cases with the subject, whence it comes that these pronouns generally
have no nominative.

In the Aryan languages we have the pronouns originally beginning with *sw-*, but their sphere of application is not everywhere
the same, so it may be of some interest to give a short survey of
their employment in the languages best known to us.

(1) Originally the reflexive pronoun was used in all three persons
and without any regard to number, e.g. in Sanskrit and in the oldest
Greek. This use is still preserved in Lithuanian and Slav, e.g. Russian
ty vrediš' sebě ' you hurt yourself,' *my dovol'ny soboju* ' we are pleased
with ourselves ' (examples taken from H. Pedersen's grammar).

(2) In many languages the reflexive pronoun has been restricted
to the third person, whether singular or plural ; thus Lat. *se* and
the forms derived from this in Romanic languages ; further G.
sich, ON. *sik*, Dan. *sig*, though, as we shall see immediately, with
some restrictions.

(3) In the dialects of Jutland this pronoun *sig* is used only
when referring to a singular subject ; when referring to a plural

subject *dem* is used. This use of *dem* instead of the received *sig* is not at all rare in literary Danish, even in writers who were not born in Jutland; thus Kierkegaard writes, Enten Ell. 1. 294 naar de ikke kede dem.

(4) While in German the polite pronoun *Sie* (notional second person) takes the reflexive *sich* : *Wollen Sie sich setzen*, the Danish imitation *De* is always now followed by *Dem* : *Vil De ikke sætte Dem* (in the eighteenth century sometimes *sig*).

(5) Though the Fr. unstressed form *se* is used of any third person subject in both numbers, the stressed form *soi* is restricted to the singular and is generally used only when referring to an indefinite subject : *ce qu'on laisse derrière soi*, but of a definite subject : *ce qu'il laisse derrière lui, ce qu'elle laisse derrière elle* (*ce qu'ils laissent derrière eux*). Exceptions to this rule are found now and then, thus pretty frequently in Rolland, e.g. J. Chr. 7. 81 Il était trop peu sûr de soi pour ce rôle (also ib. 3. 213, 4. 6).

(6) English very early went further than any of the related languages, as the only remnant of the reflexive pronouns—and that only in the oldest period—was the possessive *sin* (see below). The old expressions, therefore, were " I wash me, thou washest thee, he washes him, she washes her, we wash us, ye wash you, they wash them." Survivals of this are found in prepositional combinations like " I have no money about me, he has no money about him," etc. In many cases the simple verb besides its transitive function has now also a reflexive meaning : " I wash, dress, shave," etc. But in most cases the reflexive meaning is expressly indicated by the combinations with *self* : " I defend myself, you defend yourself (yourselves), he defends himself," etc. In this way reflexive pronouns have developed which differ from the original Aryan ones in distinguishing the three persons and the two numbers, and thus resemble those of Finnish, which are formed by means of *itse*, to which are appended the usual possessive suffixes : *itseni* myself, *itsemme* ourselves, *itsesi* yourself, *itsensä* himself (herself), etc. Compare also the later Greek *emauton, seauton, heauton*, etc., and especially the curious Modern Greek formations *ton emauto mou* myself, *ton emauto sou* yourself, *ton emauto sas* yourselves, *ton emauto tou, tēs* himself, herself, *ton emauto mas* ourselves, etc.

The development of the reflexive possessive has followed the same lines, though it has not been completely parallel with that of *se*, etc.

(1) To begin with, it referred to all persons in all numbers. This is still the Russian usage, e.g. *ja vzjal svoj platok* ' I took my pocket-handkerchief.'

(2) It is restricted to the third person, but may refer to plurals as well as to singulars. This stage is found in Lat. *suus* and in

the old Gothonic languages, e.g. Gothic Lk 6. 18 *qemun hailjan sik sauhte seinaizo* 'they came to be healed of their diseases' | Mk 15. 29 *wipondans haubida seina* 'shaking their heads.' The OE. poetical *sin* is found corresponding to 'his' and 'her,' but only rarely referring to a plural subject, and the pronoun seems to have disappeared pretty early from ordinary conversational language. ON *sinn* may refer to plural as well as to singular subjects ; this use is still found in Norwegian : *de vasker sine hænder* 'they wash their hands,' and in Swedish.

(3) But in Danish *sin* is used only with a subject in the singular : *han (hun) vasker sine hænder ; de vasker deres hænder.*

(4) In the dialects of Jutland we have the further restriction that *sin* refers to an indefinite subject only : *enhver (en) vasker sine hænder*, but *han vasker hans hænder, hun vasker hender hænder.*

(5) In some languages this pronoun has lost its reflexive power and is used as a general possessive of the third person singular, thus in French, where *ses mains* can be used in any position, meaning 'his or her hands.'

(6) Thus also in German, only with the restriction that it means only 'his' (or 'its') : *seine hände* 'his hands,' but in the fem. *ihre hände* 'her hands.' [1]

Considerations of space prevent me from dealing here with the question of the range of reflexive pronouns, which differs widely in the languages possessing them, especially in participal and infinitival constructions and dependent clauses. [2]

Where reference is possible to two different persons in complicated combinations the existence of a reflexive pronoun is in some cases no security against ambiguity, as in Lat. " Publius dicit

[1] It may not be amiss at this point to remind the reader that the possessive pronoun in some languages besides indicating the sex (or gender) of the 'possessor' also indicates the gender of the substantive to which it is an adjunct. The various possibilities may be gathered from the following translations into French, English, German, and Danish :
Son frère = his brother, her brother = sein bruder, ihr bruder = hans broder, hendes broder, sin broder.
Sa sœur = his sister, her sister = seine schwester, ihre schwester = hans søster, hendes søster, sin søster.
Son chat = his cat, her cat = seine katze, ihre katze = hans kat, hendes kat, sin kat.
Sa maison = his house, her house = sein haus, ihr haus = hans hus, hendes hus, sit hus.
[2] A few examples may be given from old Gothonic languages. Goth. Mk 3. 14 gawaurhta twalif du wisan miþ sis 'he made twelve to be with him' | 3. 34 bisaihwands bisunjane þans bi sik sitandans 'looking round at those sitting round him' | Lk 6. 32 þai frawaurhtans þans frijondans sik frijond 'sinners love those that love them' | Sn. Edda 52 Útgardaloki spyrr hvárt hann (þórr) hefir hitt ríkara mann nokkurn en sik 'U. asks whether he has met any man more powerful than him (U.).' Cf. also Nygaard NS 338 ff., Falk and Torp DNS 130 ff., Mikkelsen DO 258 ff., Western R 145 ff., Curme GG 187 f.

Gaium se occidere voluisse," or in Dan. " han fandt Peter liggende i sin seng," which is no more clear than the E. " he found Peter lying in his bed." Cf. the German use of *dessen*, where *sein* would be ambiguous : " Der graf hat diesem manne und dessen sohne alles anvertraut " (Curme GG 168).

Closely related to the reflexive pronouns are the reciprocal pronouns, meaning ' each other ' : each part of those mentioned as the subject acting upon (or with regard to) and being in turn acted upon by all the other parts. This meaning is often expressed by the simple reflexive pronoun, either alone as in Fr. *ils se haïssent* or with some addition, as in *ils se haïssent entr'eux*, Lat. *inter se confligunt*, Goth. Mk 1. 27 *sokidedun miþ sis misso*, cf. G. *sie halfen sich gegenseitig*, or in Fr. *ils se sont tués l'un l'autre* (as *ils se sont tués* might be taken to mean ' they have committed suicide '). Combinations like *l'un l'autre* are also used without any reflexive pronouns in various languages, where they always tend to become one inseparable whole, as they have done in Gr. *allēlous*, Dan. *hinanden*, *hverandre*, Dutch *elkaar*, *mekaar*, G. *einander*. On the development of the German word see the interesting article in Grimm's *Wörterbuch*, which also gives corresponding expressions from various other languages (Romanic, Slav, Lithuanian, Keltic). In English the elements formerly separated, as in Shakespeare's *gazed each on other* or *what we speak one to another*, have now in ordinary language been fused together : *gaze on each other*, *speak to one another*. In Russian *drug druga* is separated by a preposition (*drug s drugom* with one another), but the tendency to look upon the combination as a unit is shown by the fact that it is used uniformly without regard to gender and number (Boyer and Speranski, M 273). Magyar *egy-mas* seems to be simply a translation of G. *einander*.[1]

Reciprocal pronouns are sometimes found as the subject of a dependent clause, thus in a recent English novel : " Miss C. and I are going to find out what each other are like." Similar sentences may be heard in Danish.

Many grammars deal with the theory of reflexives in a chapter about various kinds of verbs, giving " reflexive verbs " as one kind (and " reciprocal verbs " as another). But surely the verb is exactly the same in ' we hurt him," " we hurt ourselves," " we hurt one

---

[1] The formation of a single inseparable word like *einander* obviates the difficulty that sometimes presents itself when one has to choose between two numbers. In French it is usual to say *les trois frères se haïssent l'un l'autre*, but it would be more logical to say *l'un les autres* or *les uns l'autre*, and in Ido people have hesitated whether to write *la tri frati odias l'unu l'altru* or *l'unu l'altri* or *l'uni l'altri* ; it would therefore be much more convenient to have one single word, and *mutu* presents itself naturally as a back-formation from *mutuala*, which then would appear as a regularly formed adjective from *mutu* instead of being an independent root-word.

another," the only difference being the identity or non-identity of subject and object. Thus also G. " ich schmeichele mir," " ich spotte meiner " contain the same verb as " ich schmeichele dir," " ich spotte seiner." The only cases in which one might fairly speak of a reflexive verb would be those in which a verb is found idiomatically with no other object than a reflexive pronoun, as in E. *I pride myself*, Dan. *jeg forsnakker mig*, G. *ich schäme mich*. The identity of subject and object (direct or indirect) influences the choice of the auxiliary in Fr. *il s'est tué* ' he has killed himself,' *nous nous sommes demandé* ' we have asked ourselves (or one another '). It is a different thing that what is expressed in our languages with a reflexive pronoun may in some languages be expressed by a separate form of the verb, as in the Greek " middle voice " : *louomai* ' I wash myself,' etc. (the same form having also a passive signification, see Ch. XII, p. 168). In Scandinavian the reflexive pronoun *sik* has in a reduced form been fused with many verbal forms, which then generally have acquired a purely passive meaning : *han kaldes*, originally ' he calls himself,' now ' he is called.' Sometimes the meaning is reciprocal : *de slås* (with a short vowel) ' they fight (strike one another) ' ; in this verb there is another form with a long vowel (and glottal catch) for the passive *slå(e)s* ' is struck.' In Russian the reflexive pronoun tends in a similar way to be fused with verbs in the two forms *sja* and *s'* (in spite of the spelling pronounced with a non-palatalized s) ; on the various meanings (distinctly reflexive, vaguely reflexive, reciprocal, approximately passive) see H. Pedersen RG 190, Boyer and Speranski M 247.

CHAPTER XVII

SEX AND GENDER

Various Languages.   Aryan Gender.   Sex.   Common Sex.   Animate and
Inanimate.   Conceptional Neuter.

Various Languages.

By the term *gender* is here meant any *grammatical* class-division
presenting some analogy to the distinction in the Aryan languages
between masculine, feminine, and neuter, whether the division be
based on the natural division into the two sexes,[1] or on that between
animate and inanimate, or on something else. While a great many,
probably the vast majority, of languages, have no gender in this
sense, there are some languages which divide nouns into gender
classes. Only the briefest mention of some of these class-distinctions
can here be given, just enough to show, on the one hand the similarities, and on the other hand the dissimilarities with our own system.

In the Bantu languages of South Africa every substantive
belongs to one of several classes, each of these being characterized
by its own prefix, which is repeated in a more or less weakened
form as a " reminder " in all subordinate words referring to the
substantive in question, whether adjuncts or verbs. Some of
these classes imply the singular, others the plural number, but
none of them has any reference to sex, though some are used mainly
of living beings and others of things. The number of the classes
varies in different languages belonging to the group, the maximum
being sixteen, but some of the classes are apt to be confounded,
and it is not possible to indicate the ultimate reason for the division.
(See *Lang.* 352 ff. and the works there quoted.)

In Tush, one of the languages of the Caucasus, various prefixes are
used according as a rational being of the male sex, a rational being
of the female sex, or an irrational being or thing is denoted. Thus

wašo wa	the brother is
bstuino ja	the woman is
naw ja	the ship is
xaux ba	the pigeon is
bader da	the child is.

[1] It is better to keep *sex* and *gender* apart than to speak of " natural
and grammatical gender," as is often done. See p. 55 on the terminological
distinction between *male, female, sexless* and *masculine, feminine, neuter.*

'Heavy' when said of a man is *watshi*, of a woman *jatshi*, of a thing *batshi*, and heaviness correspondingly is *watshol*, *jatshol*, *batshol*. *Wašo* is brother, *jašo* sister, *woh* boy, *joh* girl.

In the related Tshetshensian 'I am' is *suo wu* when spoken by a man, *suo ju* by a woman, *suo du* by a child (Fr. Müller, *Grundriss* III, 2. 162).

In Andaman one class comprises inanimate things, another animate beings, which are subdivided into human and non-human. There is a sevenfold division of parts of the human body, but this division is transferred to inanimate things that have some relation to these several parts of the human body (P. W. Schmidt, *Stellung der Pygmäervölker*, 121).

Algonkin languages have a distinction between animate and inanimate, though the distribution presents many points that to us appear strange, as when parts of the human body are generally looked upon as inanimate, while various parts of the bodies of animals are reckoned among animate things. (See J. P. B. Josselin de Jong, *De Waardeeringsonderscheiding van Levend en Levenloos*, Leiden, 1913, which compares this system and the Aryan genders, and discusses the theories advanced about the origin of the latter.)

In Hamitic languages we have a partition into two classes, one comprising names of persons, of big or important things, and of males, and the other those of things, small things, and females, sometimes with the curious rule that words of the first class in the plural belong to the second class, and vice versa. By interchange of the same prefixes we thus turn man into small man, brother into sister, and he-dog into bitch or small dog ; in Bedauyo *ando* 'excrement' is masculine of a horse, ox, or camel, feminine of smaller animals. A woman's breast is masculine, a man's (because smaller), feminine. (Meinhof, *Spr. der Hamiten*, 23, and passim ; *Die mod. sprachforsch. in Afrika*, 134 ff.)

The genders of the Semitic languages are generally considered as most similar to the Aryan genders, though there is no neuter, and though in Semitic even verbal forms are made to agree with the gender (sex) of the subject. Thus Arabic *katabta* 'thou (m.) hast written,' *katabti* 'thou (f.) hast written,' *kataba* 'he has written,' *katabat* 'she has written,' plural 2. pers. *katabtum* (m.), *katabtunna* (f.), 3. pers. *katabū* (m.), *katabna* (f.) ; in the first person no such distinction is found : *katabtu* 'I have written,' *katabnā* 'we have written.'

Aryan Gender.

Our own family of Aryan languages in the earliest historically accessible forms distinguishes three genders, masculine, feminine, and neuter, the last of which may to some extent be considered a subdivision of masculine, characterized chiefly by making no distinction between the nominative and the accusative. The distribution of words into these three classes is partly rational, partly irrational. It is rational in so far as many names of male beings are of the masculine gender, many names of females being feminine, and many names of sexless things neuter. But by the side of this we find in some cases names of male beings as feminines or neuters, names of female beings as masculines or neuters, and names of things or ideas without a natural sex as either feminines or masculines.[1] I have spoken about various attempts to explain the origin of this singular system or want of system in *Language*, p. 391 ff.,[2] and of the practical disadvantages of it, ibid. 346 ff. It may be possible to assign reasons why some words have a certain gender ; thus Handel Jakób has recently pointed out (*Bulletin de l'Acad. polonaise des Sciences*, 1919-20, p. 17 ff.) that words meaning ' earth ' (Gr *khthōn, khōra*, Lat. *terra*, Slav. *ziemia*, G. *erde*) are made f., because the earth is thought of as a mother producing plants, etc. ; similarly names of trees, because these bring forth fruits ; he adduces some Semitic parallels. But the main problem remains, why is this classification extended to all words, even where it is not possible to see any connexion with natural sex ? Why, to take only one instance, is the common Aryan word for ' foot ' (*pous, pes, fot*, etc.) m., while the various unconnected words for ' hand ' are f. (*kheir, manus, handus, ruka*) ? Words for ' table, thought, fruit, thunder,' etc., are in one language m., in another f. It is certainly impossible to find any single governing-principle in this chaos.

Gender is shown partly by form, as when in Latin the nom. and acc. are distinguished in *rex regem* m., *lex legem* f., while the two cases are identical in *regnum* n., but it is chiefly a syntactic phenomenon, different forms of adjectives and pronouns being required with the different genders : *ille rex bonus est, illa lex bona est, illud regnum bonum est.*[3]

In the vast majority of cases the gender of words is handed down traditionally from generation to generation without any change ; but sometimes changes occur. In not a few cases these are due to purely formal accidents ; thus it has been noted that, in French,

---

[1] The sex-distinction recognized by botanists in plants must, of course, from a grammarian's point of view be considered as non-existent ; if in French *lis* is masculine, and *rose* feminine, this exclusively concerns the gender of these words and has no more to do with sex than the fact that *mur* and *maison* have different genders.

[2] Besides the literature there quoted see now also Meillet LH 199 ff., Vendryes L 108 ff.

[3] As the Russian past tense is in origin a participle, it is inflected in genders : *znal* ' knew ' m., *znala* f., *znalo* n. This to some extent constitutes a parallel to the Semitic gender-distinction in verbs.

words beginning with a vowel are particularly liable to changes in gender, because there the form of the definite article is the same in all cases, viz. *l'* (the indefinite article *un, une,* too, was formerly pronounced [yn] before a word beginning with a vowel). Words ending in the feminine *-e* (or, we might say in conformity with actual pronunciation, words ending in a consonant sound) tend to become feminine. Both these causes operate together in making *énigme, épigramme, épithète* f. instead of m. In other cases the change of gender is due to the meaning of the words. There is a natural tendency to have the same gender in words of related meaning (such words being, moreover, often mentioned in close succession), thus Fr. *été* from f. becomes *m.* on account of the other names of the seasons, *hiver, printemps, automne* (the last of these in former times vacillating between the original m. and f.) ; *la minuit* under the influence of *le midi* becomes *le minuit.* In the same way G. *die mittwoche* ' Wednesday ' has become *der mittwoch* after *der tag* and the names of the other days of the week.

Similarly the gender of new words (or newly adopted foreign words) is in many cases determined by formal considerations, as when *etage* in German is fem. (in Fr. it is m.), but in others by sense-analogies, as when in G. *beefsteak* becomes neuter (after *rindfleisch*), and *lift* masculine (after *aufzug*) or when in Danish we say *et vita* (after *et liv*), *en examen* (after *en prøve*), etc., the same word being even sometimes treated differently in different senses, e.g. *fotografien* ' photography ' (after *kunsten*), *fotografiet* ' photograph ' (after *billedet*), *imperativen* (*måden*), *det kategoriske imperativ* (*buddet*). When the metrical system was introduced, *gram* and *kilogram* (*kilo*) were made neuter after *et pund, et lod*, but we say *en liter* after *en pot, en pægl*, and *en meter* after *en alen, en fod.*

We see the influence of accidents of form on a broader scale in the way in which the original trinity of Aryan gender has been reduced to a duality in some languages. In the Romanic languages the distinctive features of masculine and neuter were obliterated, chiefly through the loss of any distinction in the sounds of the endings, while the ending of the feminine with its full vowel *-a* was kept apart, the consequence being that there are two genders only, masculine and feminine (on the remains of the old neuter see below). In Danish, on the other hand, the distinction between the masculine and feminine articles (ON. *enn, en* or *inn, in, einn, ein*, etc.), was lost, and thus the old m. and f. were fused together in one " common gender " as in *hesten, bogen, den gamle hest, den gamle bog*, as distinct from the neuter as in *dyret, det gamle dyr.* But in those Danish dialects in which the old final *-nn* and *-n* are kept phonetically apart (the former having a palatalized form of the nasal) the old trinity of m., f. and n. is preserved.

In the following remarks I am chiefly concerned with the relation between notional (that is, in this case, natural) and grammatical categories, and shall try to show how here and there languages have in course of time developed other and more rational groupings than the old traditional ones.

Sex.

Though, as has been remarked above, there are many examples of incongruity, still the correspondence between male and masculine on the one hand, and female and feminine on the other hand, is strong enough to be very actively felt, and combinations which are sometimes necessary, like G. *eine männliche maus, ein weiblicher hase*, will always be felt as inharmonious and as containing a contradiction between the form of the article and the meaning of the adjective. In a comic paper I find the following illustration : " L'instituteur. Comment donc ? Vous êtes incapable de faire l'analyse grammaticale de cette simple phrase : ' L'alouette chante.' Vous avez écrit dans votre devoir : Alouette, substantif masculin singulier. —L'élève. Sans doute. Et je maintiens energiquement ' masculin ' : chez les alouettes, il n'y a que le mâle qui chante."—Cf. also from Sweden : " Hvad heter den här apan ? —Hon heter Kalle, för det är en hanne " (Noreen VS 5. 314, i.e. What is the name of that ape ? She is called Charles, for it is a he. In Swedish *apa* is feminine). And from North Jutland i honkat nöwne wi åse me haj (Grönborg *Optegnelser* 72, i.e. we say he of a she-cat ; *kat* is m., as shown by the article *i*).

There is therefore a natural tendency to bring about conformity between gender and sex.[1] This may be achieved in the first place by a change in form, as when Lat. *lupa* was formed instead of the earlier *lupus* which had been used, for instance of Romulus's she-wolf (Havet), or when much later Sp. *leona*, Fr. *lionne* and It. *signora*, Sp. *señora* were formed from Lat. *leo*, *senior*, which did not distinguish sex. In Greek the old *neania* ' youth ' adopted the masculine ending *-s* to become *neanias* ' young man.' Or else the form is retained, but the syntactic construction is changed, as when Lat. *nauta, auriga* when applied to men (a ' sailor, charioteer ') become masculine (i.e. take adjectives in m.) : originally they were abstracts and meant ' sailoring, driving ' ; or when the Spanish say *el justicia* ' the judge,' *el cura* ' the curate,' *el gallina* ' the coward,' *el figura* ' the ridiculous fellow ' (*la justicia* ' justice,' *la cura* ' curacy,' *la gallina* ' hen,' *la figura* ' figure '). Thus also Fr. *le trompette* ' the trumpeter ' (*la trompette* ' the trumpet ') ; cp. also *la jument*

---

[1] An Italian child asked why *barba* was not called *barbo* (Sully, after Lombroso).

'the mare.' In Sw. *statsråd* 'councillor of State,' orig. 'council,'
is still neuter, but an adjective predicative is generally put in the
form common to masculine and feminine : *statsrådet är sjuk* (not
sjukt) ; in Danish the word in this sense has definitely given up
its neuter gender : *statsråden er syg.* Thus also Dan. *viv*, which
formerly was n. (like G. *das weib*, OE. *þæt wif*, Sw. *vivet*) is now of
the common gender, and instead of the old *gudet, troldet* 'the god,
the troll' we say now *guden, trolden.*

Common Sex.

It is often desirable, and even necessary, in speaking of living
beings to have words which say nothing about sex and are equally
applicable to male and female beings. Such a word is German
mensch, Dan. and Norw. *menneske*, Sw. *människa*, though it is curious
that grammatically *mensch* is masculine (whence Germans in some
connexions hesitate to use it about a woman), *människa* is feminine,
and *menneske* neuter. In English *man* has from the oldest times
been used for both sexes, but as it may also be used specifically
of the male sex, ambiguity and confusion sometimes result, as
seen, for instance, in Miss Hitchener's line, which so much amused
Shelley :

All, all are men—women and all !

Note also such quotations as the following : Atrabiliar old men,
especially old women, hint that they know what they know (Car-
lyle) | the deification of the Babe. It is not likely that Man—
the human male—left to himself would have done this. . . . But
to woman it was natural.—The generic singular *man* sometimes
means both sexes (God made the country, and man made the
town) and sometimes only one (Man is destined to be a prey to
woman), see many quotations MEG II, 5. 4. This is decidedly a
defect in the English language, and the tendency recently has been
to use unambiguous, if clumsy, expressions like *a human being*
(" Marriage is not what it was. It's become a different thing
because women have become human beings," Wells) or the shorter
human, pl. *humans* (frequent in recent books by Galsworthy, W. J.
Locke, Carpenter, and others). Note that the derivatives *manly,
mannish, manful* as well as compounds like *man-servant* refer to
male man, but *manlike* and *manhood* generally to both sexes (manhood suffrage, etc.). The old compound *mankind* (now stressed
on the second syllable) comprises all human beings, but the younger
mankind (stressed on the first syllable) is opposed to *womankind.*
(The stress-difference, as made in NED, is not, however, recognized
by everybody.)

French *homme* is just as ambiguous as E. *man*, and one is there-fore sometimes obliged to say *un être humain* ; in scientific books one finds even the long-winded *un être humain, sans acception de sexe*, where other languages have simple words like *mensch*, by the side of *mann*, Greek *anthrōpos*, by the side of *anēr*, etc. (Cf. Meillet LH 273 ff.)

While a great many special names for human beings are applic-able to both sexes, e.g. *liar, possessor, inhabitant, Christian, aristo-crat, fool, stranger, neighbour*, etc., others, though possessing no distinctive mark, are as a matter of fact chiefly or even exclusively applied to one sex only, because the corresponding social functions have been restricted either to men or to women. This is true of *minister, bishop, lawyer, baker, shoemaker* and many others on the one hand, *nurse, dressmaker, milliner* on the other. It is curious that some words have in course of time been restricted to women, though originally applicable to men as well, thus *leman* (Oe. *leof-man* ' dear man,' in Chaucer and even in Shakespeare of a man, later only of a woman, now obsolete), *bawd, witch, girl*.

Where it is desired to restrict common-sex words to one sex, this may be done in various ways, thus *man-servant* or *servant-man, maid-servant, servant-girl*, a *he-devil*, a *she-devil*, her *girl-friends*, a *poetess* (but it is a higher praise to say that Mrs. Browning was a great poet, than to call her a great poetess). *Author* is still to a great extent a common-sex word, though the word *authoress* exists, but there is no corresponding formation to denote the female *teacher* or *singer*. Most languages present similar inconsistencies, and in many cases linguistic difficulties have been created through the recent extension of the activities of women to spheres that used to be reserved for men.[1] Of the artificial languages there is only one that has successfully tackled the problem of having on the one hand common-sex words and on the other hand special-sex words, namely Ido, where all denominations without any special ending are applicable to both sexes, while male is denoted by the ending *-ulo* and female by *-ino*, e.g. *frato* brother or sister, *fratulo* brother, *fratino* sister, *frati* G. geschwister, *homo* mensch, *homulo* mann, *homino* woman, *sposo* spouse, *spozulo* husband, *spozino* wife, and thus *dentisto, dentistulo, dentistino*, etc.[2]

In the plural there is naturally even greater need for common-sex words than in the singular, but it is only few languages that

---

[1] An example from long before the days of the emancipation of women, Laxd. saga 54. 11 Þorgerðr húsfreya var ok mikill [m.] hvatamaðr, at þessi ferð skyldi takaz ' she was a great instigator (instigating-man) of this raid.'

[2] Nations differ very greatly in the extent to which they have designations for married women according to the rank or profession of their husbands (*Duchess*, Swed. *professorska*, G. *frau professor*). But details would be out of place here.

can use the plural masculine in the same way as It. *gli zii* ' uncle
and aunt ' (lo zio e la zia), *i fratelli* (il fratello e la sorella), *i suoceri*
(but not *i padri* instead of *i genitrici*) or Spanish *los padres* ' father
and mother,' *los hermanos* ' brother(s) and sister(s),' *sus dos hijos,
Juan y Perfecta* (Galdós, D. Perf. 29).

With regard to animals, only those few that have the greatest
importance to men have separate common-sex and special-sex
words or forms (as *horse, stallion, mare*) ; from these we have several
gradations (e.g. *dog, he-dog* or simply *dog* for the male, *bitch* or
she-dog ; *sparrow, cock-sparrow, hen-sparrow*) down to animals
whose sex has no interest to ordinary speakers (*fly, worm*).

In pronouns and adjectives, where a common-sex form is
not available, as it is in *somebody, everybody, each,* the masculine
is most often used, as in Fr. *quelqu'un, chacun,* Jean et Marie
étaient très *contents d'eux-mêmes* ; some incongruity is inevitable
in sentences like " Was Maria und Fritz so zueinander zog, war,
dass *jeder* von ihnen *am anderen* sah, wie *er* unglücklich war "
or " Doña Perfecta . . . su hermano . . . pasaron unos pocos
años sin que *uno y otro* se vieran " (Galdós, D. Perf. 32).

It seems to be of special importance to have a common-sex
interrogative pronoun, because in asking " Who did it ? " one does
not know beforehand whether it is a he or a she ; hence most
languages have only one form here (not infrequently a form which
has a masculine ending), thus Gr. *tis,* Goth. *hwas* (the fem. form
hwo given in grammars, probably never occurs as an interrogative
primary), OE. *hwa,* E. *who,* G. *wer,* Du. *wie,* Dan. (*hvo*), *hvem,*
Russ. *kto,* etc. Exceptions are ON. m. *hverr,* f. *hver,* m. *hvárr,*
f. *hvár* and Lat. m. *quis,* f. *quæ,* but in modern Icelandic the difference has disappeared, at any rate in the nominative (*hver, hvor*), and
in the Romanic languages only the masculine form survives as a
common-sex form : It. *chi,* Fr. *qui,* Sp. *quién.*

In the personal pronouns for the third person *he* and *she* are
distinguished in English as in the other languages of our family ;
when a common-sex pronoun is wanted, *he* may be used instead
of *he or she,* but colloquially the pl. *they* is often used (" Nobody
prevents you, do they ? " etc., Lang. 347, MEG II, 5. 56). In
the plural most Gothonic languages have now generalized one form
for both sexes (E. *they,* G. *sie,* Dan. *de,* etc.), which is very natural
as one has very often to talk of groups of persons of different sex.
Thus also in Russian except in the nom., where *oni, one* are kept
apart. In the Romanic languages the two sexes are kept apart :
eglino, elleno ; ellos, ellas ; ils (*eux*), *elles,* except in the dative :
loro, les, leur, and in the Fr. acc. with verbs : *les.* ON. has separate
forms in the nom. and acc. ; *þeir, þær* ; *þá, þær,* but not in the
dat. : *þeim* ; in the nom. and acc. it has also a separate form for

the neuter : *þau*, and this is also used as a common-sex plural, a phenomenon which is generally accounted for from the accidental fact that the old dual (which would often be used for ' he and she ') came to be phonetically identical with the neuter plural. If that is so, the use of the neuter *singular* as a common-sex form may be transferred from the dual-plural ; an example of both is found in Laxd. S. 59. 20 Eptir þetta skilja þau Guðrún talit, ok bað hvárt þeira annat vel fara ' after this G. and he (Snorri) stop talking, and bade each other farewell ' (*þau* n. pl., *hvárt* and *annat* n. sg.). On the corresponding rule in Gothic and OHG see Willmanns DG 3. 768, Streitberg GE 166. Old Dan. Jysk l. 4. 3. *hwat* lengær liuær mothær æthe barn ' which lives longer, mother or child.'

Animate and Inanimate.

A distinction between living and lifeless, or animate and inanimate, or sometimes between human and extra-human, personal and non-personal (things which are not always easy to keep apart), pervades many parts of the grammars of many languages, sometimes in close connexion with sex-gender, sometimes independent of sex-gender. This distinction may be shown grammatically in the most different ways, and I cannot claim that the following survey is complete even for the languages with which I am most familiar.

In English the distinction is shown most clearly in the pronouns, as seen in this survey :

ANIMATE.	INANIMATE.
he, she	*it*
who	*what* (interrogative)
who	*which* (relative)
somebody, someone	*something*
anybody, anyone	*anything*
nobody, no one	*nothing*
everybody, every one	*everything*
all (pl.)	*all* (sg.)
the good (pl.)	*the good* (sg.)

From the oldest times there has been a strong tendency to use the pronoun *it* (OE. *hit*) to represent things. It was so even when the old threefold gender, m., f., n., was still living and showed itself in the forms of adjuncts (articles, pronouns, adjectives). Thus (to give some of the examples adduced in the interesting article " Grammatical and Natural Gender in Middle English," by S. Moore, Publ. Mod. L. Ass. 1921) *hlœw* . . . *beorhtne* (acc. m.) . . . *hit* | *anne arc* . . . *hit* | *œnne calic* . . . *hit* | *þisne calic*, *hit* | *þeos race* . . . *hit.* From the Ancrene Riwle : *þene kinedom* . . . *hit* | *þeo ilke scheadewe* . . . *hit* | *þene drunch* . . . *hit.* (In Moore's article this phenomenon is mixed up with the use of *heo* (*she*) when referred to such words as the neuter *wif*, *mægden* or the masculine *wifman*, or of *he* referring to the neuter *cild* ; it would have been better to treat these things separately : the latter, but not the former usage is pretty frequent in Modern German.) This use of *it* quite naturally became even more predominant after the old distinctions of case and gender in adjunct pronouns and adjectives had disappeared, and about 1600 it led to the creation of a new genitive case *its*, where formerly *his* was in use both for the masculine and the neuter ; *its* also superseded the dialectal gen. *it*, which had begun to be used in Standard English.

It is, however, impossible to draw a hard and fast line of demarcation in English between an animate gender, represented by *he* or *she*, and an inanimate gender, represented by *it*. For *it* may be used in speaking of a small child or an animal if its sex is unknown to the speaker or if his interest in the child or animal is not great : the greater personal interest one takes in the child or animal, the less inclined one will be to use *it*, and *he* or *she* is even used in many cases of an animal independently of any knowledge of the actual sex of the individual referred to (a hare . . . she, a canary-bird . . . he, a crocodile . . . he, an ant . . . she, etc.). On the other hand, things may, in more or less jocular style, be mentioned as *he* or *she*, by way of indicating a kind of personal interest. The best-known and most universal example of this is the sailor's *she* of a ship ; in Dickens a coach is *she*, and this is nowadays the fashion among motorists in talking of their cars.

A country may from different points of view be treated either as inanimate or animate. On the one hand, in speaking of France, we may say "it certainly is smaller than Spain, but then it is much more fertile," and on the other hand, "I do not approve of her policy in the reparations question " : in the latter case France is viewed as a personal agent, hence the sex-indicating pronoun is chosen, and if this is in the feminine in spite of the fact that the political leaders are (still !) men, this is due to literary tradition from French and Latin, where the names of countries happened to be feminine. In German and Danish, where this influence is not so strong, states even as political agents are mentioned in the neuter, *es*, *det* (though we may sometimes substitute the personal name *Franskmanden* ' the Frenchman ' and say " Ja, Franskmanden, han veed nok hvad han vil " without having any individual Frenchman in view).

A somewhat similar case in seen with *heaven*, which may be referred to as *he*, when it is a veiled expression for God. *Nature* when viewed as an agent is *she* from the Latin (and Fr.) gender, and this is transferred to *Fate* by Browning (" Let fate reach me how she likes ") in spite of the Latin gender.[1] When the sun is mentioned as *he*, and the moon as *she*, this has very little to do with a real feeling of them as animate, but is purely artificial literary tradition from Latin : it is well known that in OE. as in the other Gothonic languages the sun was f. and the moon m.

There can be no doubt that the poetic tendency to personify lifeless things or abstract notions, for instance to apostrophize Death as if it were a living being, and the related representation in plastic art of such notions, are largely due to the influence of languages with sex-gender, chiefly, of course, Latin. But it has been justly remarked (among others by Jenisch, 1796) that such personification is more vivid in English than it can be, for instance, in German, because the pronoun *he* or *she*, where everyday language has *it*, at once draws attention to the idealization, which in German is not so noticeable because every chair and every stone is *er*, and every plant and every nose is *sie*. English poets have also greater freedom to choose which sex they will attribute to such notions.[2] Thum compares Shakespeare's passage " See how the morning opes *her* golden gates, And takes her farewell of the glorious sun," in which the morning is the mistress who takes leave of her lover, with Schlegel's translation " Sieh, wie *sein* tor der goldene morgen öffnet, Und abschied von der lieben sonne nimmt," where the relation has been inverted on account of the gender of *morgen* and *sonne*. In Milton, *Sin* is talking to Satan who has begotten on her his son *Death* ; this is rendered impossible in a French translation, because *le péché* cannot be the mother, and *la mort* cannot be the son. Note also Brunot's remark (PL 87) " le hasard des genres a créé aux artistes de grands embarras. *La Grâce, la Beauté, la Science,* prenaient facilement figure de femme, mais *la Force* ? On a eu recours à *Hercule* ! "

Some of the distinctions tabulated on p. 234 are comparatively recent ; thus the relative *which* down to the beginning of the seventeenth century might be used of a person. When *this* and *that* are

---

[1] " Donnerwetter ! was ist doch manchmal diese verdammte welt niederträchtig schön ! Man sollte gar nicht glauben, dass sie dabei einen so hundsgemein behandeln kann ! "—" Kein wunder," meinte Hermann Gutzeit, " es heisst ja *die* welt ! "—" *Frau* welt ! " rief doktor Herzfeld und lachte (G. Hermann). This flippant remark is made possible only because the German word *welt* is of the feminine gender and means (1) the whole exterior world or nature—which is neither male nor female—and (2) mankind—which comprises male and female beings. It would not be possible either in French (*le* monde) or in English or Turkish.

[2] Thy wish was *father*, Harry, to that thought (Shakespeare).—Your wish is *mother* to your thought (Galsworthy, *Loyalties*, Act II).—It is small wonder—the wish being *parent* to the thought—that some accepted the rumour (McKenna, *While I Remember*, 149).

used as primaries, they are inanimate ; note also the difference in such dictionary definitions as " Rubber—*one who*, or *that which* rubs.'' When the prop-word *one* is anaphorical (i.e. refers to a word mentioned already) it may be either animate or inanimate (this cake . . . the only one I care for), but when it does not in that way refer to a word just mentioned, it is always personal (' the great ones of the earth '). All these things are dealt with in greater detail in MEG, Vol. II, passim.

It is also worth mentioning that collectives can take the verb in the plural only if they denote living beings (*family, police*), but otherwise always take it in the singular (*library, forest*). It is also noteworthy that the genitive (in -*s*) is extinct except in the case of names of living beings (*the man's foot*, but *the foot of a mountain*)—apart from some survivals of set phrases (*out of harm's way | a boat's length from the ship*).[1]

In German the distinction between animate and inanimate is not so marked as in English : many things are referred to as *er, sie, dieser, jene*, etc., that is, by the same pronouns as are used for persons. Yet there are some indications of the difference besides the obvious instance *wer* and *was* : the datives *ihm, ihr*, are not often used of things, and instead of *mit ihm, mit ihr, in ihm, in ihr*, etc., the compounds *damit, darin*, etc., are used. There is a greater inclination to use *derselbe, dieselbe* of inanimates than of living beings ; the possessive pronoun *sein* is generally reserved for living beings : sie legte die hand auf den stein und empfand *dessen wärme*, or *die wärme desselben* (Curme GG 168). The old dative has disappeared from the neuters *was, etwas, nichts*, and the compounds with *wo- (womit, wovon)* are used where with animates we have *mit wem, von wem*.

How important the neuter conception is in some cases is shown by the curious fact that it has been allowed to override the idea of plurality in *beides*, which means ' both things ' as distinct from *beide* ' both persons ' ; thus also *mehreres* ' several things,' but *mehrere* ' several persons,' and in pretty much the same way *alles* (cf. Lat. *omnia* pl. n.), to which we have, of course, parallels in other languages : E. *all* sg. n. (which tends to be superseded by *everything, all* being reserved when used alone for persons in the pl.), Dan. *alt*, etc. Dan. *alting* was originally a pl. ' all things,' but is now used as a neuter sg. : *alting er muligt*. Cf. also *much* (*viel, vieles*) = many *things* (*viele dinge*).

In Danish the distinction between animate and inanimate is not well-defined grammatically. But we have the interrogative

---

[1] " If we substitute the expression ' England's history ' for the more usual ' the history of England,' we indicate that the name of the country is used with some approach to personification " (Bradley ME 60).

pronoun *hvem* of human beings and *hvad* of things corresponding to *who* and *what*, and instead of using *begge* 'both' alone as a primary there is a tendency to use *begge to* of two persons and *begge dele* of things, corresponding to *alle* (*allesammen*) 'all' (pl.) and *alt* (*alting*) 'all, everything.' The sex-indicating pronouns *han, hun* 'he, she' are used of human beings and of such of the higher animals as the speaker takes a personal interest in ; other animals are referred to as *den* or *det* according to the gender of the word : *lammet, svinet* . . . *det, hesten, musen* . . . *den* 'the lamb, swine, horse, mouse '—exactly as the same pronouns refer to things, e.g. *huset* . . . *det, muren* . . . *den* 'the house, the wall.' As in English, though not to the same extent, there is some disinclination to use the genitive in *-s* with names of inanimates : we say *taget på huset, træerne i haven* more often than *husets tag, havens træer* 'the roof of the house, the trees of the garden.'

Swedish literary language has retained much more of the old gender system than Danish, but the tendency is towards the same use as in Danish of *den* instead of the older m. and f. *han, hon*, in speaking of things, see the extremely able discussion in Tegnér, *Om genus i svenskan*, 1892.

In French we have, of course, *qui* (qui est-ce qui) over against *que* (*qu'est-ce que*) and *quoi* ; further *en* refers to something inanimate, where with animates the possessive pronoun is used : *j'en connais la précision* in speaking of a watch, *je connais sa précision* in speaking of a man (but there are instances in which *son* is necessary even of a thing, and the relative corresponding to *en*, viz. *dont*, is used of both classes).

In Spanish we have the rule that the object takes the preposition *á* before it if it denotes a living being : *he visto al ministro* 'I have seen the minister,' but *he visto Madrid*. In Russian and the other Slav languages the rule prevails that with names of living beings the genitive is used instead of the accusative. In some of the modern languages of India, such as Hindustani, the object form with living beings is marked by the ending *-ko*, while in names of inanimate things the object has the same form as the nominative (S. Konow in *Festskrift til A. Torp*, 99). In various languages, therefore, a distinction between these two classes is seen reflected in their manner of indicating the object, but as the means by which this is achieved are entirely different, we seem here to have a trait that has its root in the psychological sameness of men all over the world. (Cf. also the Aryan nominative ending *-s* if that was originally characteristic of the names of living beings —which, however, is more than doubtful, as on the one hand *-s* is found in inanimates like Lit. *naktis*, L. *nox*, and on the other hand many animates seem never to have had -*s*, e.g. *pater*, G. *kuōn*.)

The distinction between animate (or personal) and inanimate (or impersonal) is sometimes shown indirectly in the way in which some case-forms are allowed to survive while others disappear The dative is more often used in words denoting living beings than with inanimates ; hence the acc. forms found in the oldest English, *mec*, *þec*, *usic*, *eowic* were early ousted by the dat. *me*, *þe*, *us*, *eow* (now *me*, *thee*, *us*, *you*), and somewhat later the old datives *hire* (*her*), *him*, *hem* (mod. *'em*), *hwam* (*whom*) displace the old accusatives *heo*, *hine*, *hie*, *hwane* ; *them* also is a dative. On the other hand, in the neuter it is the old accusatives *hit* (*it*), *that*, *what* that are preserved at the cost of the datives. Similarly in Dan. the old datives *ham*, *hende*, *dem*, *hvem* have ousted the accusatives (though it is true that in *mig*, *dig* the acc. has outlived the dative) ; in North German *wem* instead of *wen*, in Fr. *lui*, It. *lui*, *lei*, *loro* (when not used with a verb) we see the same tendency, while the acc. has carried the day in G. *was*, Fr. *quoi*, etc.

In substantives the old nominative has sometimes prevailed over the oblique cases in names of living beings, while the inverse is the case in names of inanimates. Thus it has been remarked by Behaghel, Bojunga and Tegnér that in the G. *n*-declension the old nom. without -*n* has held its own in names of living beings only : *bote*, *erbe*, *knabe*, while inanimates have generalized the oblique cases : *bogen*, *magen*, *tropfen*. In Swedish similarly the acc. has prevailed over the nom. in words like *maga*, *båga*, *strupa*, *aga*, *vana*, while names of persons have retained and generalized the nom. in -*e* : *gubbe*, *granne*, *bonde* (Tegnér G. 221). Another nom. ending has likewise been preserved in names of persons only : *slarver*, *spjuver*, *luver* (ibid. 225). Old French had a distinction between a nominative and an oblique case ; generally the latter has been generalized, but it has been remarked by Bréal (MSL 6. 170) that all the old nominatives that have been preserved denote human beings, e.g. *traître*, *sœur*, *fils*, *maire*.

As lifeless things are naturally reputed inferior in value to living beings, and as the neuter gender in those languages that have one is preferably used of things, this gender comes to have a certain depreciatory tinge when applied to human beings and animals : in Dan. it is noteworthy that many terms of abuse are neuter : *et fjols*, *pjok*, *fæ*, *bæst*, *drog* ; some words for animals that are chiefly used in a depreciatory sense, have in historical times changed their gender and have become neuter : *øg*, *asen*, *æsel*, *kreatur*. This may be compared with the well-known fact that diminutives in various languages are often neuter, even if the words from which they are derived have another gender : Gr. *paidion* ' little boy ' from *pais*, G. *fischlein, fräulein, bübchen, mädchen*, etc.[1] I suppose that when Italian has so many diminutives in *-ino* from feminines they were originally not real masculines but neuters : *casino, tavolino, ombrellino* from *casa, tavola, ombrella*, also *donnino, manino* by the side of *donnina, manina*, and I venture the conjecture that it is the same depreciatory neuter that is behind the curious occurrence of some forms in *-o* for smaller things by the side of words in *-a* for bigger things : *buco* ' a small hole,' *coltello* ' a small knife,' by the side of *buca, coltella*, etc. In the dialects of South-Eastern Jutland some names for young animals, which otherwise in Danish are of the common gender, have become neuter : *et kalv, hvalp, gris, kylling* (M. Kristensen, *Nydansk*, 1906, 57). In Swedish *individ* is always *en* if used of a human being, often also of higher animals, but in speaking of a lower animal *ett individ* is said (Tegnér G. 39) ; in Danish it is always neuter as Lat. and G.

Here and there we find a tendency to establish a grammatical distinction between thing-words (countables) and mass-words (uncountables) apart from the difference dealt with in the chapter on Number (XIV, p. 198 f.). In the south-western dialects of England "full shapen things " are referred to as *he*, acc. *en* (from OE. *hine*) and take the pronominal adjuncts *theäse, thik*, while " un-shapen quantities " are referred to as *it* and take *this, that : Come under theäse tree by this water | goo under thik tree, an zit on that grass* (Barnes, *Dorset Gr.* 20, Ellis EEP. 5. 85, Wright, *Dial. Gr.* § 393, 416 ff.). In other languages there is a tendency to use the neuter gender preferably with mass-words, thus G. *das gift, das kies* ' poison, gravel ' has taken or is taking the place of the older *die gift, der kies*. In the same way we have now in Danish *støvet* for older *støven* ' dust.' But in Danish this is carried further. Neuter forms of adjuncts are used to indicate quantity with mass-words even where these in other respects are of the common gender. Thus we say *mælken, osten* ' the milk, the cheese,' but *alt det mælk, noget andet ost* ' all that milk, some other cheese ' (as mass,—' another cheese ' as thing-word is *en anden ost*) ; *jeg kan ikke nøjes med det te* ' I cannot rest content with that (much) tea,' but . . . *med den tea* if the kind or quality is meant. Many dialects in Jutland go still further, all mass-words being made neuter without regard to the original gender. and in Hanherred a complementary change has taken place, all thing-names having been made of the common gender : *iset, jordet, skiben, husen* ' the ice, earth, ship, house,' where Standard Danish has *isen, jorden, skibet, huset*.

[1] It is curious that when these endings, which are otherwise always neuter, are added to proper names, it is possible to use the feminine article with *-chen : die arme Gretchen*, but not with *-li* (dial.) : *das Bäbeli*, though with male names one can say *der Jaköbli* (Tobler VB 5. 7).

Conceptional Neuter.

Before concluding this chapter on gender we still have to consider something which for want of a better name I propose to term " the conceptional neuter." It might be said to be the real or notional or universal neuter in opposition to the specified or concrete neuter which we have when in English we refer to a previously mentioned house or worm, etc., as *it*, and to the arbitrary neuter which we have when in German we refer to a previously mentioned *haus* or *mädchen* as *es* because the word happens to be of the neuter gender. It will appear from the following paragraphs that there are certain natural or notional functions for a neuter gender to fulfil, even though in many languages, which have not otherwise a neuter gender, there is nothing but a few pronominal forms to show the existence of this neuter in their grammatical system.

The first application of this unspecified or conceptional neuter is seen in such sentences as E. *it rains*, G. *es regnet*, Dan. *det regner*, Fr. *il pleut* (colloquially *ça pleut*), further *it snows, thunders*, etc., where it is difficult or impossible to define what *it* stands for : the whole situation of the atmosphere, if you like, but at any rate something thought of as definite in the same way as we use the definite article in " the weather is fine " or " the day is bright." Many languages here have no pronoun, Lat. *pluit*, It. *piove*, etc., and Brugmann and others see in the use of *it* a purely grammatical device, called forth by the habit of always having an express subject (*he comes, il vient*, where Lat. or It. has often merely the verbal form *venit, viene*). There is undoubtedly much truth in this consideration, but it does not give the whole truth, and Grimm (*Wörterbuch*) is not wholly wrong when he speaks of " das geisterhafte, gespenstige, unsichtbare, ungeheure " as expressed in the " impersonals " ; Spitzer uses the expression " das grosse neutrum der natur," and thinks that this *it* is just as much an outcome of man's mythopoetic imagination as *Juppiter tonat*.[1] I may here adduce on the one hand the following bit of conversation from one of Bennett's novels : " It only began to rain in earnest just as we got to the gate. Very thoughtful of it, I'm sure ! " and on the other hand, from a totally different sphere, Brownings use of *That* with a capital letter as a synonym for God : " Rejoice we are allied To That which doth provide And not partake, effect and not receive ! " (Rabbi Ben Ezra) and Hardy's similar use of *It* :

[1] In an article " Das synthetische und das symbolische neutralpronomen in französischen " in *Idealistische neuphilologie, Festschrift für Karl Vossler* 1922. The great neuter of Nature is seen also (without any pronoun) in Russian *otca derevom ubilo* 'it killed my father with a tree, my father was struck by a tree ' (Pedersen RG 110).

" Why doth It so and so, and ever so, This viewless, voiceless
Turner of the Wheel ? " which he justifies by saying that " the
abandonment of the masculine pronoun in allusion to the First
or Fundamental Energy seemed a necessary and logical consequence
of the long abandonment by thinkers of the anthropomorphic
conception of the same " (The Dynasts).

I find the same unspecified or conceptional *it* (though not the
great neuter of Nature) as an object in idiomatic combinations
like *to lord it* | *you are going it !* | *we can walk it perfectly well* | *let
us make a day of it*, etc. In the following sentence a comic effect
is produced by the ambiguity of *it* as specified and unspecified :
He never opens his mouth but he puts his foot in it.

Corresponding uses are found idiomatically in other languages,
for instance G. *sie hat es eilig* | *er treibt's arg* | Dan. *han har det
godt, sidder godt i det* | *han skal nok drive det vidt* | Fr. *l'emporter, le
prendre sur un certain ton*. In Dan. the n. *det* curiously inter-
changes with the common-gender form *den* : *ta den med ro* ' take
it easy ' during recent times has supplanted *ta det med ro*, and *den*
is found in many idiomatic phrases : *brænde den a, holde den gående*,
etc.

Note here also G. *es klopft an der tür*, Dan. *det banker på døren*,
corresponding to E. *someone* is knocking at the door (there is a
knock at the door) and Fr. *on* frappe à la porte.

Next we have a conceptional neuter in words like *what, nothing,
everything, something*, and it is interesting to notice that in Danish,
where *ting* is of the common gender, *ingenting* and *alting* ' nothing,
everything ' take the predicative in the neuter gender : *den ting
er sikker*, but *ingenting er sikkert*, etc. We see the same in the
Romanic languages where the Lat. neuter has been merged in the
masculine, but where these words, even those which were originally
feminine, are treated as masculines, i.e. neuters. Thus Fr. *rien*
from the Lat. f. *rem : rien n'est certain*, further *quelquechose de
bon*. In It. *qualche cosa, ogni cosa, che cosa* (and the abbreviated
interrogative *cosa = che cosa*) take the predicative in the masculine,
i.e. neuter : *che cosa fu detto ?* Thus also *nulla fu pubblicato* | *una
visione, un nulla che fosse femminile* (Serao, Cap. Sansone 87, 123).

A conceptional neuter is also found in connexion with adjectives
in the generic *the beautiful*, i.e. ' everything beautiful,' *the good*,
etc. Note that Spanish here has retained the Lat. neuter in the
form of the article : *lo bueno*, different from the masculine *el bueno*
' the good one.'

A further function of the conceptional neuter is to represent
a predicative as in : All men my brothers ? Nay, thank Heaven,
that they are not (Gissing, cf. MEG II. 16. 377) | you make him
into a smith, a carpenter, a mason : he is then and thenceforth

that and nothing else (Carlyle) | Marian grew up *everything* that her father desired (Gissing) | his former friends or masters, *whichever* they had been (Stevenson) | She had now become *what* she had always desired to be, Amy's intimate friend (Gissing) | she treated him like a tame cat, *which is what* he was (McKenna) | *What* is he ? Just *nothing* at all as yet. Sweet NEG § 212 has not understood this function of *what* when he speaks of it as " used in a personal sense " ; note that the answer to the question " What is he ? " may contain any predicative : " a shoemaker " or " kindhearted," etc.

We have exactly the same neuter in other languages. Dan. Er de modige ? Ja, *det er* de. *Hvad* er han ? G. Sind sie mutig ? Ja, *das* sind sie. Vom papst ist es bekannt, dass er, als er *es* noch nicht war, seine verhältnisse geregelt hatte. *Was* ist er ? Er ist noch *nichts*. Fr. Si elles sont belles, et si elles ne *le* sont pas. It. Pensare ch'egli era libero e che anche lei *lo* era ! (Fogazzaro). Sp. Personas que parecen buenas y no *lo* son (Galdós). Cf. also Gr. Ouk *agathon* polukoiraniē, and the G. n. sg. *Welches* sind Ihre bedingungen ? [1]

A notional neuter is also found where a pronoun represents a verb or a nexus : Can you forgive me ? Yes, *that* is easy enough | The Duke hath banished me. *That* he hath not (Sh.) | I'll write or, *what* is better, telegraph at once. Infinitives and whole clauses also always take articles, adjectives, etc., in the neuter gender in those languages which have one : Gr. *to pinein*, G. *das trinken* ; Lat. *humanum est errare*, etc.

[1] Cf. also the use of *that* in " Are there not seven planets ?—That there are, quoth my father " (Sterne).

CHAPTER XVIII

COMPARISON

Comparative and Superlative. Equality and Inequality. Weakened Superlatives and Comparatives. Latent Comparisons. Formal Comparatives. Indication of Distance. Secondaries and Tertiaries.

Comparative and Superlative.

IN all ordinary grammars we are taught that there are three "degrees of comparison,"

1.	positive : *old*	*dangerously*
2.	comparative : *older*	*more dangerously*
3.	superlative : *oldest*	*most dangerously.*

This tripartition no doubt corresponds with the actual *forms* found in the best-known languages, in which the "positive" is the fundamental form from which the two others are derived either by means of endings or by the addition of adverbs (subjuncts) like *more* and *most*. In some well-known instances the two higher degrees are taken from other stems than the positive : *good, better, best | bonus, melior, optimus*, etc.[1]

Let us now look a little more closely into this system from a *logical* point of view. In the first place, it does not require much thought to discover that the "positive" cannot strictly be called a "degree of comparison," for when we speak of a horse or a book as *old*, we do not compare it with any other horse or book ; the form, then, is rather "negative of comparison" than "positive," as the old grammarians termed it with their curious scorn of a good or consistent terminology. The term does not, however, do much harm, as it cannot very well be confounded with positive in the sense 'not negative.'

The way in which the three degrees are generally given makes us imagine that they represent a graduated scale, as if *old : older : oldest* formed a progression like, say, the numbers 1 : 2 : 3 (arithmetical progression) or 1 : 2 : 4 (geometrical progression). But this is only exceptionally the case, as in " The clowne bore it [my sonnet], the foole sent it, and the lady hath it : *sweete* clowne, *sweeter* foole, *sweetest* lady (Sh.) | We dined yesterday on *dirty*

---

[1] Some adjectives and adverbs are incapable of comparison, e.g. *other, several, half, daily, own*. On comparison of substantives see p. 80.

bacon, *dirtier* eggs, and *dirtiest* potatoes (Keats). This way of placing the three forms together [1] may really be due to the teaching of grammar ; but it is important to insist on the fact that in ordinary usage the superlative does not indicate a higher degree than the comparative, but really states the same degree, only looked at from a different point of view. If we compare the ages of four boys, A, B, C, and D, we may state the same fact in two different ways :

> *A is older than the other boys,* or
> *A is the oldest boy (the oldest of, or among, all the boys).*

In both cases A is compared with B, C, and D ; but the result is in the former case given with regard to these three (the *other* boys), in the latter with regard to *all* the boys, *himself included*. The comparative must thus be supplemented by a member (expressed or understood), added by means of *than* and different from the object compared, hence the frequent use of the word *other*. This kind of supplement is not possible in the case of a superlative, which, on the other hand, is often followed by *of* or *among all*. But as both forms really express the same idea, we should not be surprised to find a rather frequent confusion, resulting in such blendings as *the best of all others* ; see, e.g., a king, whose memory of all others we most adore (Bacon) | parents are the last of all others to be trusted with the education of their own children (Swift).

Now we can see how easy it was for languages that formerly possessed a real superlative, to give up this form and content themselves with the comparative. In the Romanic languages the only expression for the superlative idea is the comparative rendered definite either by the article or by some other defining word : *le plus grand malheur* | *mon meilleur ami*, etc. (Sometimes no defining word is required, as in " la vie, dans tout ce qu'elle a de *plus intensif*.") In Russian, the comparative similarly is often used as a kind of superlative, which is facilitated by the fact that the second member of comparison is added in the genitive, and that the same case is used as a partitive and thus corresponds both to Eng. *than* and *of* : *lúčše vsegó* = ' better than all ' or ' best of all ' | *bogáče vsěx* = ' richer than all ' or ' richest of all.' (Besides, the superlative may be expressed by *nai-* placed before the comparative or by *sámyj* ' self ' (H. Pedersen RG, p. 89 ; cf. Vondrák SG 1. 494 and 2. 71 ff.)

We have what might be called a limited superlative meaning ' better (etc.) than all the others with the exception of one (two,

---

[1] In which the superlative denotes what is otherwise indicated by *still:* still sweeter, still dirtier.

etc.) in *the next best, the largest but one* (*two*, etc.), *the third best*, etc. Similarly in Danish and German, where, however, no expressions exist corresponding to the English ones with *but*. There are many languages, on the contrary, which have no such easy ways of expressing this kind of superlative.

In German a curious confusion arises when a superlative is qualified by 'possible,' this word being put in the superlative form instead of the other adjective (adverb); both expressions are combined in a speech by Professor Jodl "das problem der *grösstmöglichen* glücksbefriedigung für die *möglichst grosse* zahl "; in English it would be "the greatest happiness possible for the greatest number possible."

Equality and Inequality.

If, then, we disregard the superlative as being really a kind of comparative, we may establish the following system of virtual comparison :

1. ($>$) more dangerous (better) than — superiority
2. ($=$) as dangerous (good) as — equality
3. ($<$) less dangerous (good) than — inferiority.

Obviously 1 and 3 are closely connected, as both denote inequality. English uses *than* with 1 and 3, and *as* with 2, while other languages use the same word in all three cases, thus Fr. *meilleur que, aussi bon que*. Danish distinguishes *end* and *som* as E., but some parts of Denmark (Fyn) use *som* even after comparatives. In the same way some parts of Germany use *wie* in all three kinds of comparison, while other parts of Germany use *wie* for equality only, and *als* with the comparative. Hence it is possible in Fr. to say, for instance, "il a autant ou peut-être plus d'argent *que* moi," where other languages have no such easy expression, for the sentence "he could box as well or better *than* I " (Wells) is felt as somewhat slipshod English.

In many cases our languages provide us with two expressions of opposite signification, which allow us to some extent to reverse the relation between stages 1 and 3 : *worse than* means the same thing as *less good than*. As *old* and *young* are opposites, we may establish the following equations :

1. older than = less young than
2. as old as = as young as
3. less old than = younger than.

But in practice the expressions with *less* are naturally little used; besides the two forms sub 2 are not exact synonyms : it would obviously be impossible to say *as young as the hills* instead of *as old as the hills.* This is a natural consequence of the fact, that *old*, besides having the neutral signification (as *vox media*) of ' having (this or that) age ' as in " baby is only two hours *old* " also signi-fies ' having a great age, advanced in years ' ; it is, indeed, in the latter sense that it forms a contrast to *young.* In some languages the two senses are kept distinct, as in Fr. *âgé de deux heures* | *vieux*, in Ido *evanta du hori* | *olda.*

Similarly, though *more unkind than = less kind than*, the terms *as unkind as* and *as kind as* are not synonyms, because the former implies that both persons compared are unkind, and the latter that both are kind. Comparison by means of *as* is therefore generally by no means neutral or indifferent, though it may occa-sionally be, as in " I don't think man has much capacity for development. He has got *as far as* he can, and that is not far, is it ? " (Wilde).

On the other hand, comparisons with *than* are as a rule indifferent or neutral ; " Peter is older than John " does not imply that Peter is old, and the comparative may really therefore indicate a lesser degree than the positive would in " Peter is old." Nor does the sentence " Peter is older than John " say anything about *John's* being old ; but that is implied if we add the sub-junct *still* : " Peter is still older than John " (thus also : Pierre est *encore* plus vieux que Jean | Peter er *endnu* ældre end Jens | Peter ist *noch* älter als Hans—by the way an interesting parallel development in different languages, for this use of *still* is not at all self-evident ; it is also found in Russian.

If we negative stage 1 (Peter is not older than John), the meaning may be either stage 2 (equality) or 3 (inferiority) ; in English a curious distinction is made between *not more than*, which is indistinct and may mean either 2 or 3, and *no more than*, which implies stage 2, equality. A negative stage 2 takes the form *not so old as* and practically always means stage 3 ' less old than, younger than ' ; a negative with *as* is not so frequent and may sometimes mean stage 1 if it has extra emphasis on *as*, as when the assertion " A is as old as B " is contradicted : " Oh no, not *as* old as B, but much older."

Weakened Superlatives and Comparatives.

There is a natural tendency to exaggerate by using the super-lative for a very high, instead of the highest, degree. This is sometimes termed the " absolute superlative," sometimes the " elative." Thus " with the greatest pleasure," " a most learned man," etc. This has become the rule in Italian and Spanish to such an extent that the old Latin superlative form is never used as a real superlative ; It. *bellissimo* ' very fine,' Sp. *doctìsimo* ' very learned,' etc.[1] In colloquial Norwegian we have the same with a negative : *ikke så værst* ' not so very bad.' In Danish a difference is made between the uninflected and the inflected superlative form, the former alone (without the article) meaning the real superlative, the latter the elative : med *störst* veltalenhed (more eloquently than anyone else) | med *störste* veltalenhed (very eloquently indeed).

Sometimes the comparative form is similarly used without implying a comparison, as Dan. " en *bedre* middag " (a good, or a pretty good, dinner). Thus also E. *rather*, e.g. " Does it rain ?— *Rather !* "

A similarly weakened comparative is found in Dan. *flere*, as in " ved flere lejligheder," where E. generally says more explicitly *more than one*, a plural of *one*. Curiously enough in this case, in which there is no comparison, some languages have a double comparative ending, G. *mehrere* (this could formerly take *als*, which is now impossible), late Lat. *plusiores*, whence Fr. *plusieurs*— which, in spite of its form, is really weaker than the ' positive ' *viele, beaucoup*.

Latent Comparisons.

In some linguistic expressions the comparative idea is latent. Thus in the verb *prefer* : I prefer A to B = I like A better than B (je préfère A à B | ich ziehe A dem B vor) ; in Ido the ordinary comparative connective is in this case used : me preferas A kam B = me prizas A plu kam B. This may be found very rarely in English, too, as in Thackeray Sk 138 preferring a solitude, and to be a bachelor, than to put up with one of these for a companion.— Further we have a latent comparative in *too* (*trop*, Dan. *for*, G. *zu*), which means ' more than enough,' or ' more than decent, or proper, or good.' Here, also, the distance may be indicated : *an hour too late* | *en time* for sent | *eine stunde* zu spät | trop tard *d'une heure*.—Cf. also *outlast* = ' last longer than,' *outlive* (*survive*), Dan. *overleve*, G. *überleben* ; *exceed*.

As latent comparatives must also be considered *before* and its opposite, Fr. *avant, après*, G. *vor, nach*, etc. ; note that E. *after* and Dan. *efter* are also formal comparatives ; the indication of distance is seen in " *an hour* before sunrise | *une heure* avant le lever du soleil | *eine stunde* vor dem sonnenaufgang," etc. But when we say " *after an hour* he came back " and similarly " *après une heure* il rentra," etc., we have really a confusion of the indication of distance and the object of the preposition, as it means

---

[1] Note also It. *medesimo*, Sp. *mismo*, Fr. *même* from *metipsimus* ; Sp. even *mismìsimo*.

'an hour after (his departure, or whatever was mentioned).' This may be compared to what has taken place in the mathematical use of *plus* and *minus* = augmented (lessened) by, cf. the translations "four less two," "quatre moins deux," "vier weniger zwei."

Fr. *cadet* and *aîné* are also latent comparatives, *il est mon cadet de deux ans* = 'he is two years younger than I (me).' Cf. also "il avait un frère *cadet, de dix ans moinds âgé,* ingénieur comme lui" (Rolland). A similar syntax is seen in English with some words taken over from Latin comparatives, though from a formal point of view they cannot in English be considered as comparatives ; thus " he is *my senior by two years,*" etc.

The irrationality of grammatical expressions is seen in the following facts. While Lat. *post* and *ante* are, as we have seen, virtual comparatives, they take *quam* only when the second member of comparison is a whole clause ; this is expressed in ordinary grammatical terminology by saying that *post* and *ante* are prepositions, but *postquam* and *antequam* are conjunctions ; but it is easy to see that this is not the usual function of *quam*, which here corresponds to E. *that* rather than to *than*. E. *after* and *before* can take both words and clauses (are both prepositions and conjunctions), cf. " he came after (before) the war " and " he came after (before) the war was over." In Danish the two words are treated differently, for *efter* requires the addition of *at* in order to be made a conjunction : " han kom efter krigen " | " han kom efterat krigen var forbi," while no *at* is required with *för* : " han kom för krigen " | " han kom för krigen var forbi " ; in both cases *förend* may be substituted (*end* means " than," the connective after comparatives), but vulgar speech inclines to add *at* to make it into a conjunction ; " han kom förend at krigen var forbi." In G. the dative case of the demonstrative-relative pronoun *dem* is required to change the preposition *nach* into the conjunction *nachdem,* while *vor (früher als)* is the preposition corresponding to the conjunction *ehe.* In Fr. we have *après* and *avant* as prepositions, *après que* and *avant que* as conjunctions, where it is impossible to tell whether *que* is 'than' or 'that' ; cf. also It. *poscia che.* (With an infinitive, French has, or had, the following constructions : *avant que de partir, avant de partir, avant que partir, avant partir.*)

Formal Comparatives.

On the other hand, we have a class of words which are, formally considered, comparatives, but are not notional comparatives in so far as they cannot take *than* : *upper, outer* and its doublet *utter, former*, etc. These have probably at no time had the true comparative functions ; but *latter* and *elder*, which now share the same inability to take *than*, were formerly true comparatives of *late* and *old*, and we still in Shakespeare find *elder than*. These, then, may be called ex-comparatives.

Other is a formal comparative, though there is no corresponding positive ; it can take *than* (thus also in other languages *autre que*, etc.). In English *other* sometimes infects its synonym *different*, which then takes *than* instead of the regular *from*, for instance : things will be made different for me than for others (Wilde) ; inversely one may find *from* after *another* : I hope to be another man from what I was (Dickens).

There are other well-known words in our languages formed with the same ending and still less to be considered as comparatives, namely pronominal words relating to the number of two like Lat. *uter, neuter*, OE. *ægðer, hwæðer*, E. *either, neither, whether*, etc.

It may be doubtful, perhaps, whether this Aryan suffix *-ter-* belonged originally to these pronominal words referring to two or was from the first a comparative ending.[1] But however that may be, we find in many languages the rule that when there is no direct comparison (with *than*) the comparative is used if two, and the superlative if more than two are referred to ; cf. Latin *major pars* if something is divided into two parts, *maxima pars* if there are three or more parts. In English we have, correspondingly, e.g. " If Hercules and Lychas plaie at dice Which is *the better* man, *the greater* throw May turne by fortune from *the weaker* hand " (Sh.), but apart from some set phrases like *the lower lip* and *the upper end* the natural tendency in modern English is to use the superlative everywhere, as in " whose blood is reddest, his or mine " (Sh.), see MEG II, 7. 77. This tendency has completely prevailed in Danish. It is curious to note that German here has a form composed of an old superlative with the comparative ending superadded : *ersterer*, and that the English equivalent *the former* is similarly formed from the OE. superlative *forma* (= *primus*) and the comparative ending *-er*.

Indication of Distance.

With comparisons of inequality the degree of difference (the distance) is often indicated, e.g. " he is *two years* older than his brother " ; also with *by* ; in Latin the ablative is here used, in G. frequently *um*, etc.

---

[1] Cp. the fact that in Finnic the interrogative *kumpi* ' which of two ' and the relative *jompi* ' which of two ' are formed and inflected like comparatives.

It is, accordingly, possible to combine the two kinds of com parison as in the sentence " She is *as much better than* her husband *as* champagne is *better than* beer " (cf. she is as superior to her husband as champagne is to beer ; the distance between her and her husband is like that between, etc.).

The distance with a comparative is in some instances indicated by means of the form *the* from the OE. instrumental case *þy*. This is a demonstrative pronoun in such combinations as " I like him all the better on account of his shyness " | " that makes it all the worse " | " so much the better " (in the two last examples *all* and *so much* also indicate the distance in addition to *the*, which is hardly felt to be more than an unmeaning expletive). But in " the more, the merrier " and similar collocations of two members, the first *the* is relative, while the second *the* is demonstrative ; the first member may be called the determinant, and the second the determined. In ordinary E. the two members have exactly the same construction, and there is nothing to show which is the dependent and which the principal clause in " the more he gets, the more he wants " ; but in Dan. and G. (and formerly also in E.) the word-order in such cases shows that the first is the deter minant, and the second the determined ; cf. " jo mere han fâr, des mere ønsker han " and " je mehr er bekommt, desto mehr wünscht er." The same relation between the two is sometimes indicated by the addition of *that* after the former *the*, e.g. The nearer that he came, the more she fled (Marlowe).

In the Russian construction with *čěm* . . . *těm*, the former is shown by the form to be a relative, and the latter a demonstrative pronoun in the instrumental denoting difference. But in French there is as little formal difference between the two as in English, and there is not even a word like *the* : " *plus* on est de fous, *plus* on rit." The two parts are therefore, even more than in English, felt to be grammatically on an equality, and this often manifests itself in the insertion of *et* as between two independent sentences : " plus il a, et plus il désire." [1]

The English (Old English) and similarly the Russian expression would seem to indicate exact proportionality (' by how much more . . . by so much more ') ; but in practice no such exact proportion exists, and the only mathematical formula to render such a combination as, for instance, " the more books he reads, the more stupid he becomes " would be something like

$$S_{(n + 1)} > S_{(n)}$$

[1] Thus also in It. : ma più ti guardo, e più mi sento commuovere (Serao). Cf. on the other hand : Quanto più ti costa, tanto più devi parlare (Giacosa). On earlier expressions in French with *que plus*, *quant plus*, etc., see Tobler VB 2. 59 ff.

where $S_{(n)}$ means the degree of stupidity found after reading n books.

In most cases the determinant is placed first, and it is this nearly fixed custom which allows of the grammatical conformity between the two members in English and French. If the order is reversed, other more explicit or more clumsy formulas than the usual ones must be used in F. " la figure est *d'autant plus* admirable *qu'*elle est *mieux* proportionnée " (= mieux la figure est proportionnée, plus elle est admirable) | " Si la vie réalise un plan, elle devra manifester une harmonie *plus* haute *à mesure qu'*elle avance *plus* loin " (Bergson). In English a change in the word-order generally is all that is required to make the sense clear : they liked the book the better, the more it made them cry (Goldsmith).

There is an interesting sub-class of these expressions of proportional correlation, in which the determinant is the length of time, but is not explicitly expressed as such. Different languages have different ways of indicating this : the usual English way is by means of a repeated comparative, as in " it grew *darker and darker* " (= the longer it lasted, the darker it grew) | he became "*more and more* impatient," etc. Similarly in Danish and other languages. Poets often substitute the positive for the first comparative, as " and swift and swifter grew the vessel's motion " (Shelley) ; another expression is seen in " her position was becoming *daily more* insecure." A third expression is by means of *ever* : he spoke ever more indistinctly. This is rare in English, but the corresponding formula is the usual one in German : es wurde immer dunkler | er sprach immer weniger. The usual French equivalent is *de plus en plus* (de plus en plus obscur | il parla de moins en moins, etc.). The idea here is that it was already at the starting point darker (than previously) and that it then became darker still (but ' still ' is not expressed).

Secondaries and Tertiaries.

The comparison is in the vast majority of cases between two primaries as in " John is older than Tom | this house is bigger than ours | I like claret better than beer." But sometimes two secondary or tertiary notions (' qualities ') may be compared as in " his speech was more eloquent than convincing | he spoke more eloquently than convincingly." Here English requires the periphrasis with *more* [1] (similarly in Danish and German), while Latin has the well-known illogical expression with the comparative

---

[1] Cf., however, the dictionary definition of *oblong* : longer than broad. Somewhat differently : Aunt Sarah, *deafer than deaf*.

in the second adjective (adverb) as well as in the first : *verior quam gratior*.

Two verbs may also be compared : he felt rather than saw her presence in the room. This really implies a stylistic rather than a real comparison, and means something like "*felt* would be a more correct expression than *saw*." A similar idea is at the bottom of such expressions as " this rather frightened him," where the second term of comparison is left unexpressed, but where the original idea is "*frightened* is a more adequate expression than any other verb." This then leads us to such expressions as " there are some things which I *more than dislike*," where the first term is omitted : *dislike* is too weak an expression.

TIME AND TENSE

The Nine-Tense System. Seven Tenses. Main Divisions of Time. Sub-ordinate Divisions of Time. Economy of Speech. Non-temporal Use of Tenses.

The Nine-Tense System.

In this chapter we shall deal with the linguistic expressions for the natural (or notional) concept "time" and its subdivisions. In many languages we find time-indications expressed in verbal forms, the so-called "tenses," and this has appeared to many grammarians so natural that they have considered tense-distinction the chief characteristic of verbs (hence G. *zeitwort*). But there are languages whose verbs do not distinguish tenses, and even in English, which ordinarily distinguishes tenses, we find such verbs as *must, ought*, which in the modern language have only one "tense"; on the other hand, time is often indicated by means of other words than verbs, and this way of indicating time is often much more precise than that effected by means of verbal forms can ever be, as when we say "on the third of February, 1923, at 11.23 p.m."

Let us, however, confine ourselves in the first place to those time-distinctions that find expression in the verbs of the best-known languages. The first question then is, can we establish a scheme of "tenses" of universal application?

In Madvig's *Latin Grammar* we find the following system. Anything said may be referred either simply to one of the three chief tenses, present, past, and future, or be indicated relatively with regard to some definite point (past or future) as present, past or future at that time. Thus we get the following nine divisions, which I mention here in Madvig's terms and with his examples, adding only the numbers I, II, III and 1, 2, 3 for later references.

	I præsens	II præteritum	III futurum
	1 *scribo*	*scripsi*	*scribam*
in præterito	2 *scribebam*	*scripseram*	*scripturus eram (fui)*
in futuro	3 *scribam*	*scripsero*	*scripturus ero*

[1] Chapters XIX and XX are a re-written, re-arranged, in many parts shortened, in other parts expanded edition of a paper "Tid og tempus" in *Oversigt over det danske videnskabernes selskabs forhandlinger*, 1914, 367–420.

The first line has no special designation ; parallel to the others it should be " in præsenti."

Closely connected systems with three times three tenses are found in other works (by Matzen, Kroman, Noreen, see details and criticism in *Tid og tempus*, 374) and are there given as purely logical systems without any regard to the way in which those nine categories are represented in actual language. Madvig probably meant his system as an empirical one for Latin exclusively (in his Greek Syntax he does not give the scheme and would have had difficulties in finding a place for the aorist in it), but even as a description of the Latin tenses the system has certain drawbacks. *Scribam* is found in two places, as præsens in futuro (I 3) and as futurum in præsenti (III 1) while other forms are given only once. In the III series it would be natural to expect 1. *scripturus sum*, parallel with the other forms, and the reason for the discrepancy evidently is that *scripturus sum* implies a near future, and Madvig did not want to have the element of distance in time mixed up with his system. It is, however, difficult to keep this element of nearness apart from the other composite forms with *scripturus*, and in his Greek Syntax, § 116, Madvig applies the terms futurum in præsenti and futurum in præterito to the combinations with *mellō* and *emellon*, which admittedly imply nearness in time, and the same element is also present in the III-series as given by Kroman and Noreen. If, on the other hand, this element is discarded, there is no necessity for having both a præsens in futuro and a futurum in præsenti. These must be regarded as one, represented by *scribam*, but then analogy would require us to identify also I 2 præsens in præterito with II 1 præteritum in præsenti : the difference between *scribebam* and *scripsi* is not indicated with sufficient precision by their places in the system, as shown incidentally by Madvig's placing *scripturus eram* and *scripturus fui* at one and the same place (III 2). These two are not synonymous, being distinguished exactly in the same way as *scribebam* and *scripsi*, but the distinction, to which we shall have to revert, has really nothing directly to do with the other time-distinctions contained in the scheme. It would be best, therefore, to reduce the scheme from nine to seven places, merging into one I 2 and II 1 and in the same way I 3 and III 1.

Seven Tenses.

If now we want to arrange these seven tenses in a consistent scheme we encounter first the difficulty of terminology. It would be best to have two separate sets of terms, one for the notional or natural divisions of time and one for the grammatical (syntactic) tense-distinctions. In Danish, and also in German, it is very convenient to use native terms for the former, and Latin terms for the latter; thus *nutid, fortid, fremtid* (*jetztzeit, vorzeit, zukunft*) of the three chief divisions of time, and *præsens, præteritum, futurum* for the three verbal tenses. But in English we cannot do exactly the same thing, because there are no native (Anglo-Saxon) words corresponding to present and future, which thus must be used both for natural time and for grammatical tense (for it would hardly do to distinguish between *present* and *præsens*, between *future* and *futurum*). We may, however, reserve the word *past* (*past time*) for the notional past and use *preterit* about the corresponding tense. Wherever it is required for the sake of clearness, I shall say *present time* or *present tense, future time* or *future tense* respectively. For subdivisions I would propose the employment of the prefixes *before* and *after* as notional and the prefixes *ante* and *post* as syntactic designations (e.g. *before-past, ante-preterit*).

The next question that arises is how to arrange the seven "times" recognized above? One method would be to place them in a triangle:

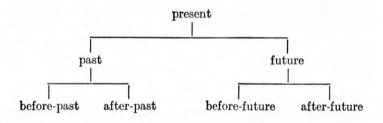

But this arrangement is not satisfactory, and it is much better to arrange the seven "times" in one straight line. Before-past is evidently "past in past," and in the same way after-past becomes "future in past," and analogously before-future is "past in future," and after-future is "future in future," to use clumsy terms reminding one of Madvig's system.

We thus get a system which avoids Madvig's two serious logical errors, (1) that of a tripartition of "now," which as a point has no dimensions and cannot be divided, and (2) the even more serious mistake of arranging time in a two-dimensional scheme with three times three compartments. For there can be no doubt that we are obliged (by the essence of time itself, or at any rate by a necessity of our thinking) to figure to ourselves time as something having one dimension only, thus capable of being represented by one straight line.

The three main divisions of time accordingly have to be arranged in the following way :

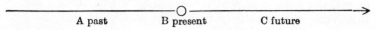

| A past | B present | C future |

The insertion of the intermediate " times " gives us this scheme, in which we place the notional terms above, and the corresponding grammatical terms below, the line which represents the course of time :

	A past				C future	
before-past	past	after-past	present	before-future	future	after-future
Aa	Ab	Ac	B	Ca	Cb	Cc
ante-preterit	preterit	post-preterit	present	ante-future	future	post-future

This figure, and the letters indicating the various divisions, show the relative value of the seven points, the subordinate " times " being orientated with regard to some point in the past (Ab) and in the future (Cb) exactly as the main times (A and C) are orientated with regard to the present moment (B).

The system thus attained seems to be logically impregnable, but, as we shall see, it does not claim to comprise all possible time-categories nor all those tenses that are actually found in languages.[1] It will now be our task to go through these seven divisions, taking first the main ones and then the subordinate ones, and to examine how they are actually expressed in various languages.

Main Divisions of Time.

(A) *Simple past time.*—For this there is in English one tense, the preterit, e.g. *wrote*. Other languages have two tenses, e.g. Lat. *scripsi, scribebam* ; on the difference see below, p. 275. While in these languages the distance of time from the present moment is quite immaterial, some languages have separate preterits for the distant and for the near past. The latter is expressed in French by means of the periphrasis *je viens d'écrire*.

---

[1] A somewhat similar arrangement, in which an attempt has been made to comprise a great many distinctions, which according to my view have nothing to do with the simple straight time-line, is found in Sheffield GTh 131. For criticism see "Tid og Tempus," 383 f.

Among expressions for the simple past we must here also mention the so-called historic present, which it would be better to call the unhistoric present, or, taking a hint thrown out by Brugmann, the *dramatic present*. The speaker in using it steps outside the frame of history, visualizing and representing what happened in the past as if it were present before his eyes. As Noreen has it, it serves to produce an artistic illusion. But however artistic this trick is, it must not be imagined that it is not popular in its origin ; one need only listen to the way in which people of the humblest ranks relate incidents that they have witnessed themselves to see how natural, nay inevitable, this form is. Yet Sweet thinks that in English it is due to literary influence from French and Latin, and that in the Icelandic sagas, where it is extremely frequent, it was borrowed from Irish (Philol. Soc. Proceedings, 1885–87, p. xlv, NEG § 2228). Einenkel and others think that its use in Middle English is due to Old French. But in Middle English it is especially frequent in popular poetry, where foreign influence of a syntactic character is highly improbable. The non-occurrence or rare occurrence of this present in Old English must, I think, be explained by the fact that Old English literature gives us none of those vivid narratives in natural prose for which Iceland is justly famous. On the whole the dramatic present belongs to that class of everyday expressions which crop up comparatively late in writing, because they were looked upon as being below the dignity of literature. It is never found in Homer, but is frequent in Herodotus. Delbrück is no doubt right when he says that it is " gewiss uraltvolkstümlich " (Synt. 2. 261).

(B) *Simple present time*.—For this those languages that have tense distinctions in their verbs generally use the present tense.

But what is the present time ? Theoretically it is a point, which has no duration, any more than a point in theoretic geometry has dimension. The present moment, " now," is nothing but the ever-fleeting boundary between the past and the future, it is continually moving " to the right " along the line figured above. But in practice " now " means a time with an appreciable duration, the length of which varies greatly according to circumstances ; cf. such sentences as " he is hungry | he is ill | he is dead." This is exactly what happens with the corresponding spatial word " here," which according to circumstances means very different things (in this room, in this house, in this town, in this country, in Europe, in this world), and with the word " we," which may embrace a varying number of individuals beside the speaker, the only thing required being (with *here*) that the spot where the present speaker is at the moment, and (with *we*) that the present speaker, is included. With regard to the present tense all languages seem to agree in having the rule that the only thing required is that the theoretical zero-point, " now " in its strictest sense, falls within the period alluded to. This definition applies to cases like : he lives at number 7 | knives are sharp | lead is heavy | water boils at 100 degrees Celsius | twice four is eight. With regard to such " eternal truths " it has sometimes been (wrongly) said that our languages are faulty because they state them only in reference to present time without having means to express that they were equally valid in the past and will be so in the future. The remark loses its sting when we take into consideration that most or all of our pronouncements about present time necessarily concern some part of what belongs strictly to the past and to the future. If " present time " is defined as is done here, it is applicable even to intermittent occurrences like the following : I get up every morning at seven (even when spoken in the evening) [1] | the train starts at 8.32 | the steamer leaves every Tuesday in winter, but in summer both on Tuesdays and Fridays. In the last sentence the present moment falls within the limits of what is spoken about, for the saying concerns the present arrangement, valid for the present year as well as for the last few years and presumably for the next few years as well.

This manner of viewing things seems to me preferable to that adopted by Sweet, who writes (NEG, § 289) that " for the purpose of such statements (as *the sun rises in the east, platinum is the heaviest metal*) the present is best suited, as being in itself the most indefinite of the tenses "—why indefinite ? Still less can we call such sentences " timeless " (zeitlos), as is often done.[2] It would be better to speak of " generic time " in the same way as we have spoken of " generic number " and " generic person." If for such statements the present tense is generally used, it is in order to affirm that they are valid now. But other tenses may occasionally be used : we have the so-called " gnomic preterit " as in Shakespeare's " Men were deceivers ever " (cf. the Greek gnomic aorist)—a sort of stylistic trick to make the hearer himself draw the conclusion that what has hitherto been true is so still and will remain so to the end of time. On the other hand, the future tense is used " gnomically " in Fr. " rira bien qui rira le dernier," where the corresponding proverbs in other languages

---

[1] If we represent each act of getting up (at seven) by a dot, and the present moment by O, we get the following figure, which shows that the condition for using the present tense is fulfilled :

. . . . . . O . . . , etc.

[2] Brunot says : " *la terre tourne autour du soleil* présente une action située hors du temps " (PL 210) and " Les actions situées hors du temps s'expriment au présent " (ib. 788).

use the present tense : the reason for the French tense is that the proverb is most often quoted when somebody else is laughing and the speaker wants to say that he will laugh later and that that will be better.[1]

(C) *Simple future time.*—It is easy to understand that expressions for times to come are less definite and less explicit in our languages than those for the past : we do not know so much about the future as about the past and are therefore obliged to talk about it in a more vague way. Many languages have no future tense proper or have even given up forms which they had once and replaced them by circuitous substitutes. I shall here give a survey of the principal ways in which languages have come to possess expressions for future time.

(1) The present tense is used in a future sense. This is particularly easy when the sentence contains a precise indication of time in the form of a subjunct and when the distance in time from the present moment is not very great : I dine with my uncle to-night. The extent to which the present tense is thus used is different in different languages ; the tendency is strongest with verbs denoting ' go ' : I start to-morrow | ich reise morgen ab | jeg rejser imorgen | je pars demain | parto domani, etc. Gr. *eîmi* ' I go ' nearly always means ' I shall go.' The present tense is also extensively used in clauses beginning with *when* and *if* : " I shall mention it when I see him (if I see him) " ; in French with *si* : " Je le dirai si je le vois," but not with *quand* : " quand je le verrai."

(2) Volition. Both E. *will* and Dan. *vil* to a certain degree retain traces of the original meaning of real volition, and therefore E. *will go* cannot be given as a pure ' future tense,' though it approaches that function, as seen especially when it is applied to natural phenomena as *it will certainly rain before night*. There is also an increasing tendency to use (*wi*)*ll* in the first person instead of *shall*, as in *I'm afraid I'll die soon* (especially in Sc. and Amr.), which makes *will* even more the common auxiliary of the future. In German *wollen* has to be used in " es scheint regnen zu wollen," because the usual auxiliary *werden* cannot be used in the infinitive. The future is expressed by volition also in Rumanian *voiu canta* ' I will (shall) sing ' ; cp. also occasional It. *vuol piovere* (Rovetta, Moglie di Sua Eccel. 155). In Modern Greek the idea of volition seems to have been completely obliterated from the combinations with *tha* : *tha graphō* and *tha grapsō* ' I shall write ' (regularly, or once) ; *tha*, formerly *thena*, is derived from the

---

We may have a generic past time : last year the early morning train started at 6.15. This is not the place to discuss some interesting uses of the present tense, as in " I *hear* (I *see* in the papers) that the Prime Minister is ill | I *come* to bury Cæsar, not to praise him," etc.

third person *the* = *thelei* + *na* 'that' from *hina* and has now become a pure temporal particle.[1]

(3) Thought, intention. ON *mun*. This cannot easily be kept apart from volition.

(4) Obligation. This is the original meaning of OE. *sceal*, now *shall*, Dutch *zal*. In English the meaning of obligation is nearly effaced, but the use of the auxiliary is restricted to the first person in assertions and to the second person in questions, though in some classes of subordinate clauses it is used in all three persons.[2] The meaning of obligation also clung at first to the Romanic form from *scribere-habeo* 'I have to write,' which has now become a pure future tense, It. *scriverò*, Fr. *écrirai*, etc. Under this head we may also place E. *is to* as in "he is to start to-morrow."

(5) Motion. Verbs meaning 'go' and 'come' are frequently used to indicate futurity, as in Fr. *je vais écrire*, used of the near future, E. *I am going to write*, which sometimes, though by no means always, has the same nuance of nearness, and finally with out that nuance Swed. *jag kommer att skriva*, Fr. *quand je viendrai à mourir*, E. *I wish that you may come to be ashamed of what you have done | they may get to know it*. (But Dan. *jeg kommer til at skrive* denotes either the accidental or the necessary, either 'I happen to write' or 'I (shall) have to write'.)

(6) Possibility. E. *may* frequently denotes a somewhat vague futurity : *this may end in disaster*. Here we may mention those cases in which an original present subjunctive has become a future tense, as Lat. *scribam*.

(7) There are other ways in which expressions for futurity may develop. G. *ich werde schreiben* according to some is derived from a participial construction *ich werde schreibend*, but this is not always recognized ; it is not mentioned in Paul Gr 4. 127 and 148, where the treatment of the future is very unsatisfactory. The Gr. future in -*sō* (*leipsō*, etc.) is said to have been originally a desiderative.

A notional imperative necessarily has relation to the future time. Where, as in Latin, there are two tenses in the imperative, both really refer to the future, the so-called present imperative referring either to the immediate future or to some indefinite time

---

[1] In It. *sta per partire* 'he is going to start' the notion of future seems to be due to *per* denoting an intention ('in order to') ; cf. also *la bottega è per chiudersi* 'the shop is going to be closed.'

[2] In German *sollen* is sometimes used as an auxiliary of the future, as in "Es handelt sich hierbei freilich meist um dinge, die erst werden sollen" (Bernhardi), where *werden werden* would, of course, be awkward. In French I find : "L'ouvrage semble devoir être très complet et précis" (Huchon, *Hist. de la langue angl.* vii, in speaking of a work of which he has only seen one instalment): *devoir être* stands for the missing fut. inf. = 'sera, à ce qu'il semble.'

in the future, and the so-called future imperative being used chiefly
with regard to some specially indicated time. A "perfect imperative" also refers to future time, the use of the perfect being a
stylistic trick to indicate how rapidly the speaker wants his command executed : *be gone!* When we say *Have done!* we mean
the same thing as "Stop at once!" or "Don't go on!" but this
is expressed circuitously : 'let that which you have already done
(said) be enough.'

Subordinate Divisions of Time.

Next we come to consider the subordinate divisions of time,
i.e. points in time anterior or posterior to some other point (past
or future) mentioned or implied in the sentence concerned.

(Aa). Before-past time. This requires to be mentioned so
frequently that many languages have developed special tenses
for it : ante-preterit (pluperfect, past perfect), either simple as
Lat. *scripseram* or periphrastic, as E. *had written* and the corresponding forms in the other Gothonic and in the Romanic languages. In OE. before-past was often indicated by means of the
simple preterit with the adverb *ær* : *þæt þe he ær sæde* 'what he
had said,' literally 'that which he before said.'

The relations between the two "times," the simple past and
the before-past, may be represented graphically thus, the line
denoting the time it took to write the letter, and the point c the
time of his coming :

I had written the letter before he came = *he came after I had
written the letter* : —— c.

He came before I had written the letter = either *I finished writing
the letter after he had come*, or *I wrote the letter after he had come* :
—— or c ——.
c

(Ac). After-past time. I know of no language which possesses
a simple tense (post-preterit) for this notion. A usual expression
is by a verb denoting destiny or obligation, in E. most often *was
to* : Next year she gave birth to a son who *was to cause her great
anxiety* | It was Monday night. On Wednesday morning Mon-
mouth *was to die* (Macaulay) | he *was not destined to arrive* there
as soon as he had hoped to do (Kingsley). Similarly in other languages. Dan. : Næste år fødte hun en søn som skulde volde
hende store bekymringer | G. Im nächsten jahre gebahr sie einen
sohn, der ihr grosse bekümmernis *verursachen sollte* | Fr. Quand
Jacques donna à l'électeur Frédéric sa fille qui *devait être* la tige
des rois actuels d'Angleterre (Jusserand) | Je ne prévoyais point

tous les malheurs qui *allaient nous frapper* coup sur coup (Sarcey). Sometimes in Fr. the future is used, which corresponds to the dramatic present : Irrité de l'obstination de Biron et voulant donner à la noblesse un de ces exemples que Richelieu *multipliera*, Henri IV laissa exécuter la sentence. Gr. : tēn hodon hēi de *emellen* enıoi kaka kēde' *esesthai* (Od. 6. 165 ' the expedition that was to bring about sufferings ' ; cf. ibid. 7. 270, 8. 510).[1]

(Ca). Before-future time. The corresponding tense (the ante-future) is usually termed futurum exactum or the future perfect. Lat. *scripsero*, in our modern languages periphrastic : *I shall have written (he will have written), er wird geschrieben haben, il aura écrit*, etc. In Dan. the element of futurity is generally left unexpressed : Hvis du kommer klokken 7, *har han skrevet* brevet (. . . *har vi spist*, . . . *er solen gået ned*). Thus also in E. and G. after conjunctions of time : I shall be glad when her marriage *has taken place* | ich werde froh sein wenn die hochzeit *stattgefunden hat*.

As above, under Aa, we may here give a graphical representation of the time-relation :

I shall have written the letter before he comes = *he will come after I have written (shall have written) the letter* :—— c.

He will come before I (shall) have written the letter = either *I shall finish writing the letter after he has come*, or *I shall write the letter after he has come* : $\frac{}{c}$ or c ——.

(Cc). After-future. This has chiefly a theoretic interest, and I doubt very much whether forms like *I shall be going to write* (which implies nearness in time to the chief future time) or *scripturus ero* are of very frequent occurrence. Madvig has an example from Cicero : " Orator eorum, apud quos aliquid aget aut acturus erit, mentes sensusque degustet oportet," but it will be seen that here the future *aget*, which drags the after-future along with it, is really a generic present, put in the future tense on account of *oportet* : it is (now and always) the duty of the orator to consider those before whom he is talking or will talk (is going to talk). Otherwise it must be said that the natural expression for what at some future time is still to come is a negative sentence : If you come at seven, *we shall not yet have dined* (. . . *the sun will not yet have set*) | *si tu viens à sept heures, nous n'aurons pas encore dîné* (. . . *le soleil ne se sera pas encore couché*). In Dan. generally with the element of futurity unexpressed : hvis du

---

[1] The use of *came* in the following quotation from Dickens is to be compared with C nr. 5, p. 261 above : the influence for all good which she came to exercise over me at a later time . . .

kommer kl. 7, *har vi ikke spist endnu* (. . . *er solen ikke gået ned endnu*).[1]

Economy of Speech.

Languages differ very much in their economy in the use of tenses as well as in other respects. Those languages which admit sentences like " I start to-morrow " use one sign for the future time (the adverb) where other languages force their speakers to use two, as in " cras ibo " (I shall start to-morrow). This is parallel to the economical expression in " my old friend's father " with only one genitive mark as compared with " pater veteris mei amici," or to " ten trout " as against " ten men " or " decem viri." Latin is often praised for its logic in such things, as when Weise writes : " Der gesunde menschenverstand befähigte den römer besonders zu genauer scheidung der begriffe, schärfe der darstellung, klarheit und durchsichtigkeit der rede. . . . Der gebildete römer ist peinlich sorgfältig in der tempusbezeichnung : ' Ich werde kommen, wenn ich kann ' heisst bei ihm : *veniam, si potero* ; ' wie du sähest, so wirst du ernten ' : *ut sememtem feceris, ita metes* ; ' so oft er fiel, stand er auf ' : *cum ceciderat, surgebat*." English and Danish in these matters generally agree with German. But it must be remembered that it cannot be called illogical to omit the designation of what goes without saying : situation and context make many things clear which a strict logician in a pedantic analysis would prefer to see stated. Nor should it be forgotten that Latin in other cases is economical enough. *Postquam urbem liquit* : here the before-past time is expressed by the combination of *postquam* (before) and *liquit* (past) ; English allows both the shorter and the more explicit expression : *after he left the town, after he had left* ; Danish and German requires the double expression : *efterat han havde forladt byen | nachdem er die stadt verlassen hatte*. Latin is also economical in omitting the mark of past time in *hoc dum narrat, forte audivi* ' while she was telling this tale I happened to overhear it.' There are really two (relative) time-indications saved in Shakespeare's " our vizards wee will change after we *leaue* them " (after we shall have left them, Ca), and in " you must leave the house before more harm is done " (= shall have been done). Such savings of time-indications in the tense of the verb are particularly frequent after conjunctions of time and of condition ; note thus the difference between the two *when*-clauses : " We do not know when he will come, but when he comes he will not find us ungrateful "—the first *when* is interrogative,

---

[1] It is clear that we have not after-future, but simple future in " (To-morrow he will go to Liverpool, and) not long after that he will sail for America."

and the second a relative adverb or a conjunction. In French with *quand* we should have *il viendra* in both clauses, but if we substitute *if*, we see the same difference as in English : " Nous ne savons pas s'il viendra, mais s'il vient il ne nous trouvera pas ingrats."

Non-temporal Use of Tenses.

What is usually a grammatical sign for a time relation may sometimes be used for other notional purposes. Thus a future tense is often used to express a mere supposition or surmise with regard to the present time : *il dormira déjà* = *he will already be asleep* = *er wird schon schlafen* (I suppose that he is asleep) and in the same way *il l'aura vu* = *he will have seen it* = *er wird es gesehen haben* (he has probably seen it). It is true that we can assert nothing with regard to a future time but mere suppositions and surmises, and this truth is here linguistically reversed as if futurity and supposition were identical. Or it may be that the idea is this : ' it will (some time in the future) appear that he is already (at the present moment) asleep,' in the same way as we may use *hope*, which implies the future, with a subordinate clause in the present or perfect : " I hope he is already asleep," " I hope he has paid his bill," i.e. that it will turn out later that he is now asleep or has now paid.

The most important non-temporal use of preterit forms is to indicate unreality or impossibility. This is found in wishes and in conditional sentences. If we want to find a logical connexion between this use and the normal temporal use of the preterit, we may say that the common link is that something is in all these cases denied with regard to the present time. " At that time he had money enough," " I wish he had money enough," and " If he had money enough "—each of these sentences is in its own way a contrast to " he has money enough."

" I wish he had money enough " expresses by its preterit a wish with regard to the present time, and at the same time its impossibility or unreality (unfortunately he has not money enough) ; in the same way the ante-preterit in " I wish he had had money enough " expresses a wish with regard to some past period and at the same time denies that he had money enough then. But with regard to future time it is not as a rule possible to deny anything so categorically, and the corresponding tense-shifting (*would* instead of *will*) therefore merely serves to express uncertainty of fulfilment : " I wish he would send the money to-morrow," whereas " I hope he will send the money to-morrow " expresses the wish without saying anything about the probability of its fulfilment.

In conditional clauses we see the same shiftings. "If he had money enough" has reference to the present time and denies that he has; "if he had had money enough" has reference to the past and denies that he had money enough; "if he should have money enough" has reference to the future, but instead of denying it only leaves it uncertain whether he will get it or no. But the last form may be used also to express a doubt with regard to the present time: "if he should be innocent"—meaning perhaps in most cases "if it turns out (fut. time) that he is (now) innocent," etc.—In speaking of the future the simple preterit (without *should*) may also be used: "It would be a pity if he missed the boat to-morrow." [1]

We may sometimes, chiefly in colloquial speech, meet with a further shifting, the ante-preterit being used not only of the past, but also of the present time, simply to intensify the unreality irrespective of time. Thus we may say: "If I had had money enough (at the present moment), I would have paid you," and "I wish I had had money enough (now) to pay you."

It is also interesting to observe that the use of the preterit to denote unreality at the present time leads to the consequence that it may be used in speaking of the future, as in "It is high time the boy went to bed."

In wishes and conditions the unreality or impossibility was not originally denoted by the tense-shifting in itself, but required also the shifting from the indicative to the subjunctive, as still in German. But in Danish there is now in the preterit (and ante-preterit) no formal distinction between the two moods, and the modification of meaning is thus made contingent on the tense only. It is the same in English in more than 99 per cent. of the cases, as the old preterit subjunctive is identical with the indicative, except in the singular of the one verb *be*, where *was* and *were* are still distinct. It is easy to understand, therefore, that the instinctive feeling for the difference between these two forms cannot be vivid enough to prevent the use of *was*, where *were* would have been required some centuries ago. Since ab. 1700 *was* has been increasingly frequent in these positions: I wish he was present to hear you (Defoe) | a murder behind the scenes will affect the audience with greater terror than if it was acted before their eyes (Fielding). In literary language there has recently been a reaction in favour of *were*, which is preferred by most teachers; but in colloquial speech *were* is comparatively rare, except in the phrase "if I were you," and it is worth remarking that *was* is

---

[1] The tense-shifting is also found in cases where the hypothetical character of the clause is not indicated expressly by means of such a conjunction as *if*: Fancy your wife attached to a mother who *dropped* her *h*'s (Thackeray).

decidedly more emphatic than *were*, and thus may be said to
mark the impossibility better than the old subjunctive form :
" I'm not rich. I wish I was " | " I am ill. If I wasn't, I should
come with you "—thus often in the negative form. In this way
we get a distinction between " If he were to call " with weak
were, denoting vaguely a future possibility, and " If he was to
call " with strong *was*, denying that he *is* to call (now),
with the use of *is to* which is nearly synonymous with *has to*,
is bound to : " If I was to open my heart to you, I could show
you strange sights " (Cowper) | " If I was to be shot for it I
couldn't " (Shaw).

In French we have the corresponding use of the preterit and
ante-preterit in conditional sentences, and here too the indicative
has prevailed over the subjunctive, though the forms were more
different than was the case in English and Danish : " s'il avait
assez d'argent, il payerait," formerly " s'il eût . . ."

I have here spoken of the tense in the conditional (subordinate)
clause only, but originally the same rules applied to the conditioned
(principal) clause as well. Thus we have : " But if my father
had not scanted me. . . . Yourselfe, renowned Prince, than *stood*
as faire As any commer (Sh.) | She *were* an excellent wife for Bene-
dick (Sh.). Correspondingly in the ante-preterit : " If thou hadst
bene here, my brother *had not died* " (A.V.). But just as there is
a strong tendency to express the future more clearly in principal
sentences than in subordinate clauses (which in English is effected
by the use of *will* or *shall*), in the same way the shorter expression
has in these conditioned sentences been supplanted by a fuller
one with *should* or *would* : *you would stand* | *she would be* | *my
brother would not have died*, etc. *Could* and *might* are still used
in the old way in principal sentences because these verbs have
no infinitives and thus cannot be combined with *should* or *would* ;
e.g. How *could* I be angry with you ? | He *might* stay if he liked.
In French we witness a similar development, *il vînt* (*venait*) in
a conditioned sentence having been ousted by *il viendrait*, which
originally denoted an obligation in the past (' he had to come '),
but is now chiefly used as what is generally termed " le conditionnel,"
e.g. in " s'il pouvait, il viendrait." Similarly in the past : *mon
frère ne serait pas mort, s'il l'avait su*.

Special applications of the preterit of unreality are seen in
the use of *should* and *ought* to indicate an obligation or duty, etc.,

---

[1] To designate the use of the preterit indicative to denote unreality
the terms " modal past tense " (NED) and " mood-tense " (Sweet) are
sometimes used ; they do not seem adequate, as moods have no fixed notional
value : at any rate one does not see from the term what mood the tenses
stand for.

in the present time, and in the " modest " use of *could* for *can*. (Could you tell me the right time), of *would* for *will* (Would you kindly tell me . . .) and of *might* for *may* (Might I ask . . .). It has finally led to the change of *must* from a preterit into a present tense ; cf. also Swed. *måste.* Further details must be left to special grammars.

CHAPTER XX

TIME AND TENSE—*concluded*

The Perfect. Inclusive Time. Passive Tenses. Aorist and Imperfect. The English Expanded Tenses. Terms for the Tenses. Time-Relations in Nouns (including Infinitives). Aspect.

The Perfect.

THE system of tenses given above will probably have to meet the objection that it assigns no place to the perfect, *have written, habe geschrieben, ai écrit,* etc., one of the two sides of Lat. *scripsi,* and in Latin often called perfectum absolutum or "perfect definite." This, however, is really no defect in the system, for the perfect cannot be fitted into the simple series, because besides the purely temporal element it contains the element of result. It is a present, but a permansive present : it represents the present state as the outcome of past events, and may therefore be called a retrospective variety of the present. That it is a variety of the present and not of the past is seen by the fact that the adverb *now* can stand with it : "Now I have eaten enough." "He has become mad" means that he is mad now, while "he became mad" says nothing about his present state. "Have you written the letter ? " is a question about the present time, "Did you write the letter ? " is a question about some definite time in the past. Note also the difference of tense in the dependent clause in " He has given orders that all spies are to be shot at once " and " He gave orders that all spies were to be shot at once." We may perhaps figure this by means of the letters BA or B(A)— the letters A and B being taken in the sense shown on p. 257 above.

It is highly probable that the old Aryan perfect was at first an intensive present or " permansive " ; this view is advocated very cogently by Sarauw (Festschrift Vilh. Thomsen, 1912, p. 60) : " The perfect originally denoted the state : *odi* I hate, *memini* I remember, *hestēka* I stand, *kektēmai* I possess, *kekeutha* I contain hidden within me, *heimai* I wear, *oida* I have before my eyes. The meaning of perfect was gained by an inference : he who possesses has acquired ; he who wears a garment has put it on."

The two sides of the perfect-notion cannot easily be maintained in a stable equilibrium. Some of the old perfects are used exclusively as real presents, e.g. Lat. *odi, memini* ; in the Gothonic languages the so-called præteritopræsentia, which would be better called perfectopræsentia,[1] e.g. E. *can, may,* Gothic *wait,* corresponding to Gr. *oida,* ON. *veit,* OE. *wat,* obsolete E. *wot,* etc. But apart from these what were perfects in the Gothonic languages have lost the present-element and have become pure preterits, as E. *drove, sang, held,* etc. To express the perfect-meaning compounds with *have* were then formed : *I have driven, sung, held,* etc. In quite recent times one of these combinations has become a pure present (thus a new perfectopresent verb) : *I have got* (*I've got*) : the retrospective element is quite absent in *I've got no time | you've got to do it.*[2]

The Latin perfect, which originated in an amalgamation of old preterits (aorists) and perfects,[3] combines the syntactic functions of those two tenses. In Romanic verbs, however, we witness the same development as in the majority of the Gothonic verbs, the old perfect forms having lost their perfect-function and having become pure preterits, though with this difference from the Gothonic verbs, that they are aorists (now termed *passé défini, passé historique, past historic*), because side by side with them there are imperfects (see below). The real perfect as in Gothonic is expressed periphrastically : *ho scritto, ai écrit,* etc. (On *have* as an element in the perfect of many languages see Meillet LH 189.)

Now, in spite of the employment of the present-tense form *have* in these new perfects, it appears difficult to keep up the sharp distinction between the idea of the present result of past events and that of these past events themselves : the perfect tends to become a mere preterit, though the tendency is not equally strong in all languages. English is more strict than most languages, and does not allow the use of the perfect if a definite point in the past is meant, whether this be expressly mentioned or not. Sentences containing words like *yesterday* or *in 1879* require the simple preterit, so also sentences about people who are dead, except when something is stated as the present effect of their doings, e.g. in *Newton has explained the movements of the moon* (the movements of the moon have been explained—namely by Newton). On the other hand : *Newton believed in an omnipotent God.* " We can say ' England *has had* many able rulers,' but if we substitute Assyria for England the tense must be changed " (Bradley ME. 67).

German is much more lax in this respect, and South German tends to use the compound perfect everywhere : *ich habe ihn gestern gesehen.* On the other hand, Germans (North Germans ?)

---

[1] E. *must* is a real preteritopresent verb, while its old present *mot* was a perfectopresent.

[2] Anglo-Irish has a curious perfect : *he is after drinking* = ' has drunk.'

[3] *Dixi* is an old *s*-aorist, *pepuli* a reduplicated perfect

will often say : *Waren Sie in Berlin ?* where an Englishman would
have to say " Have you been in Berlin ? " When an Englishman
hears a German ask " Were you in Berlin ? " his natural inclination is to retort : " When ? " Danish steers a middle course
between the strictness of English and the laxity of German ; a
Dane, for instance, will always ask " Har De været i Berlin ? "
but has no objection to combinations like " jeg har set ham
igår " (I have seen him yesterday). If, however, the indication
of time precedes, the preterit is required : " igår såe jeg ham "
—the psychological reason being that in the former case the sentence was at first framed as it would be without any time-indication, and the indication is as it were an afterthought, added to
sentence when virtually completed " jeg har set ham," whereas
if we begin with " yesterday " the tense naturally follows suit.

In Spanish the distinction seems to be accurately observed ;
Hanssen (Sp. gr. 95) has examples corresponding to the English
ones given above : *Roma se hizo señora del mundo* | *La Inglaterra
se ha hecho señora del mar.* But in French the feeling for the distinction is lost, at any rate in present-day colloquial Parisian and
North French, where the passé défini is entirely disused : *Je l'ai
vu hier* | *ils se sont mariés en 1910.* The transition from a perfect
to a preterit seems to be due to a universal tendency ; at any
rate we meet with it in so remote a language as Magyar, where
írt ' has written ' in the ordinary language has supplanted *íra*
' wrote ' (Simonyi US 365).

A retrospective past time, bearing the same relation to some period
in the past as the perfect does to the present, cannot be kept distinct
from the before-past (ante-preterit) mentioned above : *had written.*[1]

In the same way what was above called before-future (ante-
future) cannot be kept apart from a retrospective future : *will
have written.* The periphrasis with forms of the verb *have* seems
to indicate that people are inclined to look upon these two tenses
as parallel with the perfect rather than with the simple preterit ;
hence also the terms " past perfect " and " future perfect."

Inclusive Time.

Not infrequently one may need to speak of something belonging
at once to the past and to the present time. Two tenses may be

---

[1] R. B. McKerrow (Engl. Grammar and Grammars, in *Essays and Studies
by Members of the Engl. Assoc.*, 1922, p. 162) ingeniously remarks that " Cæsar
had thrown a bridge across the Rhine in the previous autumn " generally
means that there was a bridge at the time of which the historian is speaking
but that this inference would be neutralized by some addition like " but
it had been swept away by the winter floods." In my own terminology
had thrown in the former case would be a retrospective past, but in the latter
a pure before-past.

combined : I was (then) and am (still) an admirer of Mozart | I have been and am an admirer of Mozart. But if an indication of duration is added, we can combine the two into what might be called an inclusive past-and-present. On account of the composite character of this idea some languages use the perfect, like English and Danish, and others the present tense, like German and French : I have known him for two years | jeg har kendt ham i to år | | ich kenne ihn seit zwei jahren | je le connais depuis deux ans. Note the difference in the preposition used in the different cases. In Latin we have the same rule as in French, only without a preposition : annum jam audis Cratippum. It is evident that this time relation renders it impossible to find a place for it in our time-series above ; but it might be expressed by means of the letters B&A.

Corresponding expressions are found with reference to the past and to the future time : in 1912 I had known him for two years | i 1912 havde jeg kendt ham i to år | | in 1912 kannte ich ihn seit zwei jahren | en 1912 je le connaissais depuis deux ans | | next month I shall have known him for two years | næste måned har jeg (vil jeg ha) kendt ham i to år | | im nächsten monat werde ich ihn seit zwei jahren kennen | le mois prochain je le connaîtrai depuis deux ans. It goes without saying that these latter expressions are not very frequent.

Passive Tenses.

It will be well to keep in mind the double-sided character of the perfect when we come to treat of the tenses in the periphrastic passive of the Romanic and Gothonic verbs. In classical Latin, where we had the real present passive in *-r* : *scribitur*, the composite form *scriptum est* is a perfect ' it is written, i.e. has been written, exists now after having been written.' But in the Romanic languages the *r*-passive has disappeared, and the meaning of the periphrasis has been partly modified. This subject has been treated by Diez (GRS 3. 202) better than by anybody else. He quotes from early documents examples like *quæ ibi sunt aspecta* for *aspiciuntur*, *est possessum* for *possidetur*, and then goes on to divide verbs into two classes. In the first the action is either confined to one single moment, e.g. catch, surprise, awake, leave, end, kill, or imply a final aim (endzweck), e.g. make, bring about, adorn, construct, beat ; here the passive participle denotes the action as accomplished and finished, and the combination with *sum* in Romanic as in Latin is a perfect. Ex. *il nemico è battuto, l'ennemi est battu = hostis victus est ; era battuto, io sono abandonato, sorpreso ; la cosa è tolta via.* Diez calls these verbs perfective. The second class (imperfective) comprises verbs denoting an activity which is not begun in order to be finished, e.g. love, hate, praise, blam*e*, admire, see, hear, etc. Here the participle combined with *sum* denotes present time : *egli è amato da tutti, il est aimé de tout le monde = amatur ab omnibus ; è biasimato, lodato, odiato, riverito, temuto, veduto.* In Romanic as in Latin the participles of the first class by losing their temporal signification tend to become adjectives (*eruditus est, terra ornata est floribus*). If now the notion of past time has to be attached to those participles which tend to become adjectives, the new participle of *esse* is used for that purpose : *il nemico è stato battuto, l'ennemi a été battu.* For the present time the active construction is preferred : *batton il nemico, on bat l'ennemi.* In It. and Sp. *venire* may also be used as an auxiliary of the passive for present time.

The distinction between two classes, which Diez thus saw very clearly, has been developed by H. Lindroth in two excellent papers (PBB 31. 238 and *Om adjektivering af particip*, Lund 1906). Lindroth for the first class uses the term ' successive ' (with the subdivisions ' terminative ' and ' resultative '), and for the second the term ' cursive.' Even at the risk of seeming needlessly to multiply existing terms I venture to propose the names *conclusive* and *non-conclusive*.

In German and Danish, where there are two auxiliaries, *werden, blive* on the one hand, and *sein, være* on the other, it does not matter very much whether one or the other is chosen with verbs of the second class (non-conclusive) : *er wird geliebt (ist geliebt) von jedermann, han bliver elsket (er elsket) av alle* = jedermann liebt ihn, alle elsker ham.[1] But with verbs of the first class (conclusive) the auxiliaries denote different tenses : *er wird überwunden, han bliver overvundet* = man überwindet ihn, man overvinder ham ; but *er ist überwunden, han er overvundet* = man hat ihn überwunden, man har overvundet ham. In the latter case it is possible to denote the perfect passive more explicitly by means of the composite *er ist überwunden worden, han er blevet overvundet*.

In English the old auxiliary *weorðan*, corresponding to G. *werden*, has disappeared, and matters are now pretty much as in French. If first we consider non-conclusive verbs (Diez's second class), we see that when participles like *honoured, admired, despised*

---

[1] With some non-conclusive verbs there may be a shade of difference in the meaning according as the one auxiliary is used or the other. In Danish we also have the passive in -*s* : *elskes, overvindes*, which gives rise to delicate shades of signification in some verbs.—Where *venire* is used as auxiliary in It., it corresponds to G. *werden*, Dan. *blive* : *viene pagato* is different from *è pagato*.

are used as adjuncts as in *an honoured colleague*, they say nothing about time and may according to circumstances be used about any time (an honoured colleague of Bacon). The combination *is honoured, is admired*, etc., therefore belongs to the same (present) tense as the simple *is*.

It is different with conclusive participles like *paid, conquered, lost*, etc. In adjunct-combinations they denote the result of past action : *a paid bill | conquered towns | a lost battle*. Combinations with the auxiliary *is* may have two different meanings, according as the perfect-signification inherent in the participle or the present-signification of *is* comes to predominate; cf. the two sentences : his bills are paid, so he owes nothing now (sind bezahlt ; he has paid) | his bills are paid regularly on the first of every month (werden bezahlt, he pays). The preterit " his bills were paid " may, of course, have the two corresponding meanings. Cf. the following instances : he was dressed in the latest fashion | the children were dressed every morning by their mother | at that time they were not yet married, but they were married yesterday. I take a final example from a paper by Curme, only modifying it slightly : When I came at five, the door was shut (war geschlossen), but I do not know when it was shut (geschlossen wurde). I think the best way to make the distinction clear is to point out how the opposite statement would run : When I came at five, the door was open (thus the adj.), but I do not know when it was opened.

There is evidently a source of ambiguity here,[1] but it must be recognized that some correctives have been developed in the course of the last few centuries. In the first place the combinations *has been, had been* with a participle, which were rare in Elizabethan English, have become increasingly frequent. Shakespeare very often has *is*, where a modern writer would undoubtedly use *has been*, e.g. Sonn. 76 Spending againe what *is already spent*. . . . So is my loue still telling what *is told* | John IV. 2. 165 Arthur, whom they say *is kill'd* to-night on your suggestion. Thus also in the Authorized Version, e.g. Matt. 5. 10 Blessed are they which *are persecuted* for righteousness sake, in the Revised Version : Blessed are they that *have been persecuted*.[2] In the second place the verbs *become* and, especially in colloquial speech, *get*, are more and more used where *be* would be ambiguous, e.g. taking it into his head rather late in life that he must *get married* (Dickens) | " I am engaged to Mr. W. "—" You are not engaged to anyone.

---

[1] There is no exact English way of rendering Goethe's " Was heute nicht geschieht, ist morgen nicht getan."

[2] In the beginning of St. Luke the A.V. has the following instances, thy prayer is heard | am sent | is borne this day | which was told them | it was revealed, where The Twentieth C. Version has : has been heard | have been sent | has been born | what had been said | it had been revealed.

When you do become engaged to anyone, I or your father will inform you of the fact " (Wilde).[1] Finally the comparatively recent combination *is being* is in some cases available to make the meaning unmistakable. Thus we see that present-day English has no less than three new expressions by the side of the old *the book is read*, namely *the book has been read, gets read, is being read*. This specialization has been an evident gain to the language.

Aorist and Imperfect.

We saw above that Lat. *scripsi* besides being a perfect ('have written') was a preterit ('wrote'), but that in the latter capacity it had beside it another preterit *scribebam*. We shall now discuss the difference between these two kinds of preterit, using the names found in Greek grammars, aorist and imperfect. In French grammars, as we have also seen, the aorist is variously termed le passé défini or le passé historique ; the latter name (past historic) has been adopted by the Committee on Grammatical Terminology, though the historian seems to require not only that kind of preterit, but also the imperfect.

In Greek, Latin, and the Romanic languages the two tenses are formed from the same verbs by means of different endings. In Slavic, where we have essentially the same distinction, it is brought about in a different way, by means of the distinction between the so-called perfective and imperfective verbs (which terms there mean nearly, though not exactly the same thing as in Diez's terminology above, p. 273). As a rule two verbs stand over against one another, most often, though not always, formed from the same root by means of different suffixes. They supplement one another and make it possible to express temporal shades of meaning though the Slavic verb has only two tenses. This may be thus tabulated :

	present tense	preterit
perfective verb :	future time	aorist
imperfective verb :	present time	imperfect.

Now, as to the meaning of the aorist and the imperfect. Both denote past time and they cannot be placed at different points of the time-line drawn, p. 257, for they bear the same relation to the present moment and have no relation to the subdivisions denoted by the prefixes before and after. Nor have they any reference in themselves to the duration of the action concerned, and we cannot say that one is momentary or punctual, and the

---

[1] The following sentences from one of Shaw's plays are interesting, because the emphatic form is wanted in the second speech, and "they *are* killed " would easily be misunderstood : "No man goes to battle to be killed."—" But they do get killed "

other durative. An indication of length of duration may be added
to both, e.g. in : ebasileuse tessera kai pentēkonta etea ' he reigned
fifty-four years ' | Lucullus multos annos Asiæ præfuit | Louis XIV
régna soixante-douze ans et mourut en 1715 | De retour de ces
campagnes il fut longtemps malade ; il languit pendant des années
entières.

The two tenses correspond to the two meanings of E. *then*,
(1) next, after that, as in " then he went to France " (Dan. *dœrpå*),
and (2) ' at that time ' as in " then he lived in France " (Dan.
dengang). The aorist carries the narrative on, it tells us what
happened next, while the imperfect lingers over the conditions as
they were at that time and expatiates on them with more or less
of prolixity. One tense gives movement, the other a pause. One
Latin grammarian, whom I have seen quoted I forget where,
expresses this tersely : Perfecto procedit, Imperfecto insistit
oratio. Krüger similarly says that the aorist grips (zusammen-
fasst) and concentrates, the imperfect discloses (entfaltet). Sarauw
expands this (KZ 38. 151), saying that in the former " abstraction
is made from what is inessential, from the circumstances under
which the action took place and from interruptions that may
have occurred, and what was really a whole series of actions is
condensed into one action, the duration of which is not, however,
abbreviated." It is noteworthy that, as Sarauw emphasizes, an
aorist was formed from the imperfective as well as from the perfective verbs in Old Slavic. In the same way French uses its
aorist (passé historique) with any verb, no matter what its meaning is. We may perhaps be allowed with some exaggeration to
say in the biblical phrase that the imperfect is used by him
to whom one day is as a thousand years, and the aorist by him to
whom a thousand years are as one day. At any rate we see that
terms like the G. " aktionsart " are very wide of the mark : the
distinction has no reference to the action itself, and we get much
nearer the truth of the matter if we say that it is a difference in
the speed of the narrative ; if the speaker wants in his presentation of the facts to hurry on towards the present moment, he
will choose the aorist ; if, on the other hand, he lingers and takes
a look round, he will use the imperfect. This tense-distinction is
really, therefore, a tempo-distinction : the imperfect is lento and
the aorist allegro, or perhaps we should say ritardando and
accelerando respectively.

This will make us understand also that there is often a distinctive emotional colouring in the imperfect which is wanting in
the aorist tense.

In the composite before-past the corresponding distinction
exists in Fr. *j'avais écrit* and *j'eus écrit*. Here too *ai eu* has been

substituted in popular language for *eus*, as in " Quand ma femme *a eu trouvé* une place, elle a donné son enfant à une vieille pour le ramener au pays " (Daudet).

In the same way as the Latin perfect had two functions, the imperfect in Latin, Romanic, Greek, etc., has two functions, for besides the lingering action we have just been discussing it denotes an habitual action in some past period. Here, therefore, the time-notion is bound up with the idea of repetition, which is really a numerical idea (cf. under Number, p. 210) : the plural idea with regard to the verbal action which is expressed in this use of the imperfect is of the same order as that which finds a stronger expression in iterative or frequentative formations.

We are now in a position to give the following comparative scheme of tenses in some well-known language, line 1 denoting the real perfect, line 2 the aorist, line 3 the habitual imperfect, and line 4 the descriptive imperfect. This survey shows clearly how some languages confuse time distinctions which in others are kept strictly apart.

1. gegraphe	scripsit	a écrit	has written	hat geschrieben
2. egrapse	scripsit	écrivit, a écrit	wrote	schrieb
3. egraphe	scribebat	écrivait	wrote	schrieb
4. egraphe	scribebat	écrivait	was writing	schrieb.[1]

The English Expanded Tenses.

In the survey just given we found two renderings of Lat. *scribebam* in English, *wrote* for the habitual action, and *was writing* for the descriptive imperfect. Corresponding expressions are found in the present, etc., as English possesses a whole set of composite tense-forms : *is writing, was writing, has been writing, will (shall) be writing, will (shall) have been writing, would (should) be writing, would (should) have been writing*, and in the passive *is being written, was being written*—Sweet in his tense system even gives *I have been being seen, I had been being seen, I shall be being seen, I should be being seen, I shall have been being seen*, though it would certainly be possible to read the whole of English literature without being able to collect half a dozen examples of some of these " forms." Very much has been written by grammarians about these combinations, which have been called by various names, definite tenses, progressive tenses, continuous tenses. I prefer to call them *expanded tenses*, because this name is sufficiently descriptive of

[1] On corresponding differences in the future and in the imperative in Modern Greek see A. Thumb, *Handb. d. neugriech. volksspr.*, 1895, p. 73, 2nd ed. 1910, p. 119, C. Buck, *Classical Philology*, 1914, 92.

the formation without prejudging anything with regard to its employment.

With regard to the historical development of these forms I have given a preliminary account of my researches in *Tid og Tempus*, pp. 406–420 with criticism of earlier views, and shall here give only a very short summary. My main result is that the modern construction owes very little to the OE. construction *wæs feohtende*, which in ME. plays no important rôle, but that it arose chiefly through aphesis from the construction of the verbal substantive with the preposition *on* : *is on huntinge*, *is a-hunting*, *is hunting* (as *burst out on weeping*, *a weeping*, *weeping* ; *set the clock on going*, *a going*, *going*). This explains the fact that these forms become more common just when aphesis (in *back* from *on bæc*, *aback*, etc., etc.) became particularly frequent, while it also explains the use of the prep. *of* before an object (still heard in vu gar speech), and the passive signification in *the house was building*, and—last, not least—it helps us to understand the exact meaning of the expanded tenses in Modern English, which is much more precise than was that of the OE. and ME. participial combinations. We must remember that the preposition *on* was often used where now we say *in* : *he is on hunting* means ' he is in (the middle of) the action of hunting,' and thus contains two elements, first ' being,' with which is connected the time-indication, and second ' hunting,' which forms as it were a frame round ' is.' The action described by the word *hunt ng* has begun before the moment denoted by *is* (*was*), but has not yet ceased ; cf. **Fr.** il *était à* se raser, quand est venu son beau-frère.

The purport of the expanded tenses is not to express duration in itself, but relative duration, compared with the shorter time occupied by some other action. " Methuselah lived to be more than nine hundred years old "—here we have the unexpanded *lived* indicating a very long time. " He was raising his hand to strike her, when he stopped short "—an action of very short duration expressed by means of the expanded tense. We may represent the relatively long duration by means of a line, in which a point shows the shorter time, either the present moment (which need not always be indicated) or some time in the past, which in most cases has to be specially indicated :

Verbs denoting psychological states, feelings, etc., cannot as a rule be used in the expanded tenses ; this is easily explained if we start from the combination *is on -ing*, for we can hardly say : *he is on* (engaged in, occupied in) *liking fish, etc.* Nevertheless it is possible in speaking of a passing state to say " I am feeling cold."

The expanded forms of verbs denoting movement, like *go, come*, must be specially mentioned. They are first used in the ordinary way wherever the verbs have some special signification which does not in itself call up the idea of a beginning movement : My watch has stopped, but the clock *is going* | things *are coming* my way now | you *are going* it, I must say. In the second place they may be used where a single action of coming or going is out of the question : the real hardships *are now coming* fast upon us | She turned to the window. Her breath was *coming* quickly | cigarettes *were then coming* into fashion. But in most cases *is coming, is going* are used of the future, exactly as the corresponding verbs in many languages acquire the meaning of future time in their present tense (Gr. *eimi*, etc., see p. 261). The auctioneer will say : *Going, going*, gone. Thus also : I *am going* to Birmingham next week | Christmas *is coming*, the geese are getting fat. Thus we get the expression for a near future : he *is going* to give up business ; even : *he is going to go.*

Most of the uses of the expanded tenses in Modern English will be covered by the rules given here, and what has been said about the longer time as a frame for something else will be found particularly helpful. Yet it cannot be denied that there are applications which cannot easily be explained in this way, thus many combinations with subjuncts like *always, ever, constantly, all day long, all the afternoon.* But it is worth mentioning that these were especially frequent in ME., before the great influx of cases arising from the aphesis in *a-hunting*, etc., changed the whole character of the construction.

It is a natural consequence of the use of the expanded tenses to form a time-frame round something else that they often denote a transitory as contrasted with a permanent state which for its expression requires the corresponding unexpanded tense. The expanded form makes us think of the time-limits, within which something happens, while the simple form indicates no time-limit. Compare then " he is staying at the Savoy Hotel " with " he lives in London," or " What are you doing for a living ? I am writing for the papers " with " What do you do for a living ? I write for the papers." Habits must generally be expressed by the unexpanded tenses ; see, e.g., the following sentences : A great awe seemed to have fallen upon her, and she *was behaving* as she *behaved* in church | Now he *dines* at seven, but last year he *dined* at half-past | Thanks, I *don't smoke* (cp. I am not smoking).

But if the habitual action is viewed as a frame for something else, the expanded tense is required : I realize my own stupidity when I *am playing* chess with him | Every morning when he *was having* his breakfast his wife asked him for money (while complete coextension in time may be expressed by expanded preterit in both sentences : " Every morning when he *was having* his breakfast his dog *was staring* at him ").

The use of the expanded form to express the transitory in contrast to the permanent state has in quite recent times been extended to the simple verb *be,* though the distinction between " he is being polite " of the present moment and " he is polite " of a permanent trait of his character is only now beginning to be observed. But it is curious to see how in other languages the same distinction is sometimes expressed by means which have nothing to do with the tense system of the verb. In Danish *av sig* in some cases serves to mark the quality as a characteristic trait (*han er bange av sig* ' he is naturally timid '), while *han er bange* means that he is afraid at the present moment ; but the addition has a very limited sphere of application. In Spanish we have the distinction between the two verbs meaning ' to be,' *ser* for the generic, and *estar* for the individual time : mi hermano es muy activo ' my brother is very active ' | mi hermano está enfermo ' my brother is ill ' ; I find a good example in Calderon, Alc. de Zal. 3. 275 Tu hija soy, sin honra estoy ' I am your daughter, but am dishonoured.' With other verbs we have the expansion nearly as in English : él está comiendo ' he is dining ' [1] | él come á las siete ' he dines at seven.' In Russian the predicative is put in the nominative if generic time is meant : *on byl kupec* ' he was a merchant ' (permanently), but in the instrumental if an individual time is meant : *on byl kupcom* ' he was (for the time being) a merchant ' ; this distinction, however, applies to substantives only, adjective predicatives being always put in the nominative. On a similar distinction in modern Irish see H. Pedersen, GKS 2. 76. In Finnish the predicative is put in the nominative if a generic time is meant : *isäni on kipeä* ' my father is ill ' (permanently, is an invalid), but otherwise in the essive : *isäni on kipeänä* ' my father is ill ' (at the moment). (See also the chapter on Case, p. 183.)

Finally we have to consider the passive construction in the obsolete *the house is building,* and in the still usual " while the tea *was brewing* | my MS. *is now copying.*" In my previous paper I have stated my reasons for disbelief in the early occurrence of this construction, as well as in the theory that these constructions have their origin in the notionally passive use of English verbs (his

[1] Cf. It. *sta mangiando.*

prose *reads* like poetry | it lookes ill, it *eates* drily, marry 'tis a wither'd pear (Sh.)). This latter use may assist in explaining some examples of *is -ing* (*preparing, brewing, maturing*), but not all, and in particular not the one which is perhaps of most frequent occurrence : *the house is building,* for it is impossible to say *the house builds* in a passive sense. The chief source of the construction is in my view the combination *on* with the verbal substantive in *-ing,* which as other verbal substantives is in itself neither active nor passive (see above, p. 172) and therefore admits the passive interpretation (cp. the house is *in construction*). Combinations with the preposition *a* were not at all rare in former times in the passive signification : as this *was a doyng* (Malory) | there *is* some ill *a-brewing* towards my rest (Sh.) | while my mittimus *was a making* (Bunyan). This naturally explains the construction in : while grace *is saying* | while meat *was bringing in.* There is decidedly a difference between " my periwigg that *was mending* there " (Pepys) and " he *is now mending* rapidly," for in the latter, but not in the former case, the unexpanded forms *mends, mended,* may be used. Compare also " while something *is dressing* for our dinner " (Pepys) and " while George *was dressing* for dinner " cf. George dresses for dinner).

Just as the ambiguity of some other combinations with the substantive in *-ing* in its original use as neither active nor passive gave rise to the comparatively recent construction with *being* (foxes enjoy hunting, but do not enjoy being hunted), it was quite natural that the older construction *is building* should be restricted to the active sense, and that a new *is being built* should come into existence. It is well known that this clumsy, but unambiguous construction began to appear towards the end of the eighteenth century, and that it met with violent opposition in the nineteenth century before it was finally acknowledged as a legitimate part of the English language.

Terms for the Tenses.

A final word about terminology. With the extensive use of various auxiliaries in modern languages it becomes impossible or at any rate impracticable to have a special term for all possible combinations, the more so as many of them have more than one function (*he would go* in " He would go if he could " is different from the shifted *I will go* in " He said he would go to-morrow "). Why should the combinations *would go* and *would have gone* have special terms rather than *might go* and *might have gone*, or *dared go*, etc. ? The only reason is that these forms serve to translate simple tense-forms of certain other languages. There is really no necessity for such terms as the " Future Perfect in the Past " for *would have written*, which, as we have seen, in its chief employment has nothing whatever to do with future time, and which still retains some trace of the original meaning of volition in its first element. If we give *I shall write, you will write, he will write* as a paradigm of the future tense, we meet with difficulties when we come to consider *he shall write* in " he says that he shall write " as a shifted (indirect) " I shall write." It is really easier to make our pupils understand all these things if we take each auxiliary by itself and see its original and its later weakened meaning, and then on the other hand show how futurity (future time) is expressed by various devices in English, sometimes by a weakened *will* (volition), sometimes by a weakened *shall* or *is to* (obligation), sometimes by other means (*is coming*), and how very often it is implied in the context without any formal indication. Thus we shall say, not that *I shall go* and *he will go* are " a future tense," but that they contain an auxiliary in the present tense and the infinitive. The only instance in which there is perhaps some ground for a special tense-name is *have written* (*had written*), because the ordinary meaning of *have* is here totally lost and because the combination serves exclusively to mark one very special time-relation. But even here it might be questioned whether it would not be better to do without the term " perfect."

Time-Relations in Nouns (including Infinitives).

After thus dealing in detail with time-relations as expressed by means of tenses in finite verbs, it remains to examine whether similar grammatical phenomena may not be found outside this domain. It is, of course, possible to imagine a language so constructed that we might see from the form of the word whether the sunset we are speaking about belongs to the past, to the present, or to the future. In such a language the words for ' bride, wife, widow ' would be three tense-forms of the same root. We may find a first feeble approximation to this in the prefix *ex-*, which in recent times has come into common use in several European languages : *ex-king, ex-roi*, etc. Otherwise we must have recourse to adjuncts of various kinds : the *late* Lord Mayor ; a *future* Prime Minister ; an owner, *present or prospective*, of property ; he dreamt of home, or of *what was home once* ; the life *to come* ; she was already the *expectant* mother of his child, etc. In a novel I find the combination " governors and ex-governors and prospective governors." [1]

---

[1] Cf. with an adjective : " this august or once-august body."

In some far-off languages tense-distinctions of substantives are better represented. Thus, in the Alaska Eskimo we find that *ningla* ' cold, frost,' has a preterit *ninglithluk* and a future *ninglikak*, and from *puyok* ' smoke ' is formed a preterit *puyuthluk* ' what has been smoke,' and a future *puyoqkak* ' what will become smoke,' an ingenious name for gunpowder (Barnum, *Grammatical Fundamentals of the Innuit Language of Alaska*, Boston, 1901, p. 17). Similarly in other American languages. Thus the prefix *-neen* in Athapascan (Hupa) denotes past time both in substantives and verbs, e.g. *xontaneen* ' a house in ruins,' *xoutneen* ' his deceased wife ' (Boas, *Handbook of American Indian Languages*, Washington, 1911, pp. 105, 111 ; cf. also Uhlenbeck, *Grammatische onderscheidingen in het Algonkinsch*, Amsterdam Ac. 1909).

It would seem natural to have tense-indications in those nouns that are derived from, and closely connected with, verbs. Yet agent-nouns generally are as indifferent to time as other substantives : though *creator* most often means ' he who has created ' this is by no means necessary, and *baker, liar, beggar, reader*, etc., tell us nothing of the time when the action takes place.[1] In most cases habitual action is implied, but there are exceptions (in English more often than in Danish), e.g. *the speaker, the sitter* = the person who sits for his portrait.

With active participles some languages have developed tense-distinctions, e.g. Gr. *graphōn, grapsōn, grapsas, gegraphōs*, Lat. *scribens, scripturus*. The Gothonic languages have only one active participle, G. *schreibend*, E. *writing*, cf. also in Romanic languages It. *scrivendo*, Fr. *écrivant*, which is generally called the present participle, though it is really no more present than any other tense, the time-notion being dependent on the tense of the main verb ; cf. " I saw a man sitting on a stone | I see a man sitting on a stone | you will see a man sitting on a stone." Note also the phrase " for the time being." The composite form *having written*, *ayant écrit* better deserves its name of perfect participle.

With regard to the participle found, for instance, in It. *scritto*, Fr. *écrit*, E. *written*, G. *geschrieben*, etc., some remarks on the time-relation indicated by it have already been given above, p. 272. The usual term, the past participle, or the perfect participle, may be suitable in some cases, e.g. *printed* books, but is inadequate, for instance, in " *Judged* by this standard, the system is perfect | He can say a few words in *broken* English | My *beloved* brethren | he is *expected* every moment | many books are *printed* every year in England," etc. Some grammarians, seeing this terminological

---

[1] Accordingly, agglutinations of agent nouns with *is*, etc., may develop, according to circumstances, into either future or perfect tenses. Examples from various languages, see L. Hammerich, *Arkiv för nord. filol.* 38. 48 ff

difficulty, use the words active and passive participle for *writing* and *written*, and this is correct, so far as the former is concerned (apart from the old-fashioned *the house building now = a-building*); but the other participle is not always passive in its character. It is distinctively active in " a well-*read* man | a well-*spoken* lad | *mounted* soldiers | he is *possessed* of landed propriety," and even if the participle was passive in the original construction underlying the composite perfect (*I have caught a fish*, originally ' I have a fish (as) caught '), this has long ago ceased to be true, as we see in " I have lost it " and especially with intransitive verbs " I have slept, come, fallen, been," where the whole combination is undoubtedly active. Bréal (S 224) goes so far as to say that the participle itself has (par contagion) become active, which he proves by the fact that one writes in telegraphic style : " Reçu de mauvaises nouvelles. Pris la ligne directe." As there is therefore no really descriptive name possible for the two participles as used in actual language, I see no other way out of the terminological difficulty than the not very satisfactory method of numbering the forms, calling the -*ing*- participle the first and the other the second participle.[1]

Nexus-substantives do not as a rule any more than other substantives admit of any indication of time-relations ; *his movement* may according to circumstances correspond in meaning to *he moves, he moved, he will move*. Similarly *on account of his coming* may be equivalent to ' because he comes ' or ' came ' or ' will come.' *I intend seeing the doctor* refers to the future, *I remember seeing the doctor* to the past. But from ab. 1600 the composite form with *having* has been in use, as in " He thought himself happy in *having found* a man who knew the world " (Johnson).

The infinitive, as we have mentioned above, p. 139 f., is an old verbal substantive, and it still has something of the old indifference to time-distinctions : *I am glad to see her* refers to present time, *I was glad to see her* to past, and *I am anxious to see her* to future time.[2] But in some languages, for instance Greek, tense-forms have developed in the infinitive ; cf. also Lat. *scripsisse* by the side of *scribere*. This perfect infinitive has been given up in the Romanic languages, in which we have now the composite perfect

---

[1] In some combinations an infinitive with *to* may be regarded as a kind of substitute for the missing future participle, as in " a chapter in a book soon *to appear* in London," in the passive " a book soon *to be published* by Macmillan " ; cf. also " A National Tricolor Flag ; victorious, or *to be victorious*, in the cause of civil and religious liberty " (Carlyle). In It. " Non c'era nessuna tavoletta, nè abbozzata, nè *da abbozzare* " (Giacosa).

[2] The infinitive also refers to a (relative) future when a purpose is indicated, as in *He said this (in order) to convert the other*, and in the related use in *In 1818 Shelley left England never to return*, where it denotes the after-past time mentioned p. 262.

infinitive Fr. *avoir écrit*, etc. ; the corresponding composite form
is also found in the Gothonic languages, E. *(to) have written,*
G. *geschrieben (zu) haben.*

The English perfect infinitive corresponds not only to the
perfect ('Tis better to *have loved and lost* Than never to *hcve loved*
at all), but also to an ordinary preterit (You meant that ? I suppose I must *have meant* that) and to an ante-future (future perfect :
This day week I hope to *have finished* my work). It was formerly
used fairly often to indicate an intention which was not carried
into effect (With that Leander stoopt to *haue imbrac'd* her, But
from his spreading armes away she cast her.—Marlowe) ; this cannot be separated from its use corresponding to the preterit of
unreality, a use which is generally overlooked by grammarians,
but which presents more features of interest than I can here point
out ; I must content myself with giving a few of my examples
without classification and without any comment : To *have fallen*
into the hands of the savages, had been as bad (Defoe, = it would
have been as bad if I had fallen) | it would have been wiser to
have left us (Ruskin) | it would have been extremely interesting
to *have heard* Milton's opinion (Saintsbury) | a Iew would haue
wept to *haue seene* our parting (Sh.) | she would haue made Her-
cules *haue turnd* spit (Sh.) | she was old enough to *have made* it
herself (Lamb) | it seems likely to *have been* a desirable match for
Jane (Miss Austin, = that it would have been) | We were to *have
gone and seen* Coleridge to-morrow (Carlyle). The form of the
infinitive in the phrase *it would have been better for him to have
stayed outside* implies (in the same way as *if he had stayed*) that
he did not stay outside, which the simple *to stay* in *it would have
been better for him to stay outside* does not ; the latter infinitive is
just as "neutral" with regard to the question of reality or
unreality as *staying outside would have been better* ; similarly *he
ought to have come here* implies that he has not come, as compared
with *he ought to come here.*

Hence we find as synonymous expressions *I should like to have
seen* and *I should have liked to have seen*[1] by the side of *I should
have liked to see.* In some composite verbal expressions the indication of the past might in itself with equal reason be added to
either verb : to E. *he could have done it* and Dan. *han kunde ha
gjort det* corresponds Fr. *il aurait pu le faire*, G. *er hätte es tun
können.*[2] In Dan. we may also say *han havde kunnet gøre det,*
but this is not possible in English, as *can* has no participle ; for

---

[1] In this as well as in some of the above-mentioned instances grammarians consider the perfect inf. as a redundancy or as an error.

[2] Cp. also Tobler VB 2. 38 ff. : *il a dû venir* ' er muss gekommen sein,'
il a pu oublier = il peut avoir oublié, etc.

the same reason the perfect infinitive has to be used in *he might* (*must, should, would, ought to*) *have done it*.

Instead of saying *you needed not say that* (cf. G. " das brauchten Sie nicht zu sagen "), which denies the necessity in the past time, it is now customary to shift the time-indication on to the infinitive : *you needn't have said that*.

The opposite shifting is found in *I shall hope to see you to-morrow*, which really means a present hope of a future visit ; as there is no future infinitive in English, the sign of the future is added to *hope* instead.[1]

Aspect.

I must here very briefly deal with a subject which has already been touched upon and which has been very warmly discussed in recent decades, namely what has generally in English been called the *aspect* of the verb, and in German *aktionsart*, though some writers would use the two terms for two different things. It is generally assumed that our Aryan languages had at first no real forms in their verbs for tense-distinctions, but denoted various aspects, perfective, imperfective, punctual, durative, inceptive, or others, and that out of these distinctions were gradually evolved the tense-systems which we find in the oldest Aryan languages and which are the foundation of the systems existing to-day. Scholars took this idea of aspect from Slavic verbs, where it is fundamental and comparatively clear and clean-cut, but when they began to find something similar to this in other languages, each of them as a rule partially or wholly rejected the systems of his predecessors and set up a terminology of his own, so that nowadays it would be possible, had one the time and inclination, to give a very long list of terms, many of them with two or three or even more definitions, some of which are not at all easy to understand.[2] Nor have these writers always distinguished the four possible expressions for ‘ aspects,’ (1) the ordinary meaning of the verb itself, (2) the occasional meaning of the verb as occasioned by context or situation, (3) a derivative suffix, and (4) a tense-form. In thus criticizing my predecessors, I may seem to some to live in a glass-house, for I am now going to give

---

[1] With these shiftings may be compared *I can't seem to remember* instead of ‘ I seem not to can remember ’ on account of the missing infinitive of *can*.

[2] The following is a list of what are, if I am not mistaken, the chief works and articles on this subject : Miklosich, Vergl. Gr. d. slav. spr. Vol. IV.— Streitberg PBB 15. 71 ff.—Herbig IF 6. 157 ff. (with good bibliography).— Delbrück, Synt. 2. 1. ff., cf. Streitberg, IF Anz. 11. 56 ff.—H. Pedersen KZ 37. 220 ff.—Sarauw KZ 38. 145 ff.—Lindroth, see above p. 273.—Noreen VS 5. 607 ff. and 645 ff.—Deutschbein ESt 54. 79 ff.—Pollack PBB 44. 352 ff.—Wackernagel VS 1. 153.—On the terminological confusion see also H. Pedersen IF Anz. 12. 152.

my own classification, which after all may not be much better than previous attempts. Still I venture to hope that it may be taken as a distinctively progressive step, that I do not give the following system as representing various " aspects " or " aktions-arten " of the verb, but expressly say that the different phenomena which others have brought together under this one class (or these two classes) should not from a purely notional point of view be classed together, but should rather be distributed into totally different pigeonholes. This, then, is how I should divide and describe these things.

(1) The tempo-distinction between the aorist and the imperfect ; this affects (independently of the signification of the verb itself) the tense-form in some languages ; see above, p. 276.

(2) The distinction between conclusive and non-conclusive verbs. Here the meaning of the verb affects the meaning of the second participle in Romanic and Gothonic languages, and thus has influence on the time-meaning of passive combinations ; see above, p. 272.

(3) The distinction between durative or permanent and punctual or transitory. We have seen above that this is one of the functions of the English distinction between unexpanded and expanded tenses, and that the same distinction is in other languages expressed by totally different means.

(4) The distinction between finished and unfinished. This latter is one of the functions of the expanded forms in English : *he was writing a letter*, as compared with *he wrote a letter* ; in Dan. it is often expressed by means of the preposition *på* : *han skrev på et brev* ; cf. G. *an etwas arbeiten*.

(5) The distinction between what takes place only once, and repeated or habitual action or happening. As already remarked, this really belongs to the chapter about " number." Habitual action is very frequently not expressed separately (" he doesn't drink ") ; in some languages we have suffixes to express it, in which case we speak of iterative or frequentative verbs. Many E. verbs in *-er* and *-le* belong here : *totter, chatter, babble*, etc.

(6) The distinction between stability and change. Sometimes we have a pair of corresponding verbs, such as *have : get, be : become* (and its synonyms : *get, turn, grow*).[1] Hence the two kinds of passive mentioned p. 274 above (*be married, get married*). Most verbs derived from adjectives denote a change (becoming) : *ripen, slow (down)*, and a change is also implied in the transitive verbs of corresponding formation : *flatten, weaken*, etc. (causatives).[2]

---

[1] In the predicative Finnish has a separate case-form (the translative) after verbs denoting a change or becoming.

[2] Many of these formations are used both transitively and intransitively.

But a state is expressed by the verb *halt* = ' be lame ' (from the obsolete adj. *halt*). Many verbs denote both state and change ; in *lie down* the latter meaning is denoted by the adverb. There are other ways of expressing similar changes : *fall asleep, go to sleep, get to know, begin to look,* cp. the states : *sleep, know, look.* Some languages have special derivative endings to express change into a state, or beginning (inchoative, inceptive, ingressive verbs).[1] But it is interesting to notice how this signification of beginning has often in course of time been weakened or lost ; thus in the Romanic verbs derived from the Latin inchoatives in *-isco*, e.g Fr. *je finis, je punis*, whence E. *finish, punish.* Similarly ME. *gan* lost its original force, and *he gan look* came to mean simply ' he did look, he looked.' *To* is used with a predicative at first only when a change is implied (*take her to wife*), but later also without this meaning (*he had her to wife*) ; similarly in Dan. *til.*

The opposite kind of change, where some state ceases, is sometimes expressed by a separate formation, as in G. *verblühen*, Dan. *avblomstre* ' cease blooming,' but generally by means of such verbs as *cease, stop.*

Note the three expressions for (*a*) change into a state : (*b*) being in the state : (*c*) change from the state, in *fall in love with* (*begin to love*) : *be in love with* (*love*) : *fall out of love with* (*cease to love*) | *fall asleep* : *sleep* : *wake* (*wake up*). But *wake* in that sense may also be considered as ' change *into* a state,' the corresponding stability-verb being *to be awake*, or sometimes *wake* (cp. Danish *vågne* : *våge* = Fr. *s'éveiller* : *veiller*).

(7) The distinction according to the implication or non-implication of a result. The G. compounds with *er-* frequently are resultative, e.g. *ersteigen*, and this is generally given as one of the chief examples of " perfektivierung durch zusammensetzung " ; but it is difficult to see why, for instance, *ergreifen* should be more perfective than the simple *greifen.*

I think it would be better to do without the terms perfective and imperfective except in dealing with the Slavic verb, where they have a definite sense and have long been in universal use. In other languages it will be well in each separate instance to examine carefully what is the meaning of the verbal expression concerned, and whether it is due to the verb itself, to its prefix or suffix, to its tense-form, or to the context. Different things are comprised under the term perfective. If, thus, we analyze the interesting collection of Gothic instances with the prefix *ga-* which is given by Streitberg, *Gotisches elementarbuch*, 5th ed. 1920, p. 196, we shall see that " perfectivation " here means, first,

---

[1] Thus Ido : *staceskas* ' rises ' (*stacas* ' stands '), *sideskas* ' sits down, *jaceskas* ' lies down,' *dormeskas* ' goes to sleep,' *redeskas* ' blushes,' etc.

finishing : *swalt* lay a dying, *gaswalt* was dead, *sagq* was setting, *gasagq* set (above, No. 4)—second, change : *slepan* be asleep, *gaslepan* fall asleep, *þahan* be silent, *gaþahan* become silent, and others (above, No. 6)—third, obtaining through the action : *fraihnan* ask, *gafraihnan* learn by asking, *rinnan* run, *garinnan* durch das laufen erreichen, erringen.[1] This is akin to No. 7 above, though it is not exactly the same thing, for he who *ersteigt* a mountain does not gain the mountain. On the other hand, it has some connexion with what was above, p. 159, termed object of result, as in *dig a hole* (cp. *dig the garden*), but has evidently nothing to do with time- or tense-distinctions.

[1] We see the same in OE. *winnan* fight, *gewinnan* obtain by fighting; in later English the prefix *ge-* was lost, and the verb retained only the signification of *gewinnan*, without the idea of fighting. Most of the examples of Gothic *hausjan, gahausjan, saihwan, gasaihwan* should be ranged with our No. 6 (get to hear, get to see, obtain the sight of), thus *wildedun saihwan þatei jus saihwiþ jah ni gasehwun* desired to see what you see, but did not get to see it. But the distinction is not always clear, and in the following line (Luke 10. 24) the text has *jah hausjan þatei jus gahauseiþ jah ni hausidedun*, where Streitberg boldly emends into *hauseiþ jah ni gahausidedun*. In 14. 35, too, he alters the MS. reading to bring about a consistency which was possibly far from the mind of Wulfila.

CHAPTER XXI

DIRECT AND INDIRECT SPEECH

Two Kinds.   Shifting of Tenses.   Shifting of Mood.   Questions in Indirect
Speech.   Indirect Requests.   Final Remarks.

Two Kinds.

WHEN one wishes to report what someone else says or has said
(thinks or has thought)—or what one has said or thought oneself
on some previous occasion—two ways are open to one.

Either one gives, or purports to give, the exact words of the
speaker (or writer): *direct speech* (oratio recta).

Or else one adapts the words according to the circumstances
in which they are now quoted: *indirect speech* (oratio obliqua).

The direct speech (direct discourse) may be preceded by some
sentence like " He said " or " She asked," etc., but very frequent y
the reference to the speaker is inserted after some part of the
reported speech: " I wonder, she said (or, said she), what will
become of us ? "   Latin has a separate word for ' say ' which is
used only in such insertions, *inquam, inquit.*

The direct quotation is an outcome of the same psychological
state with its vivid imagination of the past that calls forth the
" dramatic present tense " (p. 258).   Hence we often find that
tense employed in the inserted " says he, say(s) I " instead of
" said."

There are two kinds of indirect speech (indirect discourse),
which I shall call *dependent* and *represented speech.*   The former [1]
is generally made dependent on an immediately preceding verb,
" he said (thought, hoped, etc.) " or " he asked (wondered, wanted
to know, had no idea, etc.)," while in the second class this is as
a rule understood from the whole connexion.

What is meant by the second kind of indirect speech may
perhaps be best shown by an example.   After Pendennis has
been " plucked " at the University, Thackeray writes (p. 238):
" I don't envy Pen's feelings as he thought of what he had done.
He had slept, and the tortoise had won the race.   He had marred
at its outset what might have been a brilliant career.   He had

[1] Termed by Lorck " berichtete rede " (see his pamphlet *Die erlebte
rede,* Heidelberg, 1921).

290

dipped ungenerously into a generous mother's purse ; basely and recklessly spilt her little cruse. Oh ! it was a coward hand that could strike and rob a creature so tender. . . . Poor Arthur Pendennis felt perfectly convinced that all England would remark the absence of his name from the examination lists, and talk about his misfortune. His wounded tutor, his many duns, the under-graduates of his own time and the years below him, whom he had patronised and scorned—how could he bear to look any of them in the face now ? " A few pages farther on we read of his mother : " All that the Rector could say could not bring Helen to feel any indignation or particular unhappiness, except that the boy should be unhappy. What was this degree that they made such an outcry about, and what good would it do Pen ? Why did Doctor Portman and his uncle insist upon sending the boy to a place where there was so much temptation to be risked, and so little good to be won ? Why didn't they leave him at home with his mother ? As for his debts, of course they must be paid ;—his debts !—wasn't his father's money all his, and hadn't he a right to spend it ? In this way the widow met the virtuous Doctor," etc.

It is not easy to find an adequate descriptive name for indirect discourse of this kind. Lorck rightly rejects Tobler's term (mingling of direct and indirect discourse), Kalepky's (veiled speech, verschleierte rede) and Bally's (style indirect libre), but his own term " erlebte rede," which might perhaps be rendered " experienced speech," does not seem much better. I have found no better term than " *represented speech*." (In German I should say " vorgestellte rede " and in Danish " forestillet tale.") [1]

Bally thought that this phenomenon was peculiar to French, but Lerch and Lorck give a great many German instances, though thinking that in German it may be due to French influence, especially to that of Zola(!). But it is very frequent in England (where it is found long before Zola's time, for instance in Jane Austen) and in Denmark, probably also in other countries (I have recently found Spanish examples), and it seems on the whole so natural that it may easily have come into existence independently in different places. It is chiefly used in long connected narratives where the relation of happenings in the exterior world is interrupted—very often without any transition like " he said " or " he thought "—by a report of what the person mentioned was saying or thinking at the time, as if these sayings or thought were the immediate continuation of the outward happenings. The writer does not experience or " live " (erleben) these thoughts or

[1] Curme GG (1st ed. p. 248, 2nd ed. p. 245, not mentioned by Lorck) calls it " Independent form of direct discourse."

speeches, but represents them to us, hence the name I have chosen.

Represented speech is more vivid on the whole than the first class of indirect speech. As it is nearer to direct speech, it retains some of its elements, especially those of an emotional nature, whether the emotion is expressed in intonation or in separate words like " Oh ! ", " Alas ! ", " Thank God ! ", etc.

The adaptation to changed circumstances which is charac teristic of indirect speech is effected by the following means :

> the person is shifted,
> the tense is shifted,
> the mood is shifted,
> the form of a question is changed,
> the form of a command or request is changed.

It is chiefly in the last two kinds of changes that the difference between dependent and represented speech is seen. The shifting of person has already been considered in Ch. XVI ; here we shall deal with the others.

Shifting of Tenses.

Corresponding to

(1) I am ill
(2) I saw her the other day
(3) I have not yet seen her
(4) I shall soon see her, and then everything will be all right
(5) I shall have finished by noon—

indirect discourse has the shifted tenses in

He said that
—(1) he was ill (indirect present)
—(2) he had seen her the other day (indirect preterit)
—(3) he had not seen her yet (indirect perfect)
—(4) he should soon see her, and then everything would be all right (indirect future)
—(5) he should have finished by noon (indirect before-future).

The ante-preterit cannot be further shifted : " I had already seen her before she nodded " becomes " He said that he had already seen her before she nodded." The preterit of unreality is often left unshifted, " He said that he would pay if he could " may thus be a rendering of " I would pay if I could " as well as of " I will pay if I can." As *must* has now only one form, it is unchanged in indirect discourse : " He said that he must leave at once " = " He said : I must leave at once." This is practically the only way in which *must* can be used as a preterit in modern colloquial speech.

It will be seen that the indirect preterit and the indirect perfect are formally identical with the ante-preterit (before-past) ; and the indirect future is formally identical with the conditional ; thus also in French *j'écrirais* fulfils the two functions of conditional (j'écrirais si je savais son adresse) and of indirect simple future (il disait qu'il écrirait le plus tôt possible = the direct : j'écrirai le plus tôt possible).

If we now ask what is the relation between these indirect tenses and the series of tenses established above (p. 257), the answer is that they should not be placed in that series, where they have nothing to do, being orientated with another zero-point (" then ") than that of the original series (" now "). A sentence like " (He said that) *he should come as soon as he could* " tells us nothing about the moment of his coming in its relation to the present time, but only in its relation to the time when he spoke. He may already have come, or he may be coming just now, or at some future time—all this is left undecided, and the only thing we are now told is that when he spoke he mentioned his coming as due to happen at some time which then belonged to the future.

Nor is it necessary to have special terms for the tenses arising from this shifting. The NED (*shall* 14b) speaks of the " anterior future " or " future in the past " in " he had expected that he *should be* able to push forward "—this is simply a shifted (or indirect) future, and of the " anterior future perfect," no example is given, but the reference must be to cases like " he said that he *should have dined* by eight," which is = the direct : " I shall have dined by eight," thus a shifted (or indirect) before-future time (or, if it is to be designated as a tense : a shifted or indirect ante-future tense).

The shifting of tenses in indirect speech is very natural and in many cases even inevitable : *He told me that he was ill, but now he is all right*—here the use of the preterit *was* is motived by the actual facts of the matter, and *was* is at the same time the direct past and the indirect present. But this is not always the case, and very often the verb is put in the preterit for no other reason than that the main verb is in that tense and that the speaker does not stop the current of his speech to deliberate whether the thing mentioned belongs to this or that period of time, measured from the present moment. Van Ginneken mentions this : " *Je ne savais pas qui il était*. Est-ce que je veux dire par-là qu'il est quelque autre maintenant ? Nullement. *Etait* se trouve là par inertie, et par *savait* seul on comprend qu'il faut entendre la chose ainsi : était et est encore " (LP 499). Or rather, we might say, it is left unsaid whether things are now as they were. " I told you he was ill "—he may still be ill, or he may have recovered. In the following instances it is the nature of the thing signified more than the words that shows that the present time is meant, but the shifting is perfectly natural : What did you say your name *was* ? | I didn't know you *knew* Bright | How did you know I *was* here ?   The last example is particularly interesting on account of the *contradictio in adjecto* between his presence here and the form *was* : I am here now, but how did you know that ?

It requires some mental effort to leave the preterit and use the more logical present tense, even where one has to enounce some universal truth. We cannot, therefore, expect that speakers will always be consistent in their practice with regard to the *consecutio temporum*. We may hesitate in a case like this : " He told us that an unmarried man was (or, is) only half a man," but we should probably prefer the unshifted in : " It was he who taught me that twice two *is* four."

The use of the unshifted present here implies that the actual speaker is himself convinced of the truth of the assertion, whereas the shifting of the tense also shifts the responsibility for the saying on to the original speaker ; hence the difference in " He told us that it *was* sometimes lawful to kill " (but he may have been wrong) and " I did not know then that it *is* sometimes lawful to kill " (but it is). Note the preterit in Falstaff's " Did I say you *were* an honest man ? " with the continuation : " Setting my knighthood and my souldiership aside, I had lyed in my throat, if I had said so." Sometimes the tone of the sentence is decisive : " I thought he was married " with one intonation means ' I now find that I was mistaken in thinking him married,' and with another ' Of course he is married, and didn't I tell you so ? '

The present subjunctive is not shifted to a preterit in reports of proposals made at meetings, etc. : He moved that the bill be read a second time. Here the form *be* is felt as indicating futurity and therefore as more adequate than *were*, which would rather imply something unreal or hypothetical ; in other verbs there would be no difference in the preterit between the indicative and the subjunctive, and so the form of the proposal is kept unchanged in spite of the conjunction *that*.[1]

[1] In Russian the rule prevails that in indirect discourse the same tense is used that would be used in direct discourse ; the only shifting, therefore, is of person. This rule, which must always be felt as rather unnatural by Western Europeans, was (like several other Slavisms) introduced into Esperanto by its creator, Dr. Zamenhof, and from Esperanto it was taken over into Ido, where it is now taught that ' He said that he loved—that he had heard—that he should come ' has to be rendered by means of the present, the preterit, and the future respectively : *il dicis ke il amas—ke il audis— ke il venos.* The only thing to be advanced in favour of this rather artificial

In most cases of shifted tenses the main verb refers to some
time in the past ; but we may have similar shiftings after a main
verb in the future, though this will be rarer. When we imagine
a person, who is now absent, saying at some future date " I regret
I was not with them then," we naturally say " He will regret
that he is not with us now."   But Henry V in Shakespeare (IV.
3. 64) uses the preterit that belongs to the direct speech of the
gentlemen concerned (though he says *here*, which implies his own
standpoint) : And gentlemen in England, now a bed, Shall thinke
themselues accurst they *were* not here, And hold their manhoods
cheape, whiles any speakes, That *fought* with vs vpon Saint Cris-
pines day. This reminds one of the Latin " episto'ary tenses,"
in which the writer of a letter transports himself to the time when
it will be read, and therefore uses the imperfect or perfect where
to us the present tense is the only natural one.

Shifting of Mood.

The shifting of mood from the indicative to some other mood
in indirect speech is not found in modern English and Danish,
but in other related languages. Latin makes an extensive use of
the accusative with infinitive in what in direct discourse would be
a principal clause, as well as in the more independent of subordinate
clauses, and of the subjunctive in other dependent clauses. Other
languages have other rules, and the use of the subjunctive, or
optative, mood in indirect speech shows such marked divergencies
in the various ancient languages of our family that it seems to have
developed independently at different places for different reasons.
T. Frank (in *Journal of Engl. and Germ. Philol.* 7. 64 ff.), while
rejecting earlier " metaphysical " explanations from the nature
of " subjectivity " and " potentiality," gives good reasons for
supposing that the use of the subjunctive in the Gothonic languages
is a gradual extension by analogy from its use in clauses dependent
on such verbs as Goth. *wenjan*, OE. *wenan*, G. *wähnen*, which
at first meant " hope, desire " and therefore naturally required
the optative. It was retained when the verbs came to mean
' imagine, think,' and then transferred to other verbs meaning
' think, say,' etc.

The development of the forms of indirect discourse in German
is particularly instructive, because it is governed by various and
often conflicting tendencies : the tendency to harmonize the tense

---

rule is that otherwise it would perhaps be necessary to create a special tense.
form for the shifted future, for it would be against the logical spirit of such
a language to use the same form for the shifted future as for the conditional
(*venus*) as our Western languages do (*viendrait, should come, würde kommen*).

with that of the main verb (expressed or understood) and on the other hand the tendency to keep the same tense as in the original statement, further the tendency to use the subjunctive mood as an indication of doubt or uncertainty, the tendency to use the subjunctive simply as a mark of subordination even where no doubt is implied, and finally the general tendency to restrict the use of the subjunctive and to use the indicative instead. Now, as the power of these tendencies varies in different periods and in different parts of the country, German writers and German grammarians do not always agree as to which form to use and to recommend. As a matter of fact we find in actual use:

Er sagt, dass er krank ist.
Er sagt, er ist krank.
Er sagt, dass er krank sei.
Er sagt, er sei krank.
Er sagt, dass er krank wäre.
Er sagt, er wäre krank.
Er sagte, dass er krank war.
Er sagte, er war krank.
Er sagte, dass er krank sei.
Er sagte, dass er krank wäre.
Er sagte, er wäre krank.

(See, e.g., Delbrück GNS 73 ff., Behaghel, *Die zeitfolge der abhängigen rede*, 1878, Curme GG 237.) Of course, matters are not quite so chaotic as might be inferred from this list, but I have no space for detailed explanation. I want, however, to call attention to the effect of the desire for unmistakable forms, even at the cost of consistency, which is excellently stated by Curme as follows:

"Altho the new sequence [i.e. the same tense in the indirect as in the direct discourse] may be followed . . . it is more common to employ it only where its subjunctive forms are clearly distinguished from the corresponding indicative forms, and elsewhere to use the old historic sequence. Thus, as the past tense distinguishes the subjunctive more clearly than the present tense, a present tense form . . . is regularly replaced after a past tense by a past tense form . . . wherever the present is not a clear subjunctive: *Sokrates erklärte, alles, was er wisse, sei, dass er nichts wisse; v ele wüssten* (the present subjunctive would be like the indicative) *aber auch dies nicht. Sie sagten, sie hätten* (a past tense form instead of the present tense form *haben*) *es nicht getan. Sie sagten, sie würden* (a past tense form instead of the present tense form *werden*) *morgen kommen.* So strong is the feeling that a clear subjunctive form should be used, that a past tense form is used instead

of a present tense form even after a present tense, if a clear subjunctive form is thus secured : *Sie sagen, sie hätten es nicht gesehen,*
etc. *Sagen Sie ihm, ich käme schon.*—In case of unclear forms
the past tense forms are preferred even tho they themselves are
not clear subjunctive forms : *Die bildhauerei, sagen sie, könne
keine stoffe nachmachen; dicke falten machten eine üble wirkung*
(Lessing). The very fact of choosing a past tense form here is
felt as indicating a desire to express the subjunctive " (GG 240).
(This may, in part at any rate, be due to the feeling that the
preterit indicates something remote from actual reality, as in
" If he was well, he would write," etc. ; cp. p. 265.)

Questions in Indirect Speech.

Here we meet with the chief difference between the two
kinds, dependent and represented speech. We shall speak first
of dependent questions.

When a question is reported the interrogatory intonation,
which is very often the chief indication that a question is meant,
is necessarily lost or weakened, but there is some compensation,
partly in the introductory (or inserted) formula, in which the verb
ask is used instead of *say*, partly in the use of an interrogative
conjunction where there is no interrogative pronoun. The conjunction often originates in a pronoun meaning ' which of two ' :
E. *whether*, Icel. *hvárt*, Lat. *utrum*, but in other cases the origin
is different, and we frequently find the use of a conditional conjunction : E. *if*, Fr. *si*, Dan. *om*, cf. G. *ob*. Very frequently the
difference between a direct and an indirect question is marked by
a different word-order : [1] Who is she ?—He asked who she was |
How can I bear to look any of them in the face ?— . . . how he
could bear to look . . . | Hasn't he a right to spend his money ?—
. . . whether he had not. . . . In the same way in other languages,
e.g. Danish : Hvem er hun ?—Han spurgte, hvem hun var | Hvor
kan jeg holde det ud ?— . . . hvor jeg kunde holde det ud | Har
han ikke ret ?— . . . om han ikke havde ret. French : Qui
est-elle ? (Qui est-ce ?)—Il a demandé qui elle était (qui c'était) |
Comment peut-on le souffrir ?— . . . comment on pouvait le
souffrir | N'a-t-il pas raison ?— . . . s'il n'avait pas raison. In
Danish there is the further difference that an interrogative pronoun as the subject of the sentence requires the addition of *der*
in an indirect question : Hvem har ret ?—Han spurgte (om) hvem
der havde ret ? | Hvad er grunden ?— . . . hvad der var grunden
(but if *grunden* is here treated as the subject, which is also possible

---

[1] In English without the *do*, which serves to bring about the interrogative
word-order : What does she see ?—I ask what she sees.

the result is the inverse word-order : Han spurgte om hvad grunden var).

Instead of the form peculiar to dependent indirect questions it has become more and more frequent in English to use the form also found in represented discourse, with no introductory *if* or *whether*, and with inverted word-order. Thus : I know not yet, was it a dream or no (Shelley) | he said was I coming back, and I said yes ; and he said did I know you, and I said yes ; and he said if that was the case, would I say to you what I have said, and as soon as I ever saw you, would I ask you to step round the corner (Dickens). In recent writers this is very frequent indeed ; it is mixed up with the dependent form in : they asked where she was going, and would she come along with them ? (Carlyle). In German the same form is found, though rarely, e.g. " man weiss nicht recht, ist er junggeselle, witwer oder gar geschieden " (G. Hermann).

Besides being used in quotations of direct questions, indirect questions are very often used (as " clause primaries ") after verbs like *know, doubt, see*, etc., as in : I want to know if he has been there | Go and see who it is, and try to find out where he comes from | it is not easy to say why the book is so fascinating.—They may also be subjects, as in " Whether this is true or not is still an open question." Sometimes the main sentence may be omitted, and the (formally) indirect question thus becomes a (notionally) direct question : If I may leave it at that ? (I ask if . . . = May I leave it at that ?).

In represented discourse the only shiftings in questions are those shiftings of person and tense that are common to all indirect discourse ; otherwise questions remain what they would be in direct quotation. Thus the questions " How can I bear to look any of them in the face now ? " and " Hasn't he a right to spend it ? " in the passage from Pendennis simply became " How could he bear . . ." and " Hadn't he a right . . ." " What does she see ? " became " What did she see ? " [1] In French the *imparfait* replaces the *présent*, in German the preterit indicative (not the subjunctive) is used, etc.

Exclamations introduced by an interrogative word remain unchanged except for the shifting of tense and person : " What a nuisance it is to change ! " becomes " What a nuisance it was to change " both when it is dependent on such a verb as " He said " and when it forms part of a represented speech.

---

[1] The same form of indirect question is used when " he asked " is inserted into the question : " Hadn't he a right, she asked, to spend his money ? " Thus also in Danish : " Havde han ikke, spurgte hun, ret til at bruge sine egne penge ? " Note also the English formula, " Mrs. Wright presents her compliments to Mrs. Smith, and might she borrow a saucepan, please ? "

Indirect Requests.

Such requests (commands, etc.) as in direct speech are expressed in the imperative have to be changed. In dependent speech either the element of request is expressed in the main verb, e.g. when " Come at once " is made into " He ordered (commanded, told, asked, implored) me (her) to come at once " or the main verb does not express the element of request, which must therefore find expression otherwise in the dependent clause : " He said (wrote) that I (she) *was to come* at once." The latter is the form generally employed in represented speech, though occasionally the imperative may be retained, as in the following passage from Dickens : " Mr. Spenlow argued the matter with me. He said, *Look* at the world, there was good and evil in that ; *look* at the ecclesiastical law, there was good and evil in that. It was all part of a system. Very good. There you were." Imperatives with *let us* are differently rendered in the two kinds of indirect discourse : " He proposed that we (they) were to go " and " Let us (them) go."

Final Remarks.

The distinction between direct and indirect speech is not always strictly maintained. A direct quotation may be introduced by the conjunction (' that ') usually reserved for indirect quotation ; thus not unfrequently in Greek. The Greek " kai legōn autōï, hoti ean thelēïs, dunasai me katharisai " was imitated by Wulfila : " jah qiþands du imma þatei jabai wileis, magt mik gahrainjan " (Mark 1. 40, thus also ib. 1. 37). I take a modern instance from Tennyson : " she thought that peradventure he will fight for me." [1] In French we have " je crois que non," although *non* belongs to direct speech.

Human forgetfulness or incapacity to keep up for a long time the changed attitude of mind implied in indirect discourse causes the frequent phenomenon that a reported speech begins indirectly and is then suddenly continued in the direct form. Examples from Greek writers like Xenophon are given in handbooks of Greek syntax. In Icelandic sagas they abound, e.g. Vols. 1 : segir at Breði hafi riðit frá honum á skóginn, ok var hann senn ór augliti mér, ok veit ek ekki til hans ' he says that B. rode from him into the wood, and I soon lost sight of him, and I know nothing about him ' | ib. 6 mælti at hann skyldi gera til brauð þeira, en ek man sœkja eldivi ' he said that he [the other] was to prepare

---

[1] Cf. also from Dickens : she sat sobbing and murmuring behind it, *that*, if I was uneasy, *why* had I ever married ? (*I* is a shifted *you* : the question is in " represented indirect discourse.")

their bread, but I will fetch fuel ' | ib. 9 hann spyrr, hverir þar væri, eða hví eru-þér svá reiðuligir ? 'he asks who were there, and why are you so angry.' A different kind of mixture of the two discourses is seen in Goldsmith Vic. 2. 166 : But tell me how hast thou been relieved, or who the ruffians were who carried thee away ?

German and Danish have a curious way of expressing what is notionally an indirect discourse by means of the verb *soll*, *skal* : Er soll sehr reich sein (gewesen sein) | han skal være (ha været) meget rig 'he is said (reputed, rumoured) to be (have been) very rich.' As *soll*, *skal* is in most of its uses a kind of weaker *muss*, *må*, I think this usage may be classed as a kind of weaker counterpart of the *muss*, *må*, *must* of logical necessity or of compelling conclusion, as in " he must be very rich (since he can give so much to the poor)."

CHAPTER XXII

CLASSIFICATION OF UTTERANCES

Que donnee nous fut parole
Por faire nos voloirs entendre,
Por enseignier et por aprendre.
ROMAN DE LA ROSE.

How many Classes ? Questions. Sentence.

How many Classes?

BRUGMANN (*Verschiedenheiten der satzgestaltung* nach massgabe
der seelischen grundfunktionen, Sächs. ges. d. wiss. 1918) has an
elaborate classification of sentences or utterances with the following main divisions, most of them with up to 11 subclasses : (1)
exclamation, (2) desire, (3) invitation (aufforderung), (4) concession,
(5) threat, (6) warding off (abwehr und abweisung), (7) statement
about imagined reality, (8) question.[1] In the treatment of these
classes historical considerations often cross purely logical divisions,
and it is difficult to see the rationale of the whole classification
as well as to see where such simple statements as " he is rich "
have to be placed. This criticism does not hinder one from
acknowledging the high value of many things in this book, one
of the last things the revered master of comparative philology
ever wrote. The older classification is much clearer : (1) statements, (2) questions, (3) desires, (4) exclamations (see, e.g., Sonnenschein's *Grammar*). But even this division is open to criticism ;
the boundary between (3) and (4) is not clear : why are " God
save the King " and " Long may he reign " excluded from Exclamations, and why are these latter confined to those that are
" introduced by exclamatory pronouns, adjectives or adverbs "
such as *what* and *how* !

A further objection to the classification given by Sonnenschein
is that it is expressly meant as a classification of " sentences "
only, i.e. such utterances as contain a finite verb. But obviously
utterances like " What fun ! ", " How odd ! ", " Glorious ! "
or " Hurrah ! " are " exclamations " just as much as those

---

[1] It is interesting to compare this classification with the equally elaborate,
but totally different classification in Noreen VS 5. 91 ff., which I must refrain
here from resuming or criticizing.

mentioned; "Waiter, another bottle!" cannot be separated from "desires" containing an imperative; and among statements we must reckon also the "nominal" sentences considered above (p. 121). It might perhaps also be said that the term "desire" is not the best term to include "commands, requests, entreaties, and wishes," and at the same time exclude "I want a cigar" and "Will you give me a light, please?" etc. Notionally these are really desires to be classed with the imperative "Give me," though formally they are "statements" and "questions." The classification is thus seen to be faulty because it is neither frankly notional nor frankly syntactic, but alternates between the two points of view: both are important, but they should be kept strictly apart in this as in other domains of grammatical theory.

If, then, we attempt a *purely notional classification* of utterances, without regard to their grammatical form, it seems natural to divide them into two main classes, according as the speaker does not or does want to exert an influence on the will of the hearer directly through his utterance. In the former class we must include not only ordinary statements and exclamations, but also such wishes as "God save the King," etc. With regard to this class it is, of course, immaterial whether there is a hearer or not; such an utterance as "What a nuisance!" is the same whether it is spoken in soliloquy or to someone else.

In the second class the aim of the utterance is to influence the will of the hearer; that is, to make him do something. Here we have two subclasses, requests and questions. Requests comprise many utterances of different forms, imperatives, verbless expressions ("Another bottle!" | "Two third Brighton" | "A horse, a horse!" | "One minute" | "Hats off"), formal questions ("Will you pack at once!") and formal "statements" ("You will pack at once") if the situation and the tone shows them to be equivalent to commands, etc. Requests may range from brutal commands through many intermediate steps (demands, injunctions, implorations, invitations) to the most modest and humble prayer (entreaty, supplication).

Questions.

A question also is a kind of request, viz. a request to tell the original speaker something, to give him a piece of information that he wants. Questions again may range from virtual commands to polite prayers: the answer may be as it were exacted or humbly solicited. The kinship between ordinary requests and questions is seen in the frequency with which a question is tagged on to an imperative: "Hand me that box, will you?" The question " Well ? " means the same thing as the imperative " Go on ! " or " Speak ! "

There are two kinds of questions ; " Did he say that ? " is an example of the one kind, and " What did he say ? " and " Who said that ? " are examples of the other. Many names have been proposed for these two kinds : yes-or-no question or categorical question *v.* pronominal question, sentence question *v.* word question, totality question *v.* detail question or partial question, entscheidungsfrage *v.* ergänzungsfrage or tatsachenfrage, bestätigungsfrage *v.* bestimmungsfrage. Noreen (VS 5. 118 ff.) discusses and criticizes these proposed terms and ends by proposing (in Swedish) " rogation " *v.* " kvestion." This distinction would be impossible in English (and French), where the word " question " has to be used as the common term ; it has the further grave drawback that it is impossible to remember which is which. An unambiguous terminology may be easily found if we remember that in the former kind it is always a nexus the truth of which is called in question : the speaker wants to have his doubt resolved whether it is correct to connect this particular subject with this particular predicate. We may therefore call questions of this kind *nexus-questions.* In the other kind of questions we have an unknown " quantity " exactly as in an algebraic equation ; we may therefore use the well-known symbol x for the unknown and the term *x-question* for a question aiming at finding out what x stands for.

Sometimes there may be two unknown quantities in the same equation, as in the colloquial : " *Who* shall sit *where* ? " (But " I don't know *which* is *which* " and " *Who's who* ? " are different : they really mean : ' which (who) is one, and which (who) is the other ? ')

The answer to a nexus-question is either yes or no ; to an x-question it may according to circumstances be anything except yes or no. With regard to tone it is the general rule that nexus-questions have a rising and x-questions a falling tone towards the end of the sentence. But there are certain questions which in these two respects are like x-questions, and yet resemble nexus-questions in their form. If we extend the question " Is it white ? " by adding " or black ? " and alter " Do you drink sherry ? " into " Do you drink sherry or port ? " we get disjunctive or alternative questions, in which the rising tone is concentrated on the first part as in the simple question, and the added " or white," " or port " has a falling tone. These questions are the equivalents of pronominal questions (x-questions) of this type : " What colour is it ? " " Which do you drink, sherry or port ? " But it is interesting to notice that what are seemingly the same questions may have a different meaning with a different intonation, if *sherry or port* is taken as one comprehensive term for strong wines, the answer to this question (Do you drink [such strong wines as] sherry or port ?) is then naturally yes or no (cf. LPh 15. 54). Questions with *neither—nor* (Have you neither seen nor heard it ?) are nexus-questions because *neither—nor* is a negative *both—and*, not a negative *either—or*.

Mention may here be made of the phenomenon which I have termed " questions raised to the second power " (LPh 15. 52). One person asks " Is that true ? " but instead of answering this, the other returns " Is that true ? "—meaning " How can you ask ? " Here most languages use the same form as in indirect questions : " Om det er sandt ? | Ob das wahr ist ? | Si c'est vrai ? " [1] though the sentences differ from ordinary indirect questions by having a much more marked rising of the interrogatory tone. I find the same form in Caxton (Reynard 21, imitation from French ?) " Loue ye wel myes [mice] ? Yf I loue hem wel, said the catt, I loue myes better than ony thing." But otherwise the English form of the question (inversion without conjunction) is here the same as in direct questions ; I have collected a great many examples from the time of the earliest comedies to that of the latest novels. As the retorted question generally implies that it was superfluous to ask, it amounts to the same thing as an affirmation : " Do I remember it ? " = Certainly I remember it, and the curious consequence is that it often does not matter whether there is a negative or not in the question, as " Don't I remember it ? " is also equivalent to an affirmation.

Questions introduced by an interrogative word (x-questions) may be similarly retorted, and here, too, most languages use the form of indirect questions : Was hast du getan ?—Was ich getan habe ? | Hvad har du gjort ?—Hvad jeg har gjort ? In French we see a relative clause taking the place of the interrogative clause : Ce que j'ai fait ? Chaucer used an inserted *that* as in other clauses : But wherefore that I speke al this ? (Parl. 17). But from the time of Shakespeare it has been usual in Eng'ish simply to repeat the question unchanged (except for the tone) : " Where is it ?—Where is it ? taken from vs, it is " (Shakespeare).—The change in the character of the question by being " raised to the second power " is shown also in the kind of answer required : " What have you done ? "—" What have I done ? "—" Yes, that is what I wanted to know." Questions of this kind are thus always nexus-questions.[2]

---

[1] Est-ce que vous avez déjà tué beaucoup de lions, monsieur de Tartarin ?—Si j'en ai beaucoup tué, monsieur ? (Daudet).

[2] There is a different kind of retorted question in which we may have two interrogative words. A says : Why are you doing this ? and B asks : Why am I doing what ? This is an x-question referring to a part of the original question.

The formal means by which questions are expressed, are (1) tone ; (2) separate interrogative words, whether pronouns or particles, e.g. Lat. *num*, enclitic *-ne* (originally the negative word), Dan. *mon* (originally an auxiliary verb), Fr. *ti* (Lang. 358)—in spoken French we may count [ɛskə] as an interrogative particle ; (3) word-order.

But it should be noted that what from a formal point of view is a question very often is used for something which notionally is not a question, i.e. a request to solve some doubt in the mind of the speaker. Besides the so-called rhetorical questions, which retain part of the notional value of questions, we must here mention expressions of surprise, e.g. "What ! are you here ? " which certainly is not said in order to be informed whether the other person is here. Further "Isn't he stupid ! " | G. "Ist das unglaublich ! " In exclamations of this kind the tone is modified, and in so far they cannot be said to have the complete form of questions. This is even more true of conditional clauses having the same word-order as questions and developed out of original questions, e.g. "Had he been here, I should have given him a piece of my mind."

Sentence.

The definitions of ' sentence ' are too numerous and too divergent for it to be worth while here to reprint or criticize them all.[1] In so far as they are not merely bogus definitions, in which technical words are used to conceal the want of clear thought, these definitions have taken as their starting point either formal or logical or psychological considerations, while some of them have tried to reconcile two or three of these points of view. But though there is thus no consensus of theory, grammarians will generally be more apt to agree in practice, and when some concrete group of words is presented to them will be in little doubt whether or not it should be recognized as a real sentence.

According to traditional logic every sentence forms a trinity of Subject, Copula and Predicate. Logicians analyze all sentences (propositions) with which they have to deal into these three components and thus obtain one fixed scheme that facilitates their operations. But even with regard to their purely intellectual propositions the scheme is artificial and fictitious, and it does not at all fit the great majority of those everyday sentences of a

[1] See Noreen VS 5. 51. 576, Sonnenschein § 1, Sweet NEG § 447, Brugmann KG 623, Versch. 15, Paul P § 85, Gr. 3. 10, Wundt S 2. 234, Wellander, Bedeutungslehre 5, Sundén, Elliptical Words 4, E. Otto, Grundlage der sprachwissenschaft 145, Kretschmer, Einleit. in die altertumswiss. 1. 515, Sheffield GTh 47, Wegener IF 39. 1, etc., etc.

more or less emotional colouring which form the chief subject-matter of the researches of the grammarian.

Instead of the old 'threeness' it is now more customary to postulate a 'twoness': every sentence is said to be composed of two parts, Subject and Predicate. In "the sun shines" *the sun* is subject and *shines* predicate. Each of these two parts may be composite: in "The youngest brother of the boy whom we have just seen once told me a funny story about his sister in Ireland" all the words up to *seen* constitute the subject, and the rest the predicate. Opinions vary as to how this 'twoness' is brought about psychologically, whether by the bringing together of two ideas existing already separately in the mind of the speaker, or by the breaking up of one idea (gesamtvorstellung) into two special ideas for the purpose of communication. This question need not, however, occupy us here. On the other hand, it is important to keep in mind that the two parts of the sentence, subject and predicate, are the same as the two parts of a nexus, primary and adnex, but that, as we have seen, it is not every nexus that constitutes a sentence: only an *independent* nexus forms a sentence.

It is, however, being more and more recognized by linguists that besides such two-member sentences as just mentioned we have one-member sentences. These may consist of one single word, e.g. "Come!" or "Splendid!" or "What?"—or of two words, or more than two words, which then must not stand to one another in the relation of subject and predicate, e.g. "Come along!" | "A capital idea!" | "Poor little Ann!" | "What fun!" Here we must first guard against a misconception found in no less a grammarian than Sweet, who says (NEG § 452) that "from a grammatical point of view these condensed sentences are hardly sentences at all, but rather something intermediate between word and sentence." This presupposes that word and sentence are steps in one ascending hierarchy instead of belonging to two different spheres; a one-word sentence is at once a word and a sentence, just as a one-room house is from one point of view a room and from another a house, but not something between the two.

An old-fashioned grammarian will feel a certain repugnance to this theory of one-member sentences, and will be inclined to explain them by his panacea, ellipsis. In "Come!" he will say that the subject "you" is understood, and in "Splendid!" and "A capital idea!" not only the subject ("this"), but also the verb "is" is understood. In many exclamations we may thus look upon what is said as the adnex, the subject (primary) being either the whole situation or something implied by the situation (cp. Ch. X). Most grammarians would probably analyze such Latin

one-word sentences as " Canto " or " Pluit " as containing implicitly
a subject, however difficult it may be to say exactly what is the
subject of the latter verb. But grammarians should always be
wary in admitting ellipses except where they are absolutely necessary and where there can be no doubt as to what is understood—
as, for instance, in " he is rich, but his brother is not [rich]," " it
generally costs six shillings, but I paid only five [shillings]." But
what is understood in " Watercresses ! " or " Special edition ! " ?
" I offer you . . ." or " Will you buy . . . ? " or " This is . . ." ?

If the word " John ! " forms a whole utterance, it may according
to circumstances and the tone in which it is said be interpreted
in various ways : " How I love you, John," " How could you do
that ? ", " I am glad to see you," " Was it John ? I thought it
was Tom," etc. How can these various " John !"'s be reduced to
the scheme subject-predicate, and how can ellipses assist us
in analyzing them ? Yet it would not do to deny their being
sentences. Nor can we stop here. " Yes " and " No," and interjections like " Alas ! " or " Oh ! " or the tongue-clicks inadequately
spelt " Tut " and " Tck " are to all intents and purposes sentences
just as much as the most delicately balanced sentences ever uttered
by Demosthenes or penned by Samuel Johnson.

If we admit this—and I confess that I do not see at what point
of the chain between the Johnsonian construction and the click
we should draw the line, then the definition of a sentence is comparatively an easy matter.

A sentence is a (relatively) complete and independent human
utterance—the completeness and independence being shown by
its standing alone or its capability of standing alone, i.e. of being
uttered by itself.[1]

In this definition the word ' utterance " has been expressly
chosen as the most comprehensive term I could find. Generally
by an utterance is meant a piece of communication to someone
else, but this is not necessary (soliloquy !) ; however, in order to
be recognized as a sentence an utterance must be such as might
be a piece of communication were there someone to listen to it.[2]

Let us see what is implied in the word " independent " in our
definition. " She is ill " is a sentence, but if the same words enter
into the combinations " He thinks (that) she is ill " and " He is

---

[1] On a previous occasion I defined a sentence as what can stand alone
without being an answer or a retort, thus excluding " Yesterday " as a reply
to the question " When did it happen ? " and " If " in the retort mentioned
p. 95. I am now somewhat doubtful about this restriction.

[2] Some definitions of " sentence " are so narrow that it is difficult to
see how they are to comprise questions. But mine is not, for though a
question is in so far incomplete as it requires a completion in the form of
an answer, it is a relatively complete and independent utterance.

sad when (if, because) she is ill," they are no longer independent utterances, but parts of sentences, either, as in the first example, the object of *thinks*, or, as in the others, subjuncts (strictly speaking, parts of subjuncts, as the conjunctions are also required). These parts of sentences, which in English are generally termed (dependent) clauses, are in German called " nebensätze " and in Danish " bisætninger," as if they were in themselves sentences of a particular kind, which according to our definition they are not. In the same way, while " What to do ? " is a complete sentence when standing alone, it ceases to be one and becomes a mere clause in " He did not know what to do." [1]

It is also a simple corollary of the definition that when " If only something would happen ! " stands alone and means " I wish something would happen," and when " If this isn't the limit ! " means " This is the limit," these are (complete) sentences, no matter how easy it is to see that they have developed from clauses requiring some continuation to be complete.

It will be noticed that sentence as here defined is a purely notional category : no particular grammatical form is required for a word or a group of words to be called a sentence. I do not even imitate those scholars who introduce the term " normal sentence " (normalsatz) for sentences containing a subject and a finite verb. Such sentences may be normal in quiet, easy-flowing unemotional prose, but as soon as speech is affected by vivid emotion an extensive use is made of sentences which fall outside this normal scheme and yet have every right to be considered natural and regular sentences.

It would probably be better to divide sentences into the following classes :

(1) Inarticulate sentences : " Thanks ! " (Thanks very much | Many thanks) | " What ? " | " Off ! "

(2) Semi-articulate sentences : " Thank you ! " (Thank you very much) | " What to do ? " | " Off with his head ! " [2]

(3) Articulate sentences : " I thank you " | " What am I to do ? " | " You must strike off his head ! "

Articulate sentences contain both components of a nexus, and as the " nominal sentences " considered above, p. 12¼, are in the minority, this means that the great majority of articulate sentences contain a finite verb.

---

[1] There is no necessity for a special term (" complex sentence ") for a sentence containing one or more dependent clauses. Cf. the end of Ch. VII.

[2] This is an interesting type (" Away with you ! " | " On with your vizards ! " | " To the rack with him ! ") containing a subjunct implying motion and a primary introduced by the preposition *with*, whose rôle resembles that of the same preposition in " a cage with the bird flown " and " pale with the pallor of death."

In the practice of any speech-community there will always be strong forces making for order and regularity, for uniformity, for fixed patterns. Through wholesale imitation of the word-combinations in most frequent use certain types will tend to become practically universal. Hence some words which at first may have been rare and have been thought more or less super-fluous become more and more frequent and at last may come to be thought necessary because they make the whole sentence con-form to the most usual patterns. As most sentences have a subject (Petrus venit), subjects come to be introduced where at first there were none : *je viens, il vient, il pleut* as against *venio, venit, pluit,* and in the same way E. *I come, he comes, it rains.* As most sentences have something placed before the verb, the empty *there* came to be used in *there are many,* etc. As most sentences contain a verb, a verb was inserted in places where it was not at first necessary to have one, hence the use of the ' copula ' *is* and of *does* in " So John does ! " As some verbs generally take a predicative, an empty *so* (G. *es*, Dan. *det*) is used, e.g. in " In France the population is stationary, and in England it is rapidly becoming so," cp. also " To make men happy, and to keep them so " (Pope). As most adjuncts are followed by a primary, *one* is used to prop up the adjunct in " a grey horse instead of the white one " | " birds love their young ones," etc. In all these cases we have practically the same tendency to round off sentences so as to make them conform to a prevalent type.

Although this uniformizing tendency has not been carried through with perfect consistency, it has nevertheless been made the basis of the grammarian's assumption that every sentence, or every normal sentence, must contain a subject and a finite verb ; but as soon as we see that it is merely a tendency, and not a law of language, it becomes urgent to give a definition of ' sentence ' which does not require the presence of those two constituents.

In all speech activity there are three things to be distinguished, expression, suppression, and impression. Expression is what the speaker gives, suppression is what he does not give, though he might have given it, and impression is what the hearer receives. It is important to notice that an impression is often produced not only by what is said expressly, but also by what is suppressed. Suggestion is impression through suppression. Only bores want to express everything, but even bores find it impossible to express everything. Not only is the writer's art rightly said to consist largely in knowing what to leave in the inkstand, but in the most everyday remarks we suppress a great many things which it would be pedantic to say expressly. " Two third Brighton return " stands for something like : " Would you please sell me two third-class tickets from London to Brighton and back again, and I will pay you the usual fare for such tickets." Compound nouns state two terms, but say nothing of the way in which the relation between them is to be understood : *home life,* life at home, *home letters,* letters from home, *home journey,* journey (to) home ; compare further *life boat, life insurance, life member ; sunrise, sunworship, sunflower, sunburnt, Sunday, sun-bright,* etc.

As in the structure of compounds, so also in the structure of sentences much is left to the sympathetic imagination of the hearer, and what from the point of view of the trained thinker, or the pedantic schoolmaster, is only part of an utterance, is frequently the only thing said, and the only thing required to make the meaning clear to the hearer. This is especially true of certain types of sentences in which suppressions of the same kind have occurred so often that at last no one thinks of what is left out, the remainder becoming a regular idiomatic expression which the grammarian must recognize as a complete sentence. There are two types of suppression which require particular attention (cf. *Lang.* 273).

(1) The beginning of a sentence falls out by what we might learnedly term *prosiopesis* : the speaker begins to articulate, or thinks he begins to articulate, but produces no audible sound (either for want of expiration, or because he does not put his vocal chords in the right position) till one or two syllables after the beginning of what he intended to say. Examples are such forms of salutation as *Morning* instead of *Good morning,* G. (Guten) *tag,* etc. Further : colloquial *See ?* for *Do you see ?* | (Do you) *remember that chap ?* | (Will) *that do ?* | (I'm a)*fraid not* | (When you) *come to think of it* | (I shall) *see you again this afternoon* | (God) *bless you !* Similar examples occur in all languages.

(2) The end is left out : *aposiopesis* is the learned name for what I have elsewhere (*Language* 251) more colloquially called stop-short or pull-up sentences. After saying " If only something would happen " the speaker stops without making clear to himself how he would go on, were he to complete the sentence, whether " I should be happy," or " it would be better," or " things would be tolerable," or whatever he might think of. But even without any continuation the *if*-clause is taken at more than its face-value and becomes, to speaker and hearer alike, a complete expression of a wish. Other expressions of wishes are G. " Wer doch eine zigarre hätte ! " | Dan. " Hvem der havde en sigar ! " | Span. " Quién le diera ! " Further examples of pull-up sentences : Well, I never ! | The things he would say ! | The callousness of it ! | To think that he has become a minister ! | Dire qu'il est devenu ministre ! | Tænke sig at han er blevet minister ! | Figurarsi

ch'egli è divenuto ministro! In all such cases the fact that something is left out should not prevent us from recognizing the utterance as sufficiently complete to be called a sentence.

In other cases, however, the suppression is so violent that this condition is not fulfilled. I should not recognize as sentences signboards ("J. C. Mason, Bookseller"), book-titles ("Men and Women"), head-lines in newspapers ("New Conferences in Paris" or "Killed his father-in-law"), indication of speaker in plays ("Hamlet"), entries in diaries ("Tuesday. Rain and fog. Chess with uncle Tom, walk with the girls") and similar short expressions. It is, however, important to observe that all these phenomena occur in writing only and thus fall outside language proper : spoken language may indulge in many suppressions, but the result is always distinguished from that exemplified in this paragraph.

With regard to suppression a few final remarks may not be out of place here.[1] It has been said (C. Alphonso Smith, *Studies in Engl. Syntax*, 1906, p. 3) that "verbs denote activity and change : they are hustling and fussy," and that therefore the omission of verbs gives the impression of calm. This is exemplified by Tennyson's *In Memoriam*, XI (Calm and deep peace on this high wold, etc.). But as a matter of fact the impression there is produced in the first place by the constant repetition of the word *calm* and its synonyms, and secondly by the fact that the verb omitted is one of rest, "is." If verbs of motion are omitted, their suppression may inversely strengthen the impression of unrest, as in the following example : "Then rapidly to the door, down the steps, out into the street, and without looking to right or left into the automobile, and in three minutes to Wall Street with utter disregard of police regulations and speed limits," or in Longfellow's description of Paul Revere's ride : "A hurry of hoofs in a village street, A shape in the moonlight, a bulk in the dark, And beneath, from the pebbles, in passing, a spark Struck out by a steed flying fearless and fleet." As in these cases a feeling of terseness and of vigour is also produced by the omission of verbs in a great many proverbial locutions, apophthegms, party devices, and similar sayings. G. "Ende gut, alles gut" is more pithy than E. "All is well that ends well," Fr. "Tout est bien qui finit bien," Dan. "Når enden er god, er alting godt." Cp. also : "Like master, like man" | "Every man to his taste" | "No cure, no pay" | "Once a clergyman, always a clergyman" | "Least said, soonest mended," "One man, one vote," etc. By

---

[1] In the initial clauses of "When in France, he was taken prisoner" and "If in doubt, answer no!" we may say that from one point of view we have abbreviation (omission of "he was" and "you are"), but, from another, expansion of "In France he was . . ." "In doubt answer no!" Similar considerations apply to "I want to know *the reason why*."

leaving out what may seem superfluous one creates the impression of hurry or stress of business which does not allow time enough to round off one's sentences in the usual way : it is also of importance that proverbs, etc., should be easy to remember and therefore not too long. In these cases, however, it is not the fact that a *verb* is omitted which produces the effect, for we have other abbreviated proverbs, etc., in which a similar effect is produced though they contain verbs : " Live and learn " | " Rule a wife and have a wife " | " Spare the rod and spoil the child " | " Love me, love my dog." [1] In both classes of sayings the usual sentence-construction with subject and finite verb is abandoned in favour of something which may be compared to a Japanese drawing, in which the contours are not completely filled in ; the very boldness of such a drawing assists in bringing about an artistic effect by leaving more to the imagination of the beholder. And our grammatical phenomenon thus turns out to be one little part of the ever-standing war between classicism and impressionism.

[1] What is the form of the verb in these sayings ? They closely resemble the imperatives mentioned below (p. 314) which are not meant as requests, but might be transcribed as conditional clauses : the difference is that there the imperatives are followed by complete sentences which are so to speak the apodoses, but here by verbs in the same form, which it is more difficult to apprehend as imperatives.

CHAPTER XXIII

MOODS

Classification.

MANY grammars enumerate the following moods in English, etc. : indicative, subjunctive, imperative, infinitive, and participle. It is, however, evident, that infinitives and participles cannot be co-ordinated with the others ; enough has also been said of them in various other parts of this work, and we shall therefore in this chapter deal with the first three moods only. These are sometimes called fact-mood, thought-mood, and will-mood respectively. But they do not " express different relations between subject and predicate," as Sweet says (NEG § 293). It is much more correct to say [1] that they express certain attitudes of the mind of the speaker towards the contents of the sentence, though in some cases the choice of a mood is determined not by the attitude of the actual speaker, but by the character of the clause itself and its relation to the main nexus on which it is dependent.[2] Further it is very important to remember that we speak of " mood " only if this attitude of mind is shown in the form of the verb : mood thus is a syntactic, not a notional category.

Imperative.

This is true even of the Imperative, though that mood comes nearer than either the indicative or the subjunctive to being notional. It is a will-mood in so far as its chief use is to express the will of the speaker, though only—and this is very important—in so far as it is meant to influence the behaviour of the hearer, for otherwise the speaker expresses his will in other ways. Imperatives thus are requests, and, as we have seen, these range from the strictest command to the humblest prayer. But we saw also that

---

[1] As Brugmann, Oertel, and Noreen do.
[2] Thus in Fr. " ma femme veut que je lui obéisse " or " ma femme ne croit pas qu'il vienne " the subjunctive evidently says nothing about the *speaker's* frame of mind.

requests are very often expressed by other means than the imperative (" Another bottle ! " | " Wollen wir gehen " | " You will pack at once and leave this house," [1] etc.), and we may here remind the reader of the use in requests of infinitives (" Einsteigen ! " | " Nicht hinauslehnen ! " | " Non piangere ! ") and of participles (" Vorgesehen ! " | " Still gestanden ! " | " Wohl auf, kameraden, auf's pferd, auf's pferd, In's feld, in die freiheit gezogen ! ")—in other words, imperative and request are not convertible or coextensive terms.

Nor can it be said that imperatives are exclusively used to express requests. An imperative very often means permission, which is not a request, because it does not say that the speaker wants the hearer to behave in a certain way. But a permissive " Take that (if you like) ! " may also be expressed in other ways : " I allow you to take that " | " You may take that " | " I have no objection to your taking that " | " I don't mind if you take that."—On prohibition = negative command or permission see Ch. XXIV.

A further use of the imperative is seen in Hamlet's " Vse euerie man after his desart, and who should scape whipping "—the first part is no more a real request to use every man after his desert than the second is a real question ; together the two sentences mean : if we used . . ., no one would escape punishment. Other examples : Spoil foc's'le hands, make devils (Stevenson) | Give you women but rope enough, you'll do your own business (Richardson ; the use of *you* as an indirect object shows that no request to the person addressed is meant).

As the imperative has no particular ending in English, one might perhaps feel inclined to think that these sentences contained infinitives (though how used ?). Parallel uses in other languages show us, however, clearly that they contain imperatives, e.g. G. Sage das, und du wirst (so wirst du) verhöhnt | Dan. Tag hatten op eller lad den ligge, i begge tilfælde fâr du prygl | Fr. Obligez cent fois, refusez une, on ne se souviendra que du refus | Lat. Scaevae vivacem crede nepoti Matrem : nil faciet sceleris pia dextera (Hor.) | Gr. Dos moi pou stō, kai tēn gēn kinēsō.

As imperatives in this function serve to express condition, we can understand their occurrence in connexion with a preterit, e.g. " Give him time, and he was generally equal to the demands of suburban customers ; hurry or interrupt him, and he showed

---

[1] Even the Eskimo makes frequent use of a future in the sense of an imperative : *torqorumârparse* ihr werdet es aufheben = hebt es auf ! (Kleinschmidt, *Gramm. d. grönl. spr.* 69). I mention this because E. Lerch has recently drawn far-reaching conclusions as to French mentality from the occurrence in French of expressions like *tu le feras* = *fais-le* : " den herrschsüchtigen, tyrannischen charakter des heischefuturums." The spirit of the Greenlander is perhaps less domineering than that of any other nation.

himself anything but the man for a crisis " (Gissing), and the use
of a perfect imperative in " Soyez bon, pitoyable, intelligent, *ayez
souffert* mille morts : vous ne sentirez pas la douleur de votre ami
qui a mal aux dents " (Rolland).   Note also the imperative in the
middle of a dependent clause, e.g. "Darwin tells us how little
curly worms, only give them time enough, will cover with earth
even the larger kind of stones (Birrell) | an Alpine Avalanche ;
which once stir it, will spread (Carlyle) | I thought that, take them
all round, I had never seen their equals (Butler).[1]

This use of what might be called the imaginary imperative [2]
helps us to explain the fact that some imperatives have become
prepositions or conjunctions, e.g. When you feel that, *bar* accidents,
the worst is over (Quiller-Couch) | I am not in the habit of beating
women at any time, *let alone* at a lunch-party (Hope) | *Suppose*
he were to come, what then ?   Dan. *Sæt* han kom, hvad så ?

Indicative and Subjunctive.

If we pass on to the Indicative and the Subjunctive, the first
remark that obtrudes itself is that the treatment of this subject
has been needlessly complicated by those writers who speak of
combinations with auxiliary verbs, e.g. *may he come* | *he may come*
| *if he should come* | *he would come*, as if they were subjunctives of
the verb *come*, or subjunctive equivalents.   Scholars would hardly
have used these expressions if they had had only the English language to deal with, for it is merely the fact that such combinations
in some cases serve to translate simple subjunctives in German or
Latin that suggests the use of such terms, exactly as people will
call *to the boy* a dative case.   It is equally wrong to speak of *bless*
in *God bless you* as an optative, while the same form in *if he bless you*
is called a subjunctive ; we should use the term ' optative ' only
where the language concerned has a separate form, as is the case in
Greek—but there, of course, the optative is not exclusively an
" optative " in the sense just alluded to, i.e. a mood of wish, but
has other meanings as well.   A precise terminology is a *conditio sine
qua non* if one wants to understand grammatical facts.[3]

The view here presented is in direct opposition to that taken by
Professor Sonnenschein.   Though my objections to his treatment
of the theory of moods are essentially the same as those I had

---

[1] On a peculiar use of the imperative in narrative style see Brugmann,
Versch. 79.

[2] It may be said to be addressed not to the ' second person' (hearer),
but to the ' generic person ' as defined in Ch. XVI.

[3] Some comparative linguists use ' optative ' instead of ' subjunctive '
in speaking of Gothonic languages, because the form corresponds etymo-
logically to the Greek optative.

against his theory of cases, it may not be superfluous to review what he says of moods, and to show the contradictions and difficulties inherent in his conception of them. The term 'mood' must not, he says, be taken to involve a difference of inflexion. Such a definition would make havoc of the moods of any language; for example, the Latin *regam* and *rexerit* and the German *liebte* may be either indicative or subjunctive; and the Latin forms in *-ere* may be either imperative or indicative or infinitive.—My reply is, of course, that we recognize the Latin moods because the majority of forms are distinctive : *rego, regis, rexero, rexeras,* and innumerable other forms can only be one mood each, and if we substitute the forms of another verb or another person of the same verb it is quite easy to decide what is the mood of any ambiguous form in a given context. If instead of G. *liebte* in one sentence we should say *hatte,* it is the indicative ; if we should say *hätte,* it is the subjunctive, etc.[1]

Moods then, according to Professor Sonnenschein, denote categories of *meaning,* not of form. The indicative mood speaks of a matter of fact (S. § 211). But if I say " Twice four is seven " I use the indicative to express the opposite of a fact. This objection might be called captious, for the meaning evidently is that the indicative is used to *represent* something as a fact ; yet even in that form the statement cannot be always maintained, cf. the frequent use of the indicative in conditional clauses : " if he is ill," and after *wish* : " I wish he wasn't ill."

Next, we are told that " the meaning of the subjunctive is quite different from that of the indicative " (§ 214). Nevertheless we read in § 315 that in " *Take care that you are not caught* " the indicative is " used with the meaning of the subjunctive." Similar contradictions are found in other places : in § 219 the author admits that it would be possible to use *comest* and *falls* instead of the subjunctives in " stint not to ride, Until thou come to fair Tweedside " and " Who stands, if freedom fall ? ", but he says that " these present indicatives would be used with a special meaning ; they would, in fact, be *equivalent to subjunctives.*" Similarly in § 234 : " the past indicative is sometimes used after ' as if,' but it always has the meaning of a past subjunctive." But as the distinction of moods is by definition one of meaning, the simple inference is that this indicative *is* a subjunctive ! Inversely, in § 303 (note) S. speaks of a subjunctive without any clear

---

[1] Professor Sonnenschein goes on to say : " The English subjunctive, properly understood, is an admirable clue to the uses of the mood in other languages." The same educational fallacy as above (see p. 180) ! The pupil who has mastered Sonnenschein's intricate rules for conditional sentences in English " need only be told " that Latin and German employ the same moods—to be led astray, at any rate in some cases !

difference of meaning from an indicative in *when I ask her if she love me*. According to § 219 Obs. a present indicative is quite impossible in noun-clauses which express that something is to be done. We take his own sentence "Give the order that every soldier is to kill his prisoners," and we naturally ask, is this "*is* (to kill)" an indicative or a subjunctive? How are thinking pupils to find their way in this wilderness? [1]

If we start from the assumption that meaning is decisive in these matters, it is also difficult to see the logic of Sonnenschein's § 215: "The reason why the subjunctive is not so common now as it used to be is that we have got into the habit of expressing the subjunctive meaning in other ways, especially by using the verbs ' shall ' and ' may ' with the infinitive instead of the subjunctive " and § 219 " It is a mistake to say that the subjunctive mood has practically disappeared from modern English. . . . But it is true to say that the equivalent expressions mentioned in § 215 are still commoner," for here " subjunctive " must necessarily be used of the *form* if the paragraphs are to make sense.

Although Professor Sonnenschein says that the meaning of the subjunctive is distinct from that of the indicative, we are nowhere told what exactly that meaning is (though the meaning of some specified employments of the subjunctive is explained). Nor would it be possible to find one formula that should cover all the various uses of the subjunctive in any one Aryan language, let alone one comprehensive formula for all Aryan languages. The nearest approach is contained in the term thought-mood,[2] or perhaps better, " non-committal mood " (Sheffield GTh 123) as opposed to a " downright " statement: something is mentioned with a certain hesitation or doubt or uncertainty as to its reality, but even this vague definition is not always to the point, for sometimes the subjunctive is used for what is downright imaginary or unreal (" Wäre ich doch reich ! ") and sometimes for what is downright real (" Je suis heureux que tu sois venu ").[3] The truth seems to be that the subjunctive was at first vaguely used in a variety of cases which it is impossible logically or notionally to delimitate as against the use of the indicative, and that each language took

[1] Note also the treatment of *should be* in " I am glad that he should be here." In § 299 it is called a subjunctive-equivalent, but in § 475 it is said that it is " almost equivalent to a tense of the indicative mood."

[2] Noreen (VS 5. 131) says that the ' conjunctive ' expresses fictitious idea (though not permission) and wishes apart from hope ; as a separate mood he gives the ' optative ' (för permissiva och sperativa meningar). His expressions are far from clear.

[3] Note Sweet's expression (First Steps in Anglo-Saxon, § 96) : The subjunctive is sometimes used *illogically* in statements of facts. His example is taken from Beowulf 696 Gespræc þa se goda gylp-worda sum, Beowulf Geata, ær he on bed *stige*.

its own course in sometimes restricting and sometimes extending its sphere of employment, especially in dependent clauses. The vagueness of the meaning of the subjunctive facilitates the transition of a present subjunctive to a future indicative as in the Latin forms in -*am*, and the extension of the second person singular in the strong verbs from the subjunctive to the indicative, e.g. OE. *wære*. In many cases the levelling of the two moods may have been brought about by formal coalescence, but even apart from that there is in many languages a strong tendency to get rid of the subjunctive. In Danish and in Russian there are only a few isolated survivals ; [1] in English the subjunctive has since Old English times been on retreat, though from the middle of the nineteenth century there has been a literary revival of some of its uses. In Romanic the subjunctive is less used than in Latin, as seen most clearly in French in conditional sentences (" s'il était riche il payerait," the last form having sprung from the Latin indicative *pacare habebat*). This extensive movement away from the subjunctive could hardly have taken place, had one mood been felt as decidedly the mood of fact and the other as the mood of thought, and we get nearer to the actual facts if we regard the indicative as the mood chosen when there is no special reason to the contrary, and the subjunctive as a mood required or allowable in certain cases varying from language to language. Only thus can we do justice to the frequency of hesitation, e.g. in E. *if he comes*, or *come*, G. *damit er kommen kann*, or *könne*, and to the variation of mood without any change of meaning in Fr. *s'il vient et qu'il dise*. I take at random some everyday sentences from the three best-known languages to illustrate the divergence in their use of moods :

if he be ill—if he is ill ; s'il est malade ; wenn er krank ist.
if he were ill ; wenn er krank wäre—if he was ill ; s'il était malade.

sie glaubt, er wäre krank—sie glaubt, dass er krank ist ; she believes he is ill ; elle croit qu'il est malade.
sie glaubt nicht, er wäre krank ; elle ne croit pas qu'il soit malade— she does not believe that he is ill.
damit wären wir fertig—I hope we are through now ; espérons que c'est fini.

le premier qui soit arrivé—the first who has arrived ; der erste, der angekommen ist.

---

[1] Russian *by* or *b* can hardly be called a verbal form any longer : it is added to *što* 'that' or *jesli* 'if' or to the verb, e.g. *jesli b ja znal* or *znal by ja* 'if I knew,' 'if I had known.'

je cherche un homme qui puisse me le dire—I am looking for a man
who can tell me that; ich suche einen mann, der mir das
sagen kann (or : könnte).

quoiqu'il soit réellement riche—though he is really rich ; obgleich
er wirklich reich ist.

If there are thus many divergences, there are also certain
general tendencies common to languages of our family. The
indicative is generally used in relative clauses and clauses introduced by local and temporal conjunctions (*where, when, while*),
unless (in some languages) an intention is implied or the clauses
express the thought of some other person than the speaker or
writer. With regard to condition, the subjunctive is most often
required if impossibility is implied (in " clauses of rejected or,
better, of rejecting condition," or " contrary-to-fact-condition "),
though even there English tends to get rid of the subjunctive ;
greater hesitation is found when the possibility is admitted, but
the speaker " wants to guard himself from endorsing the truth or
realization of the statement " (NED) ;   and finally the indicative
is required when the two ideas are not really meant as conditioning
and conditioned, but as equally true : " if he was rich, he was open-
handed too," i.e. he was both, though these two things do not
always go together ; the meaning of the conditional form may be
said to be : if you admit that he was rich, you must admit also that
he was open-handed ; cp. " she is fifty if she is a day." [1] Similar
considerations hold good with regard to concession (*though he were,
was, be, is*).

Notional Moods.

Would it be possible to place all " moods " in a logically consistent system ? This was attempted by grammarians more than a
hundred years ago on the basis of first Wolff's and then Kant's
philosophy. The former in his Ontology had the three categories,
possibility, necessity and contingency, and the latter under the
head of " modality " the three of possibility, existence, and
necessity ; Gottfried Hermann then gave the further subdivisions :
objective possibility (conjunctive), subjective possibility (optative),
objective necessity (Greek verbal adjectives in *-teos*) and subjective
necessity (imperative). It is hardly worth while following the
subsequent development of these theories (see the able paper
" A Century of Metaphysical Syntax," by W. G. Hale, in the St.
Louis Congress of Arts and Sciences, 1904, Vol. III).

---

[1] There is really no condition implied in " If he was successful it was
because the whole situation helped him " ; cp. on the other hand " If he were
successful in that matter he would go on in the same way."

Recently Deutschbein has presented us with a somewhat similar system (SNS 113 ff., cf. also *Sprachpsychologische Studien,* Cöthen, 1918). His main division is:

I. Kogitativus,
II. Optativus,
III. Voluntativus,
IV. Expectativus,

each with four subdivisions, which are indicated pseudo-mathematically by the formulas 1, 0, < 1 and > 1. These figures are said to represent the proportion between the thought or wish on the one hand and reality or possibility of realization on the other. Thus in the sentence " Lebte mein vater doch " the proportion between wish (W) and " Realisierungsmöglichkeit " (R) is said to be = 0, though a mathematician would probably rather say that it was = ∞, as it is R which is = 0. Apart from this curious inadvertence, the meaning is evidently to give necessity as > 1, reality = 1, possibility < 1, and unreality or impossibility = 0. There is something to be said for his view if thus formulated, though my own tripartition necessity, possibility, impossibility seems to me logically preferable, as reality and unreality really belong to another sphere than necessity and possibility.

Even Deutschbein's scheme is not exhaustive, and he does not distinguish strictly enough between syntactic and notional categories. As a tentative scheme of the purely notional ideas expressed more or less vaguely by the verbal moods and auxiliaries of various languages we might perhaps give the following list, to which I cannot, however, attach any great importance. The categories frequently overlap, and some of the terms are not quite unobjectionable. The placing of the Conditional and Concessional also is subject to doubt, and a " Subordinative " should perhaps be added at the end of the list.

1. Containing an element of will :

Jussive : go (command).
Compulsive : he has to go.
Obligative : he ought to go | we should go.
Advisory : you should go.
Precative : go, please.
Hortative : let us go.
Permissive : you may go if you like.
Promissive : I will go | it shall be done.
Optative (realizable) : may he be still alive !
Desiderative (unrealizable) : would he were still alive !
Intentional : in order that he may go.

2. Containing no element of will:

Apodictive : twice two must be (is necessarily) four.
Necessitative : he must be rich (or he could not spend so much).
Assertive : he is rich.
Presumptive : he is probably rich ; he would (will) know.
Dubitative : he may be (is perhaps) rich.
Potential : he can speak.
Conditional : if he is rich.
Hypothetical : if he were rich.
Concessional : though he is rich.

Each of these can be expressed linguistically by a variety of means besides those mentioned.

There are many " moods " if once one leaves the safe ground of verbal forms actually found in a language.[1]

[1] The artificial languages, Esperanto and Ido, very wisely restrict their moods to the number of two besides the indicative, namely what may be called a desiderative, in Esp. ending in -u, in Ido in -ez, e.g. venez come, il venez let him come, por ke il venez in order that he may come, and a conditional ending in -us : se il venus, me pagus if he came, I should pay. Otherwise auxiliaries or adverbs are used : mustas must, povas can, forsan perhaps.

CHAPTER XXIV

NEGATION

Contradictory and Contrary. Some Tripartitions. The Meaning of Negation. Special and Nexal Negation. Double or Cumulative Negation.
History of Negatives. Implied Negation.

Contradictory and Contrary.

LOGICIANS distinguish between *contradictory* terms, such as *white*
and *not-white*, *rich* and *not-rich*, and *contrary* terms, such as *white*
and *black*, *rich* and *poor*. Two contradictory terms together comprise everything in existence, as any middle term is excluded,
while two contrary terms admit one or more middle terms. For
contradictory terms language generally employs either derivatives
like *unhappy*, *impossible*, *disorder* or composite expressions containing the adverb *not*. On the other hand, separate roots are
very often used to express the most necessary contrary terms.
Hence such pairs as *young—old*, *good—bad*, *big—small*, etc. Intermediate stages may be expressed negatively, e.g. *neither young nor
old*, but in some cases we have special expressions for the intermediate stage, e.g. *indifferent* in the comparatively recent sense of
' what is between good and bad.' Sometimes we have even a whole
long string of words with shades of meaning partially overlapping,
e.g. *hot (sweltering)*, *warm*, *tepid*, *lukewarm*, *mild*, *fresh*, *cool*, *chilly*,
cold, *frosty*, *icy* ; though each adjective at the head of this list is a
contrast to each of those at the tail, it is impossible to draw a sharp
line between two halves of the list.

If now we take two simple sentences like " John is rich " and
" John is not rich," these are to my mind contrary terms, not
contradictory, because they admit the intermediate " perhaps John
is rich " or " he may be rich, he is possibly rich," and as a kind of
subdivision of this middle term we must mention " John is probably
rich " or " No doubt John is rich " (for *no doubt* as actually used in
ordinary speech implies some little doubt). We therefore may
set up a tripartition :

A. Positive.
B. Questionable.
C. Negative.

A and C are absolute and imply certainty, B implies uncertainty, and in that respect B is the negative counterpart of the two positive sentences A " it is certain that he is rich " and C " it is certain that he is not rich."

It may shock the logician that the two sentences " John is rich " and " John is not rich " are here treated as contrary and not as contradictory, but I hope he will be relieved when I say that evidently " rich " and " not rich " are contradictory and admit no middle term : the tripartition given above refers only to the attitude of the speaker to the inclusion of John in one of the two classes " rich " and " not rich." Our tripartition assists us in understanding some linguistic facts with regard to questions, for a question is an assertion of the class B + a request addressed to the hearer to resolve the doubt. It is therefore immaterial whether the question is couched positively or negatively : " Is John rich ? " or " Is John not rich ? " are perfectly synonymous, because the real question is double-sided : " Is John rich, or is he not ? " (Alternative question, p. 303, above.) In the same way, in offering a glass of beer one may say either " Will you have a glass of beer ? " or " Won't you have a glass of beer ? " Positive and negative here mean the same thing, just as in " Perhaps he is rich " and " Perhaps he is not rich."

What is here said of questions is true of unemotional questions only ; a marked tone of surprise will make the two sentences into distinct contrasts : for then " Will you (really) have a glass of beer ? " comes to mean ' I am surprised at your wanting a glass of beer ? ', and " Won't you have a glass of beer ? " the reverse. While in English " Won't you pass me the salt ? " would be rude as implying unwillingness in the person addressed, in Danish " Vil De række mig saltet ? " is generally a command, and " Vil De ikke række mig saltet ? " a polite request (' Would you mind passing the salt ? '). A Dutch lady once told me how surprised she was at first in a Copenhagen boarding-house at these negative questions, which she took as requests not to pass the salt. Very often the particular interrogative form is chosen to suggest a particular answer, thus especially in tag-questions (" He is rich, isn't he ? " | " He isn't rich, is he ? "). Consequently questions often come to mean assertions of the inverse : " Am I my brother's keeper ? " = ' I am not ' | " Isn't that nice ? " = ' It is very nice.'

As exclamations have in many cases developed out of questions, we now also understand how it is that very often it does not matter whether *not* is added or not : " How often have I (not) watched him ! "

Some Tripartitions.

Next we have to consider some terms of paramount importance to the logician as well as to the linguist, namely the two absolute extremes *all* and *nothing* with the intermediate *something*. Let us call the two extremes A and C, and the intermediate B. They are most naturally represented in a descending scale :

A. everything, all, everybody (all girls, all the money)
B. something, some, somebody (some girls, a girl, some money)
C. nothing, none, nobody (no girl(s), no money).

Thus also the adverbs :

A. always, everywhere
B. sometimes, somewhere
C. never, nowhere.

It should be noted that *some* (*something*, etc.) is here taken in the ordinary meaning it has in natural speech, and not in the meaning logicians sometimes give it, in which it is the positive counterpart of *no* (*nothing*), and thus includes the possibility of *all*.[1] The intermediate stage B of course admits many subdivisions, of which we may mention some of special linguistic interest :

B 1 : many (girls)	much (money)	very sorry
B 2 : a few (girls)	a little (money)	a little sorry
B 3 : few (girls)	little (money)	little sorry.

B 1 approaches A (all) ; B 3 approaches C (none) and may even in many cases be considered negative rather than positive ; this is especially true of the adverb *little*, e.g. in " They little think what mischief is in hand " (Byron). The use of the indefinite article to distinguish B 2 and B 3 is linguistically interesting ; it is not confined to English, cp. Fr. *un peu*, It. and Sp. *un poco*, G. *ein wenig*. The difference is well brought out in Shakespeare's sentence : " When he is best, he is a little worse than a man, and when he is worst, he is little better than a beast." B 3 is felt as a contrast to B 1, but B 2 rather to C ; cp. " Few of the passengers survived " and " A few of the passengers survived."

[1] See Keynes, FL 100 : " It has, however, been customary with logicians in interpreting the traditional scheme [A = universal affirmative, I = particular affirmative, E = universal negative, O = particular negative] to adopt the other meaning, so that *Some S is P* is not inconsistent with *All S is P*." On p. 200 Keynes is bound to admit that many logicians " have not recognized the pitfalls surrounding the use of the word *some*. Many passages might be quoted in which they distinctly adopt the meaning—*some, but not all*." But, in the name of common sense, one is tempted to ask : why do logicians dig such pitfalls for their fellow-logicians to tumble into by using ordinary words in abnormal meanings ? Keynes's arguments on p. 203 are far from convincing.

The tripartition between :

A. Necessity,
B. Possibility,
C. Impossibility,

is really nothing but a special case of the tripartition mentioned above, for necessity means that *all* possibilities are comprised, just as impossibility means the exclusion of all possibilities. The verbal expressions for these three categories are :

A. must (or, need)
B. can (or, may)
C. cannot.

If to these three categories we add an element of volition with regard to another being, the result is :

A. Command,
B. Permission,
C. Prohibition.

Verbal expressions for these are :

A. You must
B. You may
C. You must not (may not, see below).

The imperative (" Take that ! ") may mean either **A** or B, see above under Requests.

The Meaning of Negation.

If we now want to inquire into the meaning of negation, the first point of importance is to emphasize the difference between a linguistic negative and a mathematical negative : — 4 means, not everything different from + 4, but a point as much below 0 as 4 is above 0. A linguistic negative, on the contrary, changes a term into the contradictory term, at any rate theoretically, for on closer inspection we shall find that in practice this rule requires some very important qualifications ; to understand these the division made above into A, B, and C-categories will prove useful and should constantly be borne in mind. Let us first look at quantities in the B-category (above, p. 324) : neither all nor nothing.

Here the general rule in all (or most) languages is that *not* means ' less than,' or in other words ' between the term qualified and nothing.' Thus *not good* means ' inferior,' but does not comprise ' excellent ' ; *not lukewarm* indicates a lower temperature than *lukewarm*, something between lukewarm and icy, not something between lukewarm and hot. This is especially obvious if we consider the ordinary meaning of negatived numerals : He does not read three books in a year | the hill is not two hundred feet high | his income is not £200 a year | he does not see her once in a week | the bottle is not half full—all these expressions mean less than three, etc. Therefore *not one* comes to be the natural expression in many languages for ' none,' e.g. OE. *nan = ne-an*, whence modern *none, no*, further ON. *eingi*, G. *k-ein*, Fr. *pas un bruit*, etc.

But the same expressions may also exceptionally mean 'more than,' only the word following *not* then has to be strongly stressed (with the peculiar intonation indicative of contradiction), and then the whole combination has generally to be followed by a more exact indication : not *luke*warm, but really hot | his income is not *two* hundred a year, but at least three hundred | not *once*, but two or three times, etc. Note that *not once or twice* always means several times, as in Tennyson's " Not once or twice in our fair island-story, The path of duty was the way to glory."

Not above 30 means either 30 or less than 30. *No more than* generally means ' as little as,' and *no less than* ' as much as,' e.g. " the rank and file of doctors are no more scientific than their tailors ; or their tailors are no less scientific than they " (Shaw) ; note the distinction between *no* and *not* in these combinations : *no more than three* 'three only ' ; *not more than three* 'three at most ' ; *he paid no less than twenty pounds* implies astonishment at the greatness of the amount, which was exactly £20 ; *he paid not less than twenty pounds* implies uncertainty with regard to the exact amount, which at the very least was £20 (MEG II, 16. 84). In Latin both *non magis quam* and *non minus quam* are favourite expressions for equality, though, of course, used in different connexions : *Cæsar non minus operibus pacis florebat quam rebus in bello gestis* | *Pericles non magis operibus pacis florebat quam rebus in bello gestis* (Cauer).

If we turn to the negatives of the terms given above as B 1, 2 and 3, we see that negativing 1 turns it into three : *not much = little; not many = few*. But a negative 2 becomes nearly synonymous with 1 (or stands between 1 and 2) : *not a little = much, not a few = many*. B 3 is not used idiomatically with *not*.

Next we turn to the A and C-categories, the two extremes. Here we have the general rule that if the negative word is placed first, it discards the absolute element, and the result is the intermediate term : Not A = B ; not C also = B. If, on the other hand, the absolute term is mentioned first the absolute element prevails, and the result is the contrary notion : A . . . not = C ; C . . . not = A.

Examples of a negative A = B :

They are not all of them fools | he is not always so sad | non omnis moriar.

Exceptionally the same effect (B) is obtained even though the negative comes *after* the A-word in such sentences as " All that glisters is not gold " (Shakespeare), and " Tout ce qui reluit n'est pas or," which correspond to the Danish and German forms of the proverb : " Ikke alt hvad der glimrer er guld " and " Nicht alles was glänzt, ist gold " ; cp. also from the Bible : All things are lawfull vnto mee, but all things are not expedient | all is not lost (Milton, Shelley) | But all men are not born to reign (Byron) | For each man kills the thing he loves, Yet each man does not die (Wilde) ; similar examples abound also in the literatures of other countries ; they are easy to explain psychologically as the result of the two tendencies, to place the subject first, and to attract the negation to the verb. Tobler (VB 1. 197) tries to justify them logically as saying " von dem subjekte ' alles glänzende ' darf ' gold sein ' nicht prädiziert werden." This is true, but does not touch the fact that the word-order makes us expect the meaning ' nothing of what glitters is gold ' (was glänzt, ist niemals gold ; C) rather than the intended meaning ' only some part of what glitters is gold ' (was glänzt ist nicht immer gold ; B).[1]

Examples of C with a negative before it = B :
Lat. *non-nulli* ' some,' *non-nunquam* ' sometimes ' | he was not the eldest son of his father for nothing | it is not good for a man to have no gods (= it is good to have some gods).

Examples of A with a negative after it = C : Tous ces gens-là ne sont pas humains (i.e. none of them is, Rolland) | the one [uncle] I was always going to write to. And always didn't (Dickens). This is rare except when the negative is in the form of a prefix or is implied, e.g. they were all of them unkind ; everybody was unkind (= nobody was kind) | he was always unkind | they all failed (= nobody succeeded).

The difference between the two possible results of negation with a word of the A-class is idiomatically expressed by different adverbs :
Result B : he is not altogether happy | pas tout-à-fait | ikke helt | nicht ganz.
Result C : he is not at all happy (he is not happy at all) | pas du tout | slet ikke | gar nicht.

---

[1] In the examples given in this section *all* has its generic meaning (everybody, anybody) ; but *all* may also be used in the ' distributive ' sense (the sum of. . . . see p 203 note). A negative may be placed with the verb, e.g. " All the perfumes of Arabia will not sweeten this little hand " (Sh.), but is often for the sake of emphasis (= not even) put before *all*, e.g. " Not all the water in the rough rude sea Can wash the balme from an anoynted king " (Sh.).

Cp. from a recent newspaper : Germany's offer is *entirely unacceptable* to the French and *not wholly acceptable* to the English Government.

Examples of words of the class C with a negative after them, result A :

Nobody was unkind (= everybody was kind) | he was never unkind | nobody failed. This is comparatively rare with *not*, and sentences like " not a clerk in that house did not tremble before her " (Thackeray = all the clerks trembled) are generally avoided as not sufficiently clear : the hearer gets easily confused ; but if the two negatives are placed in separate sentences, the combination is unobjectionable : there was no one present that did not weep | there is nothing I could not do for her ; cp. Johnson's epitaph on Goldsmith : Qui nullum fere scribendi genus Non tetigit, Nullum quod tetigit non ornavit.

We next proceed to the three categories mentioned p. 325 : A necessity, B possibility, C impossibility. If we add a negative, we see the following results : *not necessary* (A) = possible (B) ; *not impossible* (C) = possible (B) ; *it is impossible not to see* = necessary ; *no one can deny* = everyone must admit | *nobody need be present* = everybody may be absent | *he cannot succeed* = he must fail | *non potest non amare* | *il ne pouvait pas ne pas voir* qu'on se moquait de lui.

With regard to the further tripartition A command, B permission, C prohibition, we have seen that the imperative may mean either A or B. Therefore a negative imperative, e.g. *Don't take that !* may mean either a negative command (= a prohibition), or a polite request (or advice) not to take it ; and on account of this ambiguity there is in many languages a disinclination to use a negative imperative. In Latin it is only found poetically, being otherwise replaced by a paraphrase with *noli* (*Noli me tangere*) or a subjunctive (*Ne nos inducas in tentationem*) ; in Spanish the latter has become the rule (*No vengas* ' don't come '). In Dan. *Tag det ikke* is generally a piece of advice, and *La vær å ta det* (Lad være at tage det) has become the usual form for a prohibition. In other languages we find separate verb-forms (' jussive ') or else separate negatives (e.g. Gr. *mē*) used in prohibitions.

Both *may not* and *must not* may be used in prohibitions. In the former *not* logically belongs to *may* (the negation of a permission, cf. G. *du darfst nicht*), but as the same combination is often used in a different sense, e.g. in " He may not be rich, but he is a gentleman " (where *not* goes with *be* : it is possible that he is not), and as *may* is also felt to be too weak for a prohibition, the tendency is more and more to use the more brutal *must not*, except in questions implying a positive answer (*mayn't I* = ' I suppose I may ') and in close connexion with a positive *may*, e.g. in answers (" May I take that ? No, you may not "). In *you must not take that* the negative logically belongs to the infinitive : it is a positive command (*must*) not to take that ;[1] but the prevailing tendency to attract the negative to the auxiliary verb leads to the usual form *you mustn't*. In this way we get different auxiliaries in positive and negative sentences, e.g. You may call me Dolly if you like ; but you mustn't call me child (Shaw) | You mustn't marry more than one person at a time, may you ? (Dickens). Now, however, *must* is beginning to be used in tag questions, e.g. " I must not go any farther, must I ? " (G. Eliot), though it is not possible otherwise to substitute *Must I ?* for *May I ?*

Special and Nexal Negation.

We have seen already that the meaning of a sentence sometimes depends on the place of a negative element. In a more general way we may say that the negative notion may belong logically either to one single idea (special negation) or to the combination of the two parts of a nexus (nexal negation). In the former case we have either a negative prefix (as in *never*, *unhappy*, *disorder*), or the adverb *not* put before the word (*not* happy) ; in some cases a single word without any negative prefix may be regarded as containing a negative idea, e.g. *lack* (= have not), *fail* (= not succeed ; but we may also say that *succeed* is the negative counterpart of *fail*).

When a nexus is negatived, the negative adverb is generally attracted to the verb, in many languages in the form of a weak *ne* or similar particle placed before the verb, and sometimes amalgamated with it (cp. earlier E. *nis*, *nill*) ; in MnE we have the *do*-combinations (*does not come*, *doesn't come*, etc.) except with the well-known group of verbs (*is not*, *isn't*, *cannot*, etc.).

In the sentence " Many of us didn't want the war " the nexus is negatived, but in " Not many of us wanted the war " *not* belongs exclusively to *many*, which it turns into ' few.'

In many cases it seems to be of no importance whether we negative one notion only or the combination of that notion with another ; *she is not happy* may be analyzed either as a description of what she is, viz. not-happy (= unhappy), or as a negativing of her being happy (she is-not, isn't, happy). If we add *very*, however, we see the difference between " she is very unhappy " and " she is not very happy."

---

[1] Thus properly *you must not-take*, but *you may-not take*.

The general tendency is to use a nexal negative, even in some cases where a special negative would be more apposite. By the side of the logically impeccable " I came not to send peace, but a sword " (Matt. 10. 34) we frequently find sentences like " I don't complain of your words, but of the tone in which they were uttered " (= I complain, though not . . ., but of . . .) | " We aren't here to talk nonsense, but to act " (where " we aren't here " in itself is a contradiction in terms). A particular case is found with *because* : the sentence " I didn't go because I was afraid " is ambiguous and may mean either ' I went, but the reason was not fear,' or ' I did not go, and the reason for not going was fear,' though in the spoken language the tone may show which is meant ; cp. further " I didn't call because I wanted to see her " (but for some other reason), and " I didn't call because I wanted to avoid her."

With infinitival and similar constructions it is often very important to know which of two verbal notions is negatived ; various devices are used in different languages to make the meaning clear. A few examples may suffice : She did not wish to reflect ; she strongly wished not to reflect (Bennett) | Tommy deserved not to be hated | Tommy did not deserve to be loved | Dan. prøv ikke på at se derhen | prøv på ikke at se derhen | il ne tâche pas de regarder | il tâche de ne pas regarder | il ne peut pas entendre | il peut ne pas entendre | (Will he come ?) I am afraid not | I am not afraid.

The tendency already mentioned to attract the negation to the verb is not the only one found in actual language : we often find the opposite tendency to attract the negative notion to any word that can easily be made negative. In literary English " we met nobody " is thought more elegant than the colloquial " we didn't meet anybody " ; cp. also " this will be no easy matter " and " this won't be an easy matter." In many cases we find words like *nothing* used where a nexal negation would be more logical, e.g. she loves you so well that she has the heart to thwart you in nothing (Gilbert) | you need be under no uneasiness. Attraction of this kind is seen also in the idiomatic use of " he was no ordinary boy " in preference to " he was a not ordinary boy " and in sentences like " you and I will go to the smoking-room, and talk about nothing at all subtle " (= about something that is not subtle, Benson), which most people would probably censure as wrong.

Wherever it might seem possible to attract the negative element to either of two words, it is nearly always put with the first. We may say " no one ever saw him angry " or " never did any one see him angry," but not " any one never saw him angry " or " ever did no one see him angry." Cp. also Lat. " nec quisquam " (not " et nemo "), " neque ullus," etc. *Without any danger* is preferred to *with no danger*.

When the negative is attracted to the subject, the sentence is often continued in such a way that the positive counterpart of the first subject must be understood. In ordinary life this will cause no misunderstanding, and it is only the critical, or hyper-critical, grammarian that discovers anything wrong in it, e.g. Not one should scape, but perish by my sword (= but all perish, Marlowe) | none of them are hurtful, but loving and holy (Bunyan). Cp. also : Don't let any of us go to bed to-night, but see the morning come (Benson) | I quite forget the details, only that I had a good deal of talk with him (Carlyle).[1]

Double or Cumulative Negation.

It seems to be an established view among theorists, logicians as well as linguists, that two negatives ought to cancel one another, because two negatves logically make an affirmative in the same way as in mathematics $-(-4) = +4$. Languages, as well as individual writers, are consequently censured if they use a double negative as a strengthened negative. If this view were true, a consistent logician would have to find fault with Chaucer's " He *neuere* yet *no* vileynye *ne* seyde In al his lyf unto *no* maner wight," because here four negatives (thus an even number) are made to serve as a strengthened negative expression, but not with the OE. example " *nan* man *nyste nan* þing " (no man not-knew nothing), because there are here three negatives, of which two should cancel each other, leaving one over. But as a matter of fact no one seems to calculate cumulative negation in this way, and this is perfectly right from the point of view of linguistic logic.

Language is not mathematics, and, as already remarked, a linguistic negative cannot be compared with the sign — (minus) in mathematics ; hence any reference to the mathematical rule about two minus's is inconclusive. But neither are the attempts made by some linguists to justify the use of double negation perfectly satisfactory. Van Ginneken rightly criticizes the view of Romanic scholars, who speak of a half-negation in the case of French *ne*— an explanation which at any rate does not explain many of the phenomena in other languages. His own explanation is that negation in natural languages is not logical negation, but the expression of a feeling of resistance ; according to him the logical or mathematical conception of negation, according to which two

---

[1] Cp. also " It is always astonishing to me how few people know anything (or very little) about Faraday " : *or very little* is made possible only because the sentence means ' that most people know nothing,' etc.

negatives are mutually destructive, has only gained ground in a few centres of civilization and has never struck root in the popular mind. I have my doubts as to the greater primitivity of the idea of 'resistance' than that of negation understood exactly as we understand it in such a simple sentence as "he does not sleep." Other writers speak of a difference between qualitative and quantitative negation and imagine that this distinction finds a support in Kant's table of categories, though as a matter of fact Kant ranges all negation under the heading of "quality." Anyhow the distinction does not assist us at all to comprehend double negation.[1]

Language has a logic of its own, and in this case its logic has something to recommend it. Whenever two negatives really refer to the same idea or word (as special negatives) the result is invariably positive ; this is true of all languages, and applies to such collocations as e.g. *not uncommon, not infrequent, not without some fear*. The two negatives, however, do not exactly cancel one another in such a way that the result is identical with the simple *common, frequent, with some doubt* ; the longer expression is always weaker : "this is not unknown to me" or "I am not ignorant of this" means 'I am to some extent aware of it,' etc. The psychological reason for this is that the *détour* through the two mutually destructive negatives weakens the mental energy of the listener and implies on the part of the speaker a certain hesitation which is absent from the blunt, outspoken *common* or *known*. In the same way *I don't deny that he was angry* is weaker than *I assert*, etc. Cp. also Fr. *il n'était pas sans être frappé*.

On the other hand, if two (or more than two) negatives are attached to different words, they have not the same effect upon one another, and the total result, therefore, may very well be negative. We see this in a great variety of languages, where cumulative negation in this way is of everyday occurrence. Examples from Old and Middle English have already been given ; they abound in these periods, but are somewhat rarer in Elizabethan English ; in dialectal and vulgar English of our own day they are frequent, and many examples may be culled from representations of popular language in novels and plays, e.g. "Nobody never went and hinted no such thing, said Peggotty" | "I can't do nothing without my staff" (Hardy).

In other languages we find the same phenomenon more or less regularly. Thus in Middle High German : nu *en*-kan ich *niemanne* gesagen. In French : on *ne* le voit *nulle* part. In Spanish : aquí *no* vienen *nunca* soldados 'here not come never soldiers.' In

---

[1] These theories have been criticized by Delbrück, *Negative Sätze*, 36 ff., and in my own *Negation*, 69 ff. Negation is always quantitative rather than qualitative.

Slavic languages, Serbian : i *nikto* mu *ne* mogaše odgovoriti rijcči
' and nobody him not could answer word ' (Delbrück).   Russian :
Filipok *ničego ne* skazal ' F. nothing not said.'   Greek : aneu
toutou *oudeis* eis *ouden oudenos* an humōn *oudepote* genoito axios
(Plato, in Madvig).

So also outside our family of languages, e.g. Magyar : *sëmmit sëm*
hallottam, or : *nëm* hallottam *sëmmit* ' nothing not I have heard
(Szinnyei).   Congo (Bantu) : kavangidi kwandi wawubiko, kamo-
nanga kwandi nganziko, kaba yelanga kwa-u ko ' not did he evil not,
not feeling he no pain, not they sick not.'

How to account for this phenomenon, which is spread over so
many different languages ? There is one very important observation to be made, without which I do not think that we shall be able
to understand the matter, namely that repeated negation becomes
an habitual phenomenon in those languages only in which the
ordinary negative element is comparatively small in phonetic
bulk : *ne* or *n-* in Old English, in French, in Slavic, *en* or *n-* in Middle
High (and Middle Low) German, *ou* in Greek, *s-* or *n-* in Magyar.
These are easily attracted to various words (we have already seen
instances of such attraction in previous sections), and the insignifi-
cance of these initial sounds or weakly stressed syllables makes it
desirable to multiply them in a sentence so as to prevent their
being overlooked.   Under the influence of strong feeling the speaker
wants to make absolutely sure that the negative sense will be fully
apprehended ; he therefore attaches it not only to the verb, but
also to any other part of the sentence that can be easily made
negative : he will, as it were, spread a layer of negative colouring
over the whole of the sentence instead of confining it to one single
place. If this repetition is rarer in modern English and German
than it was formerly, one of the reasons probably is that the fuller
negatives *not* and *nicht* have taken the place of the smaller *ne* and
en,[1] though the logic of the schools and the influence of Latin
have also contributed towards the same result.   It may also be
said that it requires greater mental energy to content oneself
with one negative, which has to be remembered during the whole
length of the utterance both by the speaker and the hearer, than
to repeat the negative idea whenever an occasion offers itself,
and thus impart a negative colouring to the whole of the sentence.

If we are now to pass judgment on this widespread cumulative
negation from a logical point of view, I should not call it illogical,

---

[1] In classical Latin, too, *non* is more bulky than the original *ne*. I am
inclined to explain the comparative rarity in Elizabethan English of this
kind of cumulative negation (as opposed to the resumptive negation with
neither, etc., examples of which abound) from the use at that time of the
full *not*, which had not yet dwindled down to *-n't* attached to the verb as
in more recent periods.

seeing that the negative elements are not attached to the same word. I should rather say that though logically one negative suffices, two or three are simply a redundancy, which may be superfluous from a stylistic point of view, just as any repetition in a positive sentence (every and any, always and on all occasions), but is otherwise unobjectionable. No one objects from a logical point of view to combinations like these : " I shall never consent, not under any circumstances, not on any condition, neither at home nor abroad " ; it is true that here pauses, which in writing are marked by commas, separate the negatives, as if they belonged to so many different sentences, while in " he never said nothing " and all the other cases quoted from various languages the negatives belong to one and the same sentence. But it is perfectly impossible to draw a line between what constitutes one, and what constitutes two sentences : does a sentence like " I cannot goe no further " (Shakespeare) become more logical by the mere addition of a comma : " I cannot goe, no further " ?

As a separate variety of double negation must be treated what might be called resumptive negation (Delbrück's ergänzungsnega-tion). This is especially frequent when *not* is followed by a disjunc-tive combination with *neither . . . nor* or a restrictive addition with *not even* : " he cannot sleep, neither at night nor in the daytime " or " he cannot sleep, not even after taking an opiate " ; cp. also the addition in " loue no man in good earnest, nor no further in sport neyther " (Sh.). Similarly in other languages, Lat. *non . . . neque . . . neque, non . . . ne . . . quidem,* Gr. *ou . . . oude . . . oude,* etc. In such cases, with ' neither—nor ' and ' not even,' all lan-guages seem freely to admit double negatives, though even here precisians object to them.[1]

Closely connected with resumptive negation is paratactic negation : a negative is placed in a clause dependent on a verb of negative import, e.g. ' deny, forbid, hinder, doubt,' as if the clause had been an independent sentence, or as if the corresponding positive verb had been used in the main sentence. Examples : First he deni'de you had in him no right (Sh.) | What hinders in your own instance that you do not return to those habits (Lamb). It is well known how in some languages this develops to a fixed rule, e.g. in Latin with *ne, quin, quominus,* in French with *ne* (which now, like *ne* in other positions, tends to disappear). Here, too, we have redundancy and over-emphasis rather than irrationality or want of logic.

---

[1] A special case of resumptive negation is seen when *not* is softened down by an added *hardly,* which in itself would have been sufficient to express the idea : " He wasn't changed at all hardly " (Kipling).

History of Negatives.

The general history of negative expressions in some of the best-known languages presents a curious fluctuation. The negative adverb is often weakly stressed, because some other word in the sentence has to receive a strong stress of contrast. But when the negative has become a mere proclitic syllable or even a single sound, it is felt to be too weak, and has to be strengthened by some additional word, and this in its turn may come to be felt as the negative proper, which then may be subject to the same development as the original word. We have thus a constant interplay of weakening and strengthening, which with the further tendency to place the negative in the beginning of the sentence where it is likely to be dropped (though prosiopesis) leads to curious results, which can here be sketched only in the briefest outlines by examples taken from a few languages.

First, Latin and its continuation French. The starting point, here as elsewhere, is *ne*, which I take to be (together with the variant *me*) a primitive interjection of disgust consisting mainly in the facial gesture of contracting the muscles of the nose. The first stage, then, is :

(1) *ne dico.* This persists chiefly with a few verbs (*nescio, nequeo, nolo*) and with some pronouns and adverbs ; otherwise *ne* is felt to be too weak and is strengthened by the addition of *oenum* ' one thing ' ; the result is *non (ne-oenum)* :

(2) *non dico.* In course of time *non* loses its stress and becomes OFr. *nen*, later *ne*—thus practically the same sound as the Proto-Aryan adverb :

(3) *jeo ne di.* This has survived in literary French till our own days in a few combinations, *je ne suis, je ne peux*, and colloquially in *n'importe* ; but generally it has been found necessary to strengthen it :

(4) *je ne dis pas.* Next, in colloquial French, the weak *ne* disappears :

(5) *je dis pas.*

In Scandinavian, too, the original *ne* was first strengthened by additions and finally ousted by these, ON. *eigi, ekki*, Dan. *ej, ikke*, which at first had no negative meaning.

In German we had first *ni* alone before the verb, then *ni, ne* (or weakened *n-, en-*) before and *nicht* after the verb, and finally *nicht* alone.

In English the stages are :

(1) *ic ne secge.*
(2) *I ne seye not.*

(3) *I say not.*

(4) *I do not say.*

(5) *I don't say.* In some frequent combinations, notably *I don't know*, we witness the first beginning of a new weakening, for in the pronunciation [ai d(n) nou] practically nothing is left of the original negative.

The strengthening of negatives is effected either by means of some word meaning a small thing (*not a bit, not a jot, not a scrap,* etc., Fr. *ne . . . mie, goutte, point, pas*), or by means of an adverb meaning 'ever' (OE. *na* from *ne + a =* Gothic *ni aiws,* G. *nie ;* E. *never* also sometimes loses its temporal meaning and means nothing but 'not'). Finally the strengthening addition may be a word meaning 'nothing' as Lat. *non,* E. *not* (a weaker form of *nought*) or G. *nicht ;* in ME. *I ne seye not* there is a double negation.

The dropping or leaving out of a weak negative adverb changes a positive into a negative word. The most characteristic examples of this are found in French, where *pas, personne, jamais* and other words are now negative—invariably so when there is no verb : *pas de doute | Qui le sait ? Personne | Jamais de la vie,* and in vulgar and familiar speech also in sentences containing a verb, where literary language requires *ne: Viens-tu pas ? | je le vois jamais.* With regard to *plus,* ambiguity has in some cases been obviated by the popular pronunciation, [j ãn a ply] meaning 'there is no more of it' and [j ãn a plys] 'there is more of it.' An isolated *Plus de bruit* is a negative, but *Plus de bruit que de mal* a positive expression, though the pronunciation is here the same. There is a curious consequence of this negative use of *plus,* namely that *moins* may occasionally appear as a kind of comparative of *plus : Plus d'écoles, plus d'asiles, plus de bienfaisance, encore moins de théologie* (Mérimée).

In other languages the transition from positive to negative is found sporadically, as in Sp. *nada* 'nothing' from Lat. (*res*) *nata, nadie* 'nobody,' and in the ON. words in *-gi ;* in English we find *but* from *ne . . . but,* cp. dialectal *nobbut,* and the curious *more* for 'no more' in the South-Western part of England, e.g. "Not much of a scholar. More am I " (Phillpotts).

Implied Negation.

As in other provinces of grammar, we have here cases of disagreement between the notional meaning and the grammatical expression. A notional negation is often implied though the sentence contains no negative proper.

A question is often equivalent to a negative assertion : *Am I my brother's keeper ?* (See p. 323.)

Combinations like *Me tell a lie !* = ' I cannot tell a lie ' have been mentioned, p. 130.

Conditional expressions may serve the same purpose, e.g. " I am a rogue if I drunke to-day " (= I did not drink, Sh.) | I'm dashed if I know ; also with the conditional clause standing alone : If there isn't Captain Donnithorne a-coming into the yard ! (G. Eliot ; here, of course, the direct and the indirect negations cancel each other, the result being positive : he is coming).

Further may be mentioned : (you) *see if* I don't | *catch* me going there ! | Mr. Copperfield was teaching me.—*Much* he knew of it himself | When the devil was ill, the devil a monk would be ; When the devil got well, *the devil a monk* was he. Similar idiomatic and ironical expressions seem to be frequent in all languages.

A notional negative is also implied in the use of the preterit (subjunctive) in clauses of rejected condition (p. 265).

NOTE.—The whole subject of this chapter has been treated with much fuller illustration from many languages and with discussion of some points here omitted (negative conjunctions, prefixes, the contraction of *not* into *-nt*, etc.) in " Negation in English and Other Languages," Det kgl. Danske Videnskabernes Selskabs Historisk-Filologiske Meddelelser I, 5 (Copenhagen, 1917).

CHAPTER XXV

CONCLUSION

Conflicts.   Terminology.   The Soul of Grammar

Conflicts.

IT is a natural consequence of the complexity on the one hand of the phenomena of life which have to be expressed, and on the other hand of the linguistic means available to express them, that conflicts of various kind are bound to occur, in which the speaker has to make a choice and then, possibly after some hesitation, uses one form where someone else in the same situation might have used another form. In some cases we witness a tug-of-war, as it were, between two tendencies which may go on for a very long period, during which grammarians indulge in disputes as to which form or expression is " correct " ; in other cases one of the conflicting tendencies prevails, and the question is settled practically by the speaking community, sometimes under protest from the Lindley Murrays or Academies of the time, who very often prefer logical consistency to ease and naturalness. Examples of grammatical conflicts will be found here and there in this volume : the most typical ones are perhaps those mentioned in Ch. XVII of rivalry between the notional idea of sex and grammatical gender (leading, for instance, to Greek *neanias*, G. ein fräulein . . . *sie*, Sp. *el justicia*). In Ch. XIV we saw the competition between singular and plural in the verb connected with a collective. Some other conflicts of a similar character may be mentioned here.

In the Gothonic languages there is no distinction of gender in the plural ; but the want of an express indication of the " natural neuter " in speaking of more than one thing leads to the employment of what is properly a singular neuter ending in G. *beides, verschiedenes* (cp. also *alles*) ; Curme GG 149 mentions *alles dreies*, and Spitzer somewhere writes *alles drei* (" Sie sind weder germanen noch gallier noch auch romanen, sondern alles drei der abstammung nach "). Here, then, gender has been stronger than number.

Similarly the feeling for the neuter is often stronger than the feeling for the proper case. In the dative there was originally no difference between masculine and neuter ; but in English from an

early period we find *for it, to this, after what*, and finally these
nominative-accusatives were the only forms of the neuter pronouns
that were used. In German we see the same tendency, though it
has not prevailed as completely as in English : Goethe has *zu
was ; was wohnte er bei* is common, and *zu (mit, von) etwas* is the
only form used ; thus also *mit nichts*, etc. (a survival of the old
form is found in *zu nichte machen, mit nichten*) ; *wegen was* is used
colloquially instead of the ambiguous *wegen wessen* (Curme GG 198)
But the tendency has not been strong enough to allow *mit das,
von welches*, though *mit dem, von welchem* in a neuter sense is not
frequent (cp. *damit, wovon*), and the dative is required in an adjective
following the uninflected pronoun : " der gedanke von *etwas
unverzeilichem*."

G. *wem*, like E. *whom*, is common to masculine and feminine,
but where a distinctive form for the female sex is desirable, a rare
and unrecognized form *wer* may be used : " Von Helios gezeugt ?
Von wer geboren ? " (Goethe) | " Da du so eine art bruder von ihr
bist.—Von ihr ? Von wer ? " (Wilbrandt, Curme GG 191). This,
however, is only possible after a preposition, as *wer* as the first
word of the sentence would be taken as the nominative ; Raabe
therefore finds another way out : " Festgeregnet ! *Wem und
welcher* steigt nicht bei diesem worte eine gespenstische einnerung
in der seele auf ? " (= what man and woman).

On the other hand, case has proved stronger than gender in
the gradual extension of the genitival ending *-s* to feminines in
English and Danish, the chief reason being, of course, that the old
form did not mark off the genitive distinctly enough from the other
cases. In German the same tendency is sometimes found with
proper names ; Frenssen thus writes : " Lisbeths heller kopf."

A conflict between the ordinary rule which requires an oblique
case after a preposition, and the feeling of a subject-relation which
requires the nominative, sometimes leads to the latter idea gaining
the upper hand, e.g. E. " Me thinkes no body should be sad *but I* "
(Sh.) | " not a man depart, *Saue I* alone " (id.) | " Did any one
indeed exist, *except I ?* " (Mrs. Shelley) | G. " Wo ist ein gott
ohne der herr " (Luther) | " niemand kommt mir entgegen *ausser
ein unverschämter* " (Lessing) | Dan. " ingen *uden jeg* kan vide
det," etc. (cf. ChE, p. 57 ff.).

In a similar way we have in Sp. *hasta yo lo sé* ' up to I, i.e. even
I know it ' (cp. Fr. jusqu'au roi le sait). It is really the same
principle that is at the bottom of the G. nominative in *was für
ein mensch* and the corresponding Russian *što za čelovjek* ; finally
also in G. *ein alter schelm von lohnbedienter*.

The wish to indicate the second person singular is seen to have
been stronger than the desire to distinguish between the indicative

and the subjunctive by the fact that combinations like *if thou dost* and *if thou didst* became frequent at a much earlier period than the corresponding uses of the indicative instead of the subjunctive in the third person.

In Ch. XXI we have already seen the conflicts in indirect speech between the tendency to keep the tense of direct speech and the tendency to shift it into accordance with the main verb (" He told us that an unmarried man was (or, is) only half a man " | " he moved that the bill be read a second time "). In the sentence " he proposed that the meeting adjourn " we may say that mood has been stronger than tense, and the same is true in French, where " il désirait qu'elle lui *écrive* " is now the only form used in ordinary language instead of the earlier *écrivisse*. Inversely tense is stronger than mood in colloquial French in a case like " croyez-vous qu'il fera beau demain," where old-fashioned grammarians would prefer the present subjunctive *fasse*; Rousseau writes : " Je ne dis pas que les bons seront récompensés ; mais je dis qu'ils seront heureux " : although after a negative main verb the ordinary rule is that the verb is put into the subjunctive in the dependent clause.

In the matter of word-order there are a great many similar conflicts, many of which fall under the head of style rather than of grammar. Let me mention only one point of grammatical interest : on the one hand prepositions are placed before their objects, on the other hand interrogative and relative pronouns have to be put in the beginning of the sentence. Hence conflicts, which are often settled according to the more or less intimate connexion between the preposition and its object or between the preposition and some other word in the sentence : " What are you talking of ? | What town is he living in ? or, In what town is he living ? | In what respect was he suspicious ? | Some things which I can't do without | Some things without which I can't make pancakes." I find an instructive example in Stevenson : " *What* do they care *for* but money ? *For what* would they risk their rascal carcases but money ? " By the side of " this movement of which I have seen the beginning " (here it would be less natural to say " which I have seen the beginning of ") we have the literary " the beginning of which I have seen." [1] In French it is impossible to relegate the preposition to the end of the sentence, hence it is necessary to say " l'homme à qui j'ai donné le prix " and " l'homme au fils duquel j'ai donné le prix." As a genitive in English cannot be separated from the word it belongs to, the object, which in ordinary sentences comes after the verb, has to be placed before the subject after *whose* in " the man whose son I met " ; in French,

---

[1] Hesitation where to place the preposition sometimes leads to redundancy, e.g. " Of what kinde should this cocke come of ? " (Sh.).

on the other hand, there is no such inducement, and the object comes at its usual place, though separated from *dont,* in " l'homme dont j'ai rencontré le fils."

Terminology.

Any branch of science that is not stationary, but progressive, must from time to time renew or revise its terminology. New terms must be found not only for newly discovered things like *radium, ion,* but also for new ideas resulting from new ways of considering old facts. Traditional terms often cramp the minds of investigators and may form a hindrance to fertile developments. It is true that a fixed terminology, in which the meaning of every single term is plain to every reader, is a great boon, but if the terminology is fixed only in so far as the same terms are used, while their meanings vary according to circumstances or the usage of individual writers, it becomes necessary to settle what would be the best meaning to attach to these terms, or else to introduce new terms which are not liable to misunderstanding.

In grammar terminological difficulties are aggravated by the facts that many terms go back to pre-scientific ages and that many again are used outside of grammar, often in meanings which have little or no resemblance to the technical meanings attached to them by grammarians, and finally by the fact that the same set of terms is used for languages of different structure. It is, of course, an advantage to the learner that he has not to acquire a new set of terms for each new language he takes up, but this is only of value if the grammatical facts covered by the same terms are really analogous, and not so dissimilar that the use of one and the same name may create confusion in the student's mind.

The scorn of the oldest grammarians for a good terminology is shown by their term *verbum substantivum* for the verb which is the least substantial and farthest removed from any substantive, further by the use of *positive* as the first degree of comparison, thus not as usual opposed to negative, but to comparative, and by the use of *impersonal* of some functions of the third " person." It is a great disadvantage that many grammatical terms have other non-technical meanings, which sometimes make it difficult to avoid such clashings as " this case [speaking of the nominative, for instance] is found in other cases as well " or " en d'autres cas on trouve aussi le nominatif," " a singular use of the singular." When a grammarian sees the words " a verbal proposition " in a treatise on logic, he is at first inclined to think that it has something to do with a verb and may be opposed to a nominal sentence (*nominal,* by the way, is also ambiguous), until he discovers that it means a mere definition of a word. *Active, passive, voice, object, subject*—I have had occasion in various chapters to point out how the everyday use of these words may mislead the unwary ; the fact that *subject* may mean ' subject-matter ' has given rise to whole discussions about logical, psychological, and grammatical subject which might have been avoided if grammarians had chosen a less ambiguous term. *Neuter*, besides its ordinary uses outside the province of grammar, has two distinct meanings in grammar, of which one is unavoidable (neuter gender), but the other can easily be dispensed with : neuter verb—explained as " *neither* active nor passive ; intransitive " in spite of the fact that an intransitive verb is active in the only sense in which the word ' active ' should be used by a consistent linguist. Besides this, the NED gives as an additional meaning " neuter passive, having the character *both* of a neuter and a passive verb "—confusion worse confounded !

A bad or mistaken name may lead to wrong rules which may have a detrimental influence on the free use of language, especially in writing. Thus the term *preposition*, or rather the unfortunate knowledge of the Latin etymology of this word, is responsible for that absurd aversion to putting a preposition at the end of a sentence which many schoolmasters and newspaper editors profess in utter ignorance of the principles and history of their own language. These people do not consider the two possibilities which the most superficial knowledge of general linguistics would have brought to their notice, that the name may have been a misnomer from the very first, or else that the value of the word may have changed as has been the case with so many other words the etymology of which is not, or is no longer, understood by the ordinary users of the language. A ladybird is not a bird, nor a butterfly a fly, and no one is the worse for it ; blackberries are not black till they are ripe ; a barn may be used for other things than barley (OE. *bere-œrn* ' barley-house ') and a bishop has other occupations than to ' look at ' or ' overlook ' (Gr. *epi-skopos*). Why not, then, admit postpositional prepositions,[1] just as one admits *adverbs* which do not stand by the side of a verb ? (As a matter of fact, *very* is always recognized as an adverb though it never qualifies a verb.)

Terminological difficulties are sometimes aggravated by the fact that languages change in course of time, and that therefore terms which may be adequate for one period are no longer so for a subsequent period. It is true that the case following the preposition *to* in OE. *to donne* was a dative, but that does not justify us in calling *do* in the modern *to do* a ' dative infinitive,' as the NED

---

[1] Cp. also Lat. *tenus*, Gr *heneka*.

does (though under the word *dative* it does not mention this use). It is even worse when the terms *dative* and *genitive* are applied to modern prepositional groups like *to God* and *of God*; see Ch. XIII.

It would evidently be utterly impracticable to throw the whole traditional nomenclature overboard and create a totally new one, for instance by an arbitrary system analogous to that of the old Indian grammarians, who coined words like *lat* present tense, *lit* perfect, *lut* first future, *lrt* second future, *let* subjunctive, *lot* imperative, *lan* imperfect, *lin* potential, etc. (Benfey, *Gesch. d. sprachw.* 92 : I omit the diacritics). We must take most of the old terms as they are, and make the best use of them that we can, supplementing them where it is necessary, and limiting the meanings of all terms, old and new, as precisely and unambiguously as possible. But this is no easy task, and I have the greatest sympathy with Sweet, who wrote to me at the time when he brought out his *New English Grammar* : " I have had most difficulty with the terminology."

In the preceding chapters (and earlier in my MEG) I have ventured to introduce a certain number of new terms, but I make bold to think that they are neither very numerous nor very difficult. In both respects my procedure compares favourably both with the wholesale coining of new grammatical terms and perversion of old ones in Noreen's great work, and with the nomenclature of certain recent psychologists. It should also be counted to my credit that I am able to toss to the wind many of the terms used in former grammatical works ; thus I have no " use for " such terms as synalepha, crasis, synæresis, synizesis, ekthlipsis, synekphonesis, to mention only terms from one department of phonetic theory ; in the matter of " aspect " (Ch. XX) I am also more moderate than most recent writers.

Among my innovations I should like to call special attention to the terms connected with the theory of the " three ranks," where I think that the few new terms allow one to explain a great many things more precisely and at the same time more tersely than has been possible hitherto. Let me give one example that has recently come under my notice. In Tract XV of the Society for Pure English, Mr. H. W. Fowler speaks of the position of adverbs, saying : " The word *adverb* is here to be taken as including adverbial phrases (e.g. *for a time*) and adverbial clauses (e.g. *if possible*), adjectives used predicatively (e.g. *alone*), and adverbial conjunctions (e.g. *then*), as well as simple adverbs such as *soon* and *undoubtedly*." These five lines might have been spared if the writer had made use of my simple word *subjunct*.

The Soul of Grammar.

My task is at an end. A good deal of this volume has necessarily been taken up with controversial matter, but it is my hope that the criticism contained in it will be found to be constructive rather than destructive. And let me add for the benefit of those reviewers who are fond of pointing out this or that little article in some recent periodical or this or that doctor's thesis which has been overlooked, that I have very often silently criticized views which appear to me to be wrong, without giving in each particular case chapter and verse for what I take exception to. My theme is so comprehensive that the book would have swelled to unwarrantable dimensions had I treated at full length all the varying opinions of other scholars on the questions I deal with. Those who are interested in the great problems at issue rather than in grammatical detail will perhaps think that I have quoted too much, not too little, from the ever-increasing flood of books and articles on these questions.

My endeavour has been, without neglecting investigation into the details of the languages known to me, to give due prominence to the great principles underlying the grammars of all languages, and thus to make my contribution to a grammatical science based at the same time on sound psychology, on sane logic, and on solid facts of linguistic history.

Psychology should assist us in understanding what is going on in the mind of speakers, and more particularly how they are led to deviate from previously existing rules in consequence of conflicting tendencies, each of them dependent on some facts in the structure of the language concerned.

Logic as hitherto often applied to grammar has been a narrow strictly formal kind of logic, generally called in to condemn certain developments in living speech. Instead of that, we should cultivate a broader-minded logic which would recognize, for instance, that from the logical point of view the indirect object may be made the subject of a passive sentence just as much as the direct object, the question as to the permissibility of such sentences as " he was offered a crown " being thus shifted from the jurisdiction of logic to that of actual usage. Fr. " je m'en souviens " was only illogical so long as the original meaning of *souvenir* was still felt— but at that time people still said " il m'en souvient," and the new construction is the outward symptom of the fact that the meaning of the verb has changed (cp. the change from *me dreams* to *I dream*): when *souvenir* has come to mean ' have in one's memory ' instead of ' come to one's memory,' the new construction is the only one logically possible. The paragraphs devoted in

Ch. **XXIV** to double negation also show us the applications of mistaken logical notions to grammar, and our conclusion is not that logic cannot be applied to grammatical questions, but that we should beware of calling in a superficial logic to condemn what on a more penetrating consideration may appear perfectly justifiable. On the other hand, of course, logic is of the greatest value for the building up of our grammatical system and for the formulation of our grammatical rules or laws.

The study of linguistic history is of the utmost importance to the grammarian : it broadens his mind and tends to eliminate that tendency to reprobation which is the besetting sin of the non-historic grammarian, for the history of languages shows that changes have constantly taken place in the past, and that what was bad grammar in one period may become good grammar in the next. But linguistic history has hitherto perhaps been too much occupied with trying to find out the ultimate origin of each phenomenon, while disregarding many things nearer our own days which are still waiting for careful investigation.

Grammatical phenomena can and should be considered from various (often supplementary) points of view. Take the concord between a substantive and its adjective (in gender, number and case) and between a subject and its verb (in number and person). The traditional grammarian of the old type states the rules and looks upon deviations as blunders, which he thinks himself justified in branding as illogical. The linguistic psychologist finds out the reasons why the rules are broken in this or that case : it may be that if the verb comes long after its subject, there is no more mental energy left to remember what was the number of the subject, or that if the verb precedes the subject, the speaker has not yet made up his mind as to what the subject is to be, etc. The historian examines his texts over various centuries and finds a growing tendency to neglect the forms distinctive of number, etc. And then the linguistic philosopher may step in and say that the demand for grammatical concord in these cases is simply a consequence of the imperfection of language, for the ideas of number, gender (sex), case and person belong logically only to primary words and not to secondary ones like adjective (adjunct) and verb. So far, then, from a language suffering any loss when it gradually discards those endings in adjectives and verbs which indicated this agreement with the primary, the tendency must, on the contrary, be considered a progressive one, and full stability can be found in that language alone which has abandoned all these clumsy remnants of a bygone past. (But don't let me be tempted to say more of this than I have already said in the fourth book of *Language*.)

My concern in this volume has been with what might be called the higher theory of grammar. But it is clear that if my views are accepted, even if they are accepted only partially, they must have practical consequences. First they must influence those grammars that are written for advanced students (the second volume of my own *Modern English Grammar* already bears witness to this influence, as does August Western's *Norsk Riksmaalgrammatik*); and through such grammars the new views may also in course of time penetrate to elementary grammars and influence the whole teaching of grammar from the very earliest stage. But how that should be brought about, and how many of the new views and terms may advantageously be adopted in primary schools—those are questions on which I should not like to pronounce before I have seen how this book is received by those scholars to whom it is addressed. Let me only express the hope that elementary teaching of grammar in future may be a more living thing than it has been up to now, with less half-understood or unintelligible precept, fewer "don't's," fewer definitions, and infinitely more observation of actual living facts. This is the only way in which grammar can be made a useful and interesting part of the school curriculum.

In elementary schools the only grammar that can be taught is that of the pupils' own mother-tongue. But in higher schools and in the universities foreign languages are taken up, and they may be made to throw light on each other and on the mother-tongue. This involves comparative grammar, one part of which is the historical grammar of one's own language. The great vivifying influence of comparative and historical grammar is universally recognized, but I may be allowed to point out here before I close that the way in which the facts of grammar are viewed in this volume may open out a new method in comparative grammar, or a new kind of comparative grammar. As this subject is always taught now, it starts from the sounds and forms, compares them in various related languages or in various periods of the same language in order to establish those correspondencies which are known under the name of phonetic laws, and to supplement them by developments through analogy, etc. In the scheme given above in Ch. III, this means starting from A (form), and proceeding to B (function) and C (notion or inner meaning). Even Comparative Syntax goes in the same direction, and is tied down by forms, as it is chiefly occupied in examining what has been the use made by different languages of the forms and form categories which Comparative Morphology has ascertained. But we can obtain new and fruitful points of view, and in fact arrive at a new kind of Comparative Syntax by following the method of this volume, i.e. starting from C (notion or inner meaning) and examining how each of the fundamental ideas common to all mankind is expressed in various languages, thus proceeding through B (function) to A (form). This comparison need not be restricted to languages belonging to the same family and representing various developments of one original common tongue, but may take into consideration languages of the most diverse type and ancestry. The specimens of this treatment which I have given here may serve as a preliminary sketch of a notional comparative grammar, which it is my hope that others with a wider outlook than mine and a greater knowledge of languages may take up and develop further, so as to assist us in gaining a deeper insight into the innermost nature of human language and of human thought than has been possible in this volume.

APPENDIX

In the chapter on Nexus (p. 117) I have mentioned a phenomenon which may be described as an accusative + a finite verb dependent on a verb inserted after the accusative. All books on correct English look upon the use of *whom* in sentences like "We feed children whom we think are hungry" as a gross or heinous error, the reasoning being evidently this : the relative is the subject of *are hungry*. A subject should stand in the nominative. *We think* is an insertion that cannot change anything in the relation between the pronoun and *are*. *Who*, not *whom*, is the nominative. Ergo : the sentence should be : "We feed children who we think are hungry." It is admitted that the use of *whom* is common, but the books mentioned give only a couple of examples from reputable writers besides some from less known writers and recent newspapers. My first contention is that this gives a false impression of the extent to which *whom* is used in these combinations, for as a matter of fact it is much more frequent in good writers than most people suspect. I reprint the examples I have collected from my own reading, which is not very extensive, and in which I have not paid more attention to this than to hundreds of other syntactic phenomena.

(Chaucer ?) Ros 3021 To spye and take whom that he fond Unto that roser putte an hond | Chaucer B 665 yet wol we us avyse Whom that we wole that (some MSS. omit that) shal ben our justise | Caxton R 86 his fowle hound whom I neuer see doth good | Shakesp. John IV. 2. 165 Arthur, whom they say is kill'd to night | Alls II. 1. 202 thy vassall, whom I know Is free for me to aske | Cymb. I. 4. 137 What lady . . . ? Yours, whom in constancie you thinke stands so safe | Meas. II. 1. 72 thy wife ? I Sir : whom I thanke heauen is an honest woman | Cor. IV. 2. 2 the nobility . . . whom we see haue sided in his behalfe | Temp. III. 3. 92 Ferdinand (whom they suppose is droun'd) | Tim. IV. 3. 120 a bastard, whom the oracle Hath doubtfully pronounced thy throat shall cut (= who according to the or. shall cut) | A.V. 1. Sam. 25. 11 Shall I . . . giue it vnto men, whom I know not whence they be ? | John Speed (1626, quoted Lowes, Conv. and Revolt 163) Pliny places the perosites here whom hee saith bee so narrow-mouthed that they live only by the smel of rost meat | Goldsm. Vic. 1766 2. 41 Thornhill, whom the host assured me was hated | ib. 47 Mr. Thornhill, whom now I find was even worse than he represented him (both passages 'corrected' in recent reprints) | Franklin Aut. 148 I advise you to apply to all those whom you know will give something; next, to those whom you are uncertain whether they will give any thing or not . . . and, lastly, do not neglect those who you are sure will give nothing | Shelley Lett. 453 to any-one, whom he knew had direct communication with me | Keats 5. 72 I have met with women whom I really think would like to be married to a poem | Kingsley Y 35 I suppose that the God whom you say made me . . . | Darwin

1. 60 to assist those whom he thought deserved assistance | Muloch Halif, 2. 11 one whom all the world knew was so wronged and so unhappy | Kipling DW 36 the Woman whom we know is hewn twelve-armed | Wells Sleeper 118 the Sleeper—whom no one but the superstitious, common people had ever dreamt would wake again | id Marr. 1. 246 college friends, whom he gathered from Marjorie's talk were destined to play a large part | Churchill Coniston 237 Janet . . . whom she had been told was the heiress of the state | Benson Arundel 150 I met a man whom I thought was a lunatic |

Ingpen Shelley in Engl. 624 his kindness to his grandson, whom he hoped and believed would be grateful | Oppenheim People's M. 149 people ask me to dinner, people whom I feel ought to hate me | id. Laxw. 111 In ten minutes, the man whom you must believe, since the breaking up of your band, has been your secret enemy for all these months, will be here | ib. 276 I am going to watch the man whom your little friend Miss Thorndyke believes is concerned in her father's disappearance | Burt Brand. Ir. 89 with the lover whom Prosper had told her was dead | Rev. of Rev. Oct. '05. 381 the police had the right to lock anyone up whom they suspected contemplated committing political crime | Times 2. 9. '20 the leader, whom I learned afterwards was D. L. Moody | Newsp. '22 Writers whom we must all admit are honest in their intentions have treated unpleasant subjects | Report of Royal Comm. on Honours, Dec. 1922 the person whom the Prime Minister considers was the original suggestor of the name | Times Lit. Suppl. 1. 3. '23 a German Princess, whom she hopes will help her to gain her independence.

Compare also the following cases of predicative : OE. Matt. 16. 13 Hwæne secgað men þæt sy mannes sunu ? | A.V. Whom do men say that I the son of man am ? (Wyclif has here : Whom seien men to be mannus sone ? but Luke 9. 18 and 20 : Whom seien the puple that Y am ? . . . But who seien ȝe that Y am ?) | Walpole Fort. 83 asking him whom he thought that he was | Farnol Am. Gent. 476 And whom do you think it is ? | Oppenheim People's M. 122 Never mind whom you thought it might have been.—In the biblical quotations we have here possibly influence from the Latin accusative with infinitive.

The frequency of *whom* in such sentences is all the more noteworthy because the tendency in English has gone for centuries in the opposite direction, towards using *who* instead of *whom* as an object. There must therefore be a very strong feeling that the relative in " children whom we think are hungry " does not stand in the same position as in " children who are hungry," where no one would think of substituting the form *whom*. The relative must accordingly be felt as somehow dependent on *we think*, from which it is not separated by any pause whatever : a pause would be unnatural, and, as a matter of fact, it is quite impossible to use the form *whom*, if we add *as* and make a pause before the inserted clause : " children, who, as we think, are hungry," where we have a real insertion without any influence on the sentence which is broken up by the intercalated passage.[1] In " children, whom we think are hungry," on the other hand, we have a peculiar compound relative clause, in which I should not say that *whom* in itself is the object of *think*, but rather, as in other cases considered in Ch. IX, that the object of *think* is the whole nexus, whose primary is *whom* (which is put in the accusative, because the nexus is dependent) and whose adnex is the finite combination *are hungry*. The form *whom* is used because in " who we think " the speech-instinct would be bewildered by the contiguity of two nominatives, as it were two subjects in the same clause.

There is a second test by which we can show that the speech instinct does not take the relative as a real subject, namely the possibility of omitting the relative pronoun, which, as a general rule, can only be omitted in English when it is not to be the subject. Zangwill writes (Grey Wig 326) : " Is it so with everything they say is wrong ? "—he would not have omitted the relative except for the insertion of *they say*, for " Is it so with everything is wrong ? " is not English. I give a few other examples : Keats 4. 188 I did not like to write before him a letter he knew was to reach your hands | Thurston Antag. 227 count the people who come, and compare them with the number you hoped would come | London Adv. 32 They chose the lingering death they were sure awaited them rather than the immediate death they were sure would pounce upon them if they went up against the master | ib. 50 puzzled over something untoward he was sure had happened | Lloyd

---

[1] *Who* is the form used before a pause, marked in the folio by the parenthesis, in Shakesp. Cæs. III. 2. 129 I should do Brutus wrong, and Cassius wrong : Who (you all know) are honourable men.

George Speech May 1921 In Central Europe there were blood feuds they all thought had been dead and buried for centuries | Times Lit. Suppl. 22. 3. '23 a piratical anthology in which he included certain poems he knew were not Shakespeare's | Lawrence Ladyb. 193 she's just the type I always knew would attract him.

The correctness of this analysis is confirmed by a comparison with similar constructions in Danish and French (see my paper " De to hovedarter av grammattiske forbindelser," Copenh. Acad. of Sciences, 1921, p. 20 ff.). In Danish the relative *der* can be used only as a subject, but *som* both as subject and object : now *der* is never used instead of *som* in " den mand som jeg tror har taget pungen." In the same way *hvem der*, the combination required in the subject, cannot be used instead of *hvem* in " jeg veed ikke hvem man tror har taget pungen." The relative is frequently omitted as object, not as subject, but may be omitted in " den mand jeg tror har taget pungen." The word-order in " den mand som jeg ikke tror har taget pungen " with *ikke* preposed also shows that we have not an ordinary parenthetical insertion. In French we have the somewhat obsolete construction " Mais quelle est cette femme que je vois qui arrive ? "—the first relative is put in the oblique form because the speaker dares not say *qui* on account of the immediately following subject, but after *je vois* the relative pronoun is taken up again and this time can be put in the nominative. It is easily seen that on account of the different word-order there is not the same inducement to shift the case of the Latin relative in " Cicero qui quantum scripserit nemo nescit," while in " Cicero, quem nemo nescit multa scripsisse " the sentence is continued in a different form.

In other words, two of the premises in the orthodox reasoning mentioned above cannot hold water before a closer inspection : a subject need not always be in the nominative, and the insertion of the words *we think* can and does change the relation between the relative pronoun and its verb.

INDEX

GEORGE ALLEN & UNWIN LTD

London: 40 Museum Street, W.C.1

Auckland: 24 Wyndham Street
Bombay: 15 Graham Road, Ballard Estate, Bombay 1
Buenos Aires: Escritorio 454-459, Florida 165
Calcutta: 17 Chittaranjan Avenue, Calcutta 13
Cape Town: 109 Long Street
Hong Kong: F1/12 Mirador Mansions, Kowloon
Ibadan: P.O. Box 62
Karachi: Karachi Chambers, McLeod Road
Madras: Mohan Mansions, 38c Mount Road, Madras 6
Mexico: Villalongin 32-10, Piso, Mexico 5, D.F.
Nairobi: P.O. Box 4536
New Delhi: 13-14 Ajmeri Gate Extension, New Delhi 1
São Paulo: Avenida 9 de Julho 1138-Ap. 51
Singapore: 36c Prinsep Street, Singapore 7
Sydney, N.S.W.: Bradbury House, 55 York Street
Tokyo: 3 Kanda-Oganmachi 3-Chome, Chiyoda Ku
Toronto: 91 Wellington Street West, Toronto 1